N

R. M. MacIVER

THE MODERN STATE

OXFORD UNIVERSITY PRESS

Oxford University Press, Amen House, London E.C.4

GLASGOW NEW YORK TORONTO MELBOURNE WELLINGTON
BOMBAY CALCUTTA MADRAS KARACHI LAHORE DACCA
CAPE TOWN SALISBURY NAIROBI IBADAN ACCRA
KUALA LUMPUR HONG KONG

FIRST EDITION 1926

Reprinted lithographically in Great Britain
by LOWE AND BRYDONE (PRINTERS) LTD.,
LONDON, N.W.10, from sheets of the first
edition
1928, 1932, 1941, 1945, 1947, 1950, 1955, 1960, 1962, 1964
First issued in Oxford Paperbacks 1964

TO

ETHEL MARION MacIVER

PREFACE FOR THE
PAPERBACK EDITION

THE first edition of this book opened with the words: 'The state has no finality.' At that time no one dreamed of the magnitude of the changes that were even then impending, most of them midwifed by the monstrous upheavals of the Second World War. It is highly significant that many of them involved a retreat from the ancient and once sacrosanct doctrine of sovereignty. The hitherto separatist states of Western Europe have entered into a 'common market' that already has important political implications and may well lead to a new kind of international union. All but five of the states within the United Nations have agreed to renounce, in favour of a decision by a majority of the Security Council of the U.N., their 'sovereign right' to resort to war. An international peace force has successfully intervened in outbreaks between the Arab states and Israel, and in the Congo. Two great powers abruptly ended an incipient invasion of the territory of an offending state under strong pressures that, however motivated, were sustained by a great majority in the United Nations. The ancient system of empire has crumbled over most of Africa and South-East Asia and the reaches of the Pacific, and scores of new nations have arisen as the successors of perished empire, and these new peoples, some born before their time, some nurtured to statehood by their former metropolitan countries, are advancing out of tribalism with the aid, albeit the not disinterested aid, of the great nations—itself a new phenomenon in human history.

In our first edition we spoke of war—war between great powers—as an anachronism. Now it is something else altogether. The bombs that fell on Hiroshima and Nagasaki ended not only a war but also an era. Each of the two nuclear-armed superpowers already possesses enough destructive might—far more than enough—to wipe human life off the face of the earth. We live in the perilous incubation period between two eras. It is surely a drama worthy of the Gods men profess to worship—on the one hand the promise of a poverty-rid law-ruled earth and on the other the threat of the abrupt ending of the life-urge that has guided evolution on this earth through the billion of years that at length produced man, self-styled *homo sapiens*.

Cooperative with these other changes have been the new triumphs of technology and its expansion to the remotest of the earth's undeveloped areas. Since culture, no matter how resistant, must accommodate itself to the demands of the prevailing technology, there is in process a diminution of cultural 'distance' between nations corresponding to the technological conquest of spatial distance. Its impact on peoples newly exposed to it has been a source of serious disturbances and creates new problems for the world at large, the most apparent being the rapid increase of population that, if continued for only a few generations, would endanger all the gains and amenities of civilization.

Advancing technology, with its ramifying specializations, makes for more elaborate organization. Special interests of all kinds form their defensive and offensive associations. Like interests combine into large-scale corporations. Every organization becomes a focus of power, so that power becomes many-peaked—in sharp contrast to the unicentered system of feudal times—and the state, under the pushes and pulls of these competing and conflicting forces, follows a changing diagonal of policy-making. These forces at the same time counter the separatist traditions and ideologies of states, making them somewhat less unlike—as is happening even to such extremes as those of communism and the Western form of capitalism—and entangling them in a net of common interests that has already led to the international and multinational developments to which we have referred.

The state has no finality, but human nature is as stable as human needs, and what human beings need from government—if we think not of the few, but of men generally, men as social beings—is the same under all conditions. These are liberties secured by restraints, justice under law, order that provides opportunity, the economy of the good life. The modes of satisfying these needs change with the changing conditions. To satisfy any need whatever, even the most spiritual, a modicum of power is necessary, for power is simply the effective control of means. From the beginning of human history government has been recognized as the overall holder and regulator of power, maintaining order by limiting all other expressions of power and thereby turning permitted powers into rights. In that concept lay the rudiments of the principles of government. In every age men have sought to clarify the application of these principles to the changing times. In every age the abuse of power by governments has led to disasters and uprisings, oppressions and vainglorious wars, and sometimes to experiments in the control of power, seeking to make it responsible, or more responsible, subject in some manner to the will of the people, of the majority or those who represented them. The gamut of experience is wide enough. The principles involved are reasonably well attested, though the challenge of change is perennial. Here is the subject to which this book is devoted.

TABLE OF CONTENTS

INTRODUCTORY

WHAT *IS* THE STATE?

BOOK ONE

THE EMERGENCE OF THE STATE

I

ORIGINS

II

THE EARLY EMPIRE

III

THE EMERGENCE OF CITIZENSHIP

IV

THE FORMATION OF THE COUNTRY-STATE

BOOK TWO

POWERS AND FUNCTIONS

V

THE LIMITS OF POLITICAL CONTROL

VI

THE RESIDENCE OF AUTHORITY

VII

MIGHT AND SOVEREIGNTY

VIII

LAW AND ORDER

IX

POLITICAL GOVERNMENT AND THE ECONOMIC ORDER

BOOK THREE
FORMS AND INSTITUTIONS

X
FORMATION AND DISSOLUTION

XI
THE FORMS OF THE STATE

XII
THE ARTICULATION OF GOVERNMENTAL POWERS

XIII
THE PARTY SYSTEM

BOOK FOUR

THEORIES AND INTERPRETATIONS

XIV

THE EVOLUTION OF MODERN THEORIES OF THE STATE

XV

POLITICAL THOUGHT OF THE PRESENT

XVI

A RE-INTERPRETATION OF THE STATE

INTRODUCTORY

WHAT *IS* THE STATE?

I. THE STATE AS AN ASSOCIATION

THE whole of this volume is devoted to answering the question, What *is* the State? For we are to be concerned not with the skeletons of constitutions, which can be catalogued and described, but with the living fact, which can be understood only in the light of its functioning, as that clarifies and changes and grows. But since we must use the term 'state' from the very first sentence, and since even to-day men attach most diverse ideas to that term, a preliminary definition, the justification of which will appear only as we proceed, must here be offered.

It may seem curious that so great and obvious a fact as the state should be the object of quite conflicting definitions, yet such is certainly the case. Some writers define the state as essentially a class-structure, 'an organization of one class dominating over the other classes'[1]; others regard it as the one organization that transcends class and stands for the whole community. Some interpret it as a power-system, others as a welfare-system, this being the line of cleavage between the two great series of political thinkers who in the modern world trace their descent back respectively to Machiavelli and to Grotius or Althusius. Some view it entirely as a legal construction, either in the old Austinian sense which made it a relation-

---

[1] So Oppenheimer, Preface to second American edition of *The State*. This is, as is well known, the Marxian doctrine but it is held by many who belong to other camps.

ship of governors and governed, or, in the language of modern jurisprudence, as a community 'organized for action under legal rules'.[1] Some identify it with the nation, others regard nationality as incidental or unnecessary or even as a falsifying element which perverts the nature and function of the state. Some regard it as no more than a mutual insurance society, others as the very texture of all our life. To some it is a necessary evil, and to a very few an evil that is or will some day be unnecessary, while to others it is 'the world the spirit has made for itself'. Some class the state as one in the order of 'corporations', and others think of it as indistinguishable from society itself.

It is true that these contradictions arise in part from conflicting notions of what the state *ought* to be, for in this study we are in the perilous region wherein ideals may shape not only the future of actualities but our present conception of them. It is likewise true that the evolution of states and the diversity of character revealed in present-day examples afford ground for varying interpretations. It is easier to agree on the nature of a particular state than on the nature of *the* state. But if we can speak of *the* state at all, we must define it in terms of what is common to all states, while perhaps laying stress on those aspects which become more prominent in the process of historical development. In no attitude of worship, as did Hegel, and in no attitude of belittlement, as did Spencer, but in the spirit of scientific exactitude must we seek the criterion of the state.

In the first place we must distinguish the state from society. To identify the social with the political is to be guilty of the grossest of all confusions, which completely

[1] So Vinogradoff in *Historical Jurisprudence*.

bars any understanding of either society or the state. It is perfectly obvious, if only we look at the facts of the case, that there are social forms, like the family or the church or the club, which owe neither their origin nor their inspiration to the state; and social forces, like custom or competition, which the state may protect or modify, but certainly does not create ; and social motives like friendship or jealousy, which establish relationships too intimate and personal to be controlled by the great engine of the state. The state exists within society, but it is not even the *form* of society. We see it best in what it does. Its achievement is a system of order and control. The state in a word regulates the outstanding external relationships of men in society. It supports or exploits, curbs or liberates, fulfils or even destroys, the social life over which it is invested with control—but the instrument is not the life. In the earliest phases, among hunters, fishers, root-diggers, and fruit-gatherers there have been social groups which knew nothing or almost nothing of the state. To-day there remain simple peoples, such as certain groups of Eskimos, which have no recognizable political organization. And at the other extreme, in the highest civilizations which have been attained, the long struggle against the insatiate claims of power has revealed the great intrinsic aspects of individual and social life, the things that are not Caesar's, and withdrawn them wholly, or in great part, from the competence of the state.

This distinction once established, it remains that the state must either be an institutional system or an association. There is no third alternative. All social forms may be classed as areas of society (as we shall call them, communities) ; organizations established within society for the achievement of conscious and therefore limited purposes (as we shall call them, associations); and institutions, the recognized modes in accordance with which communities and associations regulate their activities. The distinction between association and institution I have elsewhere dwelt on.[1] Here it must suffice to explain that an association denotes a group of persons or members who are associated and organized into a unity of will for a common end, whereas the term institution does not refer directly to persons at all but to the form of order along which their activities are related and directed. It is the obvious distinction between, say, the family and marriage, the church and communion, the professional association and the code. Institutions may, however, be established by the community as well as by associations, and we may include customs in the former class. There is sometimes an ambiguity because the same term may apply either to the form or the group, the institution or the association. We speak of the party, the family, the church, the department, the hospital and so forth, meaning the system of organization rather than the organized membership. And we often use the term ' institution ' loosely, in the sense which properly belongs to ' association '. But the distinction is a clear and necessary one. It is brought out in the following simple conspectus of social forms.

SOCIAL FORMS

Integral unities	COMMUNITIES :	Exx. country, city, village, nation, tribe.
Partial unities	ASSOCIATIONS :	Exx. family, church, party, class, business firm.
Modes or means	INSTITUTIONS :	Exx. inheritance, baptism, the party ' machine ', class distinctions, the market.

[1] *Community*, Bk. II, ch. iv.

Only a part of one's life is lived within or as a member of an association, but there is a sense in which the whole of one's life falls within a circle, greater or smaller, of community. There was a time when the family seemed to comprehend the whole life, but if so, it was not the family as we know it, but rather a family community which on the ostensible basis of kinship included a whole group of social interests. There were likewise times when the state *claimed* control over every sphere of life, but such claims have never been realized, for under the most absolute state, use and wont, custom and tradition, social authority underived from the state but instead the very ground of political power, were far more effective forces in the organization of communal life. Not only must we deny that the state is a community or a form of community, we must definitely declare it to be an association belonging to the same category as the family or the church. Like these it consists essentially of a group of members organized in a definite way and *therefore* for limited ends. The organization of the state is not all social organization ; the ends for which the state stands are not all the ends which humanity seeks ; and quite obviously, the ways in which the state pursues its objects are only some of the ways in which within society men strive for the objects of their desire.

The state as will presently appear is distinguished from other associations by certain peculiar characters of its own—but a like statement is true of the family or the church. One historial peculiarity must here be mentioned, because it helps to explain why the true associational character of the state has even yet scarcely been realized in our political thinking. By its very nature the state must include under its control all persons who live within its territorial bounds, whether they are properly members of the state or not. It seems accordingly, to the superficial glance, not to depend on membership, not on an organization deliberately established or maintained by the common will of men. In respect of origins we might even say that there were state-institutions before there was a state at all. As the state emerged the logic of power extended the institution beyond the association. So we may say that in the extreme case of a country subjected to foreign conquest there are state-institutions but no state. In the modern world the range of state-institutions has grown more nearly coincident with that of the state-association. To complete that transformation is the ideal of democracy, which would thus abolish the distinction between the dominant will that imposes institutions and the common will that creates them.

II

THE STATE IN TERMS OF SOVEREIGNTY

It remains for us to distinguish the state from other associations and so to complete our definition. To this end we must consider the special character of those institutions which are properly called political. Has the state any institutions peculiar to itself? These, if they exist, must give us the clue we are seeking. Let us therefore examine the two great engines of political control, sovereignty as exercised by state governments and law as the chief engine by which it is exercised. The nature of sovereignty has been the subject of much needless mystery. It is surrounded by a halo that dates back to the tribal reverence which alone, in primitive ages, could sanction the obedience it must command. It is said that men died of shock on hearing of the execution of Charles I and of Louis XVI, just as savage men have perished when they unwittingly broke the taboo surrounding the chief and his belongings.[1] This magic of sovereignty became transformed into legal prerogative, divine origin passing into divine right. When that proud title fell in turn from the relaxing grasp of monarchism, it was transferred from the person to the incarnate state. The mystic name that had exalted the obvious reality of the king now crowned a being as mystic as itself, the omnipotent majesty of the state. The fierce light that in times of stress and social revolution beats upon a throne had destroyed the ancient halo—for halos are visible only when the ' visibility ' is low—but the new sovereign dwelt apart in a shadowy realm of abstractions, powerful over the mind of men in so far as they elude his understanding.

If we think of the state as an association, unique in its kind and of incalculable significance but still an association like the rest, we are saved from these delusions. We shall also avoid those needless inquiries into the residence of sovereignty which demand whether it belongs of right or in fact to people or electorate or parliament or king. Every association of any magnitude has grades of authority and control analogous to those of the state. Consider, for example, the case of a business corporation. It has a body of shareholders who are united in the will and interest to uphold the corporation. That is, shall we say, the ' general will ' of the association, and it corresponds in its own kind with the general will of the state. But a will of this kind can only uphold, can only accept and

[1] Striking examples of this savage reverence are given in Lang's *Magic and Religion*, as also in Frazer's *Golden Bough*.

maintain the broad common purpose of an association. It cannot direct, it cannot determine policy. All who agree upon the end are not therefore agreed upon the means. The shareholders must choose a board of directors, but neither on the choice nor on the policy of the board are they likely to be unanimous. A dominant group, at most a majority, will decide. Here we have the policy-determining will, which in the sphere of the developed state is called the ' sovereign people ' or the ' sovereign electorate '. It is quite distinct from the ' general will ', since in spite of the integrity our terms imply, it is at most a majority-will. It arises out of partial conflict beneath which, and reconciling which is the broader purpose of the general will. Again, in the case of our corporation, we have the necessity for a board or ' executive ' which shall initiate, develop, and execute policy within the limits assigned or permitted by the majority or dominant membership. In the type of case we have cited, the board of directors has usually a very free hand, and the shareholders exercise their power mainly in the matter of appointment ; in other cases the members more directly control policy. In the sphere of the state the board of directors is the government, and here again we apply the term sovereignty, speaking of the ' sovereign parliament ' and, under monarchical institutions, of the ' sovereign king '. But in all cases this sovereign derives its power and its might from the broader will which elects or accepts it, and that in turn rests on the ' general will ' which is the spirit of citizenship. This is true of despotic governments, as Green has shown, as well as of democracies.

We have the various stages, as it were, of sovereignty, as follows :

A. The GENERAL WILL. This is not so much the will *of* the state as the will *for* the state, the will to maintain it. It is revealed in the feeling of loyalty or patriotism ; in the readiness to accept the decision of a majority or of a constituted government though we do not approve of its rightness ; in the trust we place in legal and constitutional methods as such, whatever their consequences for ourselves, in that sense of political unity which transcends the division of parties and policies, gathering to itself a body of tradition and sentiments which all men recognize, and which for many is the most enduring and precious of spiritual possessions.

It must of course be realized that a will of this nature, half buried in the unreflective life of every day, is no clearcut principle of political conduct. It is at the opposite extreme from that ' general will ' of Rousseau's, which continuously and directly legislates. It is unformulated though very real. It is not so much the will of the citizen as the will of the person to be a citizen—a distinction which, as we shall try to show at a later stage of our argument, leads us to the very foundations of all sovereignty. It is true that within the frontiers of every state there are many who can scarcely be said to share in its general will at all, members who do not consciously participate in the life of the state. In imperial and dynastic states government may seem to a vast majority to be something apart or alien, or else something exalted so high above themselves or so endowed with power that they are the mere objects of its will. But in the first place the state need not be regarded as comprising within its membership all who are within its law or power, any more than a business corporation counts in its membership all its employees. The *mere* subject is no part of the state-association, any more than the slave. In the second place, there are many degrees of this will for the state. The state appears, whatever its exactions, as the upholder of the customs whereby men live, and receives therefrom a reflected loyalty. Before the days of democracy this was the nearest approach to the general will.

B. The ULTIMATE SOVEREIGN. So we shall name the power which ultimately determines the policy or direction of the state. It is the will of the state, as nearly as that is ever attained, for on all questions of policy there is division. The ' will of the people ' is rarely, if ever, the will of all the people. In no democratic state certainly, and perhaps in no state of any kind, is the active government the choice of all the citizens. It is at most a fluctuating majority that here sits upon the throne. As that majority or dominant group changes, so, in direct or indirect consequence, do governments rise or fall, so do they change their policies while yet they remain in power. Here is nothing of that proud claim to be ' one and indivisible ' which a long line of theorists have ascribed to the sovereign power. It is a sovereign as elusive and as inconstant as the wind, an unstable equilibrium of will reacting to a thousand conscious and unconscious influences. But only thus is direction, with its incessant rejection of alternatives, ever achieved. If this sovereign seems a poor and precarious thing in contrast with the grandeur of the state, we should reflect that policy is but the concern of the hour. Underneath it is the deeper agreement of will. Every policy, every decision of authority and power, is achieved through difference, but as each recedes into the past, as the slow play of criticism revises or affirms it, as habituation creates first adjustment and then tradition, there is built up a sense of the integrity of the state which makes such difference relatively insignificant, which, save under very abnormal conditions, reduces every present issue to a surface-disturbance that still leaves tranquil and assured the depths of the political consciousness.

C. The LEGISLATIVE SOVEREIGN, or more comprehensively, the GOVERNMENT.

The act of the ultimate sovereign, or under less democratic conditions, its mere acquiescence, establishes a focus of political action, corresponding to the directorate of our typical association. Here sovereignty finds its clearest expression and definitive shape. It implies the exclusive right, during the term assigned by the ultimate sovereign, to make laws of universal validity within its own sphere, whether defined or undefined, together with the peculiar right to the exercise of force in the maintenance of such laws and of the authority, executive and judicial, by which they are administered. Any body which exercises these rights constitutes a political government. Our definition, however, reveals only the form and not the substance of this sovereignty, the form of right, and not the substance of power. The form is the legal aspect, on which it is most misleading to lay exclusive stress. The substance of power falls far short of the title. Within the limits set by constitutions over which the government has no direct control, there are nearer limits established by the very nature of political law, by the ever-present sense of the ultimate sovereign, and finally by the pressure of that great body of tradition whose support is the general will. The psychology of power may lead governments to break these bonds, but a stronger necessity, on which their very existence depends, is always active to restrain them or, failing that, to overthrow them. Government *may* exercise arbitrary and selfish control over a tradition-bound and ignorant people, but only if it respects their traditions, of which the habit of obedience is but one of many elements. Nor is government in itself, within these limits, ' one and indivisible '. The same unstable equilibrium of decision by majority or dominant voice, which we observed in the nature of the ultimate sovereign, operates also within this smaller circle. On the other hand, the necessary division of political functions tends to create, as it grows, some degree of independence from one another in the parts of government, which may require as a ground of unity the regulative support of the broader sovereignty on which all government depends.

Our account so far suggests little of that unique, peremptory, and universal dominion which is generally associated with the idea of sovereignty. Such legalist definitions are untrue to the political fact. ' The sovereign ', says Lewis in his *Use and Abuse of Political Terms*, ' has the complete disposal of the life, rights, and duties of every member of the community.' So say the whole school of Hobbes and Bentham and Austin. They interpret sovereignty as an extreme master-servant relationship, but their account is far more applicable to a slave plantation or to a menagerie than to the actuality of political life. We have suggested that the grades of sovereignty, in the political sphere, correspond precisely with the forms of control that exist in other associations. We have not found in the mere facts of obedience, coercion, and penalization an adequate description of the character of sovereign power. The sanction of that power lies elsewhere. If it were merely what the legalists declare it to be, it could not exist for a day. Sovereign power is an attribute of common will, made common by community of purpose. Sovereign power maintains and creates a corresponding array of institutions, and coercion is but one, and in fact a subordinate, characteristic of these.

But at least it will be said, if coercion is not the essence of sovereign power, it is surely the differentia and criterion of it. To the state alone, in its aspect of sovereignty, belongs the decisive right of force. Further there is a vast difference between the kind of authority exercised by a mere company-directorate and the mighty all-embracing sway of state. Is not the authority of the former derivative, confined to a narrow space which itself is allotted by grace of the state, owing its origin to a charter of the state, and dependent for its continued existence on the contractual fabric of rights and obligations which the state upholds ? Is not this true of every other association, and if so, how can we suggest analogy between powers so disparate ? How can we liken to any such minor authorities the majesty of the state ? Non est potestas super terram quae comparetur ei.

To answer this question aright we must examine the relation between the state and other associations, and especially we must consider whether these other associations have real, and in any sense independent, spheres of action. If, as we shall seek to show later, they do in fact own such competence ; if they have underivative control over interests no less vital than the political, interests that indeed penetrate more deeply into the significance of life, then we must reject this traditional claim of the state's universal supremacy. Meantime we may point out that in the strict sense it is not sovereignty, at least in the developed state, that owns coercive power. It is not the office but the instrument, not sovereignty but the law and the constitution that wear the legitimate armour of might. The government has power as the guardian of the constitution, as the executor of law, not in its own right. Outside of the realm of law its use of force is as irreducible to principle as that of any strong man armed. To law therefore we must turn, and not to sovereignty as such, if we are to attain a true definition of the state.

It is obviously a mistake to suppose that the mere command of a government has any attributes of political sovereignty. No parliament can issue orders for the people to obey, as its mere subjects. The tyrant who subdues men to his irresponsible will is no more exercising the function of political government than the bullying schoolboy who by his brute force cows his companions into obedience. The deep ignorance of the ages where the masses were sunk in poverty and superstition permitted kings and governments to exercise their arbitrary sway, so that still, for us, there remains in the term sovereignty some lurking shadow of the idea of personal command. But such an idea not only forms no necessary part of the principle of sovereignty ; it actually distorts our understanding of its nature, as that stands revealed in the evolved political systems of the modern world. The distinguishing authority of a developed government has relation to the laws which it enforces, laws which it too must obey, and consists in the right, within the limits of a constitution, to amend or to add to this body of law.

THE STATE IN TERMS OF LAW

Every association creates laws after its kind, but the laws of the state are sharply distinguished from all others. Political sovereignty, we have sought to show, is not, in respect of its form and mode of operation, vitally different from other types of government, such as the control of a business. Government is the exercise of will within a particular sphere, itself supported by a broader will, and this is as true of a business corporation or a church as of a state. But political law is unique, and in its uniqueness alone rests the distinctiveness of political sovereignty. Every association makes laws, but the laws of other associations, in the developed state, bind the members of them only in so far as they prefer to accept them rather than lose the benefits of membership. If I choose to disrespect the laws of my club I lose its privileges—that and nothing more. The club may fine me for non-conformity to its rules, but if I prefer to give up its advantages I need never pay the fine. If I disapprove of the laws of any economic or scientific or cultural or religious association to which I belong, I may resign at will. There is no positive penalty properly attaching to their laws. I am neither compelled to join the association nor prevented from leaving it. If I am punished, say for violating the obligations of the family, it is not because the family, but because the state insists. The law of the state alone, in a demarcated or advanced society, is coercive. That law alone binds me of necessity. If I leave one state—and even to do so is sometimes forbidden—it is at the price of leaving its territory—and then

I automatically pass within the range of the law of another
state. The law of the state is ineluctable. It binds the
rulers as well as the subjects. It is universal, in that
nowhere does it cease to function. Political law is thus an
unbroken framework over each area of society.

Here we have the explanation of a marked contrast
between the state and the other associations. These
others, the church associations, for instance, rise, disappear, and re-emerge, unite and separate with an ease
unknown in the case of the state. If a state dissolves, it is
like a convulsion of nature. If it breaks in two, it is with
violence and fierce repulsion.[1] Sometimes a temporary
unity of two or more states is achieved which again disrupts without grave commotion, as happened in the case
of Sweden and Norway or of Belgium and Holland.
But even in the federal unity of the United States the
attempted secession of the South led to a great civil war in
which the cause of indissoluble union was triumphant.
The state, then, because of its rigid, unbroken, coercive
framework of political law, has a permanence and fixity
that distinguishes it from all other associations.

If we examine further the character of political law,
we must observe that it pays a price alike for its universality and for its coercive sanction. Because of its universality, it must deal with general situations, with inclusive
and exclusive categories of actions and persons. It cannot
accommodate itself to the intricacy of individual situations. Laws which apply specially to individuals are rare

---

[1] It might be said that occasionally the dissolution of other associations,
such as the church, have been quite as convulsive as that of the state. But
the instances which present themselves, the upheaval of the Reformation
for example, occurred under conditions in which the church was itself
fused in the state.

and anomalous, so much so that by many they are regarded as contradictory to the very nature of law. A law is the resultant of an elaborate process of formation. It is the definitive expression of a formula arrived at through deliberation and adjustment, a formula which must be fitted into the complex structure of the existing code. Its very form, together with the manner of its promulgation, implies that it is to endure, not as the solution of an immediate problem of government but as the embodiment of a standing principle. It is true that certain laws, such as the budget, are enacted for a limited period, generally for a year, but these laws belong to a very special class. They do not strictly fall within the great code of the law. In any case they are renewable from year to year and they may be regarded as permanent types of legislation subject to annual revision. The vast majority of laws, on the other hand, belong to the code, the body of law, the system of established order which the state maintains.

Because then of this generality, the law cannot be more than the framework of order. To some court is given the power of interpretation and above all the power of applying the sanction of law, of adjusting penalties or assessing damages, within the limits which the law itself permits. But these adjustments, whose nature we must at a later point discuss, are possible only within relatively narrow limits. Even with their aid, the law remains a vast structural frame which cannot do more than limit the myriad relationships of men. It cannot control the operation of the spontaneous constructive activities of life. Its essential instrument, the law, is too general, too clumsy, too formal, to touch the essentials of conduct. Men feel the need for other collectivities with other methods. The state serves best when it provides the liberty and order on which other associations can build and by which they seek more intimate or more particular ends. The state cannot possibly fulfil the purpose of the family or the church or the trade union or the cultural organizations. Its attempts to usurp the place of any of these have been historically futile. When the French revolutionary government declared that ' the abolition of every kind of corporation formed among citizens of the same state is a fundamental basis of the French Constitution ', it proclaimed a doctrinaire absolutism which no state could possibly enforce.

The universal and therefore formal character of its law limits the sphere of the state in another respect. It can only concern itself, if true to the nature of law, with those interests which can reasonably be regarded as universal. It is, for example, an incongruity on the part of the state to endow one of several religions professed by its citizens, still more to identify itself with such a religion. There are many interests which are shared by only a part of the citizen body. All cultural interests are exceedingly diversified, and the advance of culture seems to involve an ever greater differentiation of human purposes and ideals. For this reason, as for another to be mentioned presently, the state is unfitted to comprise these within its own organization. It must stand for what is recognized, by the political consciousness of the times, as the common concern of the people. No doubt the determination of what is the common concern must be arrived at by (at most) a majority-decision and is liable to be consciously and unconsciously perverted by particular dominant interests. But the principle is sufficiently clear. It is obvious that partial as well as intimate interests belong properly to special associations and not to the state.

The wider the state-area, the more comprehensive, in one sense, are its laws. The government of city or county regulates, within and under authority of the state, matters too localized for the direct care of the state. At the other extreme a world-government, should such ever arise, would concern itself with the conditions requisite for world-wide order and justice, and the ' international law ' we already possess is but a rudimentary expression of that ideal. But within the smallest area of local government, as within the widest range of its possible extension, the character of political law remains the same. It is not locality that delimits the varieties of interest and marks one off from another. A single locality, nay, a single individual, might be a microcosm revealing all the range of interests of the wide world. Political law keeps its own universality in the small as in the great. In the village as in the world empire there is the same need for those other associations which pursue, on a basis of common order, the manifold free social purposes of the human spirit.

Not only because of its universality but still more because of its coercive sanction, the law of the state has a limited competence. The root of obedience to law is not coercion but the will to obey; nevertheless law takes the form of an imperative. It can therefore regulate only the external order of society. Its unbending rigour is applicable only to the outer aspects of conduct. Therefore, as Green has very clearly expressed it, ' the only acts which it *ought* to enjoin or forbid are those of which the doing or not doing, *from whatever motive*, is necessary to the moral end of society.' [1] Other social

---

[1] *Principles of Political Obligation*, synopsis of § 15.

influences may indeed, must indeed, support the law, but they derive, not from the state, but from the community whose agent it is recognized to be. There are other sanctions within society that are applied with greater persuasion. Custom and tradition hold men within their ways. Mode and fashion move them as the wind moves the surface of the waters. And beyond these there lies the sense of spiritual values—of all forces the most compelling to the sensitive and creative mind, while capable, as many a crisis has revealed, of stirring the hearts of a whole people.

It is not to belittle the state that we have drawn these distinctions, but to define it. Its true sphere is so vast, its task so endless, that no rightful limitations can detract from its worth. On the contrary, they reveal the conditions under which alone it can achieve its greatest measure of success. They show us not only what the state *is*, but, as will later appear, they teach us what the state *can* be.

Now at length we have arrived at our definition. *The state is an association which, acting through law as promulgated by a government endowed to this end with coercive power, maintains within a community territorially demarcated the universal external conditions of social order.*

BOOK ONE

THE EMERGENCE OF THE STATE

ORIGINS

I. THE FAMILY AND THE SOCIAL STRUCTURE

ORIGINS are always obscure. If we endeavour to explain the genesis of any event that happens in our own days and seemingly before our very eyes, a scientific discovery, a new religion, a war, a revolution, we never get back to the simple fountain-head, the initial impulse whence it is derived. The stream we follow upwards brings us at length to difficult marshes and underground pools, never to a clear spring. If that is true of near events, how much harder is the task to trace the origins of social phenomena in the unknown and ever receding past. Such a task would in any case be out of place here, where our main object is to understand and reveal the present character, itself sufficiently perplexing, of the greatest of social structures. But we know something of its earliest forms, and even of societies where it is still unrevealed in any form ; and this knowledge may shed some light, though dim, on the essential meaning of the state. If we know that societies have lived without the state, if we know why and how the state has grown from small beginnings to its great dominance, we may be saved some misunderstandings which beset the political thinking of our time.

In our study of the state we shall not attempt to go beyond the social stage where men are already associated in kin-groups, the clan, or close union of families, the phratry or kin-brotherhood, and the tribe or gens, as we may name them in order of size. Such kin-groupings, which disappear in the process of civilization, are characteristic of primitive society when it has attained a range of unity wider than the rude family cohesion of the cave-dweller and other types of prehistoric man.[1] No elaborate theory is required to explain why the kin-group represents the normal form of social growth beyond the family life. The first of all societies, in beast and bird and man, is the family, but it cannot exist in mere isolation. The mating impulse leads the adolescent outside the old family to form a new one. Each new family is the union of two families. The web of blood-relationship is thus woven and rewoven which creates and sustains the kin with all its potentialities of extension and subdivision. The kin arises out of the recognition of consanguinity, but it grows into an order of society.[2]

As one of the many variant types of kin-articulation in primitive society we may cite the example of the Iroquois Tribes of North America.[3] Here the structure is somewhat elaborate—a not uncommon character of societies based on consanguinity—and it shows us very clearly the manner in which the extended kin-relation merges into the political relation. We have only to contrast the table which follows with a genealogical table to perceive that in the former other factors than kinship are

[1] 'Whereas families and local groups are shared by early and modern civilization, clans and gentes are known to primitive life alone ; they are equally foreign to earliest man and to historic man.' Goldenweiser, *Early Civilization*.

[2] 'Consanguinity is physical, whereas kinship in the savage sense is social.' Hartland, *Evolution of Kinship*.

[3] Morgan, *The League of the Iroquois*.

represented. A genealogical tree is the pure representation of kinship, and it shows a relationship reaching back through time and uniting by a common ancestry the dispersed family units and individuals of the present generation. But a political structure unites directly in the present the families and individuals whom it includes. The kin-relationship is, as it were, a time bracket and the political relationship a space-bracket. For the ordering of society it is not enough that men should be conscious of common descent through time, for the memory of the past grows dim and distant as the tree of life spreads its dividing branches over space; they must be conscious of common interest and common nature in the present. The kin-relationship must be fortified, and at length largely superseded, by the social relationship.

THE KIN-ARTICULATION OF PRIMITIVE SOCIETY AS ILLUSTRATED BY THE IROQUOIS TRIBES

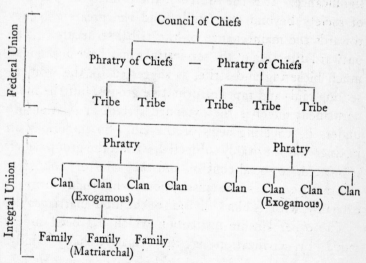

This table brings to our attention two institutions of kinship which, like the wider kin-association itself, have passed in the process of civilization but which in early society must have been important agencies of its maintenance. The institution of exogamy has been the subject of much study and of much speculation. The prohibition to marry within one's own clan or, in totemistic society very generally, one's own totem group, is extremely widespread, and is often combined with the specific injunction to marry within one other clan or totem group. This is the rigid interpretation and formulation by the ' savage ' mind of the same principle which appears in our ' table of forbidden degrees '. Whatever the fundamental instinct that explains the centrifugal tendency of sex, the fact is beyond question. It may be the expression of deep biological forces, but it acquires, if it does not from the first possess, a very clear social significance. It is the source of the primary articulation of society beyond the family, and the greatest agency towards the maintenance of the tribal structure.[1] The outward direction of the sex-instinct may have occasioned much bickering and strife, as suggested by the women-seeking raids and rapes of primitive groups, but the more permanent effect is the extended system of relationship under the covering aegis of the kin. So imperious an instinct was inevitably subjected, within the group which it created, to social control, and that control took, after the nature of savage institutions, the rigid form of exogamy, with its block-division of the inter-marriageable.

The other kinship-institution which has been superseded by civilization is the ' matriarchal ' family.

[1] Cf., e. g., Smith and Dale, *Iba-speaking Peoples of Northern Rhodesia*, pp. 283–7, 292–4.

'Matriarchal' and 'Matriarchate' are now admitted to be misleading terms for the relationship in question. There is no 'mother-rule', still less 'woman-rule' under the conditions of primitive society. Even the term 'mother-right', now commonly applied to the institution, over-emphasizes the social position of women. It was no exalted respect for women, but the logic of an age wherein maternity was a far more conclusive guide than paternity, strengthened by the permanent truth that the relation of the mother to the child is always more impressive and more profound than that of fatherhood, which must have led to the general practice of tracing descent through the female line, creating the misnamed 'matriarchal' family.

Sometimes this mode of reckoning is combined with the custom that the bridegroom must leave his own people and home and enter the family-group to which his bride belongs. Sometimes the chief or king owes his office to the right bestowed by marriage, and may actually lose it on the death of the spouse through whom his prerogative was conveyed. But in all such instances the woman is the agent of transmission, not the active wielder or even the participant of power.

A little reflection will show that this institution too played a considerable part in the extension and maintenance of the social structure. It gave the woman, the wife and mother, a social rather than a personal standing. The 'natural' dominance of the male is counterbalanced, so far as the union of families goes, by the social importance of the female. Thus the new family is bound in two different ways to its two sources, and the outward reach of the mating impulse accomplishes more than the mere adoption of wife or husband into the opposite group.

It knits very closely a whole group, and accomplishes the transition from the family to the community. In fact, all that was necessary, in order that the greater community should arise, was that men should have the *sense* of the family. For the family, though in some respects the most jealous and secluded of groups, has one essential character which distinguishes it from tribe or nation. It must, in every generation, break up. Its members must in every generation go beyond it to another family, in order that it shall re-exist. If the sense of the family persists only to the second generation, the greater society is already in being, and imperceptibly it transcends the principle of kin.

Thus the foundation of the social structure is built through the operation of the creative impulses of sex as these are controlled by the primitive understanding of the order within which they may find their least precarious satisfaction.

But another factor must be added at this point. Closely related to the control of sex is the control of property. We need only think of such institutions as the dowry, the preparation for and the maintenance of the home, the inheritance of wealth, to realize that even to-day property is to a very large degree a family rather than an individual interest. It was so even more intensely under primitive conditions. In primitive life of all types there are few goods that are consumed other than by family participation. There are in other words scarcely any luxuries, scarcely any individualized enjoyments. What scanty capital exists, the warrior's bow and spear no less than the herdsman's flock, the . fisherman's boat, and the cultivator's field, finds its normal use in the sustenance of the family life. It exists for the sake of the family as a whole, a family possession owned and controlled by the individual who is its head. It is not here implied that the instinct of property is derived from the instinct of sex. Our point is that under the conditions of early society the two are in practice indissoluble. The enjoyment of property falls within the life of the family. The problem of property, its secure possession and orderly disposal, is solved by a certain form of family organization. The problem of the family, its permanence against the waning and variability of the initial sex-impulse, is solved by its association with the unswerving desire for the control of property. It is needless to add that the woman herself, together with the offspring of the family union, took much of the aspect of property, and that the regard for woman's virtue (significant term) and the care for her well-being and maintenance depended in no small measure on this fact. The respect for personality is too weak under primitive conditions, perhaps even to this day, to be the basis of any permanent institution.

We must here pause to note that the term ' communism ' as applied to the primitive mode of property-ownership conveys a wrong impression. It lays stress on the common ownership of the productive mechanism, and particularly of the land. But in primitive life what is really owned in common within the circle of the family is the consumable product—the fruits of labour, a condition not so remote from that of our own days. The productive mechanism is owned for the sake of the family rather than by it. If we ever speak of common ownership, it must be attributed to the family, not to the community in any wider sense. Anthropological investigation has shown that the ' village community ' such as the Russian *mir* is a relatively advanced social formation, and we know that in any case it was far from being a true communistic system.[1] The householders were also, in respect of the land, shareholders. It was a method of communal land-control, guaranteeing to the family or household effectual occupancy and distinctive property-rights. Only the waste land and sometimes the meadow were really common, and the former at least came originally within the class of goods which, like water and sunlight, have, in the language of the economists, 'utility but not value'.

The interaction of the interests of sex and property in the building of the social structure is well illustrated if we turn from the 'matriarchal' to the 'patriarchal' family. The process of domestication has now advanced. The patriarch owns 'capital' in the original sense of the term, counting his wealth by *head*. The control and above all the inheritance of this self-breeding wealth, the domesticated animal, and of the land on which it breeds, must have been a strong influence against a system which sent the sons away from the home of the father to that of the father-in-law. The increase of property meant the increasing social dominance of the male, and with it went other forces which strengthened the importance, and thereby assured the fact, of paternity. We cannot here pursue the causes of this revolution, and must be content with the undoubted fact that the relatively settled pastoral life, as even more obviously the life of agriculture, accorded with, and in a sense made necessary, the patri-archal family.

With the inheritance of substantial property the importance of ancestry grew. The name of the father was the symbol of heirship; the patronymic (such as -son or -ing or -off, mac- or de- or ben-) became a permanent

---

[1] This is shown by Below, *Probleme der Wirtschaftsgeschichte*.

title. The magic of names reinforced the sense of kinship, as the course of generations enlarged the group. The blood-bond of sonship changed imperceptibly into the social bond of the wider brotherhood. The authority of the father passes into the power of the chief. Once more under the aegis of kinship new forms arise which transcend it. Kinship creates society and society at length creates the state.

II

THE SOCIAL STRUCTURE AND THE STATE

Every social phenomenon has three aspects which we may perhaps liken, though without laying stress on the comparison, to body, mind, and environment, the three primal characters of everything that lives. Thus the ' body ' of the family consists in the facts of sex, parenthood and consanguinity ; its ' mind ' or ' spirit ' in the sentiments and instincts, fear, appetite, love, and affection, which give vitality to these facts ; and its ' environment ' in the order of protection, authority, and mutual service which the ' spirit ' creates by its relation to the ' body '. To use more technical and perhaps less misleading terms, these three constitute the objective, the subjective, and the institutional factors which together form the complete social phenomenon. Likewise the community, as we saw it emerge out of the family life, has an objective factor in contiguity, assimilation, and the wider kinship ; a subjective factor in the feeling of ' brotherhood ' and ' loyalty ', the sense of common tradition and of common destiny ; and an institutional factor in the custom which permeates and regulates the conduct of its members.

Finally the state, itself a social superstructure supported by those factors that properly belong to the community, has its special outward mark of territorial inclusiveness ; its subjective character of citizenship in its various expressions, of which nationalism is perhaps the most complete ; and its institutional criterion in the form of political sovereignty and law. This political superstructure is still, in spite of these distinctive factors, too easily confounded with the community itself, to the hurt alike of our understanding and of our civilization. It will help to remove this misconception if we can show how the state in its rudimentary form, long before it could arrogate any such false claim, arose within the earlier life of society.

A brief sketch of the characteristic life of the primitive community will enable us to appreciate the feeble, experimental beginnings of the great state. Fortunately such a general description is quite possible because primitive society has certain common factors under the most diverse conditions of environment and among peoples the most remote from each other. Whether we travel with Seligman to the Veddahs or to the Melanesians of New Guinea, or accompany Spencer and Gillen to the arid heart of Australia, whether we visit the Bushmen of Africa or ascend the scale to the ' higher hunters ', such as most of the Indian tribes of North America, certain common traits, which are in marked contrast to those of every advanced civilization, stand clear before us. They belong to the very nature of primitive society, inevitable as the conditions, the necessities and the privations, under which it lived.

In the first place these primitive societies are all small and relatively isolated groups. Their ignorance of science, with its fruitful applications and saving previsions, made the supply of the elementary needs of sustenance a hand-to-mouth affair and rendered the limitation of members a stern necessity, so that even above the heavy mortality due to their lack of defence against disease, pestilence, and malnutrition, customs such as infanticide, abortion, and various forms of preventive sexual taboos, extensively prevailed. In a certain sense all these peoples lived ' close to nature ', though not in the way prescribed by sophisticated philosophers as a cure for the evils of civilization. What filled their lives and seized their imaginations was her changing moods, her precarious bounties, her mysterious and dreadful powers. They lived ' close to nature ' because no elaborate structure separated human life from that of the wild, or masked the ruthless sweep of elemental forces. They lived ' close to nature ', because every family, not a mere tithe of the population as among ourselves, depended directly upon the chase or fishing or the gathering of fruits and roots or on rudimentary agriculture. There was accordingly but little ' division of labour ' and little exchange of products. A few men, perhaps only one or two in a community, might be set apart as the skilled makers of bows or spears or canoes or vessels of clay, or again as herdsmen or watchers or witch-doctors.

The ultimate traits of such a community are most easily understood if we try to think away the apparatus of civilization. Experience was stored in oral tradition, there being no written speech, no technique of education, no record of science. The subjective aberrations of the human mind had full play wherever the immediate lessons of experience left it uncontrolled. The ghosts of the dead peopled the night together with the monsters of the imagination. The forces of nature became dim personal powers, to be feared and placated, sometimes to be ' worked ' by the power of magic, the mechanical mysteries of the rain-maker, the exorcist, the ' medicine-man '. As Frazer puts it, ' men mistook the order of their ideas for the order of nature ', and consequently lived in an exceedingly narrow world which outside of a small circle of facts was mere mythology. The fear of misunderstood forces cramped and subdued and distorted the thoughts of men.

Within a community so lacking in the means of control over nature, so bound to the necessities of immediate sustenance on the one hand, and so free on the other to accept the irrational reasoning of the untutored mind, there could be little of that internal differentiation which is so marked among more advanced peoples. In civilization we find within a single community very marked gradations of class and culture, due to the complexity of organization, the inequality of opportunity, the vast specialization of knowledge as well as of function. A primitive community is far more homogeneous. Its culture is very strictly a ' folk-culture '. There are, as between primitive peoples, the most striking differences of customs, manners, and morals, but within each community, save for the distinction due to age and sex, an identity of customs, manners, and morals is rigorously prescribed by and for the folk.

This brings us to what is, sociologically, the most significant distinction between primitive and advanced society. In the former ' custom is the king of men '. Custom is often described as ' unwritten law ', but we must realize that it differs wholly from the political code, above all because it is supported and enforced and, though not in any conscious manner, made by the community and not at all by the state. In fact the early growth of the state depends on the transformation of customs into laws. The whole life of primitive peoples is custom-ridden. There is a right way of doing everything, and only one right way. Outside the necessary technique of hunting and fishing and canoe-building, of sowing and planting and harvesting, of carrying on trade and waging war, of preparing food and of healing the sick, there is another and often very complicated technique of ceremonial observance which to the savage is equally authoritative. There is a prescribed way for giving a feast and for making love. There are rights which are demanded at every season and conjuncture. Puberty and every life-transition become occasions of solemn recognition. The primal facts of birth, marriage, and death are given an elaborate social setting. Natural phenomena are translated into social institutions by the ritual attached to their occurrence. Such observances are guarded by rigorous sanction, and the dreadful powers of a misknown universe jealously attend their violation. If the community punishes the offender against custom, it is often to avert the less discriminate interposition of these formidable guardians of the social way. The acts which are forbidden are even more numerous than those which are enjoined, and taboo is the invariable concomitant of custom.

It is obvious that under all such systems individual incentive is closely circumscribed. Men are, as it were, nearer to the common mould of the race. They walk in predetermined ways, expressive of their own conformity to type. The individual is not self-directed in any of the important concerns of his life. He has neither the capacity nor the social sanction for liberty. He follows the narrow trail beaten by thousands of feet and dares not explore the perils of diversity. He remains always the ward of his society. Morality is the fulfilment of custom, and does not include that higher, more difficult, but truly ethical law which bids a man be loyal to his own sense of values, even where it conflicts with the accepted creed. Lacking any true conception of morality he lacks also, at the other end, the definite sense of legality. The customary is both the right and the permitted. In civilized life, apart from the supra-social control which religion may exercise, a trinity of sanctions preside over conduct, that of the law, that of the social milieu, and that of the 'heart'. In primitive life they are merged in the one pervasive form of communal custom. And religion too is in large part but the reinforcement of that custom by the invocation of another and more formidable array of guardians.

This communal morality has in the light of a more advanced civilization two grave defects. On the one hand it tends to repress that personal sense of initiative and responsibility from which all the finer processes of human achievement take their rise. On the other hand it limits the range and thus distorts the meaning of the social values which it also supports. Just as a tribal God is the contradiction of a religious idea by the addition of the adjective, so, if less obviously, are the principles of justice and honour stultified when they do not apply to men as men but only as kinsmen or members of the group. Both of these limitations may be illustrated from the attitude of any primitive people. Thus Seligman, describing the Koita people of British New Guinea, says : 'The sense of responsibility and of effort is communal and not individual. . . . The Koita system of morals does not teach or express individual effort or individual salvation, but on the contrary teaches the due subordination of the individual and his efforts in the sum of the tribal activities, which, broadly speaking, allow no room for individual initiative. Hence homicide and theft are not considered reprehensible in themselves, but only become so, when directed against members of the community or tribe, or against outsiders strong enough to avenge themselves on the tribe.' [1]

If we regard this primitive morality as a low level beyond which the communities of our civilization have in greater or less degree advanced, it should be clearly understood that we so describe it not because the principles inculcated are themselves ' low ', for sometimes they surprise us by their austerity and simplicity —nor because they are less effective in binding society, for they are often extremely effective as social bonds. But the very fact that morality is wholly determined as communal usage reveals the childishness of a people, the absence of inner strength and guidance, the weakness of personality which must move in grooves or else suffer disintegration. The system accords with the life ; its restrictiveness is the price of existence. Thus the disturbance of the system caused by contact with a freer and more flexible civilization may have fatal consequences, and the well-intentioned ' reforms ' of alien governments and of proselytizing missionaries may prove the instruments of social death.[2] The cohesion of a primitive society is quite different from that of our own. It is communistic, not so much in the narrower economic sense, but in the form of the spiritual life. Its feasts and

[1] Seligman, *The Melanesians of British New Guinea*, p. 131.
[2] See, e. g., Malinowski, *Argonauts of the Western Pacific*.

solemn occasions, its lore, its song and dance, its whole armament of traditions and customs, bind each member within the narrow circle of social security.

The foregoing sketch may help us to understand the slow beginnings of the state, and to justify our contention that the state is a structure not coeval and co-extensive with society, but built within it as a determinate order for the attainment of specific ends. The earliest forms of state are extremely narrow in their aims and powers. They scarcely touch the inner purposes of the community, which are in the far safer wardship of custom. Apart from the organization of defence and offence, and the rudimentary organization of 'justice', they are more concerned with the privileges and powers of the dominant few than with the welfare of the community. Their rulers are heroes or demi-gods or warriors, or else their descendants, who exercise authority, not strictly as law-givers but as privileged persons. If such rulers create social order, it is by quelling rival claims to power, within or without the state, not by establishing a code. They enforce custom long before they make law; the judges come before the kings.[1] As diversity increases and disturbances from within or from without trouble the ancient order, there arise leaders who set out in a code those portions of the inheritance of custom which demand conscious reinforcement. These, however, are relatively late developments, after the art of writing or inscribing on stone was well advanced. But even such surviving examples as the Twelve Tables, the laws of ' Moses ', and the code of Hammurabi show how far they still are from attaining the true criterion of political law. It is

[1] As Maine showed, *Ancient Law*, ch. i.

significant that such codes are usually represented as directly handed to the law-giver from a divine source. Hammurabi receives them from Shamash, as Moses from Jehovah. And in their content they make no distinction between ceremonial injunction, moral and religious observance, and true legal enactment.

It might generally be stated, without much exaggeration, that the activities of early government are scarcely political at all. Rulers are privileged beings who gratify their sense of personal power by the capricious and arbitrary exercise of it over their subjects. The early kings of the relatively high civilization of Egypt, such as the Thinitae, have the power of life and death, can seize the women and the property of their subjects at will, and are reverenced as incarnate Gods. But they dare to alter scarce one tittle of the ceremonies and institutions of the people whose persons and wealth they dispose of so freely.[1] There is a might greater than the majesty of kings. There is a stability which their mere privileges do not touch. It is the immanent sense of the due order of society, to protect and develop *one* great part of which the state at last comes to recognize as its true function and only justification.

The display of leadership and the exercise of authority is

---

[1] Cf. Meyer, *Geschichte des Altertums*, vol. i, Pt. II, Bk. i, ch. iii. The chiefs and kings of Western peoples had apparently more power to alter institutions than was accorded to Eastern potentates. The names of many Anglo-Saxon monarchs, such as Canute, are associated with institutional changes. This corresponds with the fact that the Western monarch was more dependent on his council, such as the Anglo-Saxon witan. Whether the witan had really the power to elect and depose kings is open to doubt (cf. Chadwick, *Studies on Anglo-Saxon Institutions*, pp. 355–66), but it did exercise a degree of control from which the Eastern monarch was free.

found wherever society exists. It gives form and character to an urchins' club as well as to a cabinet committee ; to a gang of thieves as well as to a convocation of clerics. But no one would call all such leadership and authority ' political ', and neither should we say that wherever we find a ' headman ' in a savage tribe we are in the presence of the state. We cannot say when or where the state begins. It is implicit in the universal tendency to leadership and subordination, but it only emerges when authority becomes government and custom is translated into law.

Thus the right of men and families to quarrel interfered with their service of the chief and created an indiscipline which touched his authority. What more natural than that he should restrict that liberty by pains and penalties ? The evolution of penal law is very significant here. The ancient rule of retaliation—' an eye for an eye ', ' a tooth for a tooth '—obviously goes back to the pre-political stage. It was the injured man or his group that found satisfaction in that primitive revenge, and we must in fact remember that ' revenge ' is a personal and not a political category. ' The avenger of blood himself shall slay the murderer : when he meeteth him, he shall slay him ' (Num. xxxv. 19). It is above all the kinsman's duty sanctioned by custom and often enforced by the dreadful shapes of expiatory divinities. Orestes must avenge on his own mother his father's death. Vengeance belongs to the kin, not to the state. Its mode is often prescribed in most meticulous form. The curious rigour of this barbaric logic is seen in such a case as the following. ' A boy who had climbed a tree happened to fall down right on the head of his little comrade standing below. The comrade died immediately ; and the unlucky climber was in consequence sentenced to be killed in the same way as he had killed the other boy, that is, the dead boy's brother should climb the tree in his turn, and tumble down on the other's head till he killed him '.[1] In other cases revenge is modified into the milder expiation of the fine, embodying the idea of ' damages ' later translated, for an entirely different type of offence, into a principle of the ' civil ' code. Thus it is still characteristic of Chinese society that an appeal to the family of the offender is made for compensation. But in such cases the relation of the state to the act is not yet envisaged.

The social, not the political, significance of certain offences, leads, on the other hand, to penal action undertaken by the community as a whole. We need only refer to the story of Achan by way of illustration. The offence of Achan ' troubled ' Israel, and all Israel stoned him with stones—including, for safety's sake, his family with the sinner (Joshua vii. 24–6). The motive is here transformed. It is to protect society, if not from the direct social consequences of such conduct, at least from the general ' wrath of God ', that the offender is punished. It is, in so far, the true political motive, but the instrument is not yet the state.

There are various aspects of this process which are easily discerned. The ' natural ' authority of the paterfamilias prepared the way for the tribal chief. The former wields authority over wife and children, he is the guardian and interpreter of custom, the priest and often the medicine-man within the circle. As the ' old men ' convert sporadic meetings into the regular ' council ' of elders, these functions receive in part the support of a wider community, and in part are transferred to the

[1] Parkyns, *Life in Abyssinia*, ii, 236, *apud* Westermarck, *Origin and Development of the Moral Ideas*, I, ch. ix.

chiefs or leaders who, here too, 'naturally' arise. At first there is no thought of created law, no organization of government save for the affirming of the *mores*, the conduct of ceremonies, and the punishment of offenders. As has been so clearly shown by Maine, Bagehot, and others, the making of law in the strict sense, which is the central function of the modern state, is foreign to primitive communities. 'Custom is the king of men.' Within it is woven the religious principle, which finds for human life a law that is never made by man and is fearfully enforced by powers beyond his range. Magic adds its strange mechanism, so that 'crime' is punished automatically or by the skill of the magician. There remained for the rudimentary state only a narrow group of executive functions which the logic of power as well as the necessities of order extended into the vast control exercised by the developed state.

We may observe this process in its further development in the history of the Anglo-Saxon people. At first the courts merely deliver the communal law, and they lack executive power. It is still for the family to take vengeance, and the blood-feud flourishes. But 'step by step as the power of the state waxes, the self-centred and self-helping autonomy of the kindred wanes. Private feud is controlled, regulated, put, one may say, into a legal harness; the avenging and the protecting clan of the slain and the slayer are made pledges and auxiliaries of public justice.' [1]

The indiscipline, the insecurity, the wastefulness, and the endless strife appertaining to these forms of revenge or retribution, so well illustrated by such surviving instances as the blood-feud in Albania, Montenegro, and

[1] Pollock and Maitland, *History of English Law*, vol. i.

Corsica, or again by the indiscriminate mass-punishment by lynching in America, were strong inducements for the intervention of the nascent state. At first it merely intervenes. It protects the custom rather than the society. It prevents the powerful offender from going scot-free and it prevents the strong avenger from exceeding in his anger the limits of retaliation. To achieve these ends it must take over the task of punishment. But in so doing it imperceptibly introduces the political ground of punishment. For what is the use of retaliation or even retribution to the *state* ? What satisfaction does it bring to the *state* that it should ' hurt back ' one of its own members because he has hurt another ? Why should it multiply its own corporate hurt ? Inevitably the idea of social protection, with its concomitants of reformation as well as prevention, modify the whole system. The *custom* of punishment recedes into the regions of social ostracism, and the political principle of punishment takes its place. In Anglo-Saxon England the development of the ' king's peace ' proclaims the change which made punishment a function of the state, justified by the need of public order and private protection. It is a transformation of motive that is even to-day far from being complete. Still the state is understood as intervening for the sake of assuring a duly limited, a ' just ' retribution. But the process has advanced and the state has conquered a new sphere.

III

AUTHORITY AND CLASS

Social protection and the ambition of power—these are the two most diverse but most mingled motives which stimulated the formation of state-institutions. The former impelled the rulers, as it were from below, since alike their function and their authority required them to consider the members or citizens of the state ; the latter actuated them from within. When the two motives combined to inspire the same course of action, there the state found its surest ground and its quickest development. Such is the history of the political institution of punishment, involving as it did the establishment of a judicial system, a code of criminal law, and an executive charged with its enforcement. The panoply of justice obviously increased the power of the government, while at the same time it was a necessary instrument of social order. The like combination of motives worked for the control of the state over property and for its regulation of the system of sexual relations, since in these matters the drive of human instincts is most apt to transgress the restrictions of custom and to cause social disintegration. But nowhere were the two motives so cunningly and so inextricably combined as in the provision of armed force against external foes. Here the demand for protection took on its most insistent form, and here also it most directly worked for the aggrandizement of political authority. Here too, and here alone, the power of the chief was made manifest as the power of the people as well. Elsewhere the exaltation of the ruler was the abasement of his subjects, but here his exaltation was also theirs. They shared with him the necessity of deliverance and security, the feeling of glory and triumph. So strong a conjuncture—strong still to-day as in the primitive world—turned the growing state into an agency of dominance, creating peace within and war abroad.

It would be easy to show, by many evidences, how various early states, under the influence of the motives already mentioned, gradually created for themselves an organization at length so far-reaching that with it came to be identified society itself. But the proportions of this work limit us to the mere indications we have just offered. We must, instead, turn to another aspect of the rising state, without consideration of which our idea of the process by which it developed, within and in a sense above the community, would be quite one-sided. We have hitherto spoken of the state in terms of ruler and subjects, the government and the governed. This is the legal aspect, but the internal structure of the state is not built on any such simple dichotomy. The state creates not only order but orders. Power is never a mere subordination of the many to the one. It is, always, a hierarchy. It implies a class-structure. Power is the effective exercise of will, but, even if it seems to pertain to the will of one, it requires a complex and graded organization of supporting wills, wills that participate no less than wills that acquiesce.

The growth of political power thus necessitates important changes in the social structure. These changes consist in the establishment or re-formation of social classes in terms of relative dominance and subjection. The headman of a primitive tribe might securely depend on the support of the communal custom of which he was the custodian, but the ruler who organizes armed forces, takes regular toll of the community's wealth, and settles the disputes of property and of sex, needs the support of a privileged class whose interests are more nearly identified with his own. Thus we may explain the fact that in the simpler stages of customary determination the organization of the people has a more democratic appearance than later on when the state has definitely emerged. We might cite the descriptions by Caesar and Tacitus of the Gaulish and Germanic tribes, or the accounts of such present-day peoples as the nomads of the Asiatic plains or certain tribes of American Indians. Such primitive democracies exist because of the rudimentary organization of power, in sharp contrast to modern democracies which are only possible by reason of a high development of the system of political control.

The origins of this class-structure are of course inherent in the inequality of human conditions. There are inner and outer circles of kinship. There are prouder and more humble pretensions of descent. There is authority that accrues to age and experience—until time weakens it again. There is the greater prestige and power of the successful warrior and of the man whose herds are larger or whose lands are more fertile or wider. There is a lore which becomes the jealously guarded possession of individuals or families. There are men honoured for their skill or cunning or physical powers. Thus select fraternities and cliques arise, the natural oligarchies of mankind. They claim prerogatives and superior rights. They strengthen their claims by attaching themselves to the power of the growing state. They thus at once secure their own ends and give to government the social support which its extended authority requires. In the process, however, the state becomes a class-state, tribal custom is narrowed by group privilege, and the polity of the state moves still farther towards the aims of dominance and away from those of the common welfare.

A good illustration of the way in which the graded social order develops within the community and thereby fosters political oligarchy is found in the history of the ' secret societies ' which are so characteristic of primitive life. The following passage well summarizes the evolution of these societies :

' However striking may be the difference between such an institution as the *Bora* of the Australian natives and a tribal secret society like the *Dukduk* of the Bismarck Archipelago or the *Egbo* of West Africa, they appear, in the last analysis, to be due fundamentally to the changes brought about when once the principle of limitation of membership is introduced. The process which converts the puberty-institution into the secret societies of peoples more advanced in culture, seems in general to be that of the gradual shrinking of the earlier inclusive and democratic organization consisting of all the members of the tribe. The outcome of this process, on the one hand, is a limitation of the membership of the organization to those only who are able to satisfy the necessary entrance-requirements ; and, on the other hand, the establishment in the fraternity so formed of various degrees through which candidates may pass in succession. With the fuller development of secret society characteristics, these degrees become more numerous, and passage through them more costly. The members of the higher degrees, forming an inner circle of picked initiates, then control the organization in their own interests.' [1]

This is merely an instance of the way in which, as social life grows more complex, the simpler and the more democratic rule of custom gives place to a new order of subordination and control. This is the opportunity of the

[1] Webster, *Primitive Secret Societies.*

state. It becomes more essential to social order, but it also becomes more restrictive. The state becomes identified with a privileged class. It stands for dominance and obedience, a category in terms of which the narrow legalist doctrine of the Austinians still seeks to interpret its nature. The state becomes the embodiment of power, but only in proportion as it becomes the instrument of a class, only as it is identified with a privileged order. Thus the idea of the state is narrowed as its functions increase. So the way is prepared for the form of empire, by which for so long the destinies of mankind were shaped.

THE EARLY EMPIRE

I. THE BUILDING OF EMPIRE

WE have so far been concerned with small communities within which a rudimentary political structure was evolved. But the term ' state ' is generally associated with an extended and comprehensive area, and already in the background of history we discover far-flung states exercising an imperial sway. How did these arise ? Was it by natural union, by the ramification of the system of kinship, leading to alliances, confederacies, and thus to stronger unities ? Or was it by conquest and domination ? It cannot be doubted that the latter was the pathway of the extended state. In the course of history the centrifugal forces are nearly always too strong for orderly expansion, and it is only after the habituation imposed by necessity that the worth, which even for us to-day is a matter of difficult valuation, of the greater order is accepted. Near aims and narrow jealousies, the incitements of a precarious subsistence, the love of independence and the pride of personal power, the ideas of a society which required the aegis of kinship to give it cohesion, prevented the extension of order through co-operative intelligence, though they readily adapted themselves to the spirit of conquest. Besides, the conditions of primitive communication made it impossible for men to join in free political co-operation over any great area. We scarcely realize how completely all extensive systems of democratic and responsible government depend upon a quite modern development of the means by which men can relate themselves swiftly and directly to one another over vast distances. In the absence of these means we can expect nothing beyond loose alliances or confederacies, no great system of control—save empire. For wealth and power may exercise control, being external and cumulative, over the common will of men even where that will itself can find no way to achieve its intrinsic ends.

Alliances, therefore, and confederacies we do find among relatively primitive peoples, as for example the famous five-tribe confederacy of the Iroquois, which at one time controlled an area larger than that of many a modern state.[1] But these never develop into a true state. The enlarged state was reached by a very different road. It represented the triumph of the political idea of power over the political idea of justice. It at once stimulated and depended upon a class structure that gave an age-long redirection to political institutions.

In the life of primitive man, there is no surplus of wealth on which a class-system can well be based. Existence is, for the community as a whole, a hand-to-mouth affair, so that social distinctions depend on personal qualities, on birth or initiation, or on those traditional privileges which express themselves in ceremonial office and custom-prescribed deference. Such distinctions

---

[1] 'About 1675, they attained their culminating point when their dominion reached over an area remarkably large, covering the greater parts of New York, Pennsylvania, and Ohio, and portions of Canada north of Lake Ontario.' Morgan, *Ancient Society*, ch. v.

do not vitally affect the everyday life of men. There is a certain democracy about poverty, even in a primitive tribe. But it is an unprogressive democracy. It was superseded in the very process which built the state. The evolving state established subjection in the place of equality, preferring dominion to fellowship and the class-system to the co-operative commonwealth. What made the change possible was the accumulation of mobilizable wealth. Progress in the domestication of animals, in the cultivation of the soil, in the technique of the arts of peace and of war, of production and of exchange, created by slow degrees, in regions favoured by nature, a new instrument of power which the state, the organ of power, was not slow to seize.

Those fertile valleys of the Euphrates and the Tigris, the Nile, the Yellow River, and the Yang-tse, which we call the 'cradles of civilization', were the regions in which first a surplus of wealth was accumulated. As it grew, there arose cities, small and great, for the city is the focus and the sign of mobilizable wealth. The presence of the city witnesses to the fact that a group has liberated itself from the immediate necessity of wresting a livelihood from the soil, that it has found a means by which to command the fruits of the labours of other men. The city implies the concentration of wealth and through it the concentration of power. The city is the first condition of empire. The early empires of the world, Sumerian, Assyrian, Persian, Egyptian, Chinese, were established by peoples which first had learned the art of city-life. The city organizes and elaborates the forms of social control. It tends in early times to be a state in itself, extending its influence over a rural *hinterland*. By loose alliance or mere cultural assimilation a number of cities are joined in jealous and quarrelsome contact until one more eminent in power and leadership dominates the rest and becomes the heart of an empire.

Within the city the organization of power develops to a degree quite unattainable among nomads, shepherds, or agriculturists. Of all people the soil-bound agriculturist, devoted to incessant and dispersive toil, is the least able to organize resources or bid for power. The nomad achieves a closer unity, is able to combine more rapidly for defence or aggression, and to transport his belongings where necessity or advantage dictates. The horse or camel provide him with swift locomotion, his flocks and herds he drives before him, and his wagons carry his household goods and the less mobile members of his family. Where the nomad and the peasant occupy adjoining territories, the latter is exposed to the forays of the former, as in the striking and oft-cited case of the age-long resistance offered by the settled peaceful agriculturist along the Yellow River to the attacks of the restless horsemen of the Mongolian desert. But such wandering hordes do not attain the type of civilization on which the larger state is built. They are unstable and ill-adapted to that persistent, purposeful, and ordered exploitation which is the work of empire. They form bands rather than states. Generally they seek merely to raid and withdraw. When under the impulse of unusual leadership they attain the scale of a conquering host, they may, as did the Huns, the Turks, and the Arabs, overthrow an established empire, but they cannot maintain one save as they settle down, lose their old character, and rebuild out of the ruins of what they had previously destroyed. Only the settled population of a country rich enough to permit of the order and the concentration of power involved in the life of the city can learn the secret of empire.

In the ancient city the kinship-organization of primitive society declined in importance whereas class-organization developed. Kinship, in modern as in ancient times, finds the conditions of the city less congenial than those of the country. The mode of housing and of aggregation characteristic of the city isolates the essential family group from the cluster of relatives, while new influences create new forms of association. Religion crystallizes into temple-worship overshadowing the ancient rites of the household. A priesthood develops within the temple precincts and becomes a close corporation, an exclusive and highly organized instrument of social control. A court of growing complexity, with specialized functionaries, surrounds the person of the king and elaborates a code of manners and a mode of life which sets it apart from the rest of the people. These orders make the city as well as the country their tributaries, and consolidate their position by institutions of control and dominance, establishing to that end an official array of ministers, tax-gatherers, officers of justice, and so forth. At the same time there is growing up the general ' civilization ' of the city, enhancing the division of labour and stimulating technical developments, including developments of the instruments of war. The higher forms of skill are thus demarcated from the commoner forms of labour, with corresponding class distinctions. The system of exchange is liberated from the clumsy operation of barter, and thereby not only is wealth rendered more mobilizable and cumulative than before, but also it becomes an easier means to power, commanding freely or without apparent constraint the services of men.

Nowhere does the influence of free or mobilizable wealth work more effectively than in the establishment of a permanent armed force, as distinct from the occasional levies or spontaneous musterings of clan or tribe. A military order is created, with professional officers who organize a rigorous system of subordination and make unquestioned and graded authority and obedience the rule of life. So the army becomes a strong conservative force, confirming the class-state, tending to divorce the principle of authority from that of the common service, and translating the idea of service itself into the fulfilment of command. Command, unlike law, is personal, the peremptory claim of a superior, requiring obedience in the name of power or office, ascribing to the inferior a mere duty without reference to his own purposes or interests.

A community, so organized, presents a striking contrast to the primitive tribe. We may take as illustration the earliest known stage of the ancient civilization of Egypt. Here we can find nothing to correspond to the clan or the tribe. The order of society is based not on kinship but on status determined by class and occupation. These distinctions are for the most part hereditary, though fortune and official favour may raise a man to any eminence. The divisions of the double kingdom of Upper and Lower Egypt are territorial, and each territory or province has its local usage and its local gods. But they are all set like mosaics in the framework of the state. Originally they must have been, save for a few merely administrative divisions, autonomous communities. But the conflicts of power have issued in an overruling might, wielded by the conjoint authority of king and priest. A repressive religion, for the most part grotesque, gloomy, and dread-inspiring, has elevated a few of the local gods into deities of universal range and common cult, like Osiris and Horus and Seth. The king too has become a god, and one symbol, the ' falcon of Horus ', stands alike for ' god ' and for ' king '. Thus palace and temple dominate the land, and all men are subjects. The institution has become lord of life. Its origin is forgotten, and the strong influences of superstition and rank dominate the mind. Men are no more blood-brothers or comrades, free-men of a community whose institutions are their own ; they are servants of power. The building of the king's palace or of his tomb or of another temple to one of the many gods they serve, is a duty paramount over the mere well-being of the folk. The state, doubly armed with the weapons of military force and religious awe, is over all.

No other community may have exhibited so extreme a diversion of the state from the principle of common service as did ancient Egypt, but in varying degrees all early peoples which attained the conditions of civilization, to wit, a surplus of wealth over immediate necessities and a form of city life, passed through a similar process of satisfaction and subjection. In Sumeria as in Babylonia, in India as in China, the way of empire was prepared by the subordination, within the at first small city-centred states, of the mass of the people to the class or classes which held the institutions of power. Not always is the ' spiritual ' dominance so clearly associated as in Egypt with the political—sometimes the priestly order is separate and withdrawn from the political, and sometimes it wins a superior place. But always the two powers are united in this at least, that they reinforce one another in stabilizing, along lines of authority and subordination, the order of society. The class system becomes in consequence deeply impressed upon each community. When this has been achieved the time is ripe for a leader who, with the instrument of power now forged for his hand, will carry the principle of dominance from out his own state and impose it upon others. Such was the role of leaders like Sargon of the Akkadians, Tiglath-Pileser I of the Assyrians, and Wu Wang, the founder of the Chow dynasty. These were no mere victors in common warfare ; they were men who incarnated the idea of power to which their individual states were already committed, and carried it to its logical conclusion of empire.

The coming of empire brought new political problems. To concentrate the government of a large area under one ruler was a matter of endless difficulty, especially in those ages of slow communications. The regional commanders, provincial governors, or satraps enjoyed a very large measure of autonomy and were frequently tempted to conspire against or defy the all-ruler. In the court of the emperor itself powerful nobles stood jealously ready to seize his throne when occasion offered. Especially was this true when hereditary succession transferred the sceptre to weaker hands. Heredity is the natural means of stabilizing power as ' right ', but its operation, while generally enhancing the prestige of the throne, often diminishes its effectual authority. Thus early empire presents an aspect of instability and vicissitude, at best a loose congeries of semi-independent states, while the imperial sceptre shifts not only from dynasty to dynasty, but also from city to city. In truth, the conditions of imperial stability included not only the establishment of common political institutions, but also a further reformation of the class-structure. The divisions of the ruling classes created by the centralization of power weaken their united front against the subject classes. These divisions are overcome only in the rare instance when a strong monarch arises who understands and is able to practise the principle of absolutism, destroying the independence of all the lesser principalities and powers. So the Egyptian rulers of the twelfth dynasty, Amenemhat I and Sesostris III, crushed in turn the autonomous rulers who distracted their realm. But successful absolutism, as imperial Rome so conclusively showed, and as appeared even in the Egypt of Sesostris III, reduces the political distinction between classes and draws its instruments of service from the lowly as well as from the great. The pride of absolutism leads the monarch to emphasize the difference between himself and *all* his subjects, so undermining the solidarity of a ruling class. Monarchy thus prepares the way of democracy. At a later historical stage it was in fact proclaimed in the name of democracy and with the support of the consciously democratic elements, the ' commons '. In its name the Greek ' tyrants ', the Gracchi, and the early Caesars fought against ' oligarchy '; for there is never the same conflict between the interests of the one and the many as between the interests of the many and the few.

But nothing seems so hard to acquire as political wisdom. Early empires rose and fell, but they never attained political stability. Some fell directly through the invasion of outer nomad peoples, as did Sumeria and Assyria. New empires took their place, with no greater hold on the secret of political permanence. Chaldea, Media, Persia, had their day. Others, because of geographical situation, endured in name and even in form like Egypt, but subject to many conquests and transferences of power. One alone of these empires, the Chinese, has lasted in some sense from an unknown past to the present day, but its loose-membered unity has never been securely established in political solidarity, and were it not for the social tenacity of a common civilization peculiarly rooted in the life of the family it too would long ago have been numbered with the past. All early forms of empire turned the commonwealth into property, and sovereignty into the right of possession. The temptations and jealousies of power were thus set free from the control of the only sure guardian of the state, the common will. The instrument of power broke in the hands that held it too tightly. It is not because of the ' natural ' mortality of the state, but because of the defective basis of political authority, that the early empires fell, to impress mankind for ever with the sense of the transient character of pomp and power.

II

LAND POWER AND SEA POWER

The empires which we have thus far been considering were inland or continental powers. To them the sea was a barrier, not a highway, the frontier beyond which they could not pass, but which, once attained, afforded them protection against external foes. The focus of Egyptian civilization lay not at the mouths of the Delta but on the middle reaches of the Egyptian Nile. Chinese civilization spread southward and eastward from the inner valleys of the Yellow River, and even to this day, ' from the native point of view, the coasts are the ends of the earth, and the places where least of the true celestial

spirit is to be found.'[1] The sea was the great divider.
It was *dissociabile*, and the fear of the great waters still
echoes in the literature of the maritime Greeks. Navigation was confined almost entirely, save for a month or two
in the year, to coastwise traffic. The ships of the ancient
empires were according to our standards clumsy and un-
seaworthy, and to the perils of the deep were added the
constant hazards of piracy. Even in the time of Demosthenes the rate of insurance on seagoing ships was enormous. Slowly and fearfully did men discover the power and
the wealth which accrues to those who control the sea.

If any region in the world was naturally adapted to
teach the advantages of sea-enterprise it was the coast of
the Aegean. Strings of islands stretched across it, forming
bridges to connect lands most diverse in character. It is
here then that we find the first sea-empires, the beginnings
of a new and epoch-making form of political power. An
Aegean civilization, quite distinctive from the inland
civilizations of Asia Minor, of Egypt, of China, or of
India, arose and flourished for more than a millennium
before the first page of classical history was opened. Its
most remarkable development was in the island of Crete,
but it has also left illuminating memorials on the famous
site of Troy and later, in the second millennium before
Christ, at Mycenae and Tiryns. Built as these latter
cities were at some distance from the sea, they belonged
undoubtedly to a maritime civilization. It is moreover
a civilization that we recognize as akin to our own.
Compared with those of the Orient it has a curiously
European character.[2] Like our modern civilization of

[1] Parker, *China*, ch. i.

[2] Cf. Cavaignac, *Histoire de l'antiquité*, vol. i, ch. v; 'quelque stimu-
lante qu'ait été la proximité de l'Orient civilisé, la civilisation égéenne est
nettement européenne d'origine et de caractère.'

the West, this ancient order of life rested on resources and conditions that arise from the contacts established by the unified control of land and sea.

These early maritime powers had, characteristically, an influence out of proportion to their size. In Crete the little state whose capital was Knossos dominated the Cyclades and spread its influence as far as Ionia and Greece, while in the same island Phaestos was the centre of another power which established connexions with the empires of the East. Crete is represented in the Odyssey as a land of five distinct peoples. It is a meeting-place of civilizations, out of which a new and greater civilization arose. It is on the routes of traffic and represents the intermingling and fusion of diverse types. This is the process of fertilization which has brought to final birth perhaps every great civilization of the world. The sea-routes to a strategic point enabled contacts to be established there while precluding those mass movements of population which overwhelm the culture and customs of the land subjected to them. There is at such points a constant interchange not only of products but also of ideas. The minds of men are stimulated and liberated, no longer subservient to the tyranny of hardening customs. The cultural fate of Egypt could never have befallen a sea-faring people. The trader acquires inevitably a greater social flexibility and freedom from prejudice, and sea-power far more than land-power is dependent upon trade. Further, a state whose wealth is due to trading has a relatively smaller peasant population and lacks thus the element of immobility which belongs to the nature of the peasant. The wealth of commerce, while it may be more precarious, is more quickly enhanced under favouring conditions than the wealth that accrues directly from the soil. It is also more concentrated, more available for free expenditure, and thus gives a greater stimulus to the arts of life. All these conditions help to explain the distinctive character of the maritime empires.

Among inland peoples the nomads had mobility without wealth, while the agriculturists acquired resources at the cost of mobility. The sea-faring peoples retained something of both advantages. They had both wealth and striking power. It was easier and less expensive for them to establish a dominion of tolls and dues and tributes. On these, and not on the continuous occupation of the land, were the maritime empires founded. Their cities were at once forts and markets. The surplus acquired by free interchange was itself a power by means of which they sought another and more invidious surplus, that wrung by tribute from the less wealthy and the less strong. Nevertheless from the two combined they acquired a command over resources which permitted the free and very remarkable development of their native genius. The power-states of the Aegean, relatively secure as they were from invasion and the burden of armies, while yet saved by their accessibility to the outer world from the encrustation of their social forms, established a basis of leisure and opportunity on which the intrinsic arts of life flourished as never before. In this they differed from that other maritime empire which arose after their decline, Phoenicia, whose trading spirit consumed in its own development the resources which it acquired. In this too they resembled that later and yet greater sea-empire of Athens, whose best minds, learning clearly to distinguish the ends of life from the mere means, have given an immortal inspiration to the world.

There are certain distinctions between land-power and

sea-power which have much significance for the evolution of the state. The motive of imperial expansion is and always has been predominantly an economic one. In pursuit of this object the land-power annexes, generally by main force before the days of dynastic compacts and fusions, adjoining territories whose lands and peoples, through direct subjection, pay tribute to the dominant class of the state. The labour of the cultivator, often reduced to a serf, is the chief source of its wealth and the unhonoured foundation of its prestige. As the land-empire expands, its central control, inevitably in those earlier times when the world was not knit together by swift lines of communication, tends to grow weaker. It is forced to decentralize its authority, and the central government receives only a portion of the surplus which comes from domination. At the same time it must maintain ever larger forces under arms, which eat up its resources. Its exactions consequently become greater, and the production of wealth is imperilled by the depression of the producers. Meanwhile the provinces of the empire, growing more autonomous as they increase, have no bond of common interest to unite them to the centre. Their subordinate governors and landed nobles claim and exercise powers that disturb the structure of empire. It is liable to be broken up by its own centrifugal forces. This has been the repeated fate of land powers, in India, in China, in Egypt, and in the later empires of North Africa and of mediaeval Germany.

In sharp contrast stands the maritime empire. It does not annex, part after part, a bulk of adjoining territories, but instead establishes strategic colonies, fortified trading-posts commanding a *hinterland*, or it employs its wealth and strength in dominating such posts already established by weaker states. In so doing it does not require an extended line of military occupation. It combines the uses of economic and political power. It seizes the control of trade, the sinews of peace and war, sometimes by mere encroachment without the display of force. Its wealth is collected, almost automatically, at the centre, and from the centre its power goes swiftly forth, at need, to any point of its circumference. It can therefore govern without excessive decentralization, without creating a group of dangerously empowered subordinates or proconsuls. Further, it links its parts to each other and to the centre by the strong persuasions of trading facilities, customs, and other advantages. It seems to depend, and in fact does depend, to a lesser degree than the land-empire on the power of arms, and to that extent is stronger. It is less vulnerable from within and seldom breaks from disruption, though Athens, transforming too forcefully the Delian League into a subject empire and relying overmuch on exactions instead of on the advantages of trade, suffered this fate. But the downfall of maritime empire usually proceeds from other causes. The channels of trade change in the course of the centuries ; new powers arise, new conflicts with external foes. And if the single heart of a sea-empire is smitten, its fall is catastrophic and spectacular, like that of Carthage. The land-empire rests on the wealth of the soil, which is far less destructible, and endures through the ' drums and tramplings of a thousand conquests '. The slow transitions of nature, combined perhaps with the wasteful exploitation and ravage of men, may indeed impoverish it, as in Mesopotamia, Persia, Arabia, and possibly Greece. But nature generally restores, with prudent cultivation, the wealth of the soil though new powers may enter in to possess it. Whereas the advantage of the maritime empire, once lost, may have passed for ever.

Another antithesis of great moment reveals itself within the subject orders of those two types of empire. The territorial power gathers to itself the surplus produced on the land, not so much the surplus of ' nature's bounty ', in the polite phrase of the Physiocrats, as the surplus accruing to his toil which the cultivator is not permitted to consume. In the course of social evolution, two classes of cultivator appear, the serf and the ' freeman '. But the common burdens which they endure, the exacting labour which they share, the ' natural ' economy of rural life in which monetary exchange is subordinate, and the absence of that constant supervision and direct control which belong to industrial exploitation, work towards their assimilation. The serf and the freeman tend thus to a common intermediate status, that of the peasant. His is perhaps the most permanent, the most conservative, of all social conditions. The same laws which bind the peasant to the land give him a body of elementary rights. To these rights he clings with the utmost tenacity, but he does not of his own accord endeavour to transform them into active political powers. He is content with their recognition. The inner ferment of the maritime city, breeding challenges to established authority whose significance we must soon see, is unknown to him. He seeks above all things establishment, the customary way, provided it is not beyond measure intolerable. Whatever satisfactions life brings to him fall within the circle of the family and the kin or come as the scarce conscious rewards of that intimacy with nature which fills his days. They are simple and deeply impressed, direct and non-competitive. The order of things of which they are part, he is not inclined to question or disturb. The forces of nature convey to him that sense of ineluctable, abiding, yet capricious power which reflects itself in submission also to personal authority. For him the distance between God and the king is one of degree. The peasant is eminently in harmony, therefore, with the class-power of the land-empire. The internal forces that disturb it come not from below but from above, from the distracting claims of the land magnates and not from the subject population of the land.

The sea-empire is in precisely the opposite condition. Its evolution, instead of modifying, sharpened the distinction between the slave and the freeman. The freer capital of the maritime power not only enabled it to procure slaves, by purchase or raids, in greater numbers, it also assigned them to the multitude of menial and mechanical tasks which commercial and industrial development creates. The early sea-empires swarmed with slaves. As aliens, as 'living tools' subject to the will of others, and as beings dedicated to forms of toil which for that very reason were thought of as 'illiberal', they were an entirely different order from the freeman. They made life easier for the freemen, giving to numbers of them the leisure and opportunity of life in the cities. Doubtless the price was heavy. Slavery has grave social costs, and most of all when it is the necessary basis of a civilization. But at any rate, by affording leisure and a certain power and the contrast of condition to the free, it conspired with those other influences which led them to demand, in the mercantile city, a full share of political power. The power-state is here attacked from below. It is an old observation that *status* matters less in the community that lives by trade. Here at least Maine's pregnant doctrine that the progress of civilization is 'from *status* to contract' holds true. Contract is the basis of trade, and *status* is disturbed and weakened by the fluctuations of fortune which the life of trade involves. The trader is at the opposite pole from the peasant. He seeks advantage, change, novelty—finally power. The sea-empire breeds within it a new thing, democracy.

Of this later. Meantime, lest we lay overmuch stress upon the divergence of land from sea-empire, we may observe that all domination of whatever kind extended the range of common custom, common speech, common ideas. Thus civilization was widened and in some measure enriched. Empire brought a degree of peace and stability, sometimes long-lived, within which the human spirit found a greater opportunity to reveal its unexplored capacities, in philosophy, in literature, in religion, in art, in science and technique. The forces thus partially liberated must in time recreate the state also. Under the aegis of uncomprehending power the common, the universal interests of mankind were slowly growing. Of the two aspects of the state, power and service, it is nearly always the former which determines in the first instance its extension, whereas service determines its intension, its inner development. Men are nearly always subjects before they become citizens. But the very conditions of subjection prepare the way for citizenship.

III

THE EMERGENCE OF CITIZENSHIP

I. THE SPIRIT OF THE CITY

THE Aegean civilization of Troy and Crete, of Mycenae and Tiryns, rose and fell. It left scarcely a trace, save for a fabulous legend or so, on the page of recorded history. Only the spade of the excavator revealed the long-unsuspected reality, the wonder of a rich, artistic, and distinctive life whose very memory was buried along with its spear-heads of obsidian, its rings of iron, and its cups of gold, with its gems and its jars, its sculptures and its wall-paintings, in the graves of its own dead. It fell, not because its life-course was fulfilled, for there is no ' natural ' end, but only transformation, in the histories of civilization. It fell before an invading people from the north, who swept over and overwhelmed the land of Greece, the islands and the coasts of the Aegean. The conquerors were one people in the sense that, apart from dialectical variations, they spoke a common language, had common traditions attached to their name, common customs, and one Pantheon to which their local gods belonged. But they were not, nor did they ever become, one nation.[1] In a later age they adopted a common name and derived themselves from a common mythical ancestor,

[1] See ch. iv. ii.

Hellen, but neither then nor ever afterwards did they realize a common *political* consciousness.

Of all the achievements of this uniquely gifted people, the one which in this place most concerns us is the evolution, within the lands they conquered, of a new and remarkable order of society. City life did not begin with the Greeks, but it took a new emphasis and distinctive form. Before the claims of the city all other human relationships took a secondary place. Kinship, the strangest social bond of primitive life, lost its pre-eminence and found its chief recognition as admitting to a condition more highly prized, that of citizenship. The loyalty or subservience to ruler or chief which cemented the early empires lost its hold upon this people, and their 'kings', still in the Homeric tradition supreme and 'revered among the folk', either disappeared or became mere functionaries of minor note, the 'shadow of a great name'. Religion too sat less heavily upon this people, as compared with the superstition-dominated peoples of the Orient. No priestly order reinforced among them that sense of subjection to authority which their kings had failed to maintain. Their religion was rather the adaptable personified expression, set in aesthetic more than dogmatic forms, of their conception of nature, not so much the fearful sanction of the pre-scriptions of a not-to-be questioned morality. A people so minded were prepared for the great social and political experiment for which the shores of the Aegean furnished the appropriate environment.

In so saying we are not seeking to explain or trace the pedigree of the political genius of Greece. We cannot explain why the seed reveals in its growth the peculiar attributes of its own kind of life. No more can we explain why the Greeks became what they were in the history of civilization. Nevertheless the environment of Greece and its adjacent shores—a land of small plains and mountain barriers, with much indented coasts beyond which chains of islands stretched towards the civilizations of the East, a land of meagre agricultural wealth in spite of its vines and olives and wheat, turning therefore the enterprise of its settlers towards the richer rewards of trade, a land moreover that conduced by its climate to the life of the open air, even within its cities—such an environment gave the occasion without which the political life of Greece could never have taken its characteristic form. In those secluded plains and valleys guarded from the barbarian by the sea and the mountain ranges of Northern Greece, yet in ceaseless contact through their harbours with the outside world, the opportunity was provided for the development of the autonomous activity of the 'city-state' Settling at first in villages, as was natural to a previously pastoral folk, around the strong hill or the protected haven, they came presently to unite their villages within or under a single polity. The best-known instance is the 'synoecism' of Attica, whereby its groups of little towns were brought into one community, with one citizenship and one centre, Athens.

In their new environment this people devoted themselves freely and intensely to the life of the city and were peculiarly responsive to the influences which the city, always and by necessity of its nature, causes to radiate. To understand this development, it is necessary to appreciate the manner in which the city changes the mentality of all men, but most of all of those who, like the Greeks, have the temerity to accept new influences without any strong inhibitions from the older folkways.

In the city the relationship of man to man becomes vastly more determinative of character than that of man to nature. Livelihood and success depend on the matching of mind with mind, on agility, quick-wittedness, detachment. The country breeds a slow and steadier wariness, a patient endurance, a reticence, evoked by contact on the one hand with forces unknown and uncontrollable, and on the other with the processes of natural fertility which man seeks to utilize by persistent watchful toil. The seasons in their inexorable succession convey to the country-bred mind the sense of destiny, and the course of human life is reflected in the unhasting inevitable tide of natural change. Beyond this changefulness, there stand the immemorial seeming-changeless things, the returning suns, the stars, the enduring earth whose fruits and creatures pass away, the seeds of life that renew themselves in the mystery of generation. This contrast of the temporary and the eternal dominates the religion and the outlook of the countryman. It is the note of every true description of rural life, such as, in our own days, that contained in Hamsun's *Growth of the Soil*. Against the eternal background of the earth the cardinal events of life, birth, marriage, and death, gain a profound significance. The city-dweller lives in another world. To him the periodicity and the eternity of outside nature have far less meaning. He is organized, save for some abnormal and startling irruption, against its menace and its capriciousness. He deals with the products rather than the processes of nature. Death itself matters less to his mind, in the varying scenes and successions of episode, meeting and parting. His sense of the hour is sharpened, while that of the season is dulled. The contacts of art predominate over the contacts of nature. Convention rules him as well as custom. He grows at once more critical and more competitive.

This spirit of the city, where allowed free play, is the solvent of the more ' instinctive ' forms of social unity. The kin loosens its hold where varied contacts provide opportunity for the cultivation of the particular interests which appeal to different types and age-periods. Only the family remains as an effective kin-group, the essential nuclear family of parents and offspring. The other interests detach themselves more and more from kinship, even from the family relationship. The household ceases to be the centre of nearly all activities, social and economic. It remains the scene of the special activities which belong to the very nature of the family, but it sheds many of the functions which were previously associated with it. The social mobility which the city affords, and the differentiation of interests which it encourages, lead men to find other centres for one and another activity. The place of business, the club, the eating-house, the theatre, the temple, become *foci* of interests which once pertained to the home. In fact the family, once a community, is transformed into an association, and the city now appears as the essential community. Men gain the sense of belonging to the city as a whole. Men become, in a new sense, ' citizens '. They identify civilization itself with this process of incorporation into the city. Detached from the ' natural ' environment where immobility and tradition strengthen each other, they are free to make for themselves a new unity and a new life.

The forms of power undergo a corresponding change. The order of the city demands more intensive, more complex, and more continuous regulation. Both the necessity and the purpose of law are more obvious. Men perceive that which they also create—their dependence on one another and thus the relationship between order and the *common* welfare. Within the walls of the city the mystery of authority dwindles and its public uses grow more significant. The city is the home of organized democracy, deliberate, critical, restless, utterly different from the formless unpolitical democracy of the tribal life. It increases vastly the sphere over which political authority is continually exercised, but at the same time it checks and controls political power. The citizen is the antithesis of the subject. Compelled by outer necessity to extend the forms of order, the city is no less driven by inner necessity to the demand for liberty. The sharp antithesis of these twin necessities sets anew the whole political problem.

Such is in briefest outline the spirit which the city evokes, in ancient times as well as to-day. In Greece, for the first time in recorded history, this spirit prevailed over all opposing influences, breaking an ancient order to create an imperishable example.

II

POLITIES OF GREECE

The Greek settlers scattered their autonomous cities over all the coasts and islands from the Black Sea to Sicily and the West coast of Italy, and in them all they planted the seeds of the same political evolution. The tribal kings of Homeric song disappear and dwindle. The power of the monarch passes into the hands of aristocratic families who control the councils and magistracies of the city. These civic offices become the prizes of a struggle between nobles and common citizens, and the strife leads to a new constitution, either a compromise or a 'full democracy'. In the course of the struggle a dictator or 'tyrant' may come for a time to rule the city, but always the characteristic form of government emerges, the control of political affairs by a body of citizens, narrower or wider, who take an active part not only in the election of officials but in the direct conduct of the city's business.

Many examples might be taken to show the character of this evolution, but none are more striking, more significant, and more divergent than those of Sparta and of Athens. The city of Sparta represented the union of five villages which still remained distinct and straggling after the amalgamation. Probably the union meant in addition the fusion of two tribes, for Sparta had the rare institution of a double kingship. Nor did those kings pass away with the development of citizenship. They remained as kings, though with greatly limited powers. As kings, they were high priests and military leaders, but the bulk of legislative, judicial, and executive functions passed to the Senate (Gerousia) and Assembly (Apella). The Senate, whose thirty members included *ex officio* the kings, grew into an advisory body, elected for life-tenures by the Assembly. The Assembly was composed of all citizens, that is all Spartans over thirty years of age, and its will was law. All recommendations of the Senate or the kings or the magistrates came before it for decision, whether concerning internal or external politics. Yet, in the curious balance of conservatism and democracy which was characteristic of Sparta, it remained for the Senate and magistrates to proclaim the decision ere it came into effect. If they refused, they would 'secede', and proclaim instead the dissolution of the Assembly. The Assembly itself was regularly summoned, originally by the kings, later by the ' overseers ', who also had the right to dissolve it. These ' overseers ' (ephors) were a special order of magistrates, five in number, whose duties were mainly judicial—evidently, as officials elected by the citizens, they had gained power in the early contests between the kingship and the democracy—but besides they had the peculiar responsibility of maintaining general discipline throughout the city-state and of jealously supervising the exercise of the kingly functions. Any citizen might be elected overseer and the election was by a kind of lot. The lot, which we can regard as either the logical fulfilment, or the *reductio ad absurdum*, of democracy, played a considerable role in the Greek commonwealths.

This curious constitution, which remained unaltered in its essential features throughout the period of Greece's cultural supremacy, stands, in spite of its halting conservatism, quite apart from anything the contemporary civilization of Egypt or the Orient could show. Organized government is at last reduced to a ministry of the people, elected by and responsible to it. In the process the ultimate sovereign and the legislative sovereign have become one. It is a temporary solution, fit only for the city-state, but it had a profound effect in the shaping of the most brilliant civilization the world has known. The Greek cities were, in a peculiar sense, free cities. The welfare of the city as such was the ostensible aim of government, and the method of attaining it was the direct exercise by the citizen of political functions. The civil and the political were one. The spirit of the citizens, *in so far as it was a unity*, had no let or hindrance to its expression. But this meant, as Hobbes shrewdly put it, that 'the liberty, whereof there is so frequent and honourable mention in the histories and philosophies of the ancient Greeks and Romans, is not the liberty of particular men but the liberty of the commonwealth'. While this statement is particularly true of Sparta it applies in a degree to all the city-states.

The identity of political and civil rights had as its counterpart the exclusion from citizenship of a large portion of the population. The Spartan constitution was a democracy from the point of view of the citizen, an oligarchy when we include in our survey all the inhabitants of Lacedaemonia. Besides the citizens there were the serfs (Helots) and the unfranchised 'dwellers around' (Perioeci) subject to tribute and military service. The citizens were group-owners of the city, each having his own inalienable and indivisible allotment. Such a system meant the military domination of the state-territory by the relatively small citizen body. It is easy to see how this strengthened the conservatism of Sparta. The ever-present danger of the serf and the subject controlled her policy. The citizen was also a soldier, trained for ten years in the military art, inured to the rigorous semi-communistic discipline of Spartan barrack-life. All the creative energy of Sparta was used up in the vigilant maintenance of this stern order. Her control of the non-citizen subject elements was founded on the strictest subordination of these that superior power could devise. The democracy of Sparta was as inflexible as it was limited. Established as a military commonwealth, it could pass through no constructive changes, and when new needs became at last compulsive its spirit broke and it fell into rapid decay.

The constitution of Athens differed more markedly in spirit and direction than in structure from that of its great rival in the Peloponnesus. Athens too arose out of a ' synoecism ', but when it subjugated the rest of Attica it learned to include the inhabitants among its own citizens. The little state of Attica found unity and liberation through the participation of every village or town in the civil and political rights of the metropolis—an example of liberalism which, if only it could have been extended further would have anticipated the wisdom of Rome and changed the whole history of Greece and perhaps of the world. The citizens of Athens were ranged in four tribes, each tribe being subdivided into three phratries or brotherhoods, and these in turn into kindreds or family groups. This arrangement throws some light on the process of transition from the kin-organization to the city-organization. The phratries still retained in classical Athens certain functions and powers particularly in respect of religious rites and the registration of citizens. At an earlier stage these powers must have been much more extensive, as also those of the kindreds, and we know that Cleisthenes reduced considerably the jurisdiction of the latter. We can see also how the conditions of citizenship modified the kin-basis of all the groupings. The tribe-king became, like other kings, a mere dignitary. The phratries and kindreds were widened to include not only the old-established families but also the unpedigreed citizen households. Common ancestry ceased to be the rallying-point of organization, and the worship of a common deity was found to be a more serviceable and inclusive basis. The main public function of each group became in consequence the guarding of the privilege of citizenship. There are many survivals in the life and the law of classical Athens which reveal this transition from kinship to citizenship, such as the obligation, formerly customary but legal in the age of Demosthenes, on the brother to support his brother's widow. It may in fact be maintained that the struggle between oligarchy and democracy through which Athens passed, like the other cities of Greece, was one between kinship and citizenship. The aristocracy of the kin-organized, the 'Eupatrids', fought a losing battle for privilege against the commonalty, the peasant-farmers, and the 'work-people'. The patrician, at Athens as at Rome, asserted the kin-right against the plebeian's claim of civil and political rights, until the spirit of the city, reinforced at this point by the necessity arising out of a city-dominated empire, gave victory to the latter, and created, for the first time in history, a structural democracy.

The evolution of this Athenian democracy is extremely significant and illuminating. The noble families, un-reckoning of further consequences, first of all stripped the kingship of power while leaving to it the ancient pre-rogative of the control of ceremonial religion. The patrician council then ruled the city, and this governing caste, still feudal rather than civic in its character, con-firmed and developed a social system within which here-ditary landownership subjected to its rank and office the lower orders of peasant and artisan. But the trading wealth of Athens grew, and her ships, exchanging the wares of her civilization, her jars and vases, her fine-wrought ornaments of copper and gold, no less than the improving products of her soil, olive-oil and wheat and wine, carried back to her new luxuries, new resources, and new influences. By the middle of the seventh century B.C. a property classification had been reached which began to undermine the older system. Instead of three classes demarcated by social status we have three classes distinguished by degrees of wealth as measured by the amounts of wheat, oil, or wine yielded annually by their landed property, the minima being five hundred measures for the first class, three hundred for the second, and two hundred for the third. A fourth class comprised all those citizens whose income fell below the last minimum. Such a gradation, especially as a money-reckoning came to supersede the assessment in kind, opened the way not only for the transference of political privilege from the noble to the merely wealthy, but also for the extension of civic and political rights by gradual process from class to class. For since an accession of wealth now enabled a man to rise to the privileged classes the caste-line was broken and the claims of birth were no longer sacrosanct.

Accordingly we find, during the growing social unrest of the late seventh and the sixth century, that the distinctive character of the Athenian state was the diffusion of political power. Offices formerly limited to the five-hundred-measure men were opened to lower classes. Under Solon the fourth class was admitted to the popular assembly, the folk-meeting, though not yet to magisterial office. The old aristocratic council which met on the Areopagus, the hill of Mars, was transformed by a system of recruitment from ex-magistrates, and at the same time it lost its administrative and legislative functions while gaining a new dignity, of a somewhat precarious character, as 'guardian of the laws'. A new 'council of four hundred', open to all but the lowest class, was established, and the fact that its chief duty was to prepare business for submission to the assembly shows that the latter body was already in process of achieving the supremacy of control which later belonged to it. But more remarkable was the establishment of a system of popular courts of justice, which gave all citizens of every class the chance of serving in the role of judges, the panel being selected on each occasion by lot. This judicial power of the people was made all the greater by the 'indictment of illegality' which might be brought against any magistrate after his term of office. The use of the lot in the choice of judges appears less incongruous with our modern methods than the adoption of the same arbitrament of chance, after a preliminary election, in the case of the magistrates. The lot may be regarded as the logical fulfilment of a certain theory of democracy, though its introduction was probably due to the desire to obviate civic dissension and found a superstitious justification in the belief that thereby the issue passed from the decision of men to that of the gods themselves.

Notwithstanding the proverbial wisdom of Solon and the undoubted skill revealed in his reforms, there followed a period of that unmitigated turbulence and strife which in all ages has been the curse of the city-state. Kinship organized in tribe and brotherhood fought against the principle of citizenship, and in the confusion 'tyrants' arose and were overthrown. Then by a stroke of extraordinary boldness the reformer Cleisthenes swept away the old tribes and confounded the brotherhoods and kindreds. He constituted his new tribes in a most ingenious manner, making the local district or deme the basis and uniting within each tribe one deme of the city, one of the inland, and one of the coast. Thus at the same time he broke up the ancient factions associated with the larger geographical divisions and utilized the smaller geographical units to break up the kin-grouping which was the centre of resistance to democratization. Cleisthenes established a new Council of Five Hundred on the basis of his new tribes, the fifty representatives of each being a committee responsible for the transaction of public business during a tenth of the year. Behind it remained the assembly of the folk which must ratify every decision of the council ere it became effective in law.

So was achieved the determinate and typical form of the Athenian constitution, in which, for the first time in history, the political interest overcame the 'natural' grouping of family and tribe, of race and nation; in which even the tenaciously conservative instinct of religion appeared to find a new focus in the civic consciousness; in which there was offered, as the reconciliation of the disparities and distinctions which mark a growing civilization, the idea of a free and equal citizenship. Many further changes of the constitution were made in the course of Athenian history, but the seal was now upon it which gave it its meaning for the world. The changes were first towards fuller democracy. The magistracies came to be filled solely by the lot and were opened to the poorer classes. The aristocratic Areopagus was shorn of its censorial powers, and to complete the political levelling of economic advantage an extensive system of payment for public service, whether as magistrate, as councillor, or as judge, was introduced. The payment of the large popular panels, introduced by Pericles, might be defended as a necessary and reasonable condition for the evoking of democratic institutions, but it had unlooked-for consequences. Athenian citizenship now conveyed economic as well as political privilege, save for the wealthier citizens on whom the burden of the 'liturgies', the expense of religious festivals and of the state's vessels of war, was laid. It was therefore now the turn of the ' demos ', the whole citizen body, to become exclusive, and they limited the right of citizenship to those who on both sides were of Athenian birth. This action reflected also the now imperial status of Athens, enriched by the tribute of her allies. The age of Pericles was the zenith of her political as well as of her cultural triumphs. From that time the defects of her polity, or rather of the polities of all the exclusive cities of Greece, alike in nothing so much as in the fierce and obdurate autonomy which each claimed in the face of internal dissensions and of external foes, became more and more apparent. Scarce twenty years had passed from the day when Persian troops burned and desecrated the temples of the Athenian Acropolis ere the Athenians and the Spartans were arrayed against each other in the first of those fatal internecine struggles which at length brought them down in common ruin. The form of Athenian democracy was meanwhile shaken by the revolutions and counter-revolutions which sprang from the discontent of a war-broken people. The form was restored again, but under the shadow of empires old and new, first Carthage, then Macedon, and then Rome, which at last bereft it of all meaning.

III

THE CITY AS AN INCLUSIVE PARTNERSHIP

A famous sentence in Burke's *Reflections on the Revolution in France* defines the state as a ' partnership in all science ; a partnership in all art ; a partnership in every virtue, and in all perfection.' It might well be maintained that these words express the ideal of the ancient city-state. The city is described by Greek political thinkers precisely in terms of a universal partnership. It was so regarded by the privileged and exclusive body of citizens, privileged and exclusive not least in the periods of 'full democracy'. Citizenship was a function, almost a profession. It was pointed out by Beloch that at Athens, with a citizen population of only thirty thousand, there were in the Periclean age nineteen hundred official posts, and, as appointments were normally annual and re-election was on the whole discouraged, there was thus the possibility of bringing every citizen within the official round in a period of sixteen years. Furthermore, there was the vast activity of the popular courts, and there were ceremonies and festivals in which large numbers of citizens took an active part. The life of the citizen was the life of the city. His good was, in ideal, wholly identified with that of the commonwealth. Perhaps nothing in the Athenian polity seems stranger to us than the distributive aspect of this ideal, as illustrated for example by the official disbursements of theatre-money among the citizens even when the threatening power of Macedon seemed to men like Demosthenes to make the dissipation of public funds most perilous. And we are surprised to find Aristotle devoting a considerable part of his political inquiry to the subject of 'distributive justice', gravely settling the manner in which the public surpluses should be divided.

This political ideal of universal partnership has won from the immortal achievements of the Hellenic spirit a renown which is not its due. For a period the genius of Greece attained, under the conditions provided particularly by Athens, an astonishing liberation, and we can say at least that the political environment permitted and even encouraged, though it surely did not evoke, that outburst of literary and artistic power. If indeed we dared attribute such cultural fulfilment to any assignable factors, we should think rather of the conjuncture of circumstances which gave this highly endowed people deliverance from the menace of external empire at the very time when it had freed itself from the heavier bondage of ancient custom, which gave it also a surplus of wealth and leisure for the furtherance of its arts, and which, partly in consequence and partly on account of its trading opportunities, made Athens the focus of many civilizational influences. The self-governing city was certainly a supreme necessity for the evolution of the Greek spirit, but the interpretation of self-government in the form of a complete civic partnership was a hindrance and not a help. We tend to exaggerate the range of Athenian liberty. The tyrannous aspect of the universal partner-ship is revealed particularly in certain ' graphai ' or forms of accusation to which the statesman, the innovator, and even the artist, were exposed. In the age of Periclean liberty any citizen might bring an ' accusation for illegality ' against a state-official on the expiry of his office, and in practice the charge was supported not merely by evidences of ' unconstitutionality ' but by pleas that the action of the accused was undesirable or inexpedient, or even that his motives were crooked. The penalty of death was attached to the verdict of condemnation, and this menace lay in the path of every public man. Even more invidious forms of suit were the accusations for ' unserviceable legislation ' and for ' deceit of the people '. Finally there was the accusation for ' impiety ', under which Anaxagoras was fined and exiled, Pheidias thrown into prison to die there, and Socrates condemned to death. How utterly unbridled was the opportunity for accusation under this rubric we may judge from the famous case of Euripides, who was accused of 'impiety' because a character in one of his plays, the *Hippolytus*, was represented as saying: 'My tongue did swear; my heart remains unsworn.'

The doctrine of partnership 'in all art and in every virtue' is in truth a fatal misinterpretation of the nature of the state, though one to which the character of the *polis* quite naturally led. Plato and Aristotle have here a justification to which their modern followers, including such opposites as Burke and Rousseau, can lay no claim. The narrow exclusive circle of the city-community encouraged the conception of a wholly unified common life, under a single and absolute political direction. 'Truth and goodness are for all men the same', said Democritus. Plato carried the doctrine to the extreme conclusion. There is but one true type of art and of virtue, one ideal, all else being aberration and confusion. The Socrates of the *Crito* nobly refuses to evade the death penalty which has been imposed upon him, on the ground that he must not break the covenant he has made with the laws, but there is never a suggestion, on either side of the argument, that matters of religion or of opinion are outside the sphere of legality. In Plato's visionary city none may abide who do not, in art, in poetry, in music, in religion, in morality, conform to the rigorous prescriptions of authority. In his *Laws* it is proclaimed that all one's family and all one's wealth belong to the 'city'. Aristotle, in spite of significant misgivings, offers no alternative theory. He permits a doubt whether it is always the same thing 'to be a good man and to be a good citizen', but ethics is still for him the other side of the shield of politics. He allows, for example, the city-authority to be determinative of the sciences which the individual may study, and he declares that ' all associations appear to be part of the " political ".' Yet long before this time the cults of mystic universal religions had begun to create associations stretching across Greece to further lands and including non-citizens in their catholic eclecticism.

The Greek political thinker was at a loss because in Greek there was really no word corresponding to the modern term ' state '. It is only the ' city ', the *polis*, of which he could speak, and we are very apt to misinterpret his meaning when we translate it as state. It is the city-community, not our ' state ', to which he attributed those all-comprehensive functions and powers. The very word ' law ' (*nomos*) meant to the Greek also ' custom ' or ' convention '. Nor did Aristotle ever mean what we mean by his famous description of man as a ' political animal '; he understood by it a being whose life is fulfilled in the city. The Greek tradition, thus misinterpreted, has inspired a modern doctrine of universal partnership within the state which does far less than justice to its original. In respect of social forms, our world has become differentiated far beyond the Greek or even the Roman. The self-government of the city-community was a great achievement, but it could only be a step towards the solution of the great problem of liberty and order, of the union of individuals within society, until the sphere of political government began to be discovered. The failure to distinguish the state from the community left ' Athenian liberty ' itself a monument broken and defaced.

The all-inclusive state, whether its dimensions are those of the city or of the nation, cannot draw the line between law and custom, between enforcement and spontaneity, between the conditions of order and those of culture. The mere discretion of government is not an adequate guarantee against the application of political law to regions where its intrusion is harmful. So long as the theory is accepted that the state is omnicompetent there will be confusion and suppression. It may not be fanciful to regard the endless internal strife of each Greek city as stimulated by a mistaken theory of government. Under such a theory no form of life is safe, no religion, no opinion, unless its adherents control the government. So the very diversity which enriches a civilization when recognized as existing of right, creates, under the principle of the ' universal partnership ', those violent and factious oppositions which on the contrary destroy it.

We shall see more fully at a later stage how prejudicially the doctrine of all-inclusive sovereignty bears on the life of the cultural associations. At Athens this principle of citizenship may also have adversely affected the primary association of the family. It is not without significance that the expression ' to sacrifice to the hearth ' meant in later Greek to shun the society of one's fellow-citizens. The city seemed to overpower the family. While Greece found through citizenship a notable liberation from the tyranny of kinship, it failed on the other hand to give the family its needful place in the community. As the city took on its characteristic form the importance of the household as a centre of activity seemed to diminish. The tribal family with its unity of custom, of control, and of religion, lost its cohesion. Within its older organization marriage was a religious rite and celibacy a crime against the ancestral gods. The worship of the hearth was symbolized by the undying fire. The old order waned and the new made no corresponding provision. Marriage did not become associated with a civil ceremony. There was no registration of births, and the education of young children or that of girls of any age was no concern of the city. The position of women suffered. Plato, in the *Cratylus*, makes the significant statement that the women of Athens spoke an archaic dialect. Xenophon speaks of the newly married wife as of a kind of wild animal who has first to be tamed in order that she may converse with her lord. The great speech of Pericles on the liberality of Athenian culture approves the popular view that the greatest glory of woman is to be heard of neither for evil nor for good. These views are not simply the expression of a prevailing ' Eastern ' attitude towards women. There is a remarkable contrast between the life of women as depicted in the Homeric poems or even in the lyricists like Simonides of Ceos or Sappho and that which is normal in fifth-century Athens. Herodotus has many tales to tell of feminine devotion and service, whereas Thucydides, the historian of the contemporary ' democracies ' of Greece, mentions only twice, and then quite casually, a woman in his whole narrative. In the genuine city—Sparta was different, being to the end only a cluster of villages—the woman was expected to remain indoors, and even there she had her separate place. There were no feminine occupations save of the most trivial kind, such as those of the vegetable-seller and the bread-seller of the market-place. In the majority of Greek cities women filled so small a part that we cannot even obtain information about them.

One result was that the Greek citizen was liable to seek abroad, among the class of women significantly named ' companions ' (*hetairai*), the attractions which the household denied. And another form of love, that which attached to young men and boys, was so strangely pre-valent that in Greek literature it generally receives those attributes of romance which normally belong to the rela-tionship of man and woman. It is thus not surprising that the Greek married as a rule rather late in life, and that, as Aristophanes says in the *Symposium*, many were not naturally inclined to marry or beget children—'if at all, they did so only in obedience to the law'. This fact throws some light on that progressive depopulation of Greece which grew so alarming in its later days. We can trace towards the end of the fifth century B.C. a certain uneasiness in regard to the family and the position of women. But there is no real understanding of the pro-blem of the family in the city, and there is little to choose between the mischievous and grotesque ridicule of the conservative Aristophanes and the radical proposals of Plato, who would have made women the companions of men by abolishing the family institutions altogether and completely merging them in a civic communism.

Finally, it must be remembered that an all-inclusive citizenship is also bitterly exclusive. It was so in the cities of Greece. The circle of citizens was ringed about by unprivileged residents, native or alien, and beyond these by masses of serfs or slaves. Aristotle declared that 'in the best state citizenship will not be conferred on any mechanic'. As for slavery, it was the foundation of the economy of the ancient city-community. It may well be maintained that apart from slavery the leisure and liberty which made possible the culture of Greece could not have been achieved. The absence of capital in so many of its modern forms, and above all the absence of 'labour-saving' machinery and industrial technique made slave-holding not only profitable but the very condition, for the citizen, of the 'good life'. But the foundation was unsound. Even when slavery did not create, as at Sparta, the ever-present danger of revolt, it was a fatal competitor with free labour whose social status it destroyed. A genuine free working class had no place in such an economy, and sank into a shiftless proletariat. On the other hand the mass of exploited 'living instruments', constantly replenished from out the barbarian peoples of the North and East, contaminating the cities of Greece with debased and demoralizing contacts, and causing in the midst of a triumphant democracy a disregard and even a contempt for humanity as such, may well have been, as some hold, another and perhaps the most insidious and fatal of the causes of depopulation.[1] Certainly whether this accusation be justified or not, the practice of slavery could not have failed, by reason of its psychological effect, to confirm the obstinate exclusiveness which blinded the citizens of Greece to the dangers that were gathering over their little civic autonomies.

But here we arrive at the great structural problem of all city polities to which in the course of time Rome offered a form of solution very different from the vain and sporadic attempts of Greece.

IV

THE ACHIEVEMENT OF ROME

While the cities of Greece were suffering the no longer tolerable attack of inner and outer forces of disruption, the sense of the state was growing in newer Mediterranean communities, in certain Hellenic colonies

[1] Cf. Oppenheimer, *The State*, ch. iv ; Robertson, *Evolution of States*, ch. ii, § 2.

of Magna Graecia, in Carthage, and in Rome. Of them all it was Rome alone that decisively advanced the science of the state and undertook new and illuminating experiments in the formation of a greater and more enduring political structure. Her achievement so far eclipsed that of all the rest that we need consider her alone, for the period of her dominance, in this brief survey of the making of the modern state.

At the dawn of her history Rome was the focus of some rude agricultural communities, a strategic ford near seven defensible hills. For reasons now only to be guessed at, these Latins proved in the long run stronger and more cohesive than their neighbouring enemies, first the Etruscans, a people whose civilization was relatively high, and then the Gauls, who overran her from the North. Rome won no easy victories. Again, after desperate struggles, she triumphed over her fellow-Latins and over the Samnites. Her now consolidated powers brought her into conflict with the Greek cities of Italy and their champion, King Pyrrhus of Epirus. Again she came through disaster to new triumphs. One more life and death struggle awaited her as, adding sea power to land power, she grappled with Carthage and finally destroyed her. Her control over Italy, from the Arno to Sicily, was now complete, and Rome entered on the second stage of Empire, that wider dominion within which power and citizenship could no longer advance together. Her further conquests frustrated the political solution which her earlier conquests had made possible.

What Rome in that first stage achieved was a political unity based upon metropolitan citizenship, an achievement unknown in Greece or even in the world until Rome's day. To extend the range of citizenship in correspondence with the extension of the sphere of government was a natural, to our historical eyes an obvious, solution of the problem of the city-state. The civic structure of the earliest Rome we know was based upon the *curiae*, each *curia* being a group of *gentes* which in turn were unions of families. The *curiae* were themselves divisions of the three ' original ' Roman tribes, that formal classification of consanguineous units so characteristic of the transition to civic life. The *curia* had religious as well as administrative functions. Separately the *curiae* met for worship and sacrifice, together they met as the civic assembly. Together they formed a rude order of birth and privilege, cemented by religion, and below them were ranged the unorganized plebeians, who shared neither their ceremonies nor their civic rights, the landless, propertyless common men who sought employment and refuge in the city. The privileged families also provided the council of elders or senate. At the head of the little aristocratic state stood the ' King '— magistrate, monarch, and high priest in one.

The growing city set in motion social forces, above all the instant forces of wealth and of poverty, to undermine this yeoman aristocracy. The claims of wealth to office took shape in the ' Servian census ', which divided the citizens into five classes—or six, if we count the ' knights ' as a separate class—according to their landed property as reckoned in the unit of money, the copper ' as '. These classes were organized in ' hundreds ' or centuries, which henceforth became the chief basis of civic organization. They were so arranged that the wealthiest classes comprised the largest number of centuries, and as each century had one vote in the new council, the political predominance of wealth was assured.

Nevertheless, as always, the financial rating removed the stronger and more invidious cleavage between birth-determined classes. The new council of the centuries included plebeians, and thenceforth there was no insuperable bar to their attainment of power and office. The first wedge of democracy had entered the Roman state. It was driven in by the discontent of the plebeians, who saw the conquered lands for which they had fought usurped by the patricians, while they themselves fell under the power of the terrible laws which handed the debtor over to the creditor as a slave. Under insistent pressure Rome moved along towards civic democracy. The monarchy fell, and Rome became a republic with two chief magistrates, later named consuls. In the next year the Lex Valeria permitted an appeal from the magistrates to the assembly. Then came the famous first ' secession of the plebs ', one of the most remarkable actions on the part of a lower order in the whole of history. It resulted, on their return, in the establishment of special plebeian officials, in particular two tribunes who, besides being sacrosanct, were given a right of intervention which grew into the formidable right of veto. A second secession was necessary to confirm these rights, after which the number of tribunes was finally fixed at ten.

The struggle went on, its tumults aggravated by the economic consequences of many wars, especially of that Gaulish invasion which destroyed the sacred city. But the issue was already settled. Rome was an inland city, without commercial importance, a city ruled by landowners whose political power gave them in addition the usufruct and virtual ownership of huge estates. The common citizens as well as the small farmers suffered the vast economic disturbances of war without the compensations that accrued to the wealthy landlords. These constant wars might check for a time the strife of the orders, but each respite revealed a new economic chasm between the rich and the poor. The very prestige of victory brought new population to a city that had no economic place for it. But the ruling classes of Rome perceived that which the Greek cities never learned, that a city-state cannot resist its enemies without if it is torn by dissension within. They yielded with bitter reluctance, but they yielded at last to every claim of the plebeians. The council of the plebeians was recognized and its decisions were made binding on all. One of the two consuls was required to be a plebeian, as also one of the two censors. The struggle of the orders ended after a succession of compromises which strongly contrast with the polities of Greece, in a new constitution which offered rather more than equality to the plebeians.

So after centuries of strife did the Romans solve the first of their great political problems. It was indeed a strange system wherein two assemblies, one oligarchical in spirit and structure, the other confined to the populace, exercised co-ordinate rights of legislation, while ten officials representing the lower orders had severally the right to veto any act of any magistrate. Yet by these devices the Romans attained such a solidarity of citizenship that the two assemblies worked in accord for long periods. From the date of the Licinio-Sextian laws (367 B.C.), which marked the final victory of the plebs, till the days of the Gracchi, two and a third centuries went by during which the working of the Roman constitution remained under oligarchical guidance. The stability of Rome was due, above all else, to that extension of citizenship within the city which annulled the disintegrating

formal privilege of a class. The Roman oligarchy surrendered the exclusive right of government and thus
stabilized its power. It is true that the arrangement of
the centuries, and also of the 'tribes', who by a curious
development formed a third assembly of the imperial city,
was skilfully managed in the oligarchical interest. But
the long absence of dangerous clashes between these
bodies and the sovereign council of the plebs bears
eloquent witness to the fact that the division of power
matters less than the community of right.

During the same period the Romans extended the
principle of the city-state to secure the political unification of Italy. Here too they achieved a remarkable and
novel, though partial, success. There was yet no national
sense to which they could appeal—the empire of Rome
was itself to become a later condition of the development
of the Western sentiment of nationality. Even the Latins
did not form one nation with the Romans, and besides
there were the distinctive Etruscans, the Samnites, the
Volscians, the Marsians and the Apulians, the Lucanians
and the numerous other peoples whom Rome had conquered in her Italian progress. Nothing reveals so clearly
the persistent tribal divisions of conquered Italy as the
outbreak, as late as 90 B.C., of the 'Social War', in which
eight Italian peoples revolted against Rome. When the
armies of Rome again triumphed, her enemies were made
Roman citizens, under a Lex Julia which had already
granted that proud right to her allies. It was the fulfilment of a process begun long before. The bestowal of
Roman citizenship had for centuries been the real
arcanum imperii. Within the consolidated territory of
Italy itself it was a relatively easy and highly advantageous policy. Citizenship in this original sense knows

no bar of race or even of civilization. It can be extended as nationality cannot be extended, by simple conferment. It made Italy one, from the Gaulish north to the Greek cities of the far south. It might even, for all its inadequacy, have sufficed—if Italy alone had been the empire of Rome.

This citizenship of Rome was in fact a much more flexible and adaptable system of rights than Greece had ever known. Citizenship to the Romans did not mean necessarily that universal partnership which set so absolute and fatal a limit to the extension of the Greek polity. Full citizenship no doubt embraced at the first that union, natural to a primitive community, but perilous to civilization, of political, religious, moral, social rights and of kin-rights. But in practice, though formally retaining certain religious and other elements, it narrowed its character so as to accentuate only political and civil rights. Moreover, from early times the Romans had the wit to distinguish between civil rights—rights of equality before the law—and political rights—rights of membership in the sovereign body. They conferred the Roman *civitas sine suffragio*, the complex of civil rights, on a number of towns, some of which were at the same time permitted a degree of self-government while to others it was denied. This limited citizenship carried with it the right of trading with Rome and the right of intermarriage. Another category was made for the Latin towns not thus privileged. These ' allies ' were regarded as potential Roman citizens. If they exercised the right to emigrate to Rome, they could be enrolled as burgesses : meanwhile in their own towns they enjoyed the right of trade with Rome and also the jurisdiction of the Roman courts. Beyond these again lay the towns of free allies, whose internal autonomy was ratified by a treaty with Rome, though without the privilege of Roman citizenship. Here, then, were all the political devices necessary for the incorporation of Italy within the free citizenship of Rome. This gradation was of the highest significance for the establishment of the Roman power. Sometimes granted very sparingly, sometimes actually forced upon the recipients, usually regarded as a high privilege, her citizenship followed her conquests, to bind in peace what she had won, but could not retain, by war. Roman leaders learned through bitter experience a secret more rare than that of successful war, the art of enduring peace. For a time, after the subjugation of Italy, the blind pride of power was paramount, and at length issued in the Licinio-Mercian law (95 B.C.), which forbade, under heavy penalty, non-citizens from claiming admission to the sovereign body of Romans, an act which, in Mommsen's words, ' stands completely on a parallel with that famous act which laid the foundation for the separation of North America from the mother-country '.[1] Five years later the terrible ' Social War ' broke out, whose course was marked by large concessions of citizenship to Roman allies and whose conclusion was followed by the admission of all the Italian communities to burgess rights, while ' Latin rights ' were bestowed on the Gallic towns between the Po and the Alps.

It is significant that the statesman who used his power most freely to extend the ranks of citizenship beyond these limits, in Transalpine Gaul and in the farther provinces, was Julius Caesar. This was part of the preparation for that new empire, in which the meaning of Roman citizenship, extended beyond the possible limits of effective unity,

[1] *History of Rome*, Bk. iv, ch. vii.

was emptied of all sovereign attributes. That citizenship might consolidate a country like Italy, for a time at least : it could not consolidate an empire. The principle of empire, as it spread far beyond the limits of Italy, proved in fact quite incompatible with the city-state ideal, and imperially-minded Romans, from Julius Caesar onwards, deliberately extended the citizenship to destroy its association with self-government, and to empty Rome itself of the tradition of authority. A new basis of government was needed, for the logic of the city-state had reached its limit. Here was the final problem which tested and at length broke the statesmanship of Rome.

V

THE EVOLUTION OF LAW IN GREECE AND ROME

Before we pass from the strength of Rome to her weakness we must estimate the significance of the most enduring of all her political achievements, the establishment of a universal code of law. Every state has, as it were, a double framework of order, a code and a constitution, the thing administered and the agency of administration. The former grows quietly underneath, although storms rage around the other. Even the most violent revolutions leave the bulk of the code intact, when they overthrow the agency which hitherto guarded it. The most permanent, as it is also the most conservative character of the state is its body of law. Any great advance in the system of law is therefore likely to be preserved and to become part of the legacy of humanity from its past. So it was with the law of Rome.

The cities of Greece had already made very substantial advances in the science of law. We can trace a definite progress from Homeric times, when law had not yet emerged from the embrace of custom and religion. It was then a collection of 'dooms' of judgements or decrees (Themistes or Dikai), raised out of the obscurity of custom by some necessity of vindication. Such dooms were not yet law.[1] They were adjudications which incidentally revealed their unformulated principle. They were moreover the particular possessions of a tribe, the gifts or revelations of the goddesses, or rather 'angels', Themis and Dike. As the light breaks on the oligarchical age of Greece we discover that the now enlarged collection of Judgements forms the most significant part of the ' unwritten law', a heritage in the jealous keeping of the noble class. Probably the writing down of the law, the beginning of law proper, came as the result of attempts to evade this formidable monopoly. At any rate we know that in the time of Solon it was agreed under the pressure of fierce civic strife that a legislator should be appointed to write down laws, and the same process may well have occurred in earlier times. So came the great lawgivers, such as Draco of Athens, Lycurgus (if he is indeed an historic figure) of Sparta, Zaleucus of Locris, Charondas of Catana, and Gortyn of Crete.

This written law was still, as de Coulanges[2] has insisted, the translation, no doubt with modifications made necessary by the occasion, of the communal custom set so deeply in the common matrix of religion, morality, and kinship. The form of law was first delivered, long before its true nature was evolved. To be law-abiding was to observe the ritual of the altar, just as much as to deal justly with one's fellowmen. To the end the ' king ',

---

[1] Cf. Maine, *Ancient Law*, ch. i.   [2] *La Cité Antique.*

once lawgiver and now minor official, had at Athens, Sparta, and Rome the superintendence of religious rites. In early Rome, pontiff and judge were one, and jurisprudence was *rerum divinarum atque humanarum notitia*. Religious observance was an integral part of that social order which it was incumbent upon the state to maintain and defend.

The redemption of law from custom begins properly when once it is inscribed on pillars or tablets of stone for all to see. The written code gains a special sanction, and in the course of ages becomes a complete system entirely separate from the order of custom. At first it is conceived as simply such portions of the customary fabric as require explicit and formal statement. Even in the Greek cities custom or tradition was a source of law alongside of enactment, and there were groups of authorities or jurisconsults who were 'interpreters' of this unwritten lore.[1] It is also significant that both law and custom were regarded as existing for all time and scarcely susceptible of change. The code might receive additions but it could hardly be altered. Even Solon did not repeal the laws of Draco—he set up new ones alongside of the old. The older laws might fall into abeyance, but the process of obsolescence did not prevent the concurrent and confusing appeal to contradictory laws. Thus in a case mentioned by Isaeus the claimants to an inheritance brought forward two mutually irreconcilable but equally valid laws. Moreover, it was long before the making of law came to be regarded as the primary function of government. That would have seemed like delivering over the sacrosanct established order to the arbitrary will of men. As Sidgwick pointed out, to the conservative Aristotle legislature

[1] Vinogradoff, *Historical Jurisprudence*, ii, ch. iv.

holds no prominent place in the business of government. He speaks of the 'deliberative' function instead of, as in modern classifications, the legislative, and the alteration of law he deprecates as if it were a kind of 'disobedience to authority.'[1]

Nevertheless the Greek cities, and perhaps Athens most of all, broke through this conception of law. To do so was itself a revolution, a vast unsettlement of a whole order of society. It was a chief part of the work of that 'enlightenment' of which the Greek sophists were the protagonists. The spirit of inquiry had revealed the sheer contradictions that lay between the custom, morality, and law of different peoples, each of which yet believed its own to be the sacred and eternal form of right. To the naïve Herodotus these contradictions were merely part of the picturesque mystery of things, as appears in his famous story of the banquet given by King Darius.[2] Darius asked certain Greeks whom he was feasting ' for how much money ' they would devour their dead parents, and neatly exhibited the nature of their horrified revulsion by summoning certain Indians who followed this custom and asking them for what price they would consent, after the Greek fashion, to burn their dead. But to the sophists such contradictions had another meaning. Did they not show that law was only convention, a superficial thing, in contrast and sometimes in conflict with nature ? It is hard, when ancient thought-foundations quickly dissolve, to discover new ones, nor did the Greek thinkers who opposed the sophists achieve in turn a true philosophy of law. We may perhaps liken the Greeks, in this as in other political

---

[1] Sidgwick, *Development of European Polity*, Lecture XII.
[2] Herodotus, iii. 38.

respects, to voyagers who for the first time leave the shores of tradition, seeking new worlds, voyagers endowed with daring and courage and not ignorant of the art of navigation, but careless of the seaworthiness of their ship, and engaged in mutinous strife amid the storm.

The Greeks made very important advances in the science of law, but they never attained to the consistent doctrine or the logical practice which the Romans built up. To begin with, they did not possess (any more than we do in English) a term corresponding to the Roman *ius*, the ordered system of which an individual *lex* is merely an example. Their laws were a ' collection ' still, a collection of heterogeneous rules, religious, moral, and political. The distinction between civil and criminal actions, between private prosecution for amends or damages and public prosecution under a penal code was appreciated and evolved, but there was no proper classification of the cases falling within these categories. Often, as in the instance of theft, a plaintiff had the choice of an action for damages or a criminal prosecution.[1] And many offences whose criminal nature is to us very obvious, such as murder and arson, were regarded as subjects for private action (dikai), brought by the victim or by his family, although visited with heavy penalties. Other offences criminal in nature, such as false witness, were treated at Athens wholly as torts.

Moreover, the universality of law was far from being recognized. The protection of the law was still a political privilege, fully available only to the citizen body, which formed the smaller portion of nearly every Greek city. The stranger required a citizen patron before he could enjoy the guarantee of law. The slave was, generally

[1] Vinogradoff, *op. cit.*, ii, ch. ix.

speaking, outside the law. Law was a respector of persons. Legal rights and political rights were co-extensive. The idea that law has a common application to all persons within a political territory was alien to the Greeks. The idea of a universal *ius gentium* was not yet born.

In another direction the universality of law was not liberated from arbitrary or irrelevant considerations. When the law passed out of the hands of the narrow oligarchy to whom it was a class-possession it fell within the keeping of the ' demos '. In the enormous jury courts of Athens the plaintiff or the defendant, as the surviving pleas reveal, hardly ever confined himself to the real issue. He sought to win his case, by making out, for example, that the father of his opponent was a scoundrel or his mother a vegetable-seller, or by exhibiting his weeping wife and children. In the Roman courts, also, sentimental appeals or grotesque distortions were permissible, but they never were so effective or so flagrant as before the untrained assemblies of Greek heliasts. The clarity of justice was still further obscured by the extraordinary number of political offences of which the courts took cognizance. We have already made reference to the fact that at the end of their period of office, or even during it, statesmen and officials were always liable to prosecution in one court or another. A favourite method of commencing a political career came to be the accusation of some prominent official before the courts. Thus the way was opened to grave abuses of jurisdiction and the law distorted from an instrument of justice into a dangerous engine of politics.

It is clear then that important as were the legal advances achieved in Greece, they fell far short of such legal standards as are maintained by any modern state. It was Rome that liberated the universality of law, that transcended the sophistic antithesis between nature and convention, and that first embodied in one comprehensive and unified code the distinctive order of the state. She owed much to the example offered by Greece, but more to the genius of her own people, which here found the opportunity for its purest exercise.

The law of Rome consisted at first of the same undifferentiated collection of customs, traditional rules, and religious ordinances which characterize all primitive civilization. Such is the nature of the famous Twelve Tables with which the authentic history of Rome's legal institutions may be said to begin. But it is significant that the Twelve Tables were drawn up after a study of the laws of Greece and of the Greek cities of Italy. Here is an early indication of that catholicity of mind which enabled Rome to make her unparalleled advance. What law needed most for its development was the flexibility and comprehension which reliance on custom, religion, and traditional morality are most apt to impede. The idea of a permanent law once and for all delivered and sanctified arose naturally out of the conditions of primitive civilization. Greece transcended it, but failed to discover an alternative ideal. Rome also transcended it, and found instead a true principle of universality. She saved herself from the bondage of her sacred Twelve Tables. She redeemed her *ius* from the captivity of *fas*, the Roman equivalent of *Themis*.[1]

The manner of this redemption is very interesting. It was not achieved through a revolutionary spirit of denial

---

[1] Cf. Muirhead, *Roman Law*, ch. ii, where he quotes Ausonius for the identification of *fas* and *themis*.

such as inspired the Greek sophists, but through the purposeful and gradual application of such practical devices as lay within the ambit of the original system. Of these the most obvious was the 'legal fiction', which kept the form of the established order while changing its inner character. Such was the fiction of adoption or civil heirship which gave a legatee outside of the circle of kinship the right to recover goods from the debtors of the testator, or again the fiction of sale which avoided certain difficulties in the way of the free disposal of property. Maine widens the term 'legal fiction' to include the 'answers of the learned', the *responsa prudentium*, otherwise the interpretations offered by 'experts' (who were practising lawyers, not judges) on actual or hypothetical cases. Under the Republic these interpretations were influential in modifying the law only in virtue of the reputation of particular jurisconsults. Under the Empire, from Augustus onwards, the *responsa* of certain lawyers were given official recognition as positive law, while in the latest period of the Empire the *responsa* of five great classical jurists were formally admitted into the legal code.

Underneath legal fiction and juristic interpretation there was working obscurely a principle of great moment, the principle of equity or 'the regard for substantial as opposed to formal and technical justice'.[1] This principle was itself liberated in the evolution of Roman law. The traditional law represented by the Twelve Tables applied, like the law of the Greek cities, only to citizens. It was no violation of established principle to provide a distinctive code for aliens. At first it appeared as a vindication and reservation of the peculiar right and privilege of the

---

[1] Bryce, *Studies in History and Jurisprudence*, ii.

Roman citizen, but in the course of time the *ius gentium*, built under the jurisdiction of the *praetor peregrinus* out of the principles presumed to be the common basis of justice for aliens and Romans alike, revealed a superiority over the custom-ridden complexities of the citizen code. The *ius gentium* was understood as ' the law which all men everywhere obey '. As such, it was far nearer to the true universality of law. It was in fact identified, in most respects, with the ' law of nature '. Herein was found a means of harmonizing those very concepts, law and nature, whose opposition had been most insisted upon by the Greek enlightenment. It was to the *ius gentium* that the political thinkers of Rome went to look for a philosophy of law. The gradual growth of the *ius gentium*, alongside of the *ius civile*, prevented any disruption, under the impact of new ideas, of the legal system. It facilitated the process by which deliberate law-making came to be regarded as the rational work of government, besides offering an ideal in the light of which, unrestrained by antiquated traditions, the legislator should act. Gradually the new system usurped part of the sphere of the older, until the time was prepared for that great fusion of the two whose final form was the code of Justinian.

The contrast between the first great monument of Roman Law, the Twelve Tables, and the last, the system contained in the Institutes, Digest, Code and ' Novels ' of Justinian, himself a ' barbarian ' inheritor of the Roman imperium of the East, is very striking. The old family jurisdiction of the *pater familias* has shrunk to insignificance before the universal jurisdiction of the state. The conception of personality as the basis of legal right and obligation has been disentangled from the claims of kinship. Legal rules have been redeemed from the antiquated and alien forms of priestly ordinance, though 'ecclesiastical law' still bulks largely in the law of the state. The forms of conveyance and of inheritance have been vastly simplified and rationalized. The application of the idea of 'group-personality' has begun, even if it seems most inadequate to an age such as ours which comprehends the complex realities of group-life. The nature of contract has been clarified. The whole sphere of law has been included within one system and its main divisions, civil and criminal, public and private, have been set out. So Rome left, for that far later day when again the social consciousness of the West awakened to the perception of true political ideas, at once an example and a living principle for the making and the ordering of new codes.

VI

THE CITY AND THE EMPIRE

Republican Rome made no separation between her civil and her military authorities. The superior magistrates, the consuls and the praetors, commanded armies in the field. After their year of office at home they passed, as the empire grew, to the governorship of provinces abroad, invested with the imperium, the full sovereignty of Rome. How could the various assemblies of Roman citizens control these despotic proconsuls and propraetors? They were obviously unfitted for such a task, and inevitably the Senate, which was composed mainly of ex-magistrates, and whose members were appointed for life, became the central executive of the state, determining the allocation of provinces, the levying of troops and the carrying on of wars, and the administration of finance. With these exclusive powers it was not surprising that Senate's resolutions should also come to be reckoned as no less valid than the law of the sovereign people. All the other political agencies of Rome revealed the cramping character of their city-state origin ; the Senate alone could be fitted into the imperial design.

It was a rare and a difficult opportunity which here presented itself. To become the supreme council of a great empire, the cohesive centre of authority and respect, demanded of the Senate a new statesmanship of which unfortunately it proved incapable. Set stubbornly in its aristocratic exclusiveness, it offered no provision by which the subject provinces of Rome should be guarded from spoliation. The idea of representation never occurred to it, and in any case would have been peculiarly hard to apply in an age of slow communications. But it shirked the only alternative, by which the governors of the subject provinces would have been strictly kept to account for their actions. Its members were themselves the leaders of a governing caste, enriched by the spoils of empire. Debarred from the opportunities of trade they became slave-owners and money-lenders. They acquired vast slave-worked estates. 'In whatever direction', says Mommsen,[1] 'speculation applied itself, its instrument was without exception man reduced in law to a beast of burden.' These conditions induced an outlook which totally unfitted the Senate for the tasks of empire. It failed to establish either the internal or the external conditions of security and good government. The city-state passed into the empire, and though the foundations of loyalty were destroyed in the process, no new ones were built.

[1] *History of Rome*, Book IV, ch. ii.

The state, bereft of inner principle, fell back on the sole resource of power.

The internal problem first loomed large. Slavery consumed the solidarity of citizenship, dispossessed the small cultivator, swelled the proletariat, and caused deep-seated economic and social disorder. The bold reforms of the Gracchi ended in failure that taught no lesson to the government of Rome. The wars of Rome left her ex-soldiers without civil prospects, a disturbing element unfitted for the life of peace and fretted by the encroachments of slave-labour. Moreover the armies of the new empire were no longer citizens-levies, summoned for military service in the fulfilment of civic duty; they became professional organizations permanently devoted to war. The soldier of the new order depended on his pay and on spoils. 'His only home was the camp, his only science war, his only hope the general.'[1] Political power was becoming naked force, the command of legions. The idea of the city-state was thus dissolved, and with the failure of the senate to establish a new principle the ambitions of consuls and generals led direct to civil war. The conflicts of Marius and Sulla ushered in the age of chaos which could end only when some master of force, destroying the 'republic' altogether, had imposed his will on this broken state. Henceforth all that was new and significant in the political development of Rome was obscured in the process which reduced it to the form of those oriental empires of which the world had already witnessed sufficient examples.

The momentum of the old republican order was too vast to be overcome all at once. When the politic Octavian was confirmed in the dominion established by

[1] Mommsen, *op. cit.*, Bk. IX, ch. vi.

Julius, he made a show of constitutionality, assuming the mere magistracy of the consulship at Rome and the proconsulate for the provinces henceforth designated imperatorial, while the senate administered the other provinces. But from the first the direction towards which the state was headed was sufficiently clear. Octavian became Augustus, the princeps or chief citizen, the pontifex maximus or ' high priest ', the ' father of his country ', the father by adoption of the successively designated heirs to his power, and on his death he was officially raised to the rank of a god. The aspects of oriental absolutism were all veiled in the rule of Augustus, but they were all present. The veils were withdrawn in the reigns of his successors. The principate became a monarchy, at length a dynasty. From this last step Augustus had shrunk, and it might have been better for the empire if, having gone so far, he had taken before the end the step which might have saved the state from the perilous problem of the succession. If Augustus had been the father of a son instead of only a daughter, the later history of Rome might well have been less troubled, though nothing could have averted the final fate of an empire that had lost all inner principle of cohesion. By leaving the succession undetermined by any definite system he foreshadowed the age when the shout of an army would be of more effect than the decree of the senate or the vote of the people. Under the constitution bequeathed by Augustus the comitia formally elected the emperor and the senate conferred on him the imperial power. But the day of the sovereign comitia was past. The senate was still an authority, the exclusive aristocratic council of empire. But its very exclusiveness narrowed its title to sovereign powers and weakened it as against the emperor who commanded the legions and was invested with majesty.

For two centuries the Roman world was formally governed by this unequal pair, but as early as the death of Nero the real situation was sufficiently revealed by the action of the armies which respectively proclaimed Galba, Otho, and Vitellius as rival emperors. It was military power, often fortuitous, never stable, always incapable of reading the hidden sources of political unity, that made and unmade the master of the Roman world. The ' general will ' that had expressed itself in the pride and loyalty of citizenship was dethroned and broken by the capricious will of the soldiery. It was this process that made of the empire the hollow shell of power, at length unable to resist the pressure of outer forces.

Vespasian, becoming emperor after the riot of un-principled power that followed Nero's death, sought to restore the lost unity of empire, partly by the old plan of extending the citizenship, partly by admitting to the aristocracy of the Senate a thousand leading families from the provinces. The latter was a statesman-like device that stayed for a time the disintegration of the Roman world. The Senate so reconstituted gave successive emperors a legitimacy that stabilized their authority and averted for the most part the military conflicts of aspirants to the supreme power. But the authority of the Senate was not continuously renewed by fresh elements from within the general body of the state, and, as is well known, no system of representation was ever devised to express the political will of the peoples within the empire. Rome had lost altogether the very conception of self-government, even in the narrowest interpretation of that term. The power of the emperor had no valid foundation, and therefore it could neither resist the temptations of dynastic absolutism nor fortify itself against the intrigues of ambitious generals. After the death of Domitian a new civil war revealed this truth, but it appeared in all its nakedness only after the quite despotic reign of Septimius Severus. The sense of citizenship, the basis of political order, was rotted by the lack of opportunity for its exercise. In the widespread body of empire scattered *foci* of irresponsible force caused violent disruptions. Since force could concentrate at any point the empire itself had no longer a centre, no longer a capital. So came the time of partition, the days of two emperors, or again of four, or even of six. In the process, population and wealth and culture alike dwindled, consumed by the ravage of power. Power in the service of a false ideal, power that is yoked to loyalty, however begotten, is still a servant, but power that neither inspires nor is inspired by any ideal save the reflection of its own greatness, is a destroying tyrant, until it finally destroys itself.

It is customary to tell of a mysterious and fatal decadence that befell the Romans.[1] In political science, as in all science, it is wiser to seek no refuge in the unknown until we are quite sure that we have explored the difficult and still remote recesses of the knowable. True it is that the spirit of achievement rises and falls in ways that we cannot explain, but we are so far from having probed the relation between social life and social institutions that every crucial instance, like that of Rome, is only a challenge to further endeavour. Rome's internal strength, while she was strong, depended on a tenacious principle of unity expressed in the form of citizenship. This principle had

[1] Cf. Balfour, *Decadence*.

a remarkable elasticity, so that it adapted itself for a time to the alien conditions of growing empire. But it could not be stretched beyond a certain point without breaking. The imaginative statesmanship of Rome was not great enough to devise a political basis for an empire of the civilized world. It found no new principle of unity to take the place of a now meaningless citizenship, no new principle of authority to substitute for the tradition of magistracy and city-council. Thus it fell back on the new doctrine of power which offers men no ground of solidarity. When the state failed men sought refuge in individualistic philosophies and religious kingdoms 'not of this world', of which Christianity was the chief. These doctrines accentuated by revulsion the very elements which empire ignored in the nature of man, but in doing so they still further disintegrated the state. The introduction of the Christian religion into another type of society than the Semitic revealed the true distinction (which later became lost) between church and state, but it came unprepared and at a dangerous time. This inner failure gave opportunity to the outer forces that surrounded it on all sides. Rome became at length the mere shell of empire, which could resist no longer the impact of a barbarian world of more primitive but more real loyalties.

THE FORMATION OF THE COUNTRY-STATE

I. FEUDALISM

WITH the downfall of Rome the 'state' actually disappeared from Western Europe. In the East the Byzantine Empire, little respected of historians but long enduring, maintained through consuming wars the framework of an impoverished culture. But in the West the state was killed. So far as political organization was concerned, the achievement of the great classical evolution of citizenship was as if it had never been. Traditions of the overthrown order lingered here and there in the welter of barbarian disorder. But, in the long unhappy centuries which followed, the state had once more to be built within a primitive society. This historical process we cannot here describe. We can consider only such new elements as were at length liberated towards the formation of the state we know to-day.

During these ages society crystallized around two precipitants. One was the church which by means of its own remarkable transformation survived the ruin of the state and provided not only a refuge for the minds of men but also a new form of dominion under the ancient name of Rome. The rule of Benedict was wrought into the power of Gregory. Alike the rule and the power claimed to transcend all limits of time and place. Into a world politically shattered, it brought from the first an element of cultural universality and under its aegis revived the idea of a unity which should be political as well. The other was the territorial unit which in the fragmentation of empire had fallen under the immediate rule of some warrior or noble. Far above him was the barbarian king, Frankish or Gothic or Lombard or Vandal, who could exact tribute and set in motion the greater operations of war but could not maintain order in each countryside. In the time of barbaric unsettlement protection is the first necessity and can be secured only by subservience to the strong. Each district had its lord, and there was no longer an imperial control to prevent him from building his own stronghold and enjoying the fruits of power—personal and not merely political power. Clovis and his successors sought vainly to concentrate a new imperial dominion, but both rulers and people were too ignorant, too heterogeneous, and too undisciplined. The second empire, under Charles Martel and Pepin and Charlemagne, came to accept the necessities of the situation. In place of an imperial unity they accepted an imperial hierarchy. Counts and marquises and dukes ruled the land, under the form of a grant of jurisdiction from the king. In return they were bound to render military service, to pay dues, and to swear ' fealty '.

So arose the theory and the fact—never so complete as the theory—of the feudal system. In it the state was again submerged in the community. An economic title, that to the ' fief ', the land or other good held in trust, on condition of service, homage, and fealty, conveyed an undifferentiated array of rights, political and personal. It was not the claim of the state but the claim of a lord, not the welfare of the whole but the right of a master, which inspired and maintained the obligation of men to one another. The military organization of the tribe, bereft in this new setting of the sense of tribal community, was superimposed on the land. As the system grew stable, the ownership of land became the foundation of all rights and duties. It was the title to homage and fealty, to the exacting and rendering of military service and economic dues, to control over wardship and marriage, to jurisdiction and even legislation. Public office became an appurtenance of private property—or rather the distinction between public and private was lost. Hence the acceptance of such anomalies as 'private' war, 'private' coinage, 'private' jurisdiction. Hence also the exemption of the higher nobility from taxation, for private privilege counted as public right. The king himself governed as of personal right, so that the people were 'his' people, and the country 'his' country, as the antiquated formulae of English proclamations still recall.

Mr. Jenks has described the feudal condition as a half-way house between a patriarchal and a political system.[1] The description is suggestive, but we should observe that an essential element of the patriarchate, the inclusive kin-bond, is lacking under feudalism. On the contrary, the tendency of feudalism was towards an exclusive kin-bond, towards caste. Possession and office tended to become hereditary, under the principle of primogeniture, the heir of the fief-holder being confirmed, on payment of a 'relief', in the succession. It was natural, in an age of both intellectual and economic poverty, with a population almost completely dependent on a rather primitive agriculture, that society should take a rigid form. Nor did the universal claim of the church prevent the

[1] Jenks, *The State and the Nation.*

hardening of class lines. Instead the church itself became a caste, an estate, hierarchical like the rest and teaching subservience and lordship as the order of life.

Nevertheless within this order there were slowly bred new forces which undermined it. Slowly the life of commerce revived, and trading cities, in their very nature alien and hostile to the feudal tradition, grew strong. The aristocracy of trade and industry is utterly different from the aristocracy of the land. There was no room for it within the system. It asserted and achieved its independence, and the 'free cities' of Germany and Italy arose. We have already seen how the character of city life has a transforming influence on society. This fact was again exemplified in the middle ages. In the cities commercial and industrial wealth broke through the power and tradition of a landowning class. In the cities a new socio-political unity, the gild, organized to power those elements which found no place in feudalism, and created new standards, new customs, another way of life. In the cities the idea of democracy found its most congenial soil, and the struggles between the artizans and the *popolani grassi* recorded victories which never came to the peasants in their struggles with their lords. The earlier merchant gild grew too exclusive for the new conditions, and as it decayed craft gilds, more inclusive and more fraternal, assumed importance. They too tended to become excessively tenacious of power and privilege, but by that time new movements were in progress which swept past them and finally swept them away.

Religion dominated the mentality of the middle ages to a degree unparalleled in the history of western civilization before or since. But though it proclaimed unity it brought in the end a sword of division which cut through the body of feudalism. The Holy Roman Empire never reconciled the claims of emperor and pope. The day came when a pope claimed to be ' absolute master of all princes, who were bound to kiss his feet, and whom he could depose at will, by releasing their subjects from the oath of fidelity '. Following out his word Gregory VII brought Henry IV to the subjection of Canossa, and the world beheld the astonishing spectacle of an emperor, barefooted in the snow, doing humble penance for three days and nights before his ' spiritual ' master. The triumph of Gregory was not enduring, but it was more than restored in the age of Innocent III, who had nearly all the princes of Europe, from Italy to Spain and from Sweden to England, at his feet.

This ' temporal power ' of the popes rested on the support, almost the ' general will ', of a vastly extended community of believers. But it was threatened from two sides. It touched too nearly the pride and the power of kings. There was no reconciliation of the two powers, no demarcation of spheres. If the prince claimed the right of ' lay investiture ', the church claimed the right of the ecclesiastical court. Each sought to dominate the ' universal partnership ', and the end, as always, was disruption. On the other hand the attack on the temporal power of the church was fostered by disintegration within the church. Its temporal power and spiritual principle were not in harmony. Movements for internal reform, actuated by the drive of that more profound religious conviction that appeals from authority to ' conscience ', led finally to the great schism. The unity of the church was broken, and in the cleavage its universal claim, both spiritual and temporal, was defeated. A new confusion appeared within the decaying form of feudalism.

Of this confusion the kings and princes of Europe took advantage. The feudal system, apart altogether from the pretensions of the church, gravely impeded the ambitions of the great overlord, the king. The greater vassals owed him direct service, but their subvassals and tenants only indirect service, at the bidding of their proper lords. 'The king has the ban'—the summons of the lord to military service—'but not the arrière-ban'—the summons of the under-vassals. This condition made the power of the greater vassals formidable and vexatious—to one another as well as to the king. The common people too, spent in the quarrels of their masters, were learning to cry, like the dying Mercutio in the feud of Montagues and Capulets, 'A plague o' both your houses', and to look on the power of the king as the fount of order and internal peace. From the distractions of these times of insubordinate powers men sought refuge in the unity of the state. The church had tried and failed, because the solidarity of sentiment broke beneath it. A new solidarity was arising which carried the state to success.

This was nationality. By its aid the idea of citizenship was given a character and range unknown in Greece and Rome. This was the sentiment needed to confirm the country state, and to usher in a new age of political evolution. Since this is the first time that nationality has appeared in our survey as a definite and creative force we must here pause to consider its significance.

THE SIGNIFICANCE OF NATIONALITY

By its very nature nationality is as inclusive as the state itself. It makes no distinction between the common man and the noble. Citizenship may be and generally has been exclusive, a right or a privilege with which men are invested. But nationality is not conferred as a right ; it belongs to men by nature and regardless of rank or class.[1] In this respect nationality is like the primitive sense of kinship, and it works on a higher and a far more extensive plane as kinship worked in the solidarity of the tribe. It is a free uniformity, admitting endless difference and dependent on no sanction and no coercion. Thus in the great reaction against caste domination and narrow loyalties, against, on the other hand, a tyrannous universality of thought and conduct, the spirit of nationality grew strong.

The preconditions of nationality were being laid in the later middle ages. Common elements of culture, manifested in religion, in the forms and common language of learning, in the modes and standards of life, prevailed over a great area. They were not strong enough to maintain political unity within it against the disarray of established powers. But over considerable regions, marked off as countries partly by geographical barriers, partly by historical accidents, partly by differences of speech and tradition consequent on both, they conspired to produce

[1] I am not speaking of nationality in its merely legal sense. Residence and other legal requirement suffices to confer English or French citizenship, which is also termed nationality, but it does not thereby make him English or French. A peace treaty can change in an hour the legal nationality of a group, but its intrinsic nationality is determined in the course of generations.

a new sense of community. Within these areas men learned to think of country or 'fatherland'. They learned an allegiance whose explicit bounds were narrower than those of civilization, but wider and more pervasive than those of locality. This development was vastly furthered by those technological advances which revealed the awakening spirit of science. The effect of invention, whether it was that of gunpowder or of the printing press, was to alter the distribution of power and in particular to extend it more widely. At first these new instruments of power were seized and used by the strong, but these could not use them without giving them away. Invention reduces the remoteness of things, whether spatial or social. It diffuses opportunity. It breaks the rigidity of custom. Based on inexorable law it searches the distinctions that men create, and if they are unreal it weakens and overthrows them. Arbitrary differences in a developing society cannot withstand the logic of experience. Every new power that men gain over nature may become a means to liberate a new power within themselves.

We can scarcely comprehend in these days how remote from the authorities which ruled over it was in earlier ages the life of the mass of men.

To the peasant, the land-cultivator—and until invention released them, the life of the great majority, illiterate, uniformed, and resourceless, was spent in a ceaseless struggle to subsist on the land—the operation of government was as distant and unknown as the heaven in which he dimly believed. That authority depended on himself was a conception he could not realize, while his own dependence on authority seemed as mysterious, though as real, as the order of the seasons. The sense of nationality could not develop until men learned their participation in a common life, in the service of which authority was maintained and justified.

How then shall we characterize this solidarity on which the modern state has risen to strength ? ' Nations ', says Spengler, are ' neither linguistic nor political nor biological, but spiritual (*seelische*) unities.' What ' soul-unity ' do all Englishmen possess, educated and ignorant, cockney and peasant, rich and poor, over against all Frenchmen or all Germans ?

It is vain to search for any common quality or definite interest which is everywhere associated with nationality. No one of the social possessions of mankind, whether language or distinctive custom or religion or territory or race-consciousness or economic interest, nor even the tradition of political life, is inseparable from it. In fact scarcely any two nationalities seem to find their positive support in the same objective factors.[1] The Swiss have no common language, the Jews no common territory, and as for common race, it is nearly always a delusion. When we seek for the elusive ' common ', we fall back on its positive conditions, and they in turn vary so much that they leave us bewildered. Most of the definitions of nationality beg the question, such as that famous one of Renan's : ' what constitutes a nation is not speaking the same tongue or belonging to the same ethnic group, but having accomplished great things in common in the past and the wish to accomplish them in the future '. But just who are they who, ' having accomplished great things in common ', feel themselves a nation ? The condition may be fulfilled by a family or a ship's crew or a band of conspirators, but they do not on that account become a

[1] I have sought to bring out this fact more fully in an article on *The Foundations of Nationality* (*Sociological Review*, July 1915).

nation. Nationality is the sense of community which, under the historical conditions of a particular social epoch, has possessed or still seeks expression through the unity of a state. Various as are the conditions on which it rests, the sense of nationality is itself definite and strong and moving, more so than the mere pride and vainglory of multiple egoism, so that men are aroused by its name and thought to deep stirrings of devotion, sacrifice, and even worship.

There are many spiritual unities, and nationality is but one. Why has it been in modern history so decisive as against the others ? Why has the ' soul unity ' of the English squire and coster, corporation-lawyer and coal-miner, counted for so much more, to outward seeming and in historical consequence, than the ' soul unity ' of the co-religionists or of the manual toilers of diverse lands ? Why is it that men whose manners of thought and life are poles apart and whose everyday interests belong to different worlds or are definitely opposed, nevertheless, because they belong to the same nation, feel a oneness that in the hour of crisis supersedes all obvious differences, engulfs all nearer claims, and negates all intersecting communities ?

It is true that, in the mass, there are marked similarities and dissimilarities which distinguish, in certain instances at least, the representative members of one nation from those of another, the Frenchman from the German, the Briton from the Frenchman, the Swede from the Russian, and so forth. But they are perhaps no more marked than those which distinguish the Englishman from the Scot, the Saxon from the Prussian, the Breton from the Norman. Moreover such differences are too elusive, too subtle, for definition. They are subject accordingly, within the nation, to sentimental simplification and patriotic embellishment; and, as between nations, to the most exaggerated and fanciful representation, according to the prejudices generated by political relationships. A grotesque illustration is furnished by the changing pictures of the Russian people accepted in England and France at the outbreak of the war and after the second revolution. Moreover these differences, when real, are typical rather than universal. Many Englishmen are not typical Englishmen, in physical feature or in mode of thought, who yet are conscious of their nationality. Surely these subtle similarities are not the decisive conditions of our modern civilization.

There are two great factors which account for the insistence and intensity of the national 'spirit'. One is the operation of the state itself when it reaches the stage of being a country-state, the other is found in the social conditions whence that state has historically arisen.

The state is always a defining and limiting power. From its zeal for definition and control come alike the order and the disorder which it creates—order within its bounds, disorder because it makes its bounds so determinative of all community. Once the country state had been established, it demarcated the interests of its members. The humanist features of medieval civilization, seen in its religion, its learning, its law, its custom, became 'nationalized' by degrees. The demarcating influence of the country state appears very clearly in the policy of mercantilism which interpreted the economic interests of the country as though they were bounded by its frontiers, while the fallacy of its reasoning was hidden by the zeal of its nationalism. In fact the policy created, though at no small cost, economic interests which actually were bounded by national frontiers, just as the policy of protective tariffs does to-day. Again, the very fact that administration and law have determinate boundaries knits together those who live within them and separates them from those who are subject to other administration and law. The evolution of a common order proceeds separately and therefore diversely within each state, and so the sense of likeness within and difference without is fostered. Add to this the effect of the clashes of power between states, which bind in a common cause of life and death the citizens of one against the citizens of another, most drastically uniting by a supreme act of separation and appealing in the process to the strongest emotions of love and hate, through common peril and common triumph.

The other influence making for the strong enhancement of the national spirit must be traced through the historical conditions which up to this point have liberated, repressed, and directed the fundamental instinct of society, the feeling of the group for itself. To make this plain we must here take a backward glance, as far back as our historical light avails.

We have been taught to think of peoples or tribes, integral and distinct bodies of mankind, wandering back and forth over the surface of the earth, laying waste and populating, or driven forth to seek new homes, emigrating, invading, and possessing. But such movements of whole bodies, whole groups with already formed social articulations, do not belong to the reality of human history. In the first place such folk-wanderings, save across narrow seas or deserts, or down the reaches of broad rivers, were physically impossible until after the long and painful conquest by man of the primitive, trackless, and densely

afforested earth. Mobility, like other forms of liberation, is slowly acquired by man. Primitive tribes, as
modern anthropology reveals, are for the most part
ringed about by conditions which forbid large-scale
migrations. The nomads of land and sea are exceptions
who prove the rule, inhabitants of barren steppes or
infertile shores where no settlement is possible. For
human groups settle and stay settled wherever they can.
Adventurers and pioneers and conquerors go out from
among them, but the group clings fiercely to its home, the
clearing, the mountain fastness, the protected shore.

As the earth grows settled populations expand. There
is fusion as well as strife between the spreading settlements.
Trade and exogamy, no less than conquest, bring neighbouring groups together until they call themselves by a
single name. We have at length such a condition as
Caesar found in Gaul. Already the peoples of that land
were called by a common name, the Galli ; already the
peoples within each of its three famous geographical
divisions had achieved some sense of a common character,
the Aquitani, the Celtae, and the Belgae ; though it was
so meagre and impeded that they could not act in concert
even against an external foe. The effective communities
were the tribes, the Aedui, Sequani, Helvetii, Nervii,
Arverni, Treviri, Carnutes, and many others. Yet these
tribes enter into confederacies and have friendships as
well as enmities with one another. The whole situation
is obviously unstable, and the Roman conqueror, though
he divides in order to conquer, cannot but unify when he
brings them within a common ' pacification '. The tribes
of Caesarian Gaul are themselves the product of invasion
and fusion. They are new unities born out of the endless
process of social mixture. They take pride in their race,

but that is only the universal form of group egotism
over against other groups. The inner ground of their
loyalty is not ' race ', but the felt community of place,
custom, tradition, and authority, and the common lot
and fortune which thereon depend.

The great tides of invasion and conquest which fill
the pages of history have as their pre-condition a still
larger coalescence. Now we deal with Medes and Persians,
Greeks and Phoenicians, Hebrews and Egyptians, Mongols
and Turkomans, Etruscans and Romans, Magyars and
Poles, Franks and Allemans, Saxons and Kelts. These
names in turn represent not integral and demarcated
peoples but relatively unstable fusions, formed through
historical moments and capable of united achievements
which give to their names an often brief though memorable
inscription in the vast record of change. They derive
their new title from a leader or a land or the place
of a synoecism or a dominant group, and once the name is
ratified by achievement they claim the proud integrity of
race, the harbinger of nationhood.

The flux of chance and change out of which these
unions arose is well revealed by the confusion of names
which designate them. We take the ancient ' Greek ' as
an example, because the immortal literature has preserved the variant and successive names which they gave
to themselves or received from others. What definition
can we give, in spite of the wonderful record, to the names
' Dorians ', ' Pelasgians ', ' Danaans ', ' Achaeans ', a
diversity of appellation to which no similar diversity of
peoples corresponds ? [1] Or how shall we relate them to
the ' Hellenes ' of a later age, or finally to the ' Greeks ',

---

[1] This is well brought out by Spengler : *Untergang des Abendlandes*, ii.
11, 16.

whose name in the classical period marked the extent of a civilization, in the early Christian age that of a religion, to-day that of a smaller nation ? Does not this variability show how rash it is to attach our present conception of nationality to the vague names of peoples that emerge in history in the wake of invasions and conquests ?

These greater incursions into other lands meant assuredly new fusions, new formations. They should not be likened to the colonization by modern nations of far-away lands whose aborigines were brought suddenly, after ages of separation, into contact with the exploitative methods of an utterly different and technically far superior civilization. In the latter case the former inhabitants melt away and leave the invaders supreme and racially intact. But the invasions of Huns and Mongols, Turks and Moors, Saxons and Normans, however savage and destructive, had no such effect. In times when nearly all wealth consisted in the produce of the soil it was the obvious interest of the conqueror to spare the peasant as a serf and gather the fruits of his toil. An empty land was an empty conquest. Not less desirable as booty were the young women of the conquered people, and nature provided them with a sort of revenge when as concubines or mothers they changed the spirit and the blood of their conquerors. For this reason the prophets of the fiercely exclusive Jews made it a holy command to spare neither woman nor child in the lands they strove to possess.[1] But we know from their lamentations how even the word of Jahwe did not prevail against such instincts.

So there emerged ever new peoples, new ' races ' of men, while countless old names went down to oblivion or became dim memories of former conflicts, like those of the

[1] Deut. xx. 13-19.

Amorites and Jebusites and Amalekites with whom the children of Israel fought. With the spreading out of settlements and contacts the social process revealed itself more clearly. Groups were assimilated, by intermarriage and by unperceived exchange of cultural influence, while the new and very significant diversities that arose *within* them became the condition of a more complex type of civilization. Across the surface of this deepening community feuds and dissensions appeared, partitions and wars, such as those that distracted the life of classical Greece or medieval Germany, or present-day Europe, but these were the quarrels of the like-natured who blindly clashed in the pursuit of the self-same objects. They are often the most destructive of all quarrels, but they are also the most futile, because they are internecine and waste alike the security and the resources for which they contend. When the violence and the passion are expended, there is nothing left except to build again that which has been destroyed.

It is of course the strong spirit of modern nationalism which hinders the realization of this truth. One of its grounds we have seen to be the administrative character of the modern state. The other, which makes possible, though it partly depends upon, political exclusiveness, is the sense of community which, shaken from its old foundations, clings to the fact of the state as to a rock in the midst of waters.

The sense of society is always simpler than the truth. The group never realizes the profoundity of the forces which have created and are always recreating its unity. It seizes on some one element or expression of community and makes that the criterion of it all. For most primitive tribes it is the clan element, the blood relationship, the bond of brotherhood. Nothing is more convincing of the need for a simplified expression of the social fact than the totemic system, the totem, bird or beast or fish or other natural object, being the—to us—incongruous projection of the feeling of unity, so real that it must take external form, so uncomprehended that it must suffer a mystic transformation. The highest civilization of Greece alone found the true basis of community, the solidarity born of a common life, but that which it perceived intellectually it failed to affirm politically. Rome had to content herself with a legal criterion, the far-flung right of membership within the mother-city of her empire. From this dying fiction men turned their eyes to the East. The age of faith dawned also for the West, and orthodoxy built anew the pales of citizenship. For the accommodating and many gods of classical civilization there was substituted the jealous and only true god of Judaism or some form of Christianity or Mohammedanism. Under the spell of this potent suggestion the sense of society was confined to the body of believers. The church and the community were reckoned as one and indivisible, and the unbeliever and the heretic were outcasts from society. No other allegiance was needed in this unearthly light, and so again all the problems of society were simplified and falsified.

The faith of the West broke into schisms and its fanatic zeal was cut across by other loyalties. The chaotic issue between Pope and Emperor was the focus of a struggle which ended in the triumph of territorial dynasty over all the Western world. Now men found their unity in common service and common loyalty. Monarchy with its divine right and earthly power became the keystone of society. In the thought of the age to which a belated writer like Hobbes adhered it was not a natural but an imposed cohesion which made men social beings. But underneath this dominance, and surpassing the thin logic of political thinkers, men were learning to feel themselves English and French and Germans, Italians and Poles and Russians. The unity they were realizing was the unity of nationhood, and its basis was the sense of a common and yet distinctive culture.

Here we must point out that the sense of nationality has a content more pervasive and more real than the conceptions of social unity which preceded it. It belongs to a stage where the social consciousness is diffused through the various classes of a society. It belongs to the era which advances to democracy and parliaments, where monarchy disappears or becomes a symbol of a unity it does not create. It contains a claim of equality, for nationality has no degree within its range. It applies to all men, rich or poor, high or low. It is not external, like the fact of a common subjection to dynasty. It is not transferable, except by a long process of assimilation. It cannot be merely accepted or rejected, like a creed of the days of Julian or Constantine, or of that prince of Adiabene who turned with his whole state to Judaism. No easy formula, like the famous *cuius regio eius religio*, can solve its problems of jurisdiction. It is no mere boast or subjective expression of collective pride, like the claim of distinctive race. And, though communal in character, it unites far greater areas of society than ever in the past felt themselves to be one community.

A spirit so pervasive, so complex, so subtle, and yet so strong, seeks embodiment in an association, inevitably in the state. No other association could serve its end, as the church serves the religious spirit or the family the primary needs of sex. The state becomes, or seeks to become, the body of nationality; and from this perilous but inevitable incarnation a new order of conflict and adjustment springs.

II

FROM ABSOLUTISM TOWARDS DEMOCRACY

From the break-up of feudalism there emerged the centralized monarchies of early modern Europe. The civilization of the middle ages had by the close of the thirteenth century recorded a wonderful advance over the barbaric chaos which succeeded the fall of Rome. Yet in the next centuries it was doomed to suffer changes so great as utterly to transform it. We must leave it to the historians to determine what part the various great forces of change played in this transformation. Vast wars and unparalleled visitations of pestilence undermined the weakened foundations of the social order. They seemed also to shake the morale of the survivors. The old traditions lost their power. In this prostration new social agencies were necessary, and they came at length from many sides. Two great inventions, paper and printing, prepared the way for the reception of the rediscovered thought of Greece, the most liberating of all the expressions of the human spirit. Science was not only learning slowly to control nature, it was also subtly attacking the superstitions which dominated men's minds. Many things conspired to dissolve the system of ' estates '. Gunpowder was abolishing the fighting prestige of the knight. Economic necessities were liberating the serfs. England was already feeling the first impact of a long industrial development, as she turned much arable into pasture to feed the woollen mills of Flanders. A middle class was arising, to break the great feudal line between those who owned and those who cultivated the soil.

As the estates weakened the king grew strong. Having been feudal to his loss he became anti-feudal to his gain. In England as early as the reign of Henry II, the king's prerogative, the king's court, the king's writ, overcame all local and feudal jurisdictions.[1] Law was becoming centralized, and the influence of Roman jurisprudence, as it became known and studied in Europe, reinforced the doctrine that law is the will of the king. The checks on monarchy, the semi-independent military establishments of the nobility, the 'parlements',[2] the oaths of coronation, the autonomy of the cities, were falling away. England, owing to its insular position and the conditions of the Norman Conquest, had reached absolutism at an unusually early date, and had already entered on the next stage of development when it was swung back, for a time, in the general trend. But through many vicissitudes the principle of absolutism triumphed over a great part of Europe, becoming supreme in Spain under Philip II, in France under Louis XIV and in England, though far more precariously, under the Stuarts. Germany was further removed from the new influences and attained this condition more slowly and much later. But for the

[1] Cf. Adams, *Origin of the English Constitution*, ch. iii.

[2] The 'parlement' in France was originally, like the Italian 'parlamento', a mass meeting of citizens summoned to hear and assent to some important decision. But in France it became, about the beginning of the fourteenth century, a body with judicial functions, consisting mainly of lawyers. One of these, the *parlement* of Paris, attained considerable importance, as a high judicature. It also registered and promulgated the edicts of the kings, and took the opportunity of expressing approval or disapproval, though as yet without a constitutional veto.

time the spirit of nationality, seeking unity first, was on the side of the kings. The king was the divinely appointed head of the nation, and with divine right went passive obedience. When a conflict arose between the king and the feudal nobility, as in Denmark or in France, the mass of the citizens took sides with the king. Monarchy was their first refuge against feudal privilege, the exploitation of the nobles and their exemption from the burdens of taxation. Monarchy solved also, for the mass, in an age of receding faith, the intolerable conflicts of religion. How strong was this sentiment we realize when we reflect that not only court ecclesiastics like Bossuet, not only political thinkers like the fearful Hobbes, but even so dispassionate and free a philosopher as Spinoza accorded to the state an absolute control over religion.

It was a temporary solution. The forces opposed to feudalism supported sheer monarchy for a time, but when the monarch himself, established in strength by the removal of feudal restraints, rallied around him, in opposition to the inevitably growing power of the citizens, a feudal nobility which he had no longer cause to fear, his own position was in turn assailed. Likewise the positive force of nationality, which had found both the form and the symbol of its unity in the king, demanded a fuller and more active expression. The very influences which had exalted the king, as they expanded, worked for his downfall or his reduction to the status of ' constitutional monarch '.

The nation-state grew into the heir of the dynastic state, but it was not to retain all its possessions. Together with a broadening of the basis of political authority there went a limitation of its sphere. Nationality, being common to all the members of a nation, demanded that its community should be protected, ordered, and furthered by the state. But it came also to demand that those interests which were not common to the nation should so far as practicable be left free from coercive control. The subject of religion was again the battle-ground. The first naïve formula of solution was the 'religious peace' of Augsburg, which suffered the ruler to choose between alternative faiths, his subjects being bound by the choice, save that a subject who persisted in adherence to another faith might emigrate. But the vigour of a people, in an age of increasing opportunity for its expression, could no longer tolerate this surrender of its 'personality' to any monarch or government. The confused history of the age which followed is nevertheless a history of the struggle for liberty against government in those matters where difference of opinion provides no ground and admits no necessity for common political action.[1]

In the actual struggle the issue was never so clear as the result. An occasional manifesto, like the famous *Agreement of the People*, did set forth certain of the true principles of government, especially the principle that sovereignty derives from the people and that therefore the state has limits to its rightful power, to its control over the whole body of citizens who maintain and establish it. But generally, and especially in the earlier stages, men fought against alien absolutism rather than for genuine liberty. Puritans or Catholics, when out of power, asserted their right of religious liberty, but when in power, when they saw the opportunity of controlling the state, they again magnified it for what it could do

[1] This history is traced in Acton's *History of Freedom and Other Essays*; Bury's *History of Freedom of Thought*; and Nevinson's *Growth of Freedom*.

when under their control. Men seldom fight for or against inclusive principles, but they win or they defeat them none the less. It was so also with the other differences which were bred in the national state. The new power of industry fought against alien political control of the economic life, but had no scruples against asserting its own. Even the retreating forces of feudalism, as the nation became industrialized, rallied around the banner of liberty. It was the diversity and the opposition of interests developed within the nation which forced upon men, reluctantly and through strife, a truer perception of the nature of the state.

Along with this there went a corresponding redistribution and diffusion of economic power. We have seen that the peasant, in his isolation and ignorance, was politically helpless. Under feudal conditions he was practically bound to the estate on which he worked. The village labourer could only with great difficulty leave his village. In England, the Law of Settlement, which as late as 1662 gave statutory recognition to an earlier practice, made it legal for a parish to eject an incomer provided he did not settle in a tenement worth £10 yearly. The lack of economic power meant the lack of personal liberty. The absence of a money-economy prevented the free exchange of services and assured the dependence and the immobility of labour. Even the arts and crafts were held in the net of local restrictions, and every town sought to ' protect ' itself against artisans or traders from without. The development of communications, of wider markets, of a new industrial technique, and therewith the centralization of the state, broke down these restrictions. ' The whole internal history of the seventeenth and eighteenth centuries ', says Schmoller, ' not only in Germany, but everywhere else, is summed up in the opposition of the economic policy of the state to that of the town, the district, and the several estates.'[1] The process which diminished the relative importance of agriculture in the economic life of western civilization, at first slowly, then rapidly in the age of great technical discoveries, brought a new class into being whose outlook was utterly different from that of the peasant, and whose power to influence the state was vastly greater.

Here again the first impact of the new forces strengthened the absolutism of the state while their subsequent operation helped to destroy it. The state was able to control and utilize the earlier discoveries, as Colbert did so notably in France. The further discoveries of the industrial age overwhelmed these pretensions—the state could no longer control them. Economic centres of power formed themselves quite apart from the political centres. Had it not been for their internal oppositions they would have utterly dominated the state. As it was, they exercised great influence upon it, and often without directly entering the political sphere at all.

Minor divergences of economic from political power had appeared in former ages—one may cite the conflicts of the Roman ' knights ' with the older political interests, but they never led to the sheer contrasts of this modern development. For never before the industrial age was economic power really separable from the political. The Roman ' knights ' were tax-farmers and dependents of the state. The Lombard bankers, the Genoese and South German financiers, depended on political concessions. The joint-stock companies of the seventeenth and eighteenth centuries owned politically-derived mono-

[1] *The Mercantile System.*

polies. Before the industrial age all economic power rested either on land, where ownership was closely woven with the political system, or else on particular privileges for commerce or finance which only the state could grant. The common life was so bare of superfluities, and markets were so narrow, that the producer as such or the unprivileged trader could scarcely attain to power through mere economic activity. In such times no industrial trusts or financial rings could either defy or control the state. There were no economic corporations which were not, in a very definite sense, the ' creatures ' of the state. It is true that in the ' colonies ' certain chartered companies came to exercise powers mightier than those wielded by the official representatives of the state, but they did so because invested with political authority which, directly or indirectly, by design or by negligence, proceeded from the home government.

The new economic power was no child of the state. On the contrary, government, still largely controlled by a landed class, sought to resist the forces that undermined the social importance of land and disturbed all established distinctions of class. But no political power could stay the movement that superseded the tool by the machine and made the factory instead of the household the industrial centre; that created an unheard-of and feverish productivity, bringing vast wealth to some and a new servitude to many others; that emptied the countryside into the cities; that established higher standards of living in which all might hope to share; that made possible an unprecedented increase of population; and that knit whole countries into a complex unity of interdependence. Instead of creating them, the state had with vast difficulty to adjust itself to the new conditions, a secular task which is yet a long way from accomplishment.

The most difficult adjustment was not, however, that which established the power of capital above the power of land ; here there was possible the reconciliation of a new oligarchy with an old. New wealth became endued with old titles through intermarriage and common participation in business ventures to which the one lent driving force and the other prestige. More serious was the adjustment demanded by the new economic power of the hitherto subject classes. The dependence of the industrial worker on capital was not of that static character which marked the dependence of the peasant on land. No ancient customs hallowed it. It was restless and unstable. It mobilized a class increasing always in relative numbers and in the consciousness of power. Industrial workers had an opportunity to unite which was denied to peasants. They were crowded in centres of civilization and amenable to new ideas. Their work grew specialized, but within a common technique which increased their solidarity. The state re-enacted the old laws against ' combinations ', but it might as well have legislated against the steam-engine. The economic fact was stronger than government. The workers learned the efficacy of a new economic weapon, the concerted withdrawal of their labour. The social need for the service of the humblest grade of worker is no less great, and is generally more urgent, than for that of government itself. Conscious alike of new goals and of new powers the working classes claimed and won effective citizenship. The state thus moved towards democracy, not through the temporary insurrection of a subject class but through the operation of economic forces which reconstituted the basis of society. ' The real

English revolution ', as Mr. Fisher has said, ' occurs not in 1215 nor in 1646, nor in 1689, but in 1832, 1867, and 1884, when a constitution adapted to an agricultural state was by successive stages expanded under the stress of an industrial revolution, to admit merchants and trades-people, artisans and ploughmen, to control the destinies of the nation.'

The transformation of the state under these influences will engage us throughout this work. Here it may suffice if we trace the process as it affected the most characteristic and determinative of its institutions, that of representation. Representative government distinguishes the modern state from all others. We may discover rudimentary forms of representation at any historical stage.[1] It is an obvious device that where one must act for many the one should be chosen by the many to act for them. In classical Greece we may find it in the election by demes at Athens or perhaps in the voting by cities at the assembly of the Achaean League. But in the ancient state representation was never applied as a consciously organized principle for expressing the will of the many through the few. The problem of government

[1] ' The evidence now available warrants the following statements :

i. Representative government originated as a bud put forth by monarchy.

ii. It developed first in England, not because the people were more free there, but because monarchy there was stronger than elsewhere.

iii. On making its start it got its mode and form from the church.'
Ford, *Representative Government*, Pt. I, ch. ix.

But we ought perhaps to seek the origin of political representation in judicial institutions, which always develop earlier than legislative ones. Thus it is found in the inquests of Carolingian rulers. In England, in the *Leges Henrici Primi*, we learn that in the local courts the townships are represented by the priest, the reeve, and four of the best men. Even at that time the usage was probably old.

within the Roman Empire suggests to the modern mind the representative solution, but it practically never occurred to the Romans themselves. In the last days of the gathering storm a scheme for a Gallic parliament— not a Roman one—was presented in an imperial rescript (A.D. 418), according to which deputies from districts and municipalities were to be admitted to membership, but the scheme came to nothing. This was a political direction which was left for the modern world to explore. Some historians trace the beginnings of modern representation back to the folk-meetings of pre-feudal Teutonic or Anglo-Saxon society; others derive it from the medieval system of estates or from the council of the medieval king.[1] However derived, it is indissolubly associated with the country state and gives its express character to modern citizenship

We may discern several distinctive stages in the evolution of the representative system. The king's council was the council of a hierarchy. Together with the royal officers there were assembled the greater vassals and prelates, the heads rather than the representatives of the two most important states.[2] It developed a definitely representative element when members of the 'commons' (that is, the communities) were summoned to meet with the barons and clergy. The English parliament of 1295 witnessed the completion of the first stage. 'Every sheriff is to cause two knights of each shire, two citizens of each city, and two burgesses of each borough, to be elected.' At first they were present in an inferior capacity,

[1] See note on previous page.

[2] In England the curia regis was only on special occasions composed of all tenants-in-chief. Ordinarily it included only such tenants-in-chief as were in attendance on the king. (Cf. G. B. Adams, *Origin of the English Constitution*, Appendix I.)

not to advise or be consulted, but to hear and fulfil. But the very necessity which caused their presence, the difficulty of raising funds without the consent of the class which payed, gradually increased their power. The men of substance, themselves elected by the property owners of each locality, learned to ask kings to furnish accounts of their expenditures, and kings, though at first like Henry IV they might refuse, learnt the necessity of rendering them.

The second stage was the development of a purely (though at first narrowly) representative assembly. The feudal line divided the house of the commons from the council of the nobility, but the forces which weakened feudalism strengthened the former. Nowhere is this development so continuous and so clear as in England. The feudal principle of Magna Carta was transformed by parliament into the principle that the king was bound by the laws it was learning to make. Parliament discovers a method of enforcing responsibility against the king's ministers and thus in reality against the king. The forces making for absolutism at length came into open clash with the forces which were building the power of the commons. The revolution of 1688 established the principle that, as between king and parliament, the latter was the decisive factor in legislation. Thus the way was prepared for the further evolution of representation, its broadening out until parliament became the organ of the nation itself, of the whole nation.

The English revolution contemplated no such denouement. Its ideal was the representation of property. From Locke to Burke this principle seemed a sufficient safeguard of all the liberties that counted. The changes in the social and economic life were for a time unreflected in the system of representation, with its pocket boroughs, corporation boroughs, forty shilling freeholds, burgage tenures, and other survivals. It is true that in America a new assertion of the principle that there should be 'no taxation without representation' founded a group of states which proclaimed, in bills of rights and declarations of independence, the equality of citizens and actually embodied this principle in their constitutions. Then came the great upheaval in France. Liberty, equality, and fraternity were watchwords liable to diverse and dubious interpretations, but whatever else they implied they clearly stated that personality and not property was the true basis of representation. Towards this ideal, though not without reactions, the modern state has advanced. In the realization of this principle the extensive development of representation reaches its limit.

The intensive development continues. Democracy demands far more than universal suffrage. It seeks a means of securing the responsibility of its ministers and of asserting the pre-eminence of the legislative power. It requires that not only the right to elect the representatives but also the power to select candidates for election shall be in its hands. It endeavours to improve the machinery of representation so that the various elements of public opinion shall not be misrepresented in the total result. And it finally demands that its body of representatives shall continue after election to feel the impact of the public opinion to which it owes its being.

Here are a number of problems which the modern state has endeavoured and is still endeavouring to solve. The state of our day is integrally bound to the representative principle. Perhaps the greatest problem has been in the sphere of foreign relations where ancient traditions have most successfully fought against democratic control and where ancient ideas have most tenaciously resisted the necessities created by the great changes in the social and economic order. The great war revealed the irreconcilable difference between internal democracy and oligarchical control of external relations. But it also overthrew those constitutions in which the contrast between the two was most extreme and most perilous. The nation-state, unified within, had already reached a stage in which it must relate its nationality to conditions which transcended nationality. It was a new form of a problem almost as old as history, the problem of the adjustment of the established form of political unity to a civilization which stretched beyond it. It was the problem confronted with which the state in every age had most signally failed. Nearly always the inclusive unity had been established, if at all, through the violent and often catastrophic operation of forces which the state had neither understood nor learned to master. The problem which the tribe and the city and the empire had in turn to meet was now insistently pressing on the nation-state. Its further evolution seemed likely to depend, more than on anything else, on the way in which it faced that problem, whether with the blindness of the past or with the wisdom of experience.

BOOK TWO

POWERS AND FUNCTIONS

V

THE LIMITS OF POLITICAL CONTROL

I. 'THE THINGS THAT ARE NOT CAESAR'S'

WE have seen that the very nature of political law sets effective limits to its sphere of operation. The one indubitable task for which law is the necessary, and in fact the ideal, instrument is the building and sustaining of that universal framework of social order within which the life of man, liberated from the encroachments and the confusions of unregulated desires, may more freely and more fully seek out the ways of its fulfilment. Every character of law, its definite formulation, its bindingness, its relative permanence within the code, its universality, indicates most clearly its fitness for this function. Whatever else the state may do, this it must do. But the very quality which enables the state to perform this service renders it unqualified for other forms of ministry. It is needless and futile to concentrate in one agency all the activities of life. Certain tasks the instrument can perform, but badly and clumsily—we do not sharpen pencils with an axe. Other tasks it cannot perform at all and when it is directed upon them it only ruins the material. Wherever, as Green pointed out, the worth of any activity lies solely or chiefly in its free performance, in the spirit which actuates it, in the fact that it is the spontaneous or inwardly determined expression of personality, there the state has no relevant means, has even no power, of direct control. Here is a steadfast negative principle no less invincible than the positive principle stated in the preceding paragraph. To establish order and to respect personality—these are the essential tasks positive and negative of the state, and if we can follow out their implications we shall discover aright both its sphere and its limits. Some implications are clear enough, and we shall state them first before facing the more difficult questions of demarcation. To begin with, the state should not seek to control opinion, *no matter what the opinion may be.* There are two seeming exceptions to this rule which, when examined, enable us to express it the more clearly. The state may take cognizance of incitements to break its laws or defy its authority. Such incitement or defiance is more than the expression of opinion. A citizen or group of citizens may think that an existing law is pernicious, or that an act of authority is illegitimate, or that the constitution of the state is misguided. Citizens may properly proclaim such views.[1] They may

---

[1] This principle would rule out, if the argument is sound, the claim of the state to treat as crimes a class of actions included generally under such rubrics as ' lèse-majesté ' or ' seditious utterances '. In fact the tendency of the modern state is towards the abandonment of this claim as government loses its sacrosanct character. In war time, as part of the general reversion to more primitive conditions which war renders inevitable, the claim is reasserted.

Acts to forbid the teaching of certain doctrines, such as that of the evolution of life, are still possible under the cultural conditions of certain American states. An even more vicious contradiction of political principle is found in the action of the codes committee of the New York State legislature in April 1923, which not only rejected a bill permitting information on birth-control, but actually endorsed a bill to make unlawful the dissemination of literature ' to urge the passing of legislation advocating birth-control '.

go farther and use all means of peaceful persuasion to convince others, and at the same time set in motion all constitutional methods in the endeavour to change the law and the constitution. But to urge law-breaking is to attack the fundamental order, the establishment of which is the first business of the state, and for the preservation of which it is endowed with coercive power. It is indeed a sign of weakness in the state if it feels the necessity to punish every offender who preaches disloyalty. It reveals a lack of trust in that spirit of law-abidingness which is the only permanent support of law. But we can scarcely deny it the formal right to take whatever steps it deems necessary to assure the very object of its existence.[1] Nor is the liberty of opinion thereby jeopardized. The same opinion may be no less vehemently expressed without the advocacy of law-breaking. A man may denounce a law to his heart's content while still recognizing the duty to obey it. The case is still clearer when, in any democratic state which places no constitutional obstacle in the way of the translation of opinion into law, an individual or group advocates the overthrow of government by force. The state is entitled to suppress an incitement which itself is an attempt to dethrone the rule of opinion. Here, as elsewhere, the state, as a condition of existence, must use its force in its most legitimate application, to prevent the rule of force itself. That is why, in the last resort, force can be entrusted to the state, that it may be everywhere subjected to law.

Like considerations apply to literature which clearly

[1] It does not of course follow that every citizen is always *morally* bound to obey every law. We are here discussing the responsibilities of the state, as law-maker and law-enforcer, not of the citizen as the subject of law. I have examined this latter question in my *Community*, Bk. III, ch. v, § 3.

instigates to such immoral acts *as are at the same time prohibited by law*. The instigation must be direct, not constructive. The political offence lies not in the free expression of opinion, still less in the free exercise of the literary imagination, but in the definite assault on the principle of law-abidingness. This power of the state to protect its law is a sufficient safeguard. The state does not need to exercise the dangerous office of censor, an office which treats men as though they were children and is a kind of dictatorship inevitably repressive of the free movement of thought.

The other seeming objection relates to libellous or defamatory opinion. In the common signification of libel what is involved is not merely the expression of opinion but its expression with a malicious intent, to defame or abuse or otherwise injure some person or persons. The law here is guarding the citizen against a particularly insidious form of assault. The libel may be true or false, that is not the issue. It is a libel because it is expressed not as a mere reflection on a matter of public concern but as calculated to do a particular injury. Similarly, to publish comments on a case which is *sub judice* would be to interfere with the course of justice. If the object were merely to reveal the truth, that is provided by the courts according to the rules of evidence.

Why must we deny the state this right to regulate opinion, a right which it has owned almost up to our own time ? It is not in the mere name of liberty that we must speak, for liberty must itself be justified. It is not because opinion is a personal affair and therefore outside the competence of the state. This distinction is untenable, and the insistence upon it has marred many a vindication of the ' liberty of opinion ', including the otherwise fine argument of Mill's *Essay*. It is not because we can separate opinion from action and declare the former to be innocuous. So little can we separate the two that there is perhaps nothing in the world so pernicious and destructive as wrong opinion, mistaken prejudices darkened beliefs inconsistent with the facts of nature, the springs of deplorable follies and stupidities and cruelties, of baneful antagonisms and wasteful purposes. The true reasons are found when we appreciate the pitiful irrelevance of force in the control of opinion. Force comes as a brutal alien into a sphere that is not its own, where it cannot regulate or convince, where it cannot stimulate or direct the healthy processes of thought, where its presence is destructive of good as well as of evil. Force allies itself as easily with falsehood as with truth, so that its mere invocation in support of an opinion is a blasphemy against truth. Opinion can be fought only by opinion. Only thus is it possible for truth to be revealed. Force would snatch from truth its only means of victory. Force can suppress opinion, but only by suppressing the mind which is the judge of truth. Its assault is directed against personality, and bears most strongly against those whom a conviction of truth makes courageous. Thus it attacks moral courage even more than mere belief. Nay more, it attacks the principle of life, by decreeing that the iron law of uniformity shall hold sway over its creative power. When the law of the state is exercised over opinion, then it becomes sheer coercion. For men may act voluntarily when law bids them act against their opinions, but they can never think voluntarily when law bids them think against their opinions. When law bids men believe it makes them hypocrites or rebels, and betrays its proper appeal to the mind of the citizen. The instrument of law loses its true character, and the foundations of loyalty are overthrown. Law therefore becomes false to itself when it would enforce belief.[1]

What applies to belief as such, in its mere expression, applies also to such practices and observances as depend on belief or conviction. Here too the limits of the state are definite and conclusive. They appear when we consider the relation of its law to the two great belief-determined codes, morality and religion.

The inner sanction of morality should never be confused with that of political law. We obey the law not necessarily because we think that the law is right, but because we think it right to obey the law. Otherwise the obedience of every minority would rest on compulsion, and there would be so much friction in the state that its working would be fatally embarrassed. Political obligation is based on the general recognition of the universal service of law and government, for the sake of which we accept specific enactments which in themselves we disapprove. This is the principle of the general will, and all our acquired traditions of loyalty include the assumption that we should extend our law-abidingness beyond the limits of immediate approbation. It is well that government should not unnecessarily strain the sense of loyalty by acts which are bitterly resented by a portion of the citizens, and for that very reason the proper delimitation of the political sphere is most desirable. It is also well that the general will should have as broad and deep

[1] The same argument condemns even more strongly the control of opinion by way of the domination and censorship of the press and of other organs of opinion. To prevent the people from learning the facts on which opinion should be founded is gross deception as well as tyranny. Like other forms of suppression it becomes inevitable during war, but it is still attempted by arbitrary governments even in times of peace.

a basis as possible, through the civil exercise of that sympathy and understanding which can create harmony and agreement out of prior oppositions. But no system of government can secure unanimity, and if by a miracle it were attainable it would be at the cost of something far more precious, the free individuality which must always interpret and create through indifference. To make the sanction of each law depend on the individual's sense of its complete accord with his own desires or ideals, would be to disintegrate loyalty.[1] Moreover, the law of the state, however much we are in accord with its intention, retains a certain external character. It is a law for you as well as for me, stated in precise terms which are neither yours nor mine. Even if it is within it is also without. My response to it is no less sincere, but it is different. It is not, it never can be, the law of the spirit, which is wholly within me.

Herein it differs from the ethical law. This is the imperative of the individual heart, of the ' conscience '. Seen from without it may appear as the product of custom and social training, but as a principle of conduct it is the ' self-legislating ' of a responsible person, choosing in the consciousness of his own liberty the means and ends of welfare. The ethical appeal is always to the individual's own sense of what is right and wrong, in the last resort always to *his* sense of what is good and evil. It is this immediate personal response that is the ground of all loyalties, including the loyalty to the state. But every

---

[1] Miss Follett in her fine constructive books, *The New State* and *Creative Experience*, maintains that by intelligent co-operation every law *could* be made to express a complete interest within which differences are ' integrated '. This is to set up an ideal which, whatever its value, is not likely ever to be fully attained in the political sphere. It cannot therefore provide the condition of loyalty or the sanction of law.

ethical action is the action of the person as a whole, not merely as a citizen nor as a man of business nor as the member of a family. The ethical principle is always determining a man's duty to each and to all of these, comprehending the unity of personality within its own consciousness of the unity of well-being. So stated, it may seem too reflective and deliberate a principle to express the nature of our ordinary conduct. Nevertheless, however bound we may be by habits and traditions and social conformities, we find ourselves incessantly confronted with alternatives and every choice we make has in it, obscurely or clearly, the sense of self-determination in the light of a unified conception of good. Morality is distinguished from blind slavish observance by this fact of choice.

The sphere of morality can never therefore be coincident with the sphere of political law. Morality is always individual and always in relation to the whole presented situation, of which the political fact is never more than an aspect. It is very confusing to speak, as some do, of ' state-morality ' and to contrast it with ' individual morality '. [1] If state-morality means the morality which accepts as right every action of the state, that is, of constituted authority, it is an unreasoning primitive form of *allegiance*, unmoral because the individual abjures his own sense of right and wrong, save in the one blind decision that government is always right. If it means the morality which renders unquestioning obedience to every act of

[1] Thus Mr. A. E. Zimmern quotes (*New Republic*, September 1917) with considerable approval the following statement from Troeltsch : ' Now, therefore, there abide these three, individual morality, state morality, and cosmopolitan morality, but the greatest and most important of these at the present time is state morality.'

government, whether or not the act itself is approved by the citizen, that too is a form of individual morality. For it can only be the expression of the citizen's conviction that on the whole it is better, more conducive to the general welfare, always and in all circumstances to obey—a conviction which at the same time has been opposed by the moral sense of many of the heroes of history, without whose courageous determination to be moral at all costs, that is to hold to their own burning judgement of what is good, the state might never have relinquished its once tyrannous repression of the springs of conduct. Finally, there is no morality save individual morality, even for those who abandon, to church or state or other authority, that discernment of good and evil which is the soul of morals. That is the suicide of morality, but as it is only living men who can commit suicide, so it is only moral beings who can sacrifice, whether in weariness or stupidity or fanatical devotion, the self-determination in which morality has its being.

What then is the relation of law to morality? Law cannot prescribe morality, it can prescribe only external actions, and therefore it should prescribe only those actions whose mere fulfilment, from whatever motive, the state adjudges to be conducive to welfare. What actions are these? Obviously such actions as promote the physical and social conditions requisite for the expression and development of free—or moral—personality. This general principle will of course be subject to very different interpretations, and we must return to it presently. But it shows us clearly that law does not and cannot cover all the ground of morality. To turn all moral obligations into legal obligations would be to destroy morality. Happily it is impossible. No code of law can envisage the myriad changing situations that determine moral obligations. Moreover, there must be one legal code for all, but moral codes vary as much as the individual characters of which they are the expression. To legislate against the moral codes of one's fellows is a very grave act, requiring for its justification the most indubitable and universally admitted of social gains, for it is to steal their moral codes, to suppress their characters. Here we find the condemnation of ' puritanic ' legislation, which claims that its own morals should be those of all, even to the point of destroying all moral spontaneity that is not their own. There are groups which, with good but narrow intentions, are always urging the state in this retrograde direction. They would make gambling a crime. They demand laws against adultery and the cohabitation of unmarried persons.[1] They cannot see that certain actions which they are perfectly entitled to regard as moral offences are not necessarily a proper object of political legislation. They demand a censorship of the stage, of literature, and of art, assigning thereby to some executive official the power of deciding *in advance* what a whole people shall be permitted to read and think and witness and enjoy.

[1] As an illustration we may cite the ' programme of reforms ' presented to the Baptist convention of Ontario and Quebec by their social service committee in 1923. Of the eighteen recommendations nine asked for legal restrictions in the name of morality. They were as follows :

1. The total prohibition of the liquor traffic in Canada as the ultimate goal.
2. The abolition of legalized race-track gambling.
3. The suppression of the traffic in drugs.
4. The destruction of the business of prostitution.
5. The making of adultery a crime.
6. The hindrance of hasty and ill-considered marriages.
7. Increased control of the circulation of objectionable literature.
8. Provincial censorship of speaking theatres.
9. Better supervision of pool-rooms and dance-halls.

It is an interesting commentary on this state of mind that the insistence on repressive moralistic legislation comes chiefly from certain types of religious organization. They would make universal, by coercion, their own moral particularism. In this attitude there is a double confusion of thought. It is, of course, entirely legitimate for a church to insist that its members shall adhere to certain principles of conduct deduced from or corollary to its creed. No one need belong to the church if he is not in harmony with its doctrines. But the state offers no such easy alternative of withdrawal or free acceptance, and, as we shall see later, this obdurate fact, this hard condition of universality, determines within the state, more than within any other association, certain limits beyond which majority rule is no longer expedient. Moreover, within the church the voluntary adherence of its members permits them to accept freely, as true moral obligations, the rules which it imposes upon them. Even so, because social traditions and other considerations than its specific creed and form of worship attach men to a particular church, and still more because even within the formulas of a creed there is much room for divergent opinion, it is unwise for a majority or determining group to insist on a too detailed and rigorous interpretation. This is illustrated, for example, by the difficulty in which the methodist churches of America found themselves as a result of certain official pronouncements regarding card-playing, theatre-going, and other social diversions, until wiser counsels prevailed, modifying the code and leaving to the individual conscience the application of a broader principle. But the greater confusion of thought lies herein, that demands for political legislation of this kind by a church signify a misunderstanding and an unconscious abandonment of its proper office. It is a confession of failure when, mistrusting its own moral powers, the church appeals to the state to coerce those whom the church itself cannot persuade.

The limits of the state are again revealed when we turn to the sphere of customs. Customs grow everywhere in the soil of society, unforced natural growths which reveal the underlying conditions of belief and mode of life. They may grow so strong and thick that they become suppressive of new modes of life, but in their origin they are spontaneous, not created by any deliberate will to organize, certainly not created by the will of the state. The state has little power to make custom, and perhaps less to destroy it, although indirectly it influences customs by changing the conditions out of which they spring. It has long been recognized as a rule of empire that a conquering state must not seek to change the mass of customs prevailing among a subject people. It is no less true that a state cannot legislate away the rooted customs of its own citizens. An autocrat like Peter the Great might order his own court to abandon the customs of the country —to cut off their beards and wear West-European dress and practise alien manners—and his court might obey because of their peculiar relation, itself custom-ordained, to their sovereign. But he could never have forced on the mass of the people the alien order of life whose externals were accepted by a reluctant but servile court. Here the power of any autocrat reaches its limit, or rather his power depends so intimately on the support of custom that he must be its guardian and servant in order to rule. It is in democracies that conflicts between law and custom are more apt to arise, for democracies are less homogeneous and more unstable in respect of custom, and a majority-rule is less sensitive to the power of custom and more ready to abrogate customs practised by minority-groups. But the experience of such legislation shows that the custom of minorities stubbornly resists the coercion of law. In the United States the use of intoxicating liquors, prior to the eighteenth amendment, was a minority-custom. Hence it was possible to pass an Act which undertook to suppress the custom. But the custom persists in defiance of the law and has erected around itself a system of law-defeating agencies which penetrate even to the seats of government. Custom, when attacked, attacks law in turn, attacks not only the particular law which opposes it, but, what is more vital, the spirit of law-abidingness, the unity of the general will. A grave occasion and a clear necessity may indeed justify the assault of law upon a particular custom, and a dangerous remedy may be prescribed for a dangerous disease. But such instances show at least that the main body of social customs is beyond the range of law and is neither made nor unmade by the state.

Over that minor and changeful form of custom called fashion the state has even less control. Frederick William could forbid his subjects to wear clothes made of cotton, but even he could scarcely have ordained the cut of their clothes. A king may set a mode by following it himself— but not by prescribing it. Here we have a curious illustration of the limitations of the state. A people will follow eagerly the dictates of fashion proclaimed by some unknown coterie in Paris or London or New York, but were the state to decree changes in themselves so insignificant, it would be regarded as monstrous tyranny— it might even lead to revolution.

In general the whole of that living culture which is the

expression of the spirit of a people or of an age is beyond the competence of the state. The state reflects it, and does little more. The state orders life, but does not create it. Culture is the work of community, sustained by inner forces far more potent than political law. In the realms of art and literature and music, as in those of religion and custom and fashion; in the thousand expressions of its thought and mode of living; in the endless pursuit of the satisfactions which give meaning and zest to its existence, whether on the plains of common life or on the mountains we call beauty and truth; in the intimacies of love and affection, and in its everyday joys and sufferings; in the mere toilsome acquisition of its daily bread and in the ambitious conquests of distinction and power; in all these activities a people or a ' civilization ' goes its own way, responsive to influences and conditions for the most part unknown to itself, and where known, for the most part uncomprehended and uncontrolled by the state.

These distinctions have important applications which are not yet realized in the conduct of the modern state, and in conclusion we shall dwell on one in particular which in the present circumstances needs most to be accentuated. If an association has a limited function, no matter how great it be, if there are aspects of life withdrawn from its competence, it should not exercise powers which may overwhelm these other aspects or the associations which fulfil other functions. Power should be relative to function. In one respect the state exercises without limit a power which far transcends the limits of its function. It has the power of life and death over all associations—no less than over persons—because of its unabated right to make war and peace. The possession of this power is growing intolerable. The state claims its right to settle political disputes by force. In so doing it elevates political interests to complete supremacy over all other interests. Without reference to the importance of the dispute, it is empowered to wield a weapon the use of which only a supreme need could justify as a last resort. Strangely enough, the use of this weapon creates the only kind of necessity which would justify its use—the jeopardy of the commonwealth—so that the chief ground of its condemnation becomes the reason for its continued employment.

In declaring war the state puts a particular political object above the general ends of the family, of the cultural life, of the economic order. To secure this purpose the state disrupts the family, breaks the fraternities of science and art, confounds the church, profoundly disturbs the economic system, ruins the commerce of nations, suppresses all cultural influences, and inculcates a morality of violence, robbery, falsehood and murder, as between its members and those of its enemies, which is the direct contradiction of that on which society is founded. Here we may well ask, Does the end justify the means ? Or rather, does the function of the state justify its being entrusted by the community with means so formidable, so disparate, and so absolute ? Citizenship is not the whole life or the whole duty of man. Each has a duty to family, to the community, to himself. Why should the state be given a power which assumes that a man's duty to it is supreme and absolute ?

The situation preceding the Great War gives point to our question. In 1914 the peasants of Russia had no quarrel with the peasants of Germany, nor the artizans of either country with those of the other. The business men of the various European countries had no national grievances against one another. Still less had their scientists and artists and teachers. The wives and mothers of the peoples which were soon to destroy one another had no part in the dispute whose arbitrament was to involve them in a common desolation. But the governments of Europe were embroiled, and the act of some wretched assassins at Sarajevo summoned the world to arms. We need not consider what lay behind that act, nor how far the magniloquent claims of democracy and liberty and national destiny were true—in such circumstances, once the die is cast, nations must believe what they cannot know. Our argument is only this, that each state had powers vested in it which enabled it to say : ' Forget that you are peasants, workers, business men, scientists, wives or mothers, and remember only that you are citizens. Forget all other claims upon you, for none of them compare with mine.'

Where the means are out of proportion to the end the results bear witness to it. The objects and ideals of modern warfare are magnified to make them seem worthy of the cost, and when, as seems inevitable, these objects are not attained, an equally inevitable disillusionment follows. This situation must continue so long as the limited state is permitted to wield an absolute power, or so long as, in spite of manifest facts, it is identified with the nation or the whole community. If, on the other hand, the perception of its limited character grows—if it becomes more clearly understood that the state is a particular organization of society, one of the necessary mechanisms by which it is served, society can without grave difficulty find a way of limiting its power externally as it has already done internally, and thereby prevent the catastrophic disruption of its life which the exercise of this last-surviving form of absolutism entails.

THE STATE AND THE OTHER GREAT ASSOCIATIONS

As men came to perceive the nature and the limits of the state they inevitably formed other associations, with other methods and other instrumentalities, through which to pursue those common interests for which the state did not or could not suffice. It was natural that at first the state, not yet realizing its place or properly distinguishing itself from the community, should claim that these associations were part of itself or else should suppress them as conspiracies against its divinity. 'Thou shalt have no other associations beside me,' declared the absolutist democracy of revolutionary France, in a belated renewal of the already defeated claim of monarchical and oligarchical absolutism. But the succeeding century established everywhere the right of economic ' combination ', confirmed the total or virtual separation of church from state, and developed such a rich growth of the myriad associational forms of the present world that only a tradition-blinded historian or an absolutist philosopher can fail to see therein the unusually swift process of social evolution. To-day the great associations are neither parts of the state nor its mere subjects. They exist in their own right no less than it. They exercise powers that are their own, just as surely as does the state. The family repudiates the claim that its children are merely ' born to the state '. The trade union commands a loyalty that is not to be identified with, and sometimes even clashes with, that which its members render to the state. The organizations of finance and industry, commerce and agriculture, have shaken off mercantilist control, and having ceased to be the servants of the state, seek rather to be its masters. The cultural associations have vindicated their rights to pursue without political infringement or direction the interests which are near to them. In this seething world of multifarious collectivity the state must find its place.

It has been maintained that these ' voluntary ' associations are temporary constructions which in time are rebuilt into the comprehensive structure of the state. This view is expressed as follows by Ihering :

' These new purposes being foreign to the state, led a separate and independent existence in the form of associations until they had attained the necessary degree of maturity ; and then they burst the covering in which they had existed hitherto and emptied their entire content into that form which it would seem was intended to take up everything within itself, viz., the state. What was instruction formerly ? *A private affair*. What was it next ? *The business of association*. What is it now ? *The business of the state*. What was the care of the poor formerly ? *A private matter*. What was it next ? *The business of association*. What is it now ? *The business of the state*. Individual, association, state—such is the historical step-ladder of social purposes.' [1]

We have already shown that the order of development is entirely different from that which Ihering presupposes. The individual is the last revelation, not the first, in the social process. The care of the poor was originally, like education, the concern of the kin or community. As the cohesion of the kin dissolved, its ability to discharge these responsibilities proved inadequate. In part they were taken over by the state, in part by the church. Voluntary agencies devoted to these special purposes also appeared. There arose associations for charity and social

[1] *Zweck am Recht*, Pt. I, ch. viii, § 8.

rehabilitation.   There arose educational associations, unconnected with state or church, particularly in the region of higher education, the study of educational methods, and scientific research.   The present position is somewhat as follows.   The state in most countries has assumed a general responsibility for the poor, expressed through poor laws, while leaving a wide field for the work of voluntary agencies.   Possibly the state might, possibly it should, take over the tasks which these have assigned to themselves, and if so the view of Ihering would find a partial confirmation.   But it is certainly erroneous in respect of other interests which have created 'voluntary' associations.   Take education itself as an example.   Here the general attitude of the state has been to insist on universal education and, up to a certain point, to provide the facilities therefor, while at the same time it permits, even in respect of elementary education, the independent functioning of voluntary establishments.[1]   This attitude allows for a freedom in experimentation which is highly desirable in view of the great problems which beset the discovery and application of the best educational methods.   It is highly unlikely that voluntary associations will ever abandon the whole sphere of education to the state, and such action, if possible, would suggest a failure of interest within the

[1] The people of Oregon under the initiative system adopted an Act abrogating the right of any except state schools to provide elementary education, but the Act was declared unconstitutional by the supreme court of the state, and this decision has been confirmed by the U. S. Supreme Court.   In view of the desirability of educational experiment surely a less drastic and repressive method might have been found for preventing the abuses of sectarian schools.   The chief difficulty of associational schools is that certain of them are apt to be used as propagandist agencies by religious bodies.   But even state schools have propagandist features, and there is no cure for it unless the slow cure which is inherent in education itself.

community in respect of the finer and higher possibilities of educational enterprise.

In the continuous adjustment of social life some tasks that other associations now perform will no doubt be transferred to the state. In some countries the relief of unemployment, for example, has already been transferred to the state from the trade union and other agencies. We shall presently consider the principles which determine the proper province of the state and of other associations. Meantime, since the historical confirmation of the independent role of these other associations is so clear— let us reflect simply on the evolution of the family, the church, the economic association—we may dismiss out-right the belittling interpretation which Ihering offers.

Political theory, embarrassed by false conceptions of the state, has done comparatively little to interpret the relationship between the state and the other great associations, to reveal the peculiar nature and functions of each, or even to trace the historical evolution which has created and given some degree of order to our present associational multiplicity.[1] It would engross the whole space devoted to this work were we to attempt here such a task. It must therefore suffice if we treat in more detail two such relationships which are crucial for the under-standing of the state, with a brief indication of the way in which like principles apply to the remaining fields of association. In this section we shall deal specially, because of its historic significance, with the relationship of state and church, reserving to a later chapter the more intricate and pressing problem, slower to develop and still far from being fully understood, much less resolved, of the relation-ship of the state and the economic order.

[1] A brief sketch is given in my *Community*, Bk. III, ch. iii.

There was religion long before there was a church, long before there was a state. It was at the first, as it were, a mental atmosphere which enveloped each society, clinging most densely, like mist on the hills, to the salient features and occasions of its life, to sex and birth, to spring and harvest, to death and pestilence, to darkness and to the light that pursues it, to the sudden revelations of natural power, to the kin-custom, and to the authority of the chief. It was a diffused feeling of sanctity and dread, of ecstasy and horror, expressing itself in worship and dance and ritual, sacrifice and taboo, as the groping mind of man reached everywhere the perilous verge of the unknown beyond the narrow limits of its power. The interpretation of the unknown became itself a lore, and the secret of man's powerlessness itself a power. The priest arose, and his authority was all the greater because no man could discern or question its source. Sometimes the priest and the chief were one ; sometimes they were distinct powers within the single undifferentiated re-ligious-political society. In some cases, as in classical Greece, the religious officialdom became subordinate to the political ; in others, as in ancient Egypt, the priestly power was dominant.

This situation, with endless variations, continued until the modern separation of church and state. It was threatened at times by the appearance of new ' unofficial ' religions, native or imported, which attacked the cohesion of the established political-religious order. The most serious of these assaults in the Western world was that made by Christianity, which proclaimed among the lowly a ' kingdom not of this world '. But the cohesion of the Roman Empire was at the same time decaying from within and the religion of the lowly overcame its resistance and became in turn established and official. The separation of church and state *as two associations*, each with its place and function, was thereby deferred for another age. Figgis has rightly pointed out that the medieval distinction of church and state was not, as has often been held, one between two associations, but one between the two powers of a single *civitas*.[1] Church and state were not yet associations whose respective spheres might be related within a social system, but rather two authorities, those headed by Pope and by Emperor, two 'swords', spiritual and secular, two hierarchies, clergy and governing class, two 'estates' of a single realm. There was no solution available such as we can now present—it was the uneasy co-ordination of powers unlike in nature but like in claim. Erastians and Arminians fought their battle for a ground that belonged properly to neither. Inevitably each claimed predominance, not over its own territory, but over the other. The clergy sought to turn the political government into its executive ; the government would be the head of the church. The Holy Roman Empire was in this respect a compromise of false claims and a solution of nothing. When state absolutism triumphed over Western Europe it was the end of compromise, but only because one false claim had defeated another. The church was 'established' under the headship of the king. It was farther than before from the autonomy of a true association. The two 'swords' were now both wielded by the state.

Renaissance absolutism accordingly brought a new

---

[1] Figgis, *Churches in the Modern State*, App. I.   Observe nevertheless that Figgis speaks of the church *in* the state. The church of which he speaks in such otherwise clear terms is not *in* the state any more than the state is *in* the church. Both are within the community.

intolerance, making it a form of treason and not merely of heresy to profess a religion other than that by law established. Religion became nationalized, and the medieval ideal of 'the kingdom of God on earth' shrunk back towards the Hebraic ideal of a national God guiding a favoured people. Fortunately the multiplicity of creeds through which the religious sense had begun to seek expression prevented any real identification of nationality and faith. Political parties were formed which rallied around the growing non-conformist or non-established creeds in an effort to break the dominance of the establishment, as, for example, the Presbyterian, the Independent, and the High Church parties in England during the Commonwealth. Their strength led to a partial 'toleration', based on semi-political semi-religious grounds—a toleration characteristically limited to creeds cognate to, or merely dissident from, the creed of the Established Church. Thus in England 'dissenters' were tolerated, but not Roman Catholics, Anabaptists, Jews, and Quakers—while of course 'atheists' and 'infidels' were anathema to the state.

The development of toleration was slow. It was hindered in most countries by the prestige and solidarity of the established church, by its wealth and political power, by the union of the church and the nobility. The establishment was still regarded by its adherents as part of the state, as a necessary element of the political constitution, in fact, as Burke later interpreted it for them, 'as the foundation of their whole constitution with which and with every part of which it holds an indissoluble union'. In England the Test and Corporation Acts reaffirmed the union of citizenship and faith. The Act of Toleration of 1689 was, however, a real advance towards

the distinction of church and state, since it made sub-
scription to the oaths of allegiance and supremacy the
only test. But these oaths were not merely expressions of
political loyalty, for they retained a certain religious
element. 'Atheists' were still treated as outlaws. The
assumption of a moral-religious unity of the state under-
lay toleration, and was in fact as much accepted by the
'dissenters' as by the establishment, their chief difference
being in respect of forms of worship and church government. It may be remarked that the coming of religious
liberty was prevented as much by the intolerance of
creed as by the absolutism of the state. 'It is impossible',
declared Rousseau, 'to live at peace with those we regard
as damned.'

The sense of religion, as well as the conception of the
state, had to change before liberty was possible, or rather
before the true distinction of church and state could be
attained. Two influences were working in this direction.
One was the growth of a new and more personal and
therefore more profound spirit of religion, among the
'evangelicals', for example. To such the essence of
religion was a personal conviction and consequently the
idea of the church became for them that of an association
of believers united by their belief alone. This conception,
the only one logically tenable within a community of
diverse beliefs, was in turn an influence even within the
'state' church. All along it had been paying the price
of establishment, having been subject at the same time to
the control of political expediency and to the attack on
its privileges of the non-established churches. The
acceptance of a modified associational character became
for many of its leaders the only way out of its difficulties.
The same position was accepted by the English Roman

Catholics, who were forced to deny, before they could expect emancipation, any claim of their church to political authority. In Germany, at a later date, the assertion by the state of its authority against 'ultramontane' claims forced catholicism to an associational stand. Catholic Windthorst spoke the very language of presbyterian Knox, proclaiming the independence of religion in its proper sphere.

The other influence making for the associational church was of a very different character. It was the spread of the 'enlightenment', the decline of the general hold of religion upon the people. When considerable numbers of citizens ceased to identify themselves, except possibly in name, with any church, the claim that church member-ship was integral to citizenship, or that religion was part of the state, seemed to lose all validity. Thus the separation of church and state was already achieved in fact, and it became more than ever apparent that the state could be both universal and limited, universal because its laws were binding on all within its territory, limited because its laws did not regulate all human interests. The particularism of the church was the first great wedge driven into the absolutism of the state. Political absolu-tism seemed to require a universal religion. This was true even of the absolutism of the French Revolution, which set up its articles of 'civic' religion. Universal religion had to lose itself, to meet with indifference and denial, before the true conception of spiritual association was fully attained.

In our present civilization the true demarcation of church and state has on the whole been found. The words of Stanhope have come true : 'There was a time when dissenters and Catholics begged for toleration as a grace, now they ask for it as a right, but a day will come when they will scorn it as an insult.' In the constitution of nearly all modern states it is proclaimed or implied that no man shall suffer in respect of citizenship because of his religion or lack of religion, and that every man shall be free to profess any creed or follow any form of worship. In some states, as in England, the formal relics of establishment are still associated with the titular head of the state. In England preferments to high ecclesiastical positions within the established church are still in the grant of the government, and carry the privilege of a seat in the Upper Chamber. There are also antiquated 'blasphemy laws', and Sabbatarian legislation is still in force, of which one particularly rigorous example is found in Canada.[1] But these instances are mere survivals of an old order, out of harmony with the general trend of the modern state. One of the earliest clear statements of the modern position is found in the Constitution of Belgium of 1831, which set out, among similar limitations of political authority, the express statements that ' no one shall be compelled to join in any manner whatever in the forms or ceremonies of any religious denomination, nor to observe its days of rest ', and again that ' the state shall not interfere either in the appointment or in the

[1] To ordain one common day of rest in seven and to choose Sunday for the purpose as being the most convenient day is not necessarily Sabbatarian legislation. It depends on whether a sense of social requirements or religious conviction determines the law. In Canada the law is inspired by the precepts of the Fourth Commandment, not by the requirements of the state, as is evidenced by the rigour of the enactment and by the fact that it is jealously guarded by a body known as the ' Lord's Day Alliance '. This motive is *politically* unjustifiable, especially in view of the fact that one religious communion whose members are equally citizens observes a portion of Saturday instead of Sunday.

installation of the ministers of any religious denomination whatever '.[1]

Once the principle has been accepted that the church has its own sphere autonomous and distinct from that of the state, there still remains the more subtle problem of determining the limits of each in respect of the other. On the side of the church it is obvious that the principle condemns the application of ecclesiastical law to any who are not its willing members, or any such power of jurisdiction as involves under any circumstances the physical coercion of a member, or the loss of political rights, or any other penalty than the abrogation of the services or offices or privileges of the church, save such amends or fine as the member is willing to accept in order to retain the same. But the church has exercised and still in many countries continues to exercise a certain control over education, over marriage and divorce, over probate, and other matters with which the state also and necessarily concerns itself. Since the church has rights only with respect to its own members, no church should have the exclusive or preferential right to provide any service required by citizens who may not belong to it or any other church. The celebration of marriage is a good example. The church may require of its own members a religious ceremony, but that should be no concern of the state, which is interested merely in the civil conditions of the marriage contract. The church therefore should not be in a position to make its rites a requisite of that contract, though it is perfectly entitled to require of its members, but only as a condition of their belonging to its communion, such *further* observances as it may approve. The church may lay down rules of marriage as a condition of

[1] Arts. 15 and 16 of the Constitution of 1831.

its own membership ; provided it does not seek to deny or override the *legality* of marriages which, while not ful-filling its conditions, do fulfil the requirements of the state. Further, it is entitled to teach and preach the desirability, within the state, of such regulations as on social grounds, not merely religious, it approves. On the other hand it exceeds its bounds even to demand legislation which would impose its principles, if based on religious grounds, on even a small minority which does not accept its faith, or, if based on social grounds, on a community in which there is not a consentient majority. With regard to divorce, the proper relation of church and state is well formulated by Figgis.[1] The church may properly, if it so judges, deny to its members, as a condi-tion of its membership, a right of divorce which is legally permitted to them, but it should not even advocate the retraction of this right for those who do not accept the tenets on which it takes its stand. Speaking of churchmen who demand the repeal of the English Act of 1857 Figgis says : ' They are demanding quite plainly that the morality of the Church be imposed against their will upon those who owe her no allegiance. Such demands seem to me tenable in theory only on the Puritan or mediaeval notion of a State and in practice as absurd as the proposal of John Knox to punish adultery with death.'

Education offers a somewhat more difficult problem. It is complicated by the existence of church schools and colleges, by the fact that many states include in the curricula of their schools Bible reading and other religious instruction, by the fact that moral instruction, which is in part confused with and in part based upon religious doctrine, is a proper enough element in elementary educa-

[1] *Churches in the Modern State*, ch. iii.

tion, and finally by the fact that some essential subjects, pre-eminently history, must take cognizance of religious influences and tend to be coloured by the religious attitude of the teacher. Nevertheless the wisest course for the state, and certainly that which is most in conformity with its own nature, is to abandon altogether the religious instruction of the pupils in state schools, a course adopted in countries so unlike in respect of religious development as France and the United States. It should place no difficulty in the way of its pupils being given such instruction, but it should leave to parents and churches the religious training of the young, for there are no strictly religious principles which are universally accepted in a modern community, and even if there were, the state, as we have shown, has neither right nor obligation in this matter. Nor should it be influenced in its selection of teachers by their particular religious affiliations or lack of any. This is in harmony with the principle that the state should, in respect of schools under religious denominations, take no cognizance of their religious teaching, but insist simply on the general standards of education which it provides in its own schools.

In a word, the state, if true to itself, will leave to the church its true religious function, but will not hand over to it the control of any office of a civic or political character. If a church offends against the code of law approved by the community and enacted by government it is subject to the same discipline as any other offender. The earlier practice of the Mormon Church is a case in point. But the code itself should not contain any regulations or injunctions derived from religious authority or from any esoteric principle not inherent in the experience of the common life. The state should treat the church as it would treat any other corporation, such as a club or a business or a college of art. All these have relations which bring them within the general order of society. They make contracts and they own property. Because, for example, a church has endowments it is liable, in respect of that external fact, to the jurisdiction of the state. The state must therefore take cognizance of its creed, not as a creed, but as a condition of endowment. It must, when a division arises within a church involving the disposition of property, act as arbiter, not of the difference, but of the title of the different claimants to the hitherto common possessions. Again, when two churches unite and a minority in one or both secedes, claiming to be the true repository of the doctrine of the church, the state must examine the doctrine, not as a doctrine, but as a condition of endowment. An extreme case might arise in which a church had so dwindled that it could no longer without gross waste or misapplication employ its endowments, and then the state might even, without exceeding its function, call for the surrender of its excessive wealth, derived as it must be from the present economic life of the community. But the more common situation is that in which the state is called on to allot or partition the resources of a church, because of a division or secession within it. Such a situation occurred when a minority in the Free Church of Scotland refused to follow the majority into union with the United Presbyterian Church, and similarly when a part of the Presbyterian Church of Canada repudiated the action of the majority in joining forces with two other protestant denominations. Such occasions thrust a difficult task on the judicature.[1] It may be required to establish the

---

[1] This difficulty was well illustrated by the decision of the House of

identity of a church and for that purpose to examine its creed and constitution. The state must then logically distinguish between the evolution of religious doctrine and such a sheer abandonment of creed as could negate the title of a church to control the endowments which it holds as trustee for the members, past, present, and future, of a faith. But even here the state remains outside the religious sphere. It has simply to apply, as wisely as it can, the general principles governing corporate rights to a case where these rights depend on the exercise of a defined religious function. The problem for the state is the common legal problem of determining the continuity or identity of a corporation. It has nothing whatever to do with the decision of the religious question about which the claimants differ.

There remains one other problem, beyond that of the demarcation of definite functions, the consideration of which reveals very clearly the difference between church and state. The state is essentially an order-creating organization. It exists to establish order, not of course merely for the sake of order, but for the sake of all the potentialities of life which require that basis of order. The church, on the other hand, and this is true of all cultural associations, does not exist to establish order. Order is incidental to it. It exists primarily to promote a faith, an attitude, a spirit. It would exert its influence as widely as possible. If then the state must leave the church alone, so far as the essentials of its life are concerned,

Lords (Appeal Cases, 1904) in the famous Free Church case, when it laid down the extreme principle that ' the Free Church had no power where property was concerned to alter or vary the doctrine of the church '. This crude principle of identity would bar the way to any development whatever within a church. Fortunately its effect was modified as the result of subsequent legislation.

must the church equally leave the state alone ? In one sense it cannot, for there is no delimitation of any spirit to which men can respond, save their willingness to respond to it. In another sense it should. Here it is not a question of rigorous limits, but of the discretion which saves a cultural association from forfeiting its proper quality and mode of service. This quality is confounded when, for example, a church alines itself with a political party or uses its pulpits for party purposes. Of course the tenets of a faith may lead its adherents to support certain political measures, but they should do so as citizens and not as churchmen. The churches should insist on the principles rooted in their ethical and religious nature, rather than on the policies which parties advocate, even when the latter appear in conformity with their principles. If, for example, it is a religious principle to prefer love to revenge, they should decry the idea of revenge rather than denounce the treaty of Versailles. Otherwise the churches tend, as has happened so often in history, to be drawn into political controversies which pervert their spiritual function. On the other hand, the churches cannot be true to themselves if they are swept out of their principles by a crisis in the national life. During the Great War most of the churches of all countries seemed to lose all their distinctive spiritual principles and to become mere forms of civic organization, converting their religion into a blinded national fervour.

We have dwelt at such length on the relation of church and state, not only because it affords the best historical example of a progressive differentiation, but also because here we can see in the clearest and simplest way the conditions which justify and determine the autonomy of a great association. Like considerations apply to all associations whose function is cultural, but since art and literature and music and drama and kindred interests have never been so enmeshed in the political entanglements from which religion was with such difficulty redeemed, we need not dwell upon them. More important for the student of the modern state is the case of the family. The family (as distinct from the kin) is the most restricted in size and also the shortest lived of all the great associations. It is at the same time the most intimate and perhaps the most comprehensive in interest of them all, while in some form it is absolutely necessary for the existence of the community. It exhibits the minimum of formal organization and the maximum of participation in a common life, standing in these respects in marked antithesis to the state. Its development and mode of life have been very little affected by the direct control of the state, and only an exceptional philosopher like Plato has envisaged its mere absorption in the political or civic organization, to which in fact its whole nature is repugnant. The modern state exercises a certain control over its exterior aspect, insisting on conformity to the prevailing type of monogamous union, prescribing limits of consanguinity within which marriage is prohibited, regulating divorce, and laying down certain conditions in respect of inheritance. A few states insist on certain health requirements as a condition of marriage, and nearly all states have regulations to ensure the protection and care of children and to safeguard wives against non-maintenance and other economic consequences of desertion. The state generally provides institutions to meet those cases where the family fails in its task of rearing its young, but such ' homes ' are never regarded as an adequate substitute for the family life. It has in fact become an accepted principle that the state, in caring for such children, should as far as possible restore to them the conditions of family life ; placing them out in homes under careful supervision rather than congregating them in state-barracks. There is a tendency for the state to take over, by the provision of hospitals, old-age pensions, insurance schemes, and so forth, the obligations which formerly fell upon the *kin*, and which the kin, dissipated in the development of modern civilization, no longer exists to fulfil. But the family retains all the more clearly its essential functions, because it is disembarrassed from the communal functions associated with kinship as well as from many heterogeneous economic tasks now transferred to the wider society. There is no sign that the state can either control or take over these essential functions. Moreover, it is worth while observing that, should the state seek to enforce more rigid regulations governing marriage and divorce, in opposition to tendencies prevailing within the community, it would merely drive those affected by them to other un-contractual forms of relationship which the state does not and cannot control.

We conclude therefore that in general, as our examples of the church and of the family bear witness, all the great associations have an inner life which is at least as autonomous as that of the state. The state regulates them only in respect of their common external attributes, controlling such universal institutions as contract and property so as to maintain and develop the form of social order within which they all must move. This brings us to the consideration of the positive functions of the state.

III

THE BUSINESS OF THE STATE

All men, including absolute philosophers, believe there are tasks and functions proper to the state and others which it should refrain from attempting. The believer in absolute sovereignty leaves the choice to the state as a matter of discretion, as a God might choose when He should or should not interfere in the concerns of His people. The conception of the limited state gives us a surer ground of distinction. What the state should do is what, as an organ of the community, it can do. What service it should render is that of which it is in fact capable. Our study of the nature of law revealed the range of its efficacy as a social agent.[1] The preceding sections of this chapter have confirmed that study, showing the necessity of the historical development of extra-political organizations. We can therefore, without further preliminaries, proceed to determine the positive functions of the state.

The area of business thus demarcated for the state includes, in short, those external conditions of social living which are of universal concern in view of the acknowledged objects of human desire. If we clearly grasp the character of the state as a social agent, understanding it rationally as a form of service and not mystically as an ultimate power, we shall differ only in respect of the limits of its ability to render service. The *laissez-fairist* and the socialist quarrel over the adequacy of political methods rather than over the legitimacy of ends. Their differences relate to the interpretation of experience and of history, to the ways in which certain results can be

[1] See further Bk. II, ch. iii.

attained rather than to the desirability of the results themselves. We can in fact set down the business of the state in quite scientific terms, since the objects of controversy, for those who appreciate the character of the state at all, concern the limits and not the type of political activity.

Law and order are traditionally associated, and we may regard *order* as essentially within the business of the state. To secure a universal order within its frontiers is the most obvious thing which the state can do, and it has been at all times a peculiar mission of the state. It is imposed no less by democracy than by despotism, by empire and by federation. But the form of order is always determined by a dominant purpose. Just as there is one form of order in a menagerie, another in a prison, another in an army, another in a school, another within a family, another in a fraternal society—so there is one form of order in a slave-state, another among a free people ; one form in a class-state, another in a democracy. The conception of order changes as we pass from the idea of the state as exploitative to the idea of the state as ministrative. It ceases to be order as a condition of domination and becomes order as a condition of the common welfare.

Order, so understood, is then the first business of the state. No doubt there are vast fields of social order which the state does not directly cultivate ; the order of custom, the order of morality, the order of business usage, the order of special associations. The order which the state stands for is that universal order which is so desirable or so necessary that the community empowers the state to enforce it. It involves the definition of the areas of political authority, the establishment and express formulation of those rights and obligations which are recognized as properly enforceable, as well as those conventional determinations whose convenience for the general commerce of society makes it desirable that they should be regulated from a single centre. To provide such conditions that people can lead their lives in decent relation to one another, to prevent confusion and chaos, to regulate the forms of intercourse and communication so that life shall run more smoothly for all concerned, to see that everything has and holds its appointed place—including itself, and finally to take in its sole keeping and so to minimize the exercise of coercion necessary for the fulfilment of these tasks—such is the primary function of every state. The state is a governor of the machine of civilization.

But order, so understood, is part of a larger task. Order within the community is justified only as it serves the needs of the community. It is not order for the sake of order, but for the sake of *protection* and of *conservation* and *development*. These terms sum up the universal concerns which we have seen to lie within the competence of law and therefore of the state. Order, without further definition, is a dangerous term. To insist on order as such is to make of the state a ' police-state ', which is only removed in degree from the order of a menagerie. An order that is to serve the community must be in conformity with and limited by the ideals of the community, and particularly the ideals which are understood by the terms *justice* and *liberty*. The true political conception of order extends into the conception of protection. Here is an immense task for the state, quite proper to its nature and still largely unfulfilled. To protect the weak instead of the strong is on the whole a modern reinterpretation of the state's function. Such protection is gradually taking the form of the establishment of minimal standards of living, so that the mere requisites of health and decency shall not be denied by accident or misfortune or capacity to any member of the community. It is becoming recognized that men are so bound up in families and groups that the whole suffers from the privation or degradation of any, and that the state can act as a great ministry of social assurance without destroying the initiative and responsibility of its members. How far the state should go in this direction and at what lines the minimal standards should be set is naturally a subject of controversy. But the general principle is already accepted, and modern states are experimenting in a variety of ways which are in marked contrast to an earlier role of government.

Just as the conception of order widens into that of protection, so does protection in turn find a wider interpretation in the business of conservation and development. The state with its command of resources and its universal reach can build for the future in ways that no partial organization may attempt. It can overrule the near selfish aims that would waste for immediate advantage the greater gifts of nature. It can carry on vast works of constructive enterprise whose benefits will be shared by future generations. It can control by means of the forethought which is proper to its might and permanence, the haphazard endeavours of individuals which result, when left alone, in sprawling, ill-built, congested cities and a slovenly, ill-tended countryside. It can preserve and enhance those signal beauties of forest and lake and mountain which the advance of industrialism threatens. It can carry on fruitful experiments in irrigation, the utilization of the soil, the breeding of plants and animals, the control of insect pests, and other services of great significance for the development of agriculture. It can promote the establishment of industries, by providing initial aid and by facilitating the discovery and application of scientific methods. It can mitigate the severity of economic fluctuations by its control over currency, credit, and its own expenditures. In a great variety of ways it can encourage the industry, trade, and commerce of the country, a perfectly legitimate enterprise of government so long as it does not yield to the constant temptation to benefit the part at the expense of the whole.

All these activities the state can pursue more efficiently, because more thoroughly, than individuals or private organizations, and they can be pursued in complete conformity with the character of the state and its organs of service. Of course the state may fail or blunder in the exercise of these activities, from want of intelligence or public devotion on the part of governments, but no political principle forbids it to assume national tasks for which it is intrinsically better fitted than any other association. Apart from the principles already laid down the only other limitation of function lies in the competence of legislators and of the executive service. If they are ignorant and unqualified, or else the prejudiced servants of special interests, the community must pay the price in the curtailment or distortion of the most valuable services. The more fit they are the greater the tasks they can legitimately undertake.

These tasks, moreover, extend far beyond the physical and economic developments we have outlined. The business of the state includes the conservation and development of human capacities as well as of economic resources, though here it is more necessary that it should beware of repressing the inner springs of conduct. Yet there are definite conditions requisite for the evocation of human quality, definite services of a universal character which every human being needs. Of these the first is education, a subject on which we have already touched. It is surely significant that here the state has taken over and vastly developed a task which was formerly assigned to the family and then extended by special associations such as the guild and the church. Of course the family still acts as an agency of education, and always must, but it is unqualified to give its members the continuous training requisite for life in a civilized community. It is the state which inevitably took over this function. It could do so just because (unlike the church) it has no particularist interest, because therefore it can call on every one to assist in a service and undertake obligations whose universal character is clear, because also it alone can command the resources for the greatest of those enterprises which return their ' dividend ' invisibly and to the whole community. What applies to education applies also, and for the same reasons, to the general promotion of the cultural life. Whatever can be done in this direction—and it leads into a great field of unexplored possibilities—without taking sides in the cultural issues on which men are seriously divided, and without infringing the liberty which is the source of achievement, the state can, and indeed ought to do. We have all along insisted that the state must work through external means. We must here equally insist that external means can be validly and fruitfully applied to the promotion of the cultural life. A sense of cultural or spiritual values is needed for the craftsman in wood and iron as well as for the poet or philosopher. It is needed for the statesman as well as for the prophet. The limitation of the state depends upon the instruments at its command. There is no limitation to the comprehensiveness of the understanding with which those instruments should be employed. Diversity of task requires nevertheless of each individual the unity and integrity of his nature—or else he does it ill. The demarcation of the business of the state demands none the less the appreciation by government of that communal life which it can serve only in specific ways. The state, we have insisted, is a particular social mechanism, but mechanism exists for the sake of life. This greatest of all mechanisms cannot be developed without a broad and deep understanding of the whole life which it serves.

We may now proceed to give, in the form of a table, a conspectus of the business of the state, arranged under the rubrics of order, protection, and conservation and development. These categories, as we have seen, run each into the next, so that it is often a matter of emphasis whether a particular function is included under one or another. The table is not intended to give a complete classification of all the definite functions of the state, but it should be sufficient to make clear the chief forms or provinces of its service. We have omitted altogether from present consideration the international aspect of the state's business. It is properly to be construed as the extension of the same services to its members under the conditions created by their relations to the members of other states. We should beware of regarding the state as carrying on two kinds of business, one which it transacts within its frontiers, and the other, a very different one, which it transacts with its fellow states. So regarded, the state stands illogically, in thought as often in fact, for welfare so far as its internal activities are concerned, and for power in its external activities. The true difference is only one of aspect, not of the kind of service ; and the difference of aspect exists only because the internal instrument of the state, political law, has not yet been fashioned into an international instrument. Were that achieved, even the difference of aspect would itself disappear. But this subject we shall elsewhere treat.

THE FUNCTIONS OF THE STATE
(INTERNAL ASPECT)

I	II	III
ORDER	PROTECTION	CONSERVATION AND DEVELOPMENT
A. *Physical basis.* Establishment of areas and frontiers of political authority—local, regional, national.	Exercise of the police function, securing life and property.	Promotion and regulation of the physical conditions — hygienic requirements, housing, occupational, recreational conditions—of HEALTH.
Establishment and control of the forms of communication and transportation.		Conservation and economic utilization of NATURAL RESOURCES.
Establishment of units and standards of computation, measurement, value, &c.		Planning and general control of urban and rural development.
B. *Social Structure.* Definition of political powers and spheres of authority : (1) territorial—local, regional, national. (2) functional—division and co-ordination of political services.	Maintenance and protection of authorities politically determined.	Establishment and development of facilities of EDUCATION.

Definition of general rights and obligations of citizenship and territorial residence.

Formulation of specific rights and obligations of persons and associations, e.g.:

(1) within the family association; regulation of the marriage contract, &c.

(2) within the economic order; regulation of currency, economic contracts, &c.

(3) within other social relationships; definition of professional or occupational status, registration, incorporation, &c.

Service of social information, collection and arrangement of statistics, &c., relating to population, trade and commerce, and all kinds of social phenomena.

Maintenance and enforcement of rights and obligations politically determined—JUSTICE and LIBERTY in their political significance; including protection of the community against the encroachments of specific associations, e.g. against monopoly and 'unfair competition', against social disturbance and economic dislocation through economic disputes, against racial, religious, and partisan pressure.

Assurance for the whole community of minimum standards of decent living, e.g. in respect of wage-rates, employment, upbringing of children, prevention of destitution.

Care for and prevention of 'social wreckage'.

Promotion of the external conditions of OPPORTUNITY.

Establishment of national museums, assistance of scientific research and of non-controversial cultural aims.

Promotion of industrial, agricultural, commercial, and financial development in relation to general and not particular advantage.

Provision of the means of inquiry into social problems of general significance.

The proper sphere of the state is so vast that it is absurd to regard the denial of its omnicompetence as belittlement. The functions we have defined as belonging to it constitute a task great enough for the greatest of associations and almost too great for the human agents who constitute any government. Moreover, the state cannot reasonably fulfil its own most difficult task if it meddles with concerns which are not its own. If it attempts those things which it ought not to attempt it will fail in the things which properly fall within its charge. It will create confusion instead of the order which is its foundational work. The state has shown in the course of its history the deplorable results of assumed omni-competence. It still reveals some of them to-day, though the situation is greatly improved. There are states, for example, which grotesquely forbid the teaching of evolution while they leave their unemployed to wander in resourceless despair. There are states which suppress the knowledge of birth control, concealing from the ignorant what they cannot conceal from the educated classes, while they suffer their children to be exploited in factories or cotton-fields. There are states which forbid the unhappily yoked in marriage to seek divorce, though all men know that such coercion, whether it succeeds or fails, creates a greater disharmony. There are states which censor the press and deliberately pervert education into nationalist propaganda. There are states which have no ministry of health though all states possess a ministry of war. Omnicompetence means in fact incompetence. As the vision of the state's business grows clearer, as it refrains from the futile or pernicious effort to do these things which it is unqualified to do, it appreciates better the magnitude of its proper tasks and girds itself more resolutely, and more nobly, to their fulfilment.

VI

THE RESIDENCE OF AUTHORITY

I. THE WILL OF THE PEOPLE

THE determination of state action takes on a very different aspect when we descend from the summits of philosophy to the ground of political practice. When we turn from Rousseau and Hegel and Bosanquet to, for example, Michels[1] or Ostrogorski,[2] with their elaborate demonstration of the actual working of democratic institutions, we seem to enter another world altogether. The will of the people, that 'real will' which asserts its integrity and solidarity in sovereign decision, seems to dissolve into the interested and often sordid dominance of a narrow minority, exploiting for its own ends the practical conditions of organization and leadership. Behind the liberty of association is revealed the psychological necessity of control. Instead of the clear envisagement of political situations on the part of the people we discover, against a background of ignorance and inertia, the entanglement of personal attachments and repulsions, of local interests and discriminations. Instead of the people acting through representatives and officials, we find the officials and the representatives controlling the 'machine'. The will of the people is set up as a mystical

[1] Michels, *Political Parties.*
[2] Ostrogorski, *Democracy and the Organization of Political Parties.*

god, in whose name the political priests of a new oligarchy struggle and rule.

What is the will of the people ? In the first place, what does it directly determine ? Apart from the exceptional use of the initiative and the referendum the people act through representatives. At once their choice is limited. They normally choose between candidates whom they do not nominate. The organization of party controls for the most part the selection. The party leaves to the people only the decision between its nominees and those of other parties. The 'independent' candidate is greatly handicapped and in any case he confuses the issue. Party selection is far from being a democratic process. It is influenced by considerations of service rendered, financially or otherwise, to the organization ; of the prestige attaching to well-known family groups ; of the readiness of the candidate to obey the party behests ; and of the ambitions of the inner circle which controls the machine. The mass of the people know little and care little concerning the organizations which direct their choice. In some countries, as in North America, it is a general condition that the candidate be resident in or be associated with the locality for which he stands. In others, as in Great Britain, the organization can reward its faithful supporters or placate strong interests without the constant necessity of considering local attachments.

Not only does the inner organization select the candidates on whom the will of the people shall be exercised, it also shapes the policy which the people must choose or reject. Here too strong influences are brought to bear. In the modern state these influences are predominantly economic. A manufacturers' association will secure a tariff 'plank' in the party platform, a farmers' organization will insist on agrarian interests, a trades union will demand the incorporation, as the price of its support, of a rigorous labour programme. Now a political party by its very nature seeks to appeal to a wider circle of interests than that represented by the strong and definitely opposed organizations of the economic order. It is therefore faced with the problem of reconciling economic interest with political interest. The economic associations push it farther than it would go of its own accord. It has to resort to compromise and evasion. Its programme, as it is finally shaped by a party caucus, is the diagonal of at least two lines of pressure. But the will of the people can generally only choose or reject the whole.

Once the programme is enunciated, new forces enter in. Now comes the stage of appeal and counter-appeal. The party-press—which is practically the whole apparatus of day-by-day information and publicity—applies its great engine of persuasion and denunciation. It has the vast power of selection and prominence, which even the best newspapers must exercise, while the worst go on to exploit every prejudice that will assist the cause they espouse. To discern the true proportions of the situation they are called upon to adjudge, to sift the truth from out the clamour of presentation, becomes a baffling task for the people. So many agencies are enlisted in the task of persuasion, and so few are concerned with the mere business of exploring the truth. The great endeavour is not to elicit public opinion but to make it, to control it, to use it. The will of the people is directed to objects which are seen through the high colours of interests which may not be their own and of prejudices which are only too certainly theirs.

So the decision is taken, and the ' representatives ' of

the victorious party take office. They may in fact be elected by a minority of the total vote, whether on account of the multiplicity of parties or because of the defects of the electoral system. But even if they are returned by a majority vote, the majority is often uncertain and unstable, and the ' will of the people ' is defined by that capricious element which veers with every political wind that blows. Moreover there are now new influences at work to divert the chosen ' representatives ' from carrying out the will of those who returned them to power. The office of government has its own traditions and its own strong influence on the mind. The government must work through permanent officials who understand the operation of the machine and whose professional attitude often modifies the enthusiasms and even the policies of the leaders. The very fact of power works subtly on those who wield it. For one thing it creates a feeling of superiority which is dangerous to the principle of representation. The leaders tend to acquire a sense of caste. Again, the methods by which power is gained are not necessarily those by which it is retained. Policies that were easy to profess are hard to fulfil. Opportunism offers its temptations. Leadership brings new problems in the effort to maintain solidarity against conflicting ambitions within the government or the party, and calls here too for compromise and adjustment. New situations arise on which the ' will of the people ' has not been expressed, and in any case it becomes harder than in the first flush of victory to determine what it was that the people had willed. Did they vote for a party or against a party, for a policy or against a policy ? Was it their fears or their hopes that created the government, and what relevance have either to the changing situation ?

How then shall we find the will of the people expressed in the conduct of government? Even in democracy is it reality or profession? We have briefly pointed out the serious difficulties and limitations that beset it in practice. We must now show that nevertheless the 'ultimate sovereign', though shorn of the integrity and assurance with which its exponents have endowed it, is a real presence eternally active in every modern state.

It has been well said by Hans Delbrück, observing from outside the English form of democracy, that 'in reality it is not the election which enables the people to assert themselves, but the fact that the governing parties must keep in touch with the will of the people '.[1] If there were no party system democracy in any sense would be impossible. But the government is anxious to remain in power and therefore to avoid offending the governed. The government realizes that the opposition waits the opportunity to appeal against its conduct of affairs. It must therefore conform to the prevailing sentiment of its supporters, and at the same time it seeks if possible to conciliate other elements or at least to prevent the development of a more implacable attitude on their part. To retain its position the government must so act that the popular will supports its continuance in office. This will is not so much a will for or against definite objects of legislation as a general sentiment in support of one particular government rather than another.

We should, moreover, distinguish fairly between the will of the people and the motives and influences by which that will is elicited. The will on which a government rests may be democratic, even if oligarchic or plutocratic influences are powerful in creating it. It is quite possible

[1] Hans Delbrück, *Government and the Will of the People*, Eng. tr., p. 59.

that an interested minority may so control the avenues of information and suggestion that a majority will suffer persuasion contrary to their own interests. The decision of a leader may induce millions to support measures which they would have opposed if his prestige had been thrown on the other side.[1] The will of the people rarely issues as a spontaneous expression. It is too inchoate, too inert. It must be focussed and established through an elaborate mechanism of organization, and of course such organization is an agency of control as well as of expression. If we sought for the basis of democracy after the manner of Rousseau, who believed that organization and even conference corrupts the will of the people, we should never find it at all. The fact of will and not its 'purity' or disinterestedness is the foundation of democracy. Its degree of purity can never be estimated. No doubt the will of the people becomes more clear and strong and independent in so far as education advances and intelligence grows. The quality of the will is the quality of the people.

The thing we can measure is not its quality but its volume. There is no doubt that in this respect the foundations of the modern state have been greatly broadened in quite recent times. There has been the frequent extension of the suffrage until, in many states, it has reached the practical completion of manhood and even of adult suffrage. There has been the general abolition of the system which gave unequal weight to the votes of different classes, such as prevailed in Sweden and

---

[1] There is nevertheless a point beyond which, as many statesmen have discovered, leadership and persuasion will not carry the will of the people. Joseph Chamberlain could not convert a majority to protection, nor Gladstone to Irish Home Rule. It is significant also that a policy may be strongly supported by the dominant press and yet rejected by the people.

in Austria and, until lately, in Prussia. There has been a tendency to make constituencies more nearly equal in terms of population. There have been experiments with systems of representation which promised to reflect more fairly the voting strength both of majorities and of minorities. The undoubted trend has been towards 'one man one vote', making the right of election a function no longer of property or class but of personality.

That the whole of a people should have and should exercise the right to elect a government does not mean that the people is more united than before in the election it makes. On the contrary, as new elements of the people are included a greater range of differences manifests itself, as is witnessed in the frequent break-up of the bi-party system. The more democratic the constitution the greater the disparity of policies which express the opinions of the electors. The ultimate sovereign is more precarious and unstable than ever. But the general will is on the other hand greatly strengthened. Where there are no disfranchised masses the likelihood of revolution is rendered more remote. Practically all popular revolutions have occurred under a class régime which denied to the masses a constitutional mode of sharing the power that makes and unmakes governments. In the democratic state every element of the population is embodied in the general will. The exercise of the right to vote is an implied acceptance of the general order of the state. By that act each voter affirms the principle that what the majority determines shall stand as the policy of the whole state, while his right remains effective to work for the triumph of the policy which is his own. The making of government is no longer the function of a class from which he is excluded. Each shares the common responsibility as well as the common right, and the coercion of the state is minimized.

The general will, let us once more insist, is not the will of the people, as we have been employing these terms. The will of the people, our ' ultimate sovereign ', is the will of a victorious element that wins its way through struggle and opposition. Only in rare moments of crisis does it ever transcend the strife of politics. But the general will unites those who win and those who lose. It is not the will for a policy but the will for the state. It is the will of membership, of communion, the will that identifies a citizen with all that he divines of the meaning and service, tradition and promise, of the state. It is deeper and stronger than the immediate aims of men. It is the deeper sea of devotion that knows nothing of the waves which rock the surface of politics. Actually it determines nothing, save the order within which all things may be determined. Because of it, this shifting marginal sovereign that we name the will of the people is entrusted with a dominion far more steadfast than its own nature could ever secure.

When we envisage the instability of the will of the people, exposed to all the winds of prejudice and passion, we should also realize that the forces which beat upon it generally strengthen the foundations beneath it. The agencies of persuasion, however ready they may be to exploit prejudice and distort the truth, do in fact achieve the broadening of the general will. The party, the press, the leader, insistently bring before the people the necessity of their choice between alternatives. They conjure up pictures of those alternatives which fill the minds of the people. The general will becomes more active and more real. And its very activity is after all a condition of its enlightenment. Through it the people become more critical and more discerning, perhaps even more disinterested. At any rate it is the activity of the general will which makes it impossible to ' fool all the people all the time '. Propagandism is met by criticism. The will of the people achieves not only the government which it deserves but also the government which it wants.

II

REPRESENTATION AND RESPONSIBILITY

Every modern state, in other words every state in which the will of the people is active, of necessity attaches responsibility to the powers of government. The will of the people, the ultimate sovereign, can itself have no constitutional responsibility, for to it belongs the last appeal. But it establishes the responsibility of the power which it creates. What it creates it can also overthrow. This is the real ground of its control over government, not that it can bring authority to trial for its past deeds in the crude manner of a Greek democracy, but that it can fulfil or balk the central ambition of authority, which is to keep the reins of power. By limiting the tenure of office, by making it necessary for the government to appeal for re-election within a comparatively short stated period, it has secured the formal condition of responsibility. The rest depends mainly on its own vigilance and public spirit.

This then is the meaning of responsible government, that it shall endure so long and so long only as it can claim the support of a majority (or at any rate of the largest electoral group), under a system which the minority (or the other groups) accept. It is not even necessary that the government shall act as the majority want it to act—so long as they maintain it that is enough for our definition. It is enough if the ultimate sovereign authorizes the government. It might display a blind trust in government and say in effect—Act on my behalf, but do as seems good to you. That would be not unlike the attitude of the shareholders of a company to its directorate. The shareholders admit that for the most part they have neither the time nor the experience to determine policy. They leave it to the directors and are content to trust in their discretion. If they are satisfied as to the fitness of the men they appoint, they are generally prepared to ratify their actions, in other words to re-appoint them from year to year.

But such implicit confidence is rare in the political sphere. Curious as it may seem, it is found only in the perversions of democracy, such as the ' boss-rule ' of certain American communities. No intelligent people can surrender the judgement of policy. Politics touches too many interests of their lives. Its issues are too critical and too contentious. The temptations of power are too great for it to be left in the discretion of any men. The ultimate sovereign cannot properly divest itself of the duty to determine policy and be content simply to delegate authority. In every developed state it seeks to decide the direction as well as the *personnel* of government. It elects to office those whose platform it approves, and it removes them from office when it disapproves either of their past performance or their programme for the future.

How this responsibility may be assured we must consider at a later stage. Here we are seeking to inter-pret it. The only alternative to mere delegation is representation. Delegation involves the choice of men, but representation involves also the choice of measures. Delegation in its completest form—as when the French people proclaimed Napoleon emperor—assigns no limitation of tenure, and no conditions of the exercise of power. Representation implies both direction and control. Delegation requires the consent of the governed, whereas representation requires the fulfilment of their will. Here we touch some difficult and important questions. Whom and what does the representative represent ? Is it the whole state or is it his own constituency ? Is it the party to which he belongs, or is it the particular interest or interests which may have secured his election ? Again, whatever it is, is he a mouthpiece or a mere agent, appointed to carry out instructions and to conform in every respect with the wishes of those whom he represents?

The answer to these questions is found in a consideration of the relation of means to ends. The election of representatives has an entirely different background from the expression of will in a plebiscite or referendum. In the latter case a single specific issue is formally isolated from all others. The people express their will on a proposed piece of legislation, a constitutional project or a temperance measure or a form of social insurance, or so forth. Whatever the motives that determine it, the verdict itself is clear. But the representative is elected on the ground of a general policy which he supports. The elector expresses his attitude towards that policy, not towards individual measures. Apart from such particular pledges as he may give, the representative is bound to a cause, a movement, a party, not to a whole series of individual projects. So long as he is faithful to the cause, he must use his own judgement in particular cases. There may indeed arise difficult questions of loyalty, where his attachment to his party prompts him to support measures in which he disbelieves. Here we can state only the common form of ethical solution for all such problems, which is simply the choice of the greater value in the whole situation as it presents itself to him. But it is only if he abandons the cause or general policy in respect of which he was elected that he ought to resign his office. The representative is not, under normal conditions, an agent who goes to parliament under orders, like the mediaeval delegates which the imperial free cities sent to the Reichstag. Occasionally attempts are made to bind the representative in this way, the extreme instance being that of the labour members in Australia who sign their adherence, as a clergyman signs a confession of faith, to a whole legislative programme. But this reduction of the representative to the party servant is generally and rightly repudiated.

The same considerations apply to the representative house as a whole. It would be absurd to require that for every measure which it passes the house must have a 'mandate' from the people. The practical conditions of representation preclude this possibility which, were it feasible, would deprive the house of all initiative and character. Many issues are raised by every party at an election, and, save for the cases when one supreme issue dwarfs all the rest, the most that can be inferred from the return of a party to power is that its general policy or programme is approved by the ultimate sovereign more than that of other parties. But a government so chosen must enact a variety of measures and would be surrendering its proper responsibility if it refused to act without a specific 'mandate' for each. We may go farther and admit that many acts are passed by popularly elected governments which would probably be rejected were the legislation presented to the people in the form of a referendum. The experience of Switzerland suggests that this is true of enactments involving new taxation, such as health-insurance measures. Similarly it has been declared that the German old-age and invalid insurance act 'was not passed with, but against the will of the people, and would have been unquestionably defeated by a referendum '.[1] Yet such acts receive, after they are passed, sufficient popular support to make them permanent.[2]

The proper relation of the electorate to its representatives resembles, on a different level, that of the legislative to the executive. The will of the people gives the direction only, or more strictly determines which of alternative directions presented to it shall be followed. There are general interests which should be the concern of every citizen, and on which he should express an opinion by his vote. There are broad unities and divisions of opinion which create the distinctions between parties. It is of the essence of citizenship to decide between them. But to carry out the decision in appropriate legislation is quite another affair. One must be near to the conditions of action in order to act. One must understand the pro-

[1] Delbrück, *op. cit.*, p. 29.

[2] It may be said that once a measure conferring benefits on any social group is passed, the fear of losing their votes prevents parties who would otherwise oppose it from advocating its repeal. Similarly acts may be passed for which there is no preponderance of opinion in order to conciliate minorities who earnestly desire them. Here again we must distinguish the motives which bear on will from the will itself. A majority may will an act which it does not approve for the sake of some ulterior result which it really wants. But it is still a majority will.

blems of government in order to govern. When the will of the people has chosen the government it must accept the necessities involved in its choice. The beginning is representation, the rest is responsibility, and the machinery of representation, intelligently applied, can secure responsibility as well.

To find the best means of combining responsibility with representation is one of the most important problems of the modern state. English political development created a unified responsibility through the cabinet system. Under this method, the parliamentary leaders, being also the heads of the executive, form a corporate unity responsible to parliament. In other words, their tenure of leadership depends on the support of parliament which in turn is similarly responsible to the people. The responsibility is unified because it is partly indirect. In the United States, on the other hand, responsibility is direct and therefore unco-ordinated. The chiefs of the executive are directly elected as well as the members of congress, and elected separately. There are good grounds for holding that, as applied to the executive, direct responsibility to the people is less effective than indirect. Since under the former system the activities of government are not harmonized as under the latter, since the independent and non-simultaneous election of legislative and executive permits of and in fact encourages deadlocks, unity has to be sought elsewhere, not within the government but within the party. The party-organization has thus gained strength, but at some cost to its responsibility. 'In face of the bitter political warfare which the American system of government would seem to promote, the party members will submit to action on the part of party leaders which in a more tranquil

condition of things they would not hesitate to resent.' [1]
They will cover up or ignore governmental scandals which
in other countries would mean the retirement of the
ministry.[2] Moreover the strength of the party-organization, together with the sporadic and inflexible system of
election, does not suffer the government to feel immediately or directly the consequences of popular disfavour.

Under the parliamentary system responsibility attaches
definitely to the focus of government. There is no
question of where it lies. All the people have to do is to
enforce it. The difficulty in the situation is the strong
influence which the cabinet exerts over parliament, due
to its control over appointments and political favours, and
to the fact that, as in England, it can threaten a dissolution
of parliament unless its lead is followed by the house ;
and it is probable that it was on this account that the
Irish Free State denied the Cabinet the power of dissolution. But the weakness of the system is chiefly evidenced
where party politics are ruled by local interests to the
detriment of national interests. Such a condition, pre-
valent in countries like France and Italy, enables a
centralized administration to bring the extraneous influence of its favour or disfavour to bear unduly on the
representative and the electorate. No method of
achieving governmental responsibility can succeed unless
the sense of national policy is developed. But in so far
as parties are truly national, public opinion is more
effective and more secure when in the government there
is a single centre of responsibility, such as is achieved
through the parliamentary system with its union of
legislative and executive leadership.

[1] Goodnow, *Politics and Administration*, ch. vii.
[2] The Teapot Dome scandal is a good illustration.

The reason lies in the very character of the executive function. Mill regarded it as a most important principle of good government that ' no executive functionaries should be appointed by popular election '.[1] The qualities requisite for such positions, he declared, cannot be rightly estimated by the untrained public. They cannot find the most suitable candidates, nor will the best men come forward as candidates when appointment depends on all kinds of irrelevant or narrowly political considerations. Moreover the qualities which make for popularity have no necessary relation to technical efficiency. Mill rightly points out that in the United States, under the condition of direct election, the chosen President ' is almost always either an obscure man, or one who has gained any reputation he may possess in some other field than politics '. In any case it is clear that, where expert service and guidance are needed, the public has neither the knowledge nor the opportunity to discover it. A great deal has been said and written regarding the need for experts in the increasingly complex and comprehensive business of the state ; and it is a common charge against democracy that it suffers its affairs to be badly administered because it is ignorant of, and indifferent to, the requirements of good administration. The direct election of the executive undoubtedly promotes this tendency, nor can formal responsibility avail if the executive is responsible only to the inexpert and heterogeneous public.

Considerations of efficiency demand the existence within the government service of a permanent staff of administrators, not directly dependent on a popular vote, nor selected on political grounds nor liable to replacement

[1] *Representative Government*, ch. xiv.

in the ebb and flow of party fortunes. In a word, they cannot be representatives and therefore cannot be directly responsible to the people. At the same time there is necessary a means of control over the permanent staff. Their very permanence gives them considerable power. Their experience of ways and means makes their advice weighty. They can vastly facilitate political proposals of which they approve and impede others of which they disapprove. The temporary holder of political office must rely in many matters on their judgement. The political head of a government department forms the habit of 'consulting the department' before committing himself. The tradition of the department itself becomes a force in government, and there is always the danger of its hardening into a professional and intransigeant conservatism which resists the trend of popular opinion. This is particularly true of those departments which, like the foreign office, are not primarily engaged in the task of carrying out legislative enactments, which must therefore exercise a large discretionary power, and which at the same time conduct their activities under conditions that screen them from the public eye.[1]

The only effective means of control over the permanent and professional staff is through its relation to temporary and non-professional heads of departments. This is not a case of ignorance controlling experience. It rests instead on the necessary distinction of ends and means. The permanent staff is the machinery of government, and like all machinery it must be controlled and directed. A true

[1] Marcel Proust, in his novel *À l'Ombre des Jeunes Filles en Fleurs*, well speaks of 'that negative, methodical, conservative spirit, called "governmental", which is common to all governments and, under every government, particularly inspires its foreign office'.

leader or statesman must and ought to know how the machinery of government works, without being himself a mere part of it.[1] He ought to know how to make it serve his purpose, to detect its strength and its weakness. Such oversight is recognized as essential in every large business, which properly makes the technical staff responsible to the general management or directorate. It is even more imperative in the state, because its business is greater than any other and because its competence includes so many affairs of vital concern to all its members. Moreover, while the people cannot be expected to appreciate the qualities that are requisite in the expert, it is surely within the province of a public, sufficiently educated and sufficiently disinterested, to discover and elect as their representatives men of that broad and commanding discernment which can direct and control the organization through which their policies must be fulfilled. Whatever may be the difficulties and dangers of the parliamentary or ' cabinet ' system, it does at least provide a formula, as no other system seems to do, for the integration of means and ends within the state.

We cannot rightly approach the problem of political authority unless we start from the very obvious fact that the will of the state is no mystic unity but at best and for most purposes a very imperfect and limited harmony of individual wills. The England or Germany or Russia that lives in its real multiplicity—or even in our imagination of it—is never the England or Germany or Russia which makes treaties or contracts debts or passes laws.

---

[1] This relationship was admirably explained by Bagehot in his *English Constitution*. The explanation is developed by Lowell in *Public Opinion and Popular Government*.

However great or deep we may believe to be that likeness of nature we call nationality, it does not express itself in any unitary will. A nation is united in common feeling, that is in feeling which each member experiences in common with every other, as on occasions of national triumph or disaster. It is united in common custom and tradition, as when England holds a Bank Holiday or America the Fourth of July. It may in the stress of a great crisis be inspired by 'strong prevailing sentiments' (though perhaps never universal) of love or hate, leading to like expressions of will in the activities of a common cause. But even under such conditions the definite act of the state as a unity can never be called strictly the act of the nation. As soon as will is organized it is narrowed, however 'representative' it may be. The will of a state is nothing, can be nothing, but an organization of wills so related, so limited, that a single decision prevails and is accepted by the whole.

To make this organization of will as responsive as possible to every harmony of will, every consensus, every prevailing opinion, is part of the ideal of democracy. It is a process which, in spite of all difficulties, has advanced somewhat rapidly in recent times. Both in the feudal and in the absolute state the organization of will was based on the subordination of class to class. In the modern state the will of all classes is formally admitted into the common organization. To give reality to this inclusion a new structure has been rendered necessary, and its lines are already marked out. The two guiding principles are representation and responsibility, representation to determine the ends of action and responsibility to secure the means. Both principles seem to admit of a very considerable development still unattained. Ignoring for

the present the position of the judicature, we may conclude that the relationship of will which is best calculated
to serve the democratic ideal is as follows :

Subordinate executive responsible to chiefs of per-
     manent staff ;

Chiefs of permanent staff to representative ministers ;

Representative ministers to representative cabinet ;

Cabinet to parliament ;

Parliament to people.

Each of these relations differs from every other. At each
stage there are problems of articulation which require
careful examination, though these are of a technical
nature which rules them out of this broader study. But
the general scheme seems to offer the greatest promise
towards the realization of that ' will of the people ' which
for the rest depends on the quality of the people itself.

III

AUTHORITY AND REVOLUTION

When a political régime is overthrown by force in
order to impose a new form of government, or a government which proclaims a new policy on some crucial issue,
we call it a revolution. The assassination of a king or
president or premier would not constitute a revolution if
it were inspired by personal motives or were the mere
act of a small group of desperadoes who could not hope
to establish an alternative government. A revolution
implies a deep schism within the state. It reveals a
pathological condition of the political will which shows by
contrast the normal nature of authority.

The oligarchical state is exposed to revolution from two

directions. In it government is always associated with force, and however it seeks to justify its authority, its necessary spirit of dominance binds it to the idea of power. But in every oligarchy power is detachable from the will which controls it. The direct conjunction of will and power can belong only to democracy. Oligarchy must use a power which is not its own. It enlists an armed force which is not a body of citizens but of subjects, attached by discipline to a commander. Its loyalty is not a civic loyalty. It may be transferred from one cause to another, from one leader to another. When dissension arises within the oligarchy the leader or faction which can gain control of the army may bring about a revolution.

Revolutions of this character have been common, but their significance has usually been small compared with the revolutions which involve a whole people. These too occur within oligarchy and bring about its transformation. Here it is the revolt of the suppressed, claiming the rights of citizenship. Coercion always breeds the spirit of resistance, which breaks out when some crisis of the state provides its opportunity. Frequently it is through war that the opportunity comes. Sometimes it is the sheer weight of oppression that destroys the endurance of a people. Sometimes it is the subtle growth of education which weakens the old sanctions of power such as are associated, for example, with an authoritarian religion or the reverence of kingship. Sometimes it is the development of new economic forces which undermine the established order and give to the suppressed a new consciousness of power. These influences, singly or in combination, have in modern times grown strong enough to banish from our civilization practically all the older forms of oligarchy. Part of the transformation has taken place in an orderly way, the oligarchy yielding before the menace of the new claims to power, but in scarcely any country has it been fulfilled without a revolution.

Most revolutions of the past have been either within or against oligarchy. Even in the latter case the masses have rarely succeeded unless there was also dissension among the privileged. In ancient oligarchies the revolt of slaves or helots never achieved its object. Peasant revolts, like the great uprising of the sixteenth century in Germany, have also been invariably failures. The French revolution was not brought about by the sansculottes who took advantage of the anarchy which followed. The proletarian revolution of Russia was the aftermath of a revolution accomplished by a class which had already been admitted to a share of political power. The mere mass movement of the unprivileged has never sufficed to establish a new order. A small determined group possessed of political initiative can turn to their purposes the discontent of a mass which can achieve nothing by itself.

Just as any strong man may seize a runaway horse in the impotence of its rider, so in times of stress and general unsettlement a relatively small group, if well organized and trained to power, may seize the reins of government. The general discontent with the existing régime, the fact that the minds of men have in such times become inured to force, the feeling that the strong arm is preferable to anarchy, the very fear of violence which itself is mitigated when a formidable conspiracy has assumed the legal apparatus of power, these are the psychological conditions which favour the *coup d'état*. Thus governments imposed by force or revolution are a not uncommon phenomenon of war periods. The dictatorships which have followed the 'world war' are a case in point, the soviet government of Russia, the fascist government of Italy, the militarist régime in Hungary and Spain, being good illustrations. The more unsettled the situation, the greater the likelihood of such reversals. But it must be understood that these occurrences are of an abnormal character. The Romans were right in regarding the dictatorship as a temporary expedient suitable to the hour of crisis, but necessarily discarded when the crisis was past. The sense of law and order returns, giving a new character to the newly-risen authority or else rejecting it altogether.

The general will is the only permanent foundation of government. Hence in the democratic state revolution is both more rare and more sinister. The state is more securely established to resist the shock of a great crisis. The world war evoked in England and France only the semi-constitutional, temporary, and generally approved domination of a Lloyd George or a Clemenceau, but in Russia and Germany it produced cataclysmic revolution. The very fact of revolution means the break-up of the general will. Differences become ultimate, irreconcilable. The sense of unity which under normal conditions underlies the opposition of interests no longer holds. The dividing issue is stronger or more peremptory than any common tradition, any sense of the common order, any loyalty of the whole. Revolution is the temporary destruction of the state, the substitution of dividing force for common will. After it is over, the state has to be rebuilt. A successful revolution does not rebuild the state. That does not happen until the general will is itself restored. Hence revolution often leads to further revolution or counter-revolution, until the healing processes of time have re-established the foundations of loyalty or common will.

There are certain issues that even in the democratic state may threaten revolution. These are chiefly religious, social, or economic, and a brief consideration of them throws much light on the nature of political authority. Religious dissensions have in past times often threatened and disrupted states, not because different religions could not dwell in peace under the same political authority, but because that authority refused to recognize its limits. It is significant that the earlier advocates of a ' right ' of revolution (like John of Salisbury and Manegold) founded it on the distinction between a contract with men and a contract with God, regarding the latter as paramount over the demands of the state. It was no easy task to reconcile the two, especially when churches also made imperious claims upon the state. But the lesson of religious revolution was to show the needlessness of it in an intelligently ordered state, which recognized the true nature of political authority and the conditions of social cohesion.

It is very different when we turn to the racial causes of revolution. Bitter and deep as are the divisions engendered by conflicting creeds, they are less destructive of a common order than racial or nationalistic animosities, such as occur in the attempt of a race-conscious group to achieve autonomy or at least to be separated from a state to which it is coercively bound. No other difference creates such vast and persistent unsettlement. A general will is rendered impossible by it. What it denies is the basis of unity. The difference does not concern particular and concrete interests which may be harmonized, but the very grounds of a common order. The nationalistic spirit is irreconcilable, absolute, simple. It seeks one object and cares for nothing else. If its representatives are admitted to parliament or assembly they form a permanent opposition. The intrinsic merits of opposing programmes make no appeal to them, only their possible relation to the one object they pursue. A nationalistic group has always the revolutionary mind. It is the nemesis of conquest, never permitting the conqueror to feel at peace. The only solution is that which, as in the recent surrender to the Irish Nationalists, admits the persistent claim. If the nationalistic group occupies a determinate territory, this political solution is possible ; where it is mingled inextricably with other peoples only a slow social process of assimilation can bring relief.

The third great issue which may lead to revolution is economic. Where, as in most oligarchies, government and landownership belonged together, the double exaction of rents and taxes, with no proper distinction between them, often became an intolerable burden. The resistance to this economic pressure was one of the great forces in the evolution of ancient states, as is particularly noticeable throughout the history of Rome. The overburdened yeoman or peasant made common cause with the landless citizen who had sought refuge in the city. Until the new age of industry the governing classes were also the landed classes, and this double power created the great chasm within each community. The democratic state arose with the partition of this power. But the forces which brought it into being helped to create a new division. The division between capital and labour, between the owners of the new means of production and the mere workers, has fostered much bitterness and some revolutionary feeling. The latter has been due to the belief in the control of capital over government.

This is a subject we treat of elsewhere. Here we must be content to say that the control is only partial and that the forms of democracy provide a non-revolutionary solution. Nor is the cleavage between capital and labour, great and real as it has shown itself to be, of the absolute and comprehensive character which distinguished the landowner and the cultivator. In the democratic state economic interests are of many kinds and grades. There is no supreme division on one side of which stands the power of government. The danger of revolution is less, for its spirit animates only those who have suffered the worst maladjustments and exploitations of the new system. Only to these does the extreme doctrine of the 'class-war' appeal. The modern state, through un-employment-relief, insurance, health-protection, the establishment of minimum wages, and similar measures, has advanced a long way towards removing the spirit of revolution. The economic power which the system gives to the workers, acting through constitutionally estab-lished modes, is sufficient to remove it altogether.

We conclude therefore that a truly democratic state is vastly more secure than an oligarchy against the threat of revolution. Doubtless the general will is still most imperfect and undeveloped, but at least it is sufficiently real to give a new character to political authority. The formal basis of this authority is no more the division of master and servant but the unity of agent and principal.

Authority has always and everywhere existed in human life. What has changed is not the fact of authority but the form. There was no primitive anarchy whence authority by degrees arose. There was rather a primitive authority which has evolved in a determinate direction until its ideal character has been revealed and in some measure realized in the modern state.

We may sum up the process as follows. Authority ceases to exist in its own right, or by virtue of a natural or intrinsic superiority in the wielder thereof which entitles him to demand obedience apart from the interest of the subject. It passes into a derived authority, delegated and upheld by those over whom it is exercised. It becomes authority whose justification is the general welfare, not that of a class nor yet some mystical claim of divine or predetermined right. It implies not so much fear as hope. It becomes less coercive, less peremptory, less command than regulation, less an instrument of subordination and more an instrument of co-ordination. So understood, it is perceived to have limitations which are not inherent in the relation of a master to a servant. The master can command whatever the servant can obey, but a government which seeks and understands the welfare of the governed is far less free. Its limits are inwrought in tradition and established usage, in public opinion which exacts responsibility, and in written constitutions. Thus authority abandons certain fields. It becomes authority over action as distinct from authority over thought and opinion.[1] Instead of personal command it becomes authority according to prescribed and impersonal

---

[1] Certain thinkers of the Hegelian school admit the fact of the withdrawal of the state from particular fields but not the principle above stated. Thus the late Dr. Bosanquet, in a letter to the author, wrote as follows : ' Take the relation of the State to Art and Religion—the things most out of its apparent sphere. *How* it ought to deal with them for the best at any given epoch is a fearful problem ; but if it, *prima facie*, lets them alone it is none the less dealing with them. It only lets them alone in a certain way and on certain terms, conceived in the interest of the best life.'

forms. It no longer demands a general subjection of the will to arbitrary and unheralded decrees. It becomes reciprocal instead of unilateral. Authority becomes subject to its own regulations, and derivative from those over whom it is exercised. Finally it learns to appreciate its relation to that inner control which all personality seeks for itself, and in greater measure the greater it is.

Thus authority becomes demarcated, circumscribed, and itself controlled. In so far as this takes place the residence of authority is assured, and the conditions of revolution are abolished.

VII

MIGHT AND SOVEREIGNTY

I. FORCE AS THE *ULTIMA RATIO*

THE state has always been peculiarly associated with force. In its origins, in its growth, in its present control over its members and in its relation to other states, force is proclaimed to be not only its last resort, but its first principle, not only its special weapon, but its very being. ' The state ', said Bosanquet, ' as the operative criticism of all institutions, is necessarily force.' [1] The state, conceived in violence, was born to power. ' A sound sociology ', declares another writer, ' has to recall the fact that class formation in historic times did not take place through gradual differentiation in pacific economic competition, but was the result of violent conquest and subjugation.' [2] Strife, as the ancient philosopher surmised, ' is the father of things ', and its eldest begotten, formed in its own image and at length the sole heir of its progenitor, is the state.

This doctrine, nakedly exposed by such authors as Sybel and Treitschke and decently clothed by a multitude of writers on the state, is the more misleading because of the partial truth which it contains. It belongs to that order of simplified ' realism ' which misrepresents

[1] *Philosophical Theory of the State*, ch. vi.

[2] Oppenheimer, *The State*, Preface.

the course of historical development as well as the social conditions of all achievement and the springs of human conduct. Besides, it grossly exaggerates the efficacy of force.

We have shown that the emergence of the state was not due to force, although in the process of expansion force undoubtedly played a part.[1] But force holds nothing together. Force is a substitute for unity. So far as it rules, there is no unity and no development. Force as the servant of intelligence at times prepares the way for unity, but the credit belongs more to the master than to the servant. Force always disrupts unless it is made subservient to common will. The only justification for the doctrine which attributes social origins to force is simply this, that men learn by experience the inefficacy of mere force and then learn to modify or supersede it. Thus looking backwards we perceive that force once played a greater role than now belongs to it. 'The good old rule, the simple plan' is proved to have serious drawbacks. To take and to hold by force wastes the energies of those who take and those who resist, which might have been profitably applied to their co-operative endeavour. If the world could continue to produce the objects of men's desires as a wild tree produces fruit, then forceful seizure would be less out of keeping with the conditions of success. But when the vastly greater portion of the things men seek depend on their toil and enterprise, the loss of the method of force proves too enormous for intelligent beings.[2] Men modify this method and in large part abandon it, not necessarily because they have become

[1] Bk. I, ch. ii.

[2] This is well illustrated by Angell, *Foundations of International Polity*, ch. i. See also my *Community*, Bk. III, ch. vi.

ashamed of it or scrupulous—such feelings may be more effect than cause—but because experience has revealed the fruits of the social system, the gains of conjoint and mutual service.

Within a society it is only the clumsy and the stupid who seek to attain their ends by force. Brute strength earns little reward. It enables a bully to beat his wife. It earns a pittance in the humblest forms of manual labour. But it is the least prized of human possessions, the poorest servant of intelligence. It is put under the yoke, because if suffered to go free it breaks the order of life and habit, and tramples down the amenities and satisfactions which spring from the responsive and unrepressed activity of social man. It is an intruder felt and resented and chained. If suffered to prevail, it would destroy not only material goods but also the cultural gains, the spirit of truth, the work of the mind, the fertility of thought.

Do we then, as has been suggested, make the state the legatee of those dangerous and primitive attributes of our nature which by its aid we forgo in our individual lives, as the ancient Hebrews symbolically transferred their sins to a scapegoat—or to a God ? Do we, in the language of the social contract, covenant with one another to surrender to the state the use of force, establishing a rightful master to save us from ourselves? Such a conception again unduly simplifies the case, besides exaggerating the exercise of force within the state. We do not really, in the familiar phrase, count heads to prevent breaking them. The right of a majority is not merely the socialization of the force of a majority. Coercive power is a criterion of the state, but not its essence. There are many other influences, more subtle and even more resistless, which restrain and control us.

The law forbids theft and murder under penalty, but it is not on account of that penalty that the most of us do not thieve and kill. Social instincts are born with us, the heritage of a past that knows no horizon, now the very texture of our lives. They are reinforced by training and experience, as we learn alike our dependence on society and the opportunities which it provides. Our anti-social impulses are suppressed mostly by the ' censor ' within us or by the greater censor which is the public opinion of the society around us. Exceptionally they break the bounds so as to come within the range of coercion, and that coercion itself is sanctioned by the judgement of society. Unless the people rally to the laws they lose their power. And of course there are many customs and social taboos which are supported by no law and yet command an obedience no less complete.

Just as in each of us there are these impulses which offend against the order of our lives, so in society there are individuals who are reckless of social standards and are restrained only by force. The social institutions against which they particularly offend are obviously those which determine the rights of property. Here the temptations are greatest. Here also, it may be urged, the social order is most defective. It is to a large extent because of the glaring inequalities of opportunity, combined with the extremities of need, that force is more necessary in this region than in any other. That portion of the population which is in any degree raised above the level of sheer poverty does not normally violate the laws of property. Even of the population which exists below the ' poverty line ', the larger part, so ingrained is the sense of social conformity, respect the laws which wall off the satisfaction of their animal needs. In a society delivered from the gaunt fears of starvation and homelessness the service of force would be reduced to such minimal proportions that the state would no longer assume, in the eyes of any, the semblance of the mere policeman. When force is much in evidence it is a pathological symptom.

In the sphere of legislation, majorities do not normally overawe minorities so that they surrender to their will. Minorities acquiesce because this social attitude is deep-set in their natures. When acquiescence is contrary to another principle as deeply rooted, the state is in grave trouble, even in danger. Then and then only is it wisdom for the state to waive its formal *right* of coercion, unless sheer necessity or overwhelming advantage justifies its cause to itself. The ultimate sovereign is on perilous ground when it breaks the general will. ' The attitude of Ulster before 1914 was a refusal to accept the sovereignty of an Act of Parliament which granted self-government to Ireland. The refusal was made in the name of conscience ; and, whatever be thought of the penumbra of passions and personalities by which it was surrounded, the fundamental fact has to be recorded that Parliament and the ministry found themselves jointly powerless in the face of an illegally organized opposition. The women suffragists were able, over a period of eight years, to set at defiance the ordinary rules of law ; and few people to-day seriously doubt that the reason why that defiance was so successfully maintained was the fact of its moral content. Those who refused obedience to the Military Service Act of 1916 were able to prove the powerlessness of the state to force them into subjection.' [1] Such exceptional instances offer a strong contrast to the normal conditions which determine obedience. Unhappy is the state which

[1] Laski, *Authority in the Modern State*, pp. 44–5.

has repeatedly to rely on force in the coercion of minority groups, for revolution or disruption is in sight.

So much may be conceded, but the adherent of the doctrine that the state is force will reply that the true nature of the state is seen, not in its relation to its own members, but in its unity over against other states. When the state acts in its integrity, where there is no division within it, does it not reveal itself as power ? That very use of force which it denies to its citizens as individuals it restores to them as members of the Leviathan. The reality of politics is found in the untrammelled might which a state displays in expansion and conquest, in the ' war of steel and gold ', in that diplomacy behind whose polite representations lie the persuasive arguments of land-power and sea-power.

This too is a simplified realism, inadequate to the facts. In the modern world no state is strong enough to pursue a policy of coercion over others, if only because it unites the others in resistance. The might of a state does indeed enable it to secure its ' possessions ' in the less civilized portions of the earth, though even here economic power, which carries no weapons in its hand and is the result and expression of the enterprise and intelligence of a people, may claim a greater share of the credit than political power. Here as elsewhere it is the character of a people, the intelligent direction of its energies, which is the root of superiority. The simple-minded see the resultant power and falsely convert it into the cause. If it were the cause, then mere numbers would everywhere prevail, whereas the strength of a people is not proportional to its size. Even great ' possessions ' may add nothing to the power of a state. An imperialist writer like Seeley is forced to admit that India adds to the responsibilities but not to the power of the British Empire. Power grows only where there is solidarity, co-operation, common purpose—and the more these extend the more needless and the more perilous becomes coercion.

Nor can it be maintained that the expansion of the modern state was due mainly to the use of force. The force of the state has been spent mostly in international wars which have generally proved, like the wars of England and France or the Hundred Years' War, an incalculable waste with little compensatory gain to either side. Expansion has been mainly the result of constructive energy, not of destructive force. 'The expansion of England in the seventeenth century was an expansion of society and not of the state. Society expanded to escape from the pressure of the state ; and when the state, in consequence of the duel with France and the conquest of Canada, attempted to follow up the expanding society and to re-establish its pressure, a federation of new states arose to resist the realization of an Empire which had so far existed merely for the purpose of rhetoric. In later times another but much looser federation of states has grown up which styles itself for rhetorical purposes an empire, but in which the imperial claim is so much more completely in abeyance that the state of the parent society has been able to retain the honorary presidency of the federation, and to count upon the spontaneous aid of the other states in time of war. And as the real expansion has been primarily social, so it has been essentially peaceful. English society has not expanded by the displacement, or even by the exclusion, of Spanish, Dutch, French, or German society. The defeat of the Armada, Cromwell's belated anti-Spanish crusade, and the " Jenkins's ear " war, did nothing to prevent the gradual permeation of Mexico and South America by Spanish civilization, nor is there any reason to think that if Montcalm had defeated Wolfe at Quebec, the swamps of the Mississippi and the prairies of Manitoba would have been reclaimed by French pioneers.'[1]

To attribute the expansion of England—and a like statement is true of the other 'powers' of the modern world—to mere might is to underrate grossly two decisive factors. One is the economic advantage of her position and her resources, as the new world of commerce, industry, and finance took shape under the influence of the unheralded, incessant, silently working forces of social change. The other is the character of her people, who were able to exploit that advantage by their courage and adventure, by their forethought and by their toil. Mere force is quantitative, a gross and mechanical means ; character is qualitative, upon which all creation and all development depends. In the last resort character needs to employ force only against the stupidity which relies on force.

Force saves us only from itself. Men praise the 'sword' because it gives them victory over the 'sword', or delivers them from defeat. In each country they chant paeans over the armed forces which protect them—each country from the other. But he who is considering the service of force in *the* state must not limit his vision to *a* state. And when the *pluses* and *minuses* cancel out, the residue of service to *the* state is a mighty small thing compared with its cost. Meanwhile the ideal of force is exalted because of nation-limited views, and the nations themselves are distracted and impoverished by the illusions which thus are bred.

[1] Unwin, Introduction to Conrad Gill's *National Power and Prosperity*.

One of the chief arguments in favour of the democratic state is that within it government is less dependent on the psychology of power. Always those who wield power are tempted to extol it, but the more so if that power is unchecked and irresponsible. Oligarchy develops in the ruling class a consciousness of superiority which is dissociated from their capacity for rule or for service. The rulers are the masters, the subjects are their servants. To reason why is dangerous, to question the source of authority is fatal. Servitude is therefore sanctioned by force, and in harmony with this attitude oligarchy instils in the people the illusions of national power, as a psychological condition of their own real subjection. Democracy, on the other hand, makes authority a trust, and the ruler, becoming servant as well as master, is withdrawn from certain of the temptations of power. The common interest, the common welfare, becomes not only the ostensible aim but also the sole justification of government. The place of force is narrowed, because it comes to be adjudged by its value to society rather than by its value to the ruler. The valuation may still be erroneous, but at least it is made under conditions less prejudicial to the truth.

These considerations regarding the efficacy of force leave still unanswered the initial question. Force may have a very limited operation and still be the essence of the state, so that when we deprecate the exaltation of force we are merely deprecating the exaltation of the state. This, for example, is the position to which Duguit inclines, when he makes force 'the primordial and essential character of the state' while denying that coercion is a principle of action capable of universal application.[1]

[1] *Traité de Droit Constitutionnel*, vol. i, ch. v.

It is true that there is no state where there is no over-ruling force. This is the *differentia* between the state and all other associations. There is no state where other associations arrogate to themselves the exercise of compulsion. There is no state where there is anarchy. But the exercise of force does not make a state, or a pirate ship or mutinous army would be a state. There must be force, overruling force, but the force must itself be established, recognized, accepted. The primary fact of the state is not force but a universal order constituting a foundation for all social activities. One condition of this order is that it shall be guarded by a power which can prevent or punish violations or disturbances, maintaining or restoring the fabric whenever and wherever a defect appears. But the fabric must itself be strong or it cannot be kept in repair. It is the universality of the state, within its range, which makes force a necessity. Whatever the state does must be done in the knowledge that it can secure obedience. The obedience rests on a common will. Force is necessary to prevent violations, but force is possible only because of a fundamental agreement. Enforcement is the exception, agreement the rule.

The force at the command of the state is a precious possession, because the difference between a secure and universal order and one which is liable to interruption and uncertainty is incalculable. On this account the community learns to entrust the state with the power and the right of enforcement. It is a corollary of the state's main function to establish order in accordance with the common will. But the community assigns force, not to the government as such but to the government as upholders of law. The essential function of the state is to create law. This creation is something far wider than enforcement. It is a vast work of social construction. As the state carries it on, it keeps at its side the weapon of force. But that is to prevent interruptions or attacks upon its work. The weapon is the criterion of its right, but the employment of it is only a consequence, a necessary consequence, of its greater task. Unceasingly it guards the structure which it builds, but it guards for the sake of the building, itself the main achievement of the state.

II

THE GREAT STATES AS WORLD POWERS

Until modern times every great state swung in its orbit like a single sun, surrounded perhaps by satellites but forming no constellation with other states. Usually there was one state dominant in each civilization. If another state arose to challenge its dominance the issue was fought out to the death, as between Rome and Carthage. This condition passed away when at the opening of the modern world a number of great states arose within the same Western civilization. The conflicts of power between these states were never settled by the imperial supremacy of any. Spain might rise to greatness for a time ; France might for a time become the dominant power of a continent ; England might cast her aegis over an empire of her own ; but no power could control the rest however much it might inspire them with its fear. The sources of power were too widespread, and the area of common civilization was too extensive.

From out the numerous conflicts of these rival states

a new conception of the relation of one to the other arose. It was still a conception in terms of external might, but it admitted a plurality of independent powers. These were in the first instance the great powers of Europe. After the grand attempt of Napoleon to restore the principle of hegemony, the 'big five', as we might call them in the language of to-day, formed an uneasy 'concert'. But it depended on a settlement which ignored nationalistic aspirations. As these grew stronger in the nineteenth century, accompanied by changes in the power-standing of the great states, by the formation of the German Empire and the unification of Italy, and finally by the scramble for possessions in the still un-exploited parts of the earth, the 'concert' disappeared in rival and unstable alliances, each striving to assure against the other the 'balance of power'. Such was the European situation before the Great War.

But already the powers of Europe had become 'world-powers'. The civilization of Europe penetrated the whole earth. England's empire spread over the five continents. France held a large African territory besides possessions in other parts of the globe. Germany was belatedly entering into the partition of the spoils of European civilization. Russia bestrode two continents. The great new power of the United States, European in origin and in character, reluctantly abandoned an exclusively American policy to share the problems of a world-system. Finally the non-European state of Japan, adopting the economic civilization of Europe as well as its methods of imperialism, added another to the claimants of world-power.

Before we consider the consequences of these later transformations let us observe the working out of the

power-ideal in the European sphere itself. So long as
the tradition of the absolute sovereignty of each state in
its external relations held sway, no matter how inter-
woven the interests of the nations might become, a
' concert of powers ' was the best that could be hoped
for. But such an understanding between the owners of
power is always precarious. It assumes the acceptance
and the perpetuation of the existing status. No provision is made for new situations ; every new claim
threatens it and evokes jealousies and resentments. The
powers meet in council ; but each has its hand upon the
hilt of its sword, and sooner or later the swords are drawn.
The importance of the issue is quite secondary. The
uncontrolled arbiter of power, when faced with opposition, does not, in fact cannot, weigh the cost of the
appeal to force. The means have no relation to the end.
This is the difference between irresponsible force and all
other agencies. Power refuses to yield to anything but
power, no matter what cultural or material gains are
sacrificed in the process. Subjective considerations
prevail. The feeling of pride is aroused and the sense of
' honour ' is invoked. It is the pride and the honour of
sovereign power—the peoples may share these feelings,
but chiefly as derived from the representations (and misrepresentations) of those who directly or indirectly possess
it. Their real interests are, wherever sovereignty is
uncontrolled, divorced from those of their rulers.

Such is the common psychology of power, which makes
the mere ' concert of powers ' a poor impermanent
substitute for true organization. It was sufficiently
illustrated by the fate of the concert of Europe. It is
revealed wherever power is not held accountable within
a system designed for that very purpose. If further

illustration of a truth which history inculcates in a thousand ways were needed, it may be found in the catastrophic failure on the part of the allies to establish at an earlier date a central command during the Great War. 'The difficulties', said General Dawes, 'in the determination of the allied policy, both in time of war and in time of peace, are little realized by the average citizen in all countries. To him it seems strange that eventual common sense agreements, which in times of emergency characterize allied policy, come about so slowly. He does not realize the barriers which must first be beaten down.' These barriers are 'erected by national pride and the pride and selfish interest of different allied officials, whose powers are affected by any act of coercive interallied co-ordination' and also by the incessant misrepresentations of the 'nationalistic demagogues of all countries'.[1] Even the vast urgency of a common cause can scarcely prevail, at such a juncture, over the jealousies of power.

But power is fearful as well as formidable. When the concert of powers fails, each seeks to ally itself, not with all the rest, but with a group strong enough to hold the balance against the opposition of the rest. The external history of the European states, especially since the Franco-Prussian War, presents a curious spectacle of shifting relationships based on calculations of the 'balance of power'. The *Dreikaiserbund* is rifted and renewed, only to fall asunder at last. Germany establishes a new Triple Alliance, adding Italy to Austria. Russia turns to France, which is anxiously seeking a counterpoise against Germany. England after quarrelling with France over rival colonial claims, perceives a greater peril in the

---

[1] Address by General Dawes, 14 Jan. 1924.

naval development of Germany and forms a new *entente*
with her traditional enemy. So the 'balance of power'
brings three of the great states of Europe in alliance over
against a grouping of the other three, while smaller states,
like Roumania, Bulgaria, Serbia, and Turkey, are drawn
in under the dangerous aegis of either side. At the same
time every state seeks to augment its military or naval
strength, apart from its allies, for no one really trusts the
'balance of power'. Each seeks to 'insure' itself against
the rest, which means of course that the others must all
increase their 'insurance' too. Offence and defence are
the external and internal aspects of the same thing, so
that the more each 'insures' against each the less the
security there is for any.

The history of the great powers during this last period is
a remarkable record of the incapacity of uncontrolled power
to achieve its own most limited ends. The failure to control power was in part due to the dissociation of external
from internal affairs, which in turn was a consequence of
the traditional doctrine of state-sovereignty. The result
was a series of secret treaties and stratagems, in which the
nations seemed little more than pieces moved at the will
of hidden players. When 'Russia' acts, it is the doing of
men like Sazonoff or Iswolsky ; when 'Austria' threatens
it is the 'strong' policy of Berchtold ; behind the
conduct of Germany there are at work the persuasions
of von Tirpitz and Ludendorff. In the end it becomes
a picture of defeated ambitions, dissolved hopes, calculations that come to nought. None can yield because
each is committed through pride and fear. And so the
act of some wretched assassins in a rude Balkan state
loosens the avalanche of destruction, falsehood and
hate which, while the skies resound to the appeal

of noble causes, consumes the manhood of a whole civilization.

'Blind to danger and deaf to advice as were the civilian leaders of the three despotic empires, not one of them, when it came to the point, desired to set the world alight. But though they may be acquitted of the supreme offence of deliberately starting the avalanche, they must bear the reproach of having chosen paths which led straight to the abyss. The outbreak of the Great War is the condemnation not only of the clumsy performers who strutted for a brief hour across the stage, but of the international anarchy which they inherited and which they did nothing to abate.' [1]

The power-conception of the state, in this historical light, reveals its menacing defects. In the first place the supremacy of power converts the instrument of government into the master of men. The motives of the power-holders, their pride and their prestige, are exalted above the real interests of the nations. The state assumes in consequence a transcendental character, standing in its own right apart from the welfare of the people. It is a god—or an idol—whom they serve, to whom they sacrifice. They become devotees of its glory, as though it were a glory that lay outside themselves. They become servants of its ' honour ', as if there were an honour which is greater than their own. The general will fails to inform and to direct this hypostatized being that is the power-state. The result is that a small ruling class, possessed of power and obsessed with its ideal, can make commitments which bind the whole state in the perilous game of external policies. The power-state is essentially

[1] Gooch, *History of Modern Europe, 1878–1919*, ch. 16.

anti-democratic, even when it inspires a whole people with its ethics. When it succeeds in doing so it is only to achieve its own ends, not theirs. It works in superior aloofness from the people, concerned at most to secure their adherence to policies which they never initiate and upon which they rarely express their will as ultimate sovereign.

Moreover the conception of power which underlies this misnamed *Realpolitik* is largely mistaken. The true power of a state is not a function of the force which it displays. This real power, in the last resort, is the expression of the character and the resources of its people. It is not a power that lies dormant except in the hour of collision with an opposing power. It is exerted in and through all the activities, economic and cultural, of the people. The power of Spain declined because she ceased to display this inner vitality, because she failed to keep abreast with other states of the march of culture, because, in consequence, her trade and her wealth declined. In such a case no military strength she could exert could avail to save her greatness. The power of England increased because the energies of her people enabled her to reap the advantages of her geographical position and of her mineral resources in an age which gave new values to both. It was not because she waged successful war against France and other states. The power of the United States, based on the enterprise with which her inhabitants have developed the vast resources of a new continent, has given her a foremost place among the states of the world, although she has been involved in scarcely any of the great conflicts of power. The power of Germany depended on her industrial development and the devoted application to it of her people, not on the 'shining armour' or the 'mailed fist' which her war lords falsely extolled. On the other hand that power endures beyond the disastrous overthrow of her military pretensions and cannot be permanently suppressed by the external force of her victors. The positive achievements of mere force are small and impermanent and most precarious compared with the achievements of enterprise and insight. It is the last weapon to which the intelligent resort. They can win their ends in better ways, and if they apply so wasteful a method at all, it is because the stupid present them with no alternative. So long as force is anywhere unrestrained there must also be force to oppose it.

For force, though it creates so little, can destroy everything. It can trample underfoot all spiritual and cultural gains. It can lay in dust the cathedral no less than—more easily than—the fort. It can kill the body of civilization so that the soul of culture is lost. But it cannot even envisage any but the most gross and least enduring of advantages, for no fruitful development can be based on force. This defect of enforcement grows with every advance of civilization, for not only does such advance imply cultural ends with which force is incompatible, but it makes material prosperity more dependent on economic specialization of a kind which requires the freedom of co-operation. Slavery has practically disappeared from the world, not simply because it is abhorrent to the spirit of humanity, but also because it is under modern conditions an excessively wasteful and uneconomical institution. The forceful exploitation of her colonies by Spain prevented their development. Her treatment of Mexico and Peru, instead of strengthening her position, in the end weakened it. Rome gave her

colonies law and citizenship, but Spain offered nothing
to mitigate the régime of force. Hence her empire was
short-lived. In the modern world at least, empire has
to pass into voluntary co-operation, and the world-power
must increasingly abate the exercise of force if it is to
survive at all. Free exploitation gives place to monopoly-
rights, concessions, and other privileges, and these in
turn become harder to maintain within the order of
world economics. The final form of empire would seem
to be not so much that of France, which exercises a more
jealous monopoly within her African dominion, as that
of Britain which, as it grows older, maintains itself only
as a loose co-operation within a system of free commonwealths.[1]

The interests of men become too diverse, too complex,
too interdependent to be fulfilled by their uniting
together, like some vast band of pirates, in a polity of
force. More particularly the extent and character of
world-power, comprehending different peoples, completely breaks down the conception of any such simple
unity of interests as can be asserted and furthered through
sheer dominion. The coming of the world-power means
the transition from the nation-state to the group-nation
state. The British Empire includes the most diverse
peoples, presenting great differences of civilization and
outlook, of economic as well as of cultural standing and
interest. The United States is a continent-wide amalgam
of many nations, liberated by their union from the
separatist rivalries of power, and having in their unity

---

[1] In this statement I have in mind simply the goal of empire, when
conditions are ripe for its attainment. I do not intend to detract from
the ability and excellence of administration displayed by France in the
difficult task presented by her African colonies.

little to gain and much to lose from the ancient traditions of dominion. The Mediterranean powers, France and Italy, include in their newer citizenship the peoples of a civilization quite different from that of the French and the Italians. In fact, the more truly a state can be described as a world-power, the less particularist becomes the common interest of the state, and therefore the less likely it is to be advanced by force. The world-power unites across the lines of civilization and culture. Culturally, for example, England belongs to Europe, but politically it is united with countries which belong to other systems, say with Canada, which is geographically and economically and in large measure culturally a part of America; or with India, the heart of an Oriental world. The eccentricity of the state and the civilization which marks the extension of world-power confounds the polity of force and robs it of significance. This becomes more apparent, though not more true, as democracy develops within the world-power itself.

Under these conditions external might comes to be regarded, not as a means for furthering the definite aims of the state as a whole, since for the reasons we have mentioned either there are no such aims or they are not worth the cost; not as the condition of some great crusade or noble enterprise; not as the instrument of law and order beyond the confines of the state; not even, as a rule, as a weapon by the use or threat of which material possessions can be gained; but mainly as a means of protection against alien might. So regarded, it becomes a costly and perilous substitute for the common deliverance from itself.

THE POLITICAL EVOLUTION OF WAR

War is the exercise of armed force by one social group against another social group. It is possible only because of the social unity within the group and of the absence or denial of social unity between the groups. It implies— what it also causes—a sheer separation between one area of society and another, and a sheer antagonism of their conscious interests.

War, as thus defined, belongs to a certain stage of social development, corresponding to a mentality which regards social interests as rigidly inclusive and exclusive. It is a stage into which mankind entered only after its evolution had advanced far from its unknown beginnings, and it is a stage which the logic of that evolution is already promising to close. War, as we understand it, did not belong to the primeval world in which the isolated family-group precariously struggled for existence. The god of war was one of the younger gods of mankind, and has still no place among the most primitive peoples. Sporadic fights and forays, raids for booty and for women, occur among them, but war, as a definite institution, the deliberate matching of force with force, is absent. And when it first appears it has a minor significance, in strange contrast to its character among more civilized communities.

' In many cases, savage warfare is nothing worse than a dangerous sport. In the Trobriand Islands, British New Guinea, in a big war, where a couple of thousand warriors took part, the total casualties might amount to half a dozen killed and a dozen wounded. . . . Round the east end of New Guinea, where cannibalism and head-hunting flourish, the natives had the unpleasant habit of making nocturnal raids, and of killing without any necessity, and in an unsportsmanlike manner, women and children as well as combatants. But when investigated more closely and concretely, such raids appear rather as daring and dangerous enterprises, crowned, as a rule, with but small success—half-a-dozen victims or so— rather than as a wholesale slaughter, which indeed they never were. For the weaker communities used to live in inaccessible fastnesses, perched high up above precipitous slopes, and they used to keep good watch over the coast.'[1]

War became an established thing, an institution, as society passed from its primitive cohesion to an oligarchical structure. War involves a system of authority and subordination, and until this is created there cannot be the practice of war, any more than it exists among the lower animals. Authority also creates the ends of which war is the means. In particular it creates slavery, and the capture of slaves was an important and sometimes the chief object of early warfare. Territorial expansion, the exercise of dominion over others or the permanent exaction of tribute, was not within the ambition of the tribal war-chiefs. It was scarcely possible in the rude days when men lived in small and isolated communities, separated by mountains or forests or deserts. Wars were expeditions to kill and to steal, whence the warrior might return to his people with the glory of trophies or of spoils. They were outlets for such undirected energies as the mere business of living occasionally left to the males of the tribe—except when they were desperate attempts to snatch from others the means of subsistence. Such wars did not break the exclusiveness of the small community or greatly alter its character.

With the increase of numbers, the establishment of

[1] B. Malinowski, in *Economica*, October 1922.

contacts, and the growth of organization, a stage is reached where war becomes the instrument and the source of empire. The social order becomes more strongly oligarchical under the control of a military class which has learned to organize and direct the resources of the community to the wider ambition of power, the extension of dominion and the permanent subjection of tribute-paying dependencies. The age of empire fills nearly the whole page of recorded history, which of course is only a brief span in the history of the race. There were two conditions under either of which a people has by the practice of war been able to subdue others and establish an empire. One case was that where warlike nomads, posted on the outskirts of a peaceful civilization and perhaps acquiring from it the science which they apply to war, swept over it in conquest, submerging its culture in the process. So the Dorians overcame the civilization of Tiryns and Mycenae, so the Turks and Tartars swept over the more civilized races of Asia and Europe. The other instance was that where a strong civilization, by its pre-eminence of organization or invention, was able to impose itself, like that of the Romans or of the imperial nations of the modern world, on the relatively isolated and generally less civilized peoples with which it came into contact. In both instances there was a marked disparity of life and culture between the conquerors and the conquered, permitting the establishment of an oligarchical system. When the superiority of the conqueror was evinced by a particular development of the art of war, such as the Macedonian phalanx or the Roman legion, it became under strong leadership so effective as to inspire the most ambitious dreams of world dominion. These dreams, as historical memories, have outlived the period to which they belonged, and inspired vain and catastrophic endeavours, as with Napoleon, to give them realization in an alien age. But the principle of empire was still vindicated, that it cannot be achieved except through sheer civilizational disparity. The imperial ambitions of modern states have been attained only in the regions remote from the ever-growing range of a common civilization.

The age of empire gave to the state that aspect of sovereign absolutism which is still regarded by many as revealing its true character. Under the impact of the power-impulse the state assumed a most determinate form. In the first place, since there could not be in any community more than one centre of power without disruption, it necessarily took to itself the sole right to exercise force, both within and without its borders. This not only strengthened its organization but also confirmed its oligarchical tendency. The institution of war has always been the greatest support of oligarchy. Oligarchy relies on a war-establishment as a means of self-defence, not merely as a means of establishing external dominion. A state constituted for war inculcates a discipline of unreasoning obedience, a tradition of 'loyalty' and 'duty', a spirit of subjection to the ruling class which overrides all considerations of the real interests of the many. This spirit, however, can be maintained only if within the state there are marked cultural differences between those who wield power and those who are subject to it. Such has in fact been the case in the hey-day of empire. The modern influences which have broadened the basis of culture and raised its general level have been inimical to the imperial state. War and democracy belong to different social stages.

Economic and social developments have diffused power as well as culture. But the advance of military science has abolished the distinction of the warrior and in particular has practically abolished what has always been the aristocratic arm of military service, cavalry. The revolution which the archers of Crécy inaugurated has been fulfilled in the days of the machine gun. The rules of war, under the levelling influence of a more objective and grimmer science, refused any longer to conform to the requirements of an oligarchic culture. The warrior in the old sense, who ' drunk delight of battle with his peers ', is as dead as the craftsman who wrought his armour or who wove gay caparisons for his horse.

Even before this greater transformation military power had proved a double-edged weapon, dangerous to the order which wielded it. This fact is constantly revealed in the history of dominant states. Victory and defeat alike strain the discipline of the instrument of power and have always been great agencies of political revolution. Thus the victory of the seamen of Salamis set Athens forward on the road to democracy and the defeat of the seamen of Aegospotami turned it back again. But of such consequences our recent history is so full that illustration is hardly needed. We should observe, however, that military power tends to detach oligarchy itself from its social roots and to give it another and more arbitrary character, less stable and less secure. The social structure of oligarchy enables it to establish, as the instrument of its will, a permanent force, a standing body of armed men ; but once it is established, the personal character of military command and the withdrawal of the army from the normal life of the community render this instrument serviceable to the ambitions, not of the oligarchical class as a whole, but of the military leaders. The *ethos* of class structure evokes this force, but the *ethos* of military organization may control it, and the two do not necessarily coincide. The fate of the state may thus depend on the answer to the question, Whom does the army obey? A curious constitutional illustration of the danger is found in the English Mutiny Act. Fearing the detachability of a professional army, the English parliament passed an act to give itself control over the very existence of the army, and to ensure this control it made the act of a character that required its yearly renewal.

The danger in question is greatest when the army is composed of mercenaries, in other words, when the rank and file (as well as the officers) are professional soldiers. The transition from a militia recruited on each occasion at the call of the government and a mercenary army occurred wherever empire was extended over a large area, involving continuous military control and protracted and distant expeditions. It proved especially perilous in the oligarchical states of antiquity. Mercenaries, often foreigners and sometimes ' barbarians ', were a disintegrating influence in the Hellenic world. At Rome the reorganization of the army on a professional basis by Marius inaugurated a new political era which, through vast confusion and conflict, led to the goal of Caesarism. It became an established maxim of politics that the tyrant needs the support of mercenaries. In the modern world Napoleon sought likewise to use a professional army as the means of a new Caesarism, but by this time the foundations of oligarchy itself were breaking, and the effort ended in disaster.

So we reach the stage where the political prizes of war become quite precarious and insubstantial while its costs become overwhelmingly great and more swiftly subversive of the social structure. This situation is due in part to the growth of nationalism, which is fatal to the ancient ideal of empire, in part to the increasing interdependence of national states within a common civilization. One result has been the feverish efforts of modern states to gain security by piling up armaments against one another. Although the professional army remained the nucleus of military power, it was supplemented by a system of national conscription, so that civilization returned to the principle of the armed community, but now in the form of the ' nation in arms '. This vast extension of military ' preparedness ' was rendered possible by the great developments of industrial technique and mechanical invention. It meant that in the event of war the whole population could be devoted to the struggle. It obliterated so far as adults were concerned, women as well as men, the distinction between combatants and non-combatants. War thus came to involve whole nations not only in its consequences but also in its conduct. And the new engines of war, long-distance artillery and the bombing aeroplane, were equally indiscriminate.

The age of competitive armaments and competitive alliances culminated in the ' world war ', a monstrous struggle without intrinsic purpose, involving nation after nation in a conflict whose initial issues were obscure to them and irrelevant to their interests. Mankind has never witnessed so tragic a disparity between means and ends. The struggle could not be localized because the nations were so interdependent, so bound up with one another. All the great nations of the world were embroiled, not because a single issue divided them, but because a single system held them fast. Nothing was common save the catastrophe. In the words of Viscount Grey, ' it was a victory of war itself over everybody who took part in it '.

The significance of this fact is simply that war has become an anachronism, an institution incompatible with the civilization which has overspread the world.[1] It is of course possible that the technical development of the art of war, the use of high explosives, poison gases, and perhaps other yet unknown agencies of destruction,

[1] We have not thought it necessary to consider certain arguments which claim that war has a stimulating or beneficial effect within our present civilization, since these are based on a doctrine of the state and of society which the whole of this study contradicts. We may simply mention the psychological argument which puts forward war as the great uniting force of modern nations. We are told, for instance, that ' the French and Italian nations have undoubtedly been welded more firmly by the Great War ; while England and her sister and daughter nations (with the one sad exception of the Irish) have been united, by their co-operation in the one great purpose, to a degree which no other conceivable event could have achieved and which many generations of peaceful industry and enlightened political efforts might have failed to approach ' (McDougall, *The Group Mind*, ch. x). Statements of this sort are at best gross exaggerations. War often temporarily unites, but it also divides. Permanent unity depends on permanent common interests, and if these do not already exist war cannot create them. Besides, we have reached a stage where civilization demands, not the unity of a nation simply, but unity between nations. War prevents this—even the allies of the Great War are not brought closer together in consequence, but on the contrary have tended to fall further apart than before it.

Recent developments have also shattered the economic argument that war acts to keep population within the means of subsistence by eliminating the ' surplus '. Under the conditions of modern civilization war reduces the means of subsistence even more than it reduces the population, as the fall in the standard of living since the Great War exemplifies. It may be remarked in passing that a reduction of living standards is to-day the most active source of disunion *within* a nation.

together with the ubiquitous menace of the aeroplane and airship, will render warfare so uncontrollably disastrous as finally to deter mankind from its arbitrament altogether. But whether this may or may not be expected, the development of civilization leads more directly to a like necessity. The establishment of a League of Nations, directed towards the abolition of competitive armaments and the judicial settlement of international disputes, is not so much the institutional expression of an ideal as the belated adjustment of an institution to realities. To assume the closing of the era of national wars is not an act of unscientific utopianism but a reasonable inference from the premiss that men in the long run accommodate their institutions to their necessities. No one can foretell what a future civilization may bring, but it is permissible to judge what the present civilization requires. How soon and on what terms we accept its demands remains still a matter of faith.

VIII

LAW AND ORDER

I. THE NATURE OF LAW

LAW in its broader significance reigns everywhere. Where life exists there are universal laws of life, and for each form of life after its kind. Within this great order, life-sustaining and life-sustained, there are many grades and types of law. It is outside our sphere to consider that vast region of law which works inflexibly, inviolably, and regardless of human wills.[1] Society begets another kind of law, another order reflecting no less surely its own nature, but on that very account liable to change, development, and transgression. This social law is expressed in custom, tradition, the thousand forms of use and wont. Part of this in turn is reinforced, reaffirmed, and enlarged as the law of the state.

Even within the sphere of the state there are two kinds of law. There is the law which governs the state and there is the law by means of which the state governs. The former is constitutional law; the latter we may for the sake of distinction call ordinary law. The former may be in part embodied in a 'written constitution', distinguished from ordinary laws and generally beyond the power of the ordinary legislature. Its character and sanction are necessarily different from those of other laws. Even when, as in England, a constitutional law is

---

[1] See my *Community*, Bk. I, ch. i.

enacted through the regular process of legislation, it is enacted to control the legislature, or more generally the government, and directs us back, implicitly or explicitly, to a will beyond the will of the legislature. (The fuller significance of this fact we must consider in the discussion of the problem of sovereignty.) This constitutional law is to a great extent unwritten, and consists in modes of procedure, precedents, traditions, in the ' spirit of the constitution ' which a legislature dare not violate without offending that ultimate sovereign to which it directly owes its power. Here is, except in times of violence and revolution, a sufficient sanction. The development of the law of the constitution, responsive to the solidarity of a society on the one hand and to its discernment of political function on the other, has at once narrowed and widened the sphere of legislation. It has narrowed that sphere by withdrawing from it the control of certain regions of conduct and experience. It has widened it by insisting more and more that no privilege or status, not even that of government itself, shall exempt its possessors from the common code, that legal rights and obligations shall build a common structure guaranteeing to all men certain fundamental liberties, that order shall be universal, and that law shall be administered without respect of persons.

It is obvious that the state cannot sanction constitutional law, the law of its being, as it can sanction the ordinary law. Some elements of constitutional law may be brought within the cognizance of the courts of the state ; others by the very nature of the case cannot. The mode of procedure of the courts themselves is part of the constitution. Besides, there is a whole set of rules, some of them of supreme importance, in the form of 'conventions, understandings, habits, and practices' governing the conduct of the sovereign power, which are not and cannot be enforced by the courts.[1] But all ordinary law is interpreted and applied by the courts, and all ordinary law, so applied, is administered and enforced by the agencies of the state.

To obtain the true conception of law we must, therefore, centre our attention not on the legislative chamber, though it has become the most important *source* of law, but on the court, which is concerned with the whole of the ordinary law, whatever its source. It is true that in the modern state the legislature can control the other sources of ordinary law and does, by its own enactment, constantly limit or modify their contribution to the whole body of law. But in no state, not even in France with its elaborate codifications, is jurisdiction solely and absolutely determined by the statute-book.

We are here concerned with the ordinary laws by which the state regulates the conduct of its members, the positive laws which express the will of the state. Any rule governing the conduct of citizens or residents within the state which is interpreted and applied by a political court comes within this category. Law must be distinguished and defined by its form, not by its content. We only confuse the issue if we introduce ethical and historical concepts which are irrelevant to the legal form. Of such confusions the greatest is that which arises from the attempt to read into the *definition* of law some statement of the ideal which it should conform to or should serve. But to define the law as its own ideal leads us into impossible identifications, where

[1] Cf. Dicey, *Law of the Constitution*, Introduction.

the ideal is substituted for the actual, or into impossible separations, where the actual is roundly denied to be law at all. Blackstone's well-known definition is of this sort, when he declared a law to be ' a rule of civil conduct, prescribed by the supreme power in a state, prescribing what is right and prohibiting what is wrong '.[1] This is as misleading as the ancient formulas which converted political law into the ' rule of reason ' or the human translation of the ' will of God '. It is as misleading, and for the same reason, as Rousseau's definition of the sovereign as the inerrant ' general will '. We can never interpret political actualities if we refuse to accept them, as Rousseau did, or while accepting them, as Blackstone did, attribute to them qualities of perfection which they do not possess. To relate the actual to an ideal is an engrossing and valuable service, but to identify the two is an operation of blind faith which confounds science in the act of perverting ethics.

For a law is still a law whether we deem it just or unjust. Otherwise the same act would be a law to some and not to others, and even a law at one time and not at another. It is a law equally whether it serves the interests of the many or of the few. It is a law whether it enlarges or contracts liberty. It is a law whether it is enacted on principles deduced from dogmatic religion (like Sabbatarian legislation) or on a theory of human equality or on practical considerations of the social welfare.

English-speaking peoples have less excuse than most for any confusion on this point. While we lack a word to denote the body of law as a whole, such terms as serve that purpose for many European peoples, *droit*, *Recht*,

[1] *Commentaries*, i. 44.

diritto, *derecho*, and the Roman *ius*, are associated with an ethical significance, the idea of 'right', which has encouraged the confusion. But the word *law* is objective and ethically neutral. It signifies the political fact alone. We can thus more easily avoid the assumption of any pre-established harmony between ethical right and political law. We can discuss what law should be without assuming that it already is so. We can the more easily show the impact of ideals in the making and changing of law, without implying that these or any other ideals were present in the institution from the first.

Another confusion arises from the definition of law in terms of some particular authority, less comprehensive than the state, on which it depends, or of some one source from which it emanates. So law has been regarded as the expression of the will of king or emperor, the notion of law being then confounded with that of command. Or it is declared to be the prescription of 'the sovereign', whether monarch or parliament or people, though there is a considerable portion of the body of indubitable law which no one sovereign power, nor yet the whole hierarchy of them, has 'prescribed'. The Austinian idea, that law is the command of political superiors addressed to political inferiors, is particularly misleading, since it conceals and even denies two of the attributes which law everywhere exhibits, its universality and its formality.

Let us return to a consideration of these attributes. In the Introduction to this volume we considered them briefly, as throwing light on the nature of the state. Let us now try to show, on the other hand, that they themselves reflect the nature of the state-organ. They are, in fact, not ideal principles of what law should be, they are necessary consequences of the structure and operation of every political system.

The universality or generality of law has been insisted on by practically all political thinkers, from Aristotle and from the Roman jurists to the present time. But here we must again distinguish between what law is and what law should be, between the generality which law of necessity possesses and any other generality which it ought to possess. If we except statute law, it is obvious that the other forms of law are concerned with general principles and their applications. The past decisions of judges, which enter into the Common Law, have significance only as like situations occur. The law which is an interpretation of custom is clearly a general principle derived from a general usage. The law which is built up as Civil Law from legal treatises rests on still broader principles. Equity itself is the most universal of all categories, the ' rule of reason '. What then of legislation ? It is a public act, creating rights and obligations. It operates through an elaborately constituted authority, which must formulate the law according to a definite procedure, must consider its relation to pre-existing laws, must enact it in a prescribed manner, and must proclaim it publicly throughout the state. The rules of law-making, essential elements of the constitution of a state, ensure that the law shall itself possess the generality which entitles it to be named a rule.

At the same time it is often said that a law *ought* to be general in some other way than the mere fact of legislation ensures. Most authorities insist that law *properly* applies only to classes, both of persons and of acts or forbearances. Some, like Austin, are content to limit generality to the acts enjoined or forbidden, without

requiring a like generality in respect of persons.[1] Others,
like Duguit,[2] go so far as to claim that an act is inherently
illegal if directed towards a specific person or group of
persons, such as the French act which banned in 1886
the heads of the once royal families of France. It is,
however, undesirable to deny the character of law to any
measure constitutionally enacted by a legislature, for
then we introduce subjective criteria which necessarily
vary and thus obscure our study of the legal fact. It is
safer to admit the title of law to all acts which conform
to the established procedure of law-making. Thus we
can with greater assurance distinguish between laws
which are and laws which are not in accord with political
principles, as we shall do in the next chapter. Duguit's
example is moreover an unfortunate one. Not only is
it *possible* for a law to apply to a specific person or group
of persons, but it may be *proper* that it should do so.
Even the single person may constitute, like the Lord
Chancellor or like the head of an erstwhile royal family,
a whole political class, so that there is no arbitrary
selection or exemption involved. If it is deemed to the
interest of the state that a special political category, even
if a single person constitute it, should be subjected to
a particular rule, why should the rule not be named
a law? Generality, even in the sense desiderated by
Duguit, is a matter of political status and not of numbers.
Certain forms of law, such as those concerned with
taxation or social legislation, must by their very nature
be often extremely specific in their designation of the

---

[1] It is significant that here Austin limits law by considerations of its
inherent nature, not of the power of the sovereign. A fuller development
of this principle might have overthrown his doctrine of sovereignty itself.

[2] *Traité de Droit Constitutionnel*, II, ch. ii, § 16.

groups affected by the law, but in such cases the precise determinations are the working out of a general principle. An income-tax law which made specific tax categories of bricklayers, freemasons, and university graduates would offend against the *ideal* of generality—though it would still be a law. On the other hand an income-tax law whose categories were in terms of income-classes, or which took relevant distinctions into account, such as that between bachelors and married men may be held to be, might be formally no more general, but would not on that account be indefensible.

In other words, when we make generality an ideal or criterion instead of simply a fact, we are really thinking of something else than generality. We are thinking of fairness or equity. This principle is opposed to the arbitrary or selective or spasmodic treatment of persons or actions. It requires that all who are alike in respect of the service or capacity envisaged by the law shall be treated in the same way, and in a different way from those who are in this respect unlike. The principle requires something else than generality. Mere generality might outrage all notions of fairness, as for example in a taxation measure which should levy the same amount from every one, whether rich or poor. Fairness dictates the content and not the form of generality. The form is a positive character of law itself, the procedure out of which law arises being such that it can deal only with general situations or with specific situations only in general terms.

This fact emerges more clearly when we dismiss the false identification, so much encouraged by Bentham and Austin, of law and command. Law is the very antithesis of command, as that term is usually understood, for command separates the giver and the receiver, separates their status always and sometimes their interest as well. But law unites, for it applies no less to the legislator than to those for whom he has authority to legislate. When an army officer issues a command, he does not have to obey it himself, any more than an employer who gives instructions to his *employé*. Besides, command belongs properly to the sphere of administration and not of legislation. It is concerned with ways and means, with specific occasions, usually with details that do not admit of a rule. It is a means of execution, not a form of enactment. Law is permanent and fundamental as compared with command. Every new law has to be fitted into a system, to be adjusted to, and made to consist with, the whole body of pre-existing law. The confusion of law and command destroys the very order of the state. Even in extreme despotisms mere command leaves intact the major realm of law—otherwise the state would break into chaos. The rule of law, the very criterion that a state exists, is possible only in so far as law is distinguished and set apart from command. And it is a mark of the modern state, in fact of the developing state at all times, that it extends the rule of law so that no classes (like the medieval clergy) and no individuals, not even the ' monarch ', are withdrawn from its authority.

On the other hand the protection and other benefits of law cease to be limited within the state. In the tribal and clan life of primitive communities customary law is the safeguard of the kin and does not apply to the stranger. In the Hellenic city-community the law was looked upon as belonging only to the exclusive body of citizens. Rome, setting out on the same path, found it necessary to construct, beside the *ius civile*, a separate body of law for aliens and other non-citizens. In the Byzantine civilization law extended its protection only to the orthodox, and the medieval civilization of Europe drew distinctions along the same line. But the modern state refuses such limitations. Here again the growing sense of political principle, the recognition of the true universality both of justice and of order, the concept of fairness as applied to function or service or need, have worked towards the transformation of actual law, so that the form of its generality corresponds more freely and more comprehensively with the ideal which was half expressed and half concealed within its narrower range in the past.

Of this later. Meantime let us consider another attribute of ordinary law which belongs to its very nature and definition. All rules which issue from any authority are imperatives, that is, they are addressed to the will, they prescribe a mode of conduct and demand conformity. They bring with them a certain sanction. The great difference between the law laid down by the state and the rules which are formulated by other authorities lies in the sanction. It is convenient and comfortable to conform to custom—it makes life easier and smoother and reacts happily on the sense of fellowship and solidarity. To follow the dictates of fashion gives people a feeling of social initiation. The rules of the club we belong to uphold and stimulate the desired sense of membership. We conform because we like to. The sanction in these cases is a positive social satisfaction which we lose unless we conform. In other cases we identify ourselves with the particular interest, economic, cultural, or whatever it be, for which the association stands, and we obey its rules for the sake of the interest.

There is also of course the *esprit de corps* which tradition, habit, and living comradeship fortify. The loss of these things would so impoverish our lives that we would not normally think of forfeiting them by non-conformity. This sanction is all the stronger because our membership is free. If we should change so that the objects of the association no longer appeal to us, then we can leave it at will. The impulse to obey lies wholly within us. But it is otherwise with the law of the state. This kind of sanction no longer suffices. Here is the other side of that generality on which we have insisted. There are general conditions which all *must* accept if order is to be insured. There are general obligations which all *must* fulfil if justice is to be done. Such conditions and obligations the state takes for its own. To secure them it imposes a further sanction. The other sanctions are conditional : this sanction, the sanction of coercion, is unconditional. The last resort of enforcement lies behind this law.

This cardinal distinction between the law prescribed by the state and all other social regulation has been obscured by the theories which made law the transcription of ' natural ' or ' eternal ' right or the rule of reason or even the fulfilment of liberty. That our ethical ideals should be determinant of our laws is simply a way of saying that we cherish these ideals. All ideals are demands upon reality. But we cannot identify the ethical rule and the political, for several reasons. In the first place the political law is objective, the same for all, indisputably fixed, while the ethical rule is subjective, variant, an inner obligation that expresses the social character of individuals and responds to all the formative influences that bear upon them. Unless all members of the state were in all respects alike, the law of the state could not, for every one at all times, be identified with the ethical rule. In the second place, law is concerned with order and system as well as with justice. It makes rules of conduct for the general convenience which are not themselves based on ethical distinctions at all.[1] The ethical aspect in such cases exists only because the law exists. If the law determines that drivers shall keep to the right (or the left), it is not because keeping to the right has any ethical significance. After the law is passed it may be morally wrong, as well as legally, to disobey it, but it is a derivative wrong. It belongs to the *mala prohibita*, whereas it is the quality of the essential rules of ethics that they persist no matter what the law, and that they for ever seek to make the law conform to themselves, instead of *vice versa*. Finally, there are ethical principles accepted by at least the majority of the members of a society which cannot or which should not be formulated into political law. There are duties inspired by ' natural affection ', within the family circle for instance, of which no external law can assure the fulfilment. There are obligations to utilize opportunity or to avoid wastefulness or to maintain standards of workmanship or of endeavour, which the law is incapable of enforcing and therefore should not attempt to regulate. There are alternatives presented to us by the circumstances of every day, on which we bring our standards of value to bear, but in respect of which the external pressure of law, even were it possible to assert it, would only confuse and irritate us. This is a subject to which we shall return. Here it suffices to point out that the ethical sphere is vastly more extensive than the legal. The law of the state has a proper and peculiar sanction. Where that sanction does not apply or

[1] For a fuller discussion see Pound, *Law and Morals*.

where its application fails to serve its object, law becomes a clumsy intruder into regions alien to it.

There are, it is true, certain types of ordinary law which at first sight seem to lack the coercive attribute, such as laws of a permissive or enabling character, or laws of the kind called 'declaratory' by Austin, that is 'acts of interpretation by legislative authority', or acts of repeal. But the apparent exceptions are easily seen to fall within the general principle. An act of interpretation defines conditions of political regulation and in that sense it has the quality and even the form of imperative control. An enabling act, such as that conferring a charter on a company or taxing power on a municipality, has also an imperative character, binding all concerned to respect the right it conveys and in the latter case enforcing upon the citizens the obligation to pay taxes levied in accord with the right thus bestowed. An act of repeal is the cancellation of a pre-existing regulation, and cancellation is an act of authority as imperative in a negative direction as the establishment of a rule is positively. It is a necessary part of the very mechanism of compulsion. The whole of political law is a system of compulsions whose fulfilment is left neither to the discretion nor to the conscience of the individual. This holds as true under democracy or 'self-government' as under despotism. The compulsion of law is not, in the last resort, the compulsion of ruler or of government, it is the compulsion of the state, a necessity of its existence, a criterion of its function and place among the other associations of community. It does not of course follow that obedience to law is chiefly due to compulsion or that it is prompted, as Hobbes says, by fear of the consequences. But without an element of compulsion there is no guarantee of the generality which we have seen to be inherent in law. Because it is general in its application the law of the state must be compulsive ; because it is external in its injunctions, the law of the state can be compulsive.

II

THE RULE OF LAW

In ethics, according to Kant's famous principle, there is but one ' categorical imperative ', which can be stated thus : ' Act in conformity with that maxim, and that maxim only, which you can at the same time will to be a universal law.' What is right for me, we may perhaps interpret it, must be at the same time that which is right for all others to whom the same alternatives under the same circumstances are presented. The logic of law leads to an objective imperative of a similar nature. It demands that what is law for me, legal right and legal obligation, must hold equally as law for all citizens, in such a way that none are by reason of privilege or any consideration extraneous to the purpose of the law exempted from the obligation or denied the right. This principle ensures the ' rule of law '. Let us try to give it a less abstract character.

The rule of law is contradicted by any arbitrary action on the part of government, and particularly on the part of the executive. If a potentate or magistrate can arrest and imprison or fine a citizen without, in the American phrase, ' due process of law ', the rule is violated. Under such conditions the order and security which law exists to ensure is interrupted for the person concerned and rendered precarious for all. Such arbitrary action is thus opposed to the very interest of law. Yet, as Dicey points out, it is only in quite recent times that most states have come to establish, in this sense, the rule of law. The conditions of it were first and longest established in England, and now it is generally accepted as a fundamental principle of government. Its acceptance enables us to interpret government as an organ of society, an agent empowered to work in appointed ways, owning a derived authority and a delegated might, no longer the master of the state.

It follows that government itself must be subject both to the laws which it makes and to the greater law which it upholds. This also is part of the rule of law. There may or there may not be special tribunals of ' administrative law '. In any case the responsibilities of government are different from those of the governed and must be adjudged by standards appropriate to its functions and its powers. There are, besides, those responsibilities of government which cannot be enforced at all by the ordinary sanctions of political law. Yet, as we shall see, there are other sanctions which can effectively bring government itself within the range of the common rule.

The rule of law has two aspects which are seldom adequately distinguished. The rule is violated if by reason of birth, status, wealth, or special privilege any individuals or groups are legally exempted from legal responsibility for acts which if committed by other individuals or groups would come within the cognizance of the courts. The rule includes the condition that whenever any form of conduct is amenable to legal control it shall be so amenable no matter whose conduct it is. In other words the order established by the state must be without exemptions. If, for example, I can seek legal reparation from a private railway company for injuries sustained through the negligence of its officials, the rule demands that I shall no less be able to sue the government (or rather the state) for like injuries sustained when its own officials have been at fault. The state, that is, must itself have legal responsibilities under the same conditions in which it imposes legal responsibilities on others—an obligation which, as we shall see, is entirely compatible with a realistic doctrine of sovereignty. This rule is not violated by a system which establishes, as in France or Germany, special courts for the decision of cases arising out of the acts of state officials. But it is violated if, because a tortious act is committed by a servant of the state, the state evades or denies a responsibility which it imposes on a private corporation.[1] And it is violated if an executive board or standing commission has the power to decide, without the right of appeal to the courts, contentions which arise in the administration of its office. It is no less violated if the state confers on any corporate or incorporate body an immunity from legal responsibility for its tortious acts, such as was established for trade unions in England under the Trades Disputes Act of 1906.

We might go farther and claim that the rule of law is violated in so far as there are not formal but substantial discriminations which prevent an equal access for all persons to legal redress. The greatest of these is the expense of the appeal to the law. Even in criminal cases the efficacy of the defence may be limited by the ability of the accused to pay for legal aid. In civil cases the

[1] See E. Barker, on the ' Rule of Law ', *Political Quarterly*, May 1914. The well-known case of *Bainbridge* v. *the Postmaster-General* revealed clearly this defect in the ' rule of law ' under the traditional English doctrine of the state.

resort to law is often impossible for the poor, and it is
obvious that an appeal to the higher courts is almost
a luxury for the rich. On this account there is a very
general dissatisfaction with the law, especially among the
working classes, and it is strengthened by the feeling
that the law and the courts are not equally favourable to
all classes of claimants, partly because the law is so slowly
responsive to new social situations, partly because the
courts are composed of persons who, through the conditions of the legal career, belong generally, by sympathy
or upbringing, to the class of the well-to-do. If Ehrlich
was right when he said that ' there is no guarantee of
justice except the personality of the judge ',[1] the social
sympathies of the judge must have a very significant
bearing on the character of justice.[2]

How these serious imperfections of the rule of law may
be removed is a question beyond the scope of this work.
We have cited them because they bring out, by contrast,
the ideal of the rule of law. It is the establishment of
a certain universality of order in conformity with the
principle of justice. On what then must such a universality rest ? In answer we are driven back to the conception of personality. Since personality is the only intrinsic
value we know, legal rights must either rest upon it or
else conflict with the social welfare. When for instance
the law safeguards property, it must not be because
property has rights in virtue of its mere existence, but
only because the legal rights of property are means for
the achievement and development of personality, and
therefore these rights should be so limited that they do

---

[1] Quoted by Cardozo, *The Nature of the Judicial Process*, p. 16, from
9 Modern Legal Philosophy Series.

[2] Cogent illustrations are given in Laski, *Authority in the Modern State*,
I, iii.

not override other means necessary to that end. That is the truth underlying the notions of 'natural rights', the 'law of nature', and so forth. If we understand it aright we see that the rule of law as at any time established cannot be regarded as a static and final order. The claims of personality are the only claims which command an underivative and indefeasible loyalty, but they are exceedingly hard to interpret and perhaps still harder to harmonize within the social order. The perception of personal values is infinitely variant in response to differences of character, education, and social environment. Within a community it varies from age to age. Who, for example, would now hold that the value secured by the prevention of the theft of a sheep was worth the value lost by the hanging of a man? All these changes in ethical valuation must in time be reflected in the law. The law can never be static except at the cost of the social process. In fact the law never is static. Its changes are in part screened by the forms through which the changes are expressed, but they are so real and so great that a legal writer can venture the statement that there is 'hardly a rule of to-day but may be matched by its opposite of yesterday'.[1]

Here we pass to the other aspect of the rule of law. The rule demands universality within its limits, but it cannot imply that all human activities fall within these limits. As the state is not all-comprehensive neither is the law. The idea that every ethical principle can be translated into a rule of law is groundless. The idea that every positive obligation which derives from an ethical principle can be formulated in law or enforced by legal judgement is absurd. Men find themselves

[1] Cardozo, *op. cit.*, Introduction.

bound by honour or custom or discretion or some form of loyalty in countless cases where law cannot enter in to determine their conduct. No matter how fully we admit that the law includes not only legal precepts of a definite character but also 'a body of philosophical, political, and ethical precepts as to the end of law'[1] which the courts apply to particular cases and social situations as they arise, the form of legal remedy is such as to preclude this universal application. The law remains a framework of social order, an organic framework if we care to call it so, since it grows and changes, but only one agency of control among the great forces which express the nature of society.

The legal structure no doubt reflects the spirit of the community, but it also contains a spirit of its own. For the law-maker and the judge are not merely representative of the community. Their own professions breed respective attitudes. In particular, the judge, with his legal training, jealous for the consistency of the code, tenacious of precedent, and generally imbued with a traditional philosophy of conservative individualism, may represent an attitude at variance with the trend of the community. To the judge belongs the duty of interpreting and applying, and thus of modifying and making law. It is highly desirable that he should be vested with discretionary power, for otherwise the fixity of law would defeat the ends of justice. Within limits he is empowered not only to temper the law to the special situations under which it must be applied, but also to accommodate the hard legal principle to changing social needs. His attitude is therefore of great significance in the moulding of the spirit of the laws.

[1] Pound, 'Theory of Judicial Decisions', 6 *Harvard Law Review*, 1923.

It seems generally true that the spirit of the community reflects its underlying social and economic conditions more quickly than does the spirit of the law. This is particularly true in an age of transition or rapid development. Law is happiest when dealing with a static environment and for that reason is apt to assume that the environment is static. Or if it concedes that conditions change it still assumes that the principles of law are immutable. This, as Mr. Pound has pointed out, causes a conflict between juristic doctrine and political theory. 'While', he says, 'the American lawyer, as a rule, still believes that the principles of law are absolute, eternal, and of universal validity, and the common law teaches that principles of decision must be found, not made, the people believe no less firmly that law may be made, and that they have the power to make it. While to the lawyer the state enforces law because it is law, to the people law is law because the state, reflecting their desires, has so willed.' [1] The trouble about eternal principles is that, like dogmatic religions, they become antiquated and obstructive. The law, faced with new situations, applies ancient formulas. The history of the dealings of the courts with industrial labour is full of illustrations of the inadequacy of 'eternal principles'. Certain cases, such as the Taff Vale decision or, in America, the Danbury Hatters' judgement and the Buck's Stove and Range judgement, have thrown into strong relief the inability of the law to appreciate the new conditions of industrial life. It has taken rubrics belonging to an old order, such as that of 'conspiracy', and applied them to situations to which they were wholly inappropriate. Above all, it has emphasized the static

[1] *Yale Law Journal*, vol. xxii, December 1912.

relation between persons and property to the neglect of the dynamic relation between persons and function. The law has been at home in dealing with the rights of property, but it has been far less successful in dealing with the less material aspects of conduct and service, where rights must be attached, not to a substantial thing but to the functions which men fulfil in the life of the community.

One consequence has been a new limitation of the region included under the rule of law. Not only for its too slow and cumbrous and expensive operation, but also for its lack of adaptability and of sympathetic perception, the resort of law has been shunned in the settlement of certain forms of dispute, especially in the economic sphere. Some states have realized the difficulty and sought to meet it by the establishment of special ' industrial courts ', composed mainly of representative persons whose experience has been gained in the field of industry and not in the profession of law.[1] Their decisions are therefore not bound by the requirements of a definite legal code ; they are more free and more experimental, often more in the nature of a compromise than the stricter system of law would admit. But it is significant that even so, compulsory settlement has proved of very limited service—and compulsion is an essential element in a legal decision. The experience of Australia and New Zealand, often cited to the opposite effect, is far from conclusive.[2] The general verdict seems rather to be that expressed in the words of the Whitley Committee : ' We are opposed to any system of compulsory arbitra-

---

[1] Such as those established in Britain under the Industrial Courts Act of 1919, the adjustment boards of Germany, and so forth.

[2] See, for example, Rankin, *Arbitration and Conciliation in Australia*.

tion.'[1] In other words, it is still in most countries taken for granted that the law is not able, or not yet ready, to bring order into one of the most contentious areas of modern life, that of industrial relations.

Nor does this limitation apply only to the problems of labour and capital. There has arisen a tendency to settle other forms of economic dispute by internal agencies of a non-legal character. We might instance the experiments of the American moving picture industry in this direction. An important reason for such developments lies in the necessarily coercive character of legal settlement. A legal judgement is a disturbing influence. It operates as an external force. The forms of satisfaction which it offers, through the imposition of damages, through forced sales, injunctions, and so forth, bring an alien and abrupt pressure into the established order of business. If the disputants can get together and settle by their own machinery their differences, the result is not only less costly but also less disturbing. Of course there lies beyond such devices the appeal to the law. But the nearer appeal is found in a great number of cases to be the more satisfactory.

We are now in a position to estimate the degree and kind of universality which pertains to the ' rule of law '. It has, on the one hand, a quantitative limit because law itself can regulate only the external aspects of conduct and because the appeal to law always implies some definite hurt or damage of an assessable character due to the violation of the rule. On the other hand it has a quantitative limit inherent in its mode of adjustment. The justice which law administers is mainly, in Aristotle's

[1] *Report on Conciliation and Arbitration.*

terms, a ' distributive ' justice. It apportions and divides. It does not so much reconcile opposing claims as apportion to each its due. It can adjudicate between opposing interests only in so far as they are presented as exclusive. A more comprehensive *rôle*, it is true, is sometimes attributed to law. Thus Miss Follett, speaking of the ' creative area of law ', maintains that its function ' is not merely to safeguard interests ; it is to help us to understand our interests, to broaden and deepen them '.[1] This, however, is certainly not the particular or peculiar function of law. It is a function to which other agencies, such as those above mentioned, apply themselves more directly. And it is a function for the fulfilment of which the necessary methods of legal settlement render it less adequate than various other institutions which society has evolved.

These limitations are not to be understood as defects *in* the law. They are the necessary conditions of its peculiar and essential service. To perform that service law must be imperative and external. Only so can it establish sure foundations in the certitude of which men can build and rebuild the many mansions of society.

III

THE LAW AND THE STATE

The state is both the child and the parent of law. We have seen that there are two distinct forms of law corresponding to these two relationships. In a few countries, most notably in England, both forms appear to proceed from the same source. Whether the law is of a constitutional character or an ordinary legislative

[1] *Creative Experience*, ch. xvi.

enactment it is passed by the same parliament without distinction. In most countries, however, the difference is emphasized by the fact that a different procedure is requisite. Sometimes an entirely distinct body is called into being, as in the United States, for the establishment of constitutional laws. Sometimes the regular legislature enacts them but under special rules, requiring for example the joint assemblage of the two legislative houses, as in France, or a new general election and a two-thirds majority, as in Belgium. But whatever method is adopted, and even where no distinction at all is made in the form of legislation, the two kinds of law have a different character and above all an entirely different sanction. And we cannot appreciate the full significance of law or its relation to the state unless we take these differences into account.

The sanction of the ordinary political law is clear and definite. The state penalizes the offender against it, using if necessary the resort of compulsion. Such law is under the express protection of the state. The state creates its elaborate system of rights and obligations, and it ensures the right by enforcing the obligation. These laws are made by the state for and on behalf of the community. They determine, within their range, not so much the order of the state as the order of society. The state upholds them as an organ of society expressly devoted to this end. Thus it regulates the obligations of its members to one another in a multitude of private (as opposed to public) capacities. Such obligations the state can enforce because it distinguishes itself as a public agency from individuals or groups acting on their own behalf. The public *aspect* is here distinct from the private. The organization of the state has powers as an organization, and one of these is to make laws and to enforce them.

The state can enforce laws against any of its citizens, but can it enforce laws against itself? It can enforce laws against its particular agents, as any other association might do. It can make laws which assign political obligations to its officials, to the *personnel* of the executive or the judicature, and sanction these by penalties. Nor is there any logical difficulty to prevent the law from legislating on the duties of the law-makers and enforcing these against individual members of the government. The government as a whole can dissociate itself from an offending member. The right of compulsion is vested in it not as being a group of individuals but as an organ of society. So that if one member offend against it, it can discipline that member, no less than a ' private ' citizen, without losing its integrity. But if the organ itself violates the law on which it is established, what then? What sanction can be applied against the body which wields the sanction of the laws? *Quis custodiet ipsos custodes?*

This is the problem of constitutional law which the older theories of state-sovereignty ignored or failed to solve. Most modern constitutions explicitly ' guarantee ' certain rights to the citizens, freedom of speech, religious liberty, the right of association, the inviolability of private domicile, and so forth. Besides such general ' guarantees ' they lay down rules determinant of the structure of government, of its composition and election, of its modes of procedure, and of the relation of its parts to one another. The problem of sanction exists no less for a country like England which makes no formal distinction between ordinary and constitutional law-making. In each case the law 'guarantees' the citizen against certain exercises of power by government, but government itself alone has the exercise of power. It is true that in some states an authority is established above the ordinary legislature, a special body to which is assigned the business of amending the constitution or a court which can declare unconstitutional and void such measures of the legislature as it deems to violate the constitution. But this arrangement only throws the problem a little further back. The constitutional law defines the duties of an ultimate authority, or a final court. If the authority is really ultimate, the court really final, where is the sanction of the law which regulates it? Concerning this political firmament we must repeat the ancient question: 'Whereupon are the foundations thereof fastened, or who laid the corner-stone thereof?'

Looking especially at the English constitution Dicey attempts to solve the problem as follows. While there are, as he acknowledges, constitutional rules of supreme importance which are yet outside the cognizance of any court, they are nevertheless of such a character that the failure to observe them involves the government in a consequential violation of ordinary law. Thus, if the English government refused to summon parliament for more than a year this violation of constitutional principle would not be itself illegal. But the Mutiny Act would lapse and the conduct of the executive in enforcing order, collecting taxes, and so forth, would become illegal in consequence.[1] To remain within the law the government must here remain within the constitution. The solution is ingenious but inadequate. A government,

---

[1] See Dicey, *Law of the Constitution*, chs. xv and xvi.

even the English government, could violate certain fundamental constitutional principles, such as that guaranteeing the right of assembly, without involving itself in any illegality. Parliament could pass an act to this effect, and the courts would accept it, even though it violated a long-established 'convention' of the constitution. What would really prevent a government from so acting would be not the force of political law—which it makes and changes—but the force of public opinion, which is beyond its reach.

The refuge of the traditional doctrine of sovereignty resembles that to which perplexed theologians resorted when seeking to reconcile the 'free will' of man with the doctrine of divine omnipotence. It is a mystical answer which leaves the problem as it was. Just as God was said to 'limit' himself in creating the will of man, so the state in its omnipotence is conceived as limiting itself in assuring the liberties of its members. Since the authority of the state is ultimate, the constitutional law which binds it is the expression of its own will to be so bound. Out of its mere good will, to secure the purposes which it has set before itself, it denies to itself certain exercises of power and binds itself to observe certain principles of action. No outside power, no higher authority, exists which can say to it, 'thus far and no further'. But from out its own nature, by virtue of its own self-control, there issues the imperative, self-imposed and self-determining, of constitutional law.[1]

Like all such theories, this doctrine saves the logic of

---

[1] The same conception underlies, in respect of ordinary legislation, the advocacy of *laissez-faire*. Many a business man who abhors the 'interference' of the state in the economic sphere regards as rank heresy any suggestion that sovereignty itself is limited.

power at the price of reality. We may leave aside for the present the personification of the state which it involves, merely remarking that unless this assumed state-person were both disinterested and intelligent beyond the ways of common men, the guarantee that it gives against its own abuse of power would be so precarious as scarce to deserve the name of law. The doctrine might be apt enough as an interpretation of the hitherto existing relationship between states. What is called international law has depended on the willingness of each state to bind itself to observe certain rules in its dealings with other states. On that account international law has been far less secure than constitutional law. The guarantees which the latter provides have been valid and enduring, save in the relatively rare cases where a revolution or *coup d'état* has overthrown the order of the state. Why this difference? Is it not because there lies behind constitutional law another form of sanction altogether?

It might be said that we ought here to distinguish between the government and the state and regard constitutional law as binding, not the state, but the government. It binds the legislator in the making of law itself. Behind the legislature lies the ultimate sovereign. It has vested in the government certain powers, including the execution of the laws, but it has learned to make the government its trustee, and not its master. If the government were to violate the constitutional conditions of trusteeship, which are in part formulated as constitutional law, it would destroy the support on which it rests. The government has only a lease of authority, revocable by the sovereign which granted it. This sense of dependence on a greater will, the will of the people, is so strong and so well-assured in modern states that constitutional law does not need—nor in fact can it have—any other sanction.

There is undoubtedly truth in this argument. All governments are sensitive to public opinion, which makes and dethrones them. In the last resort obedience to law rests on the will to obey, supported as it is by all the sentiments and traditions of citizenship. Government applies the compulsion of law against individuals and minorities, but government would be powerless to do so unless the governed as a whole willed to obey the law, unless in the last resort they willed the law. *A fortiori*, if the will of the governed established the ordinary law which they themselves obey, it establishes the constitutional law which governments obey. If they sustain the laws which impose obligations on all, they can surely sustain the laws which impose obligations on the few, on the government. Nay more, is not this an essential though unstated condition of their loyalty, that the rules of law-making and law-administering and not merely the resultant laws, are such as they approve? Could they will obedience to the laws at all unless they maintained the structure of law-making? And when, as in most countries with written constitutions, certain rights are guaranteed to the citizens, and certain rules laid down which the government as such cannot amend or repeal, is not this an express recognition that the will of the state is greater than the will of the government and assigns to the latter definite limits which it must not overstep?

The distinction here drawn between the state and the government is a true one, but it does not save the omnipotence of the state. It is a significant fact that most written constitutions cannot be amended or repealed by our ' ultimate sovereign ', which we saw to be at most a majority will of the members of the state. This is a formal recognition of a fact which is true for every state. How can a majority be denied the right to change the guarantees of liberty ? Within the state there can be no will superior to that of a majority of its members. Must we not here resort to that final conception of a ' general will ' on which the state itself depends ? Must we not say that it is the community which here limits the state ? And is it not true that in every state, whatever the express terms of its constitution, there are certain established principles which no sovereign power would venture to annul ? At a later stage we shall return to this interpretation, which we regard as crucial for the understanding of the state.

Writers like Duguit [1] are able to content themselves with the distinction between state and government, or more strictly, between the government and the governed, because they deny that the state is anything more than a relation between the few and the many. They deny the state as a unity, associational or corporate. To us the state is on the other hand a specific association, owning a definite character which distinguishes it from all other associations but no less from the community itself.

One immediate consequence of this view may be noted. On the theory of state omnicompetence, as well as on the individualistic theory of the Duguit school, there cannot be such a thing as a formal ' right against the state '. If sovereignty is absolute, are not all such rights the expression of its will ? How then can the state recognize, how it can possibly enforce, rights against itself ? As an

[1] *Traité de Droit Constitutionnel, passim,* and especially vol. i, ch. vi.

act of grace and condescension it may suffer its subjects to sue for redress of injuries which itself has caused. And this indeed is the form, though scarcely the reality, of legal process in many countries in actions against the state. In England, for example, in cases involving breach of contract, the injured party may prefer to the ' Crown ' a petition of right of which the Crown will graciously take cognizance. But the form masks the significance of the action, which is that an actual right against the state is here admitted. Nor is it, on the other hand, simply a right against the government, a right, that is, established by the state against its agents. It is the state, and not the government, which makes contracts. Why should it not be responsible for these, just as, when any other association acts (as alone it can) through its accredited agents, it makes itself, and not merely the agents, responsible? Would it not therefore be simpler, as well as more realistic, to admit that the state is an association, that it has consequent liabilities and responsibilities, and that the affirmation of these liabilities can be secured only if rights are admitted against the state itself? Nor need we fear the objection that such rights would be sanctionless and therefore unmeaning, if we properly understand the dependence, not merely of the government but of the state itself, upon the will of the community.

The supreme importance of this understanding does not appear until we envisage the relationship between states. The state makes contracts, not only with its members, but also with other states. Here there is no question of distinguishing the act of government from the act of the state. When a government contracts a foreign debt it obviously binds the state, not merely itself. Shall we then say that because the sovereignty of the state is absolute it may repudiate, save as morally bound, the obligations which it thus creates? This has been the historical attitude of the state except in so far as it has been tempered by that other consideration which impels men in the absence of law, the fear of the consequences of lawlessness. But it is an attitude which is not inherent in the nature of the state, which, on the contrary, may be claimed to be inconsistent with it. This we shall see as we now turn to the last great division of law, that of international law.

IV

INTERNATIONAL LAW

Our conclusions in the preceding section enables us to view the question of international law from a new angle. If we admit the claim of constitutional law to the title of law, if only we admit that it imposes certain definite obligations on government which are as securely established as the obligations which political law imposes on the private members of the state, then we must also admit that other sanctions than mere enforcement, and no less valid, obtain in the political sphere. This removes half the difficulty of applying the term ' law ' to those further rules which are regulative of the conduct of states in relation to one another. It also suggests the way along which a completer sanction may be assured to international law, and the other half of the difficulty be also removed.

A fairly complex structure of international rules has been created as the result of the economic and social interdependence of peoples or nations. Without such rules modern civilization would indeed present a very extraordinary spectacle. All relationships which fell completely within the ambit of any one state would be subject to a highly developed system of law and order, while all relationships which linked one state with another would hang across the void, without order or security, save as either state could extend its might over the other. There would be separate state-spheres of intensive order, with chaos reigning between them, a chaos illuminated only by the fires of their collision.

International law is the system which orders the relations between states. No part of it hitherto has emanated from a legislature nor has it ever been enforced by a court coextensive with its range. But we need not on these accounts deny to it the general title of law. Common law does not emanate from the legislature. Constitutional law has no court coextensive with its range. International law requires in the first place—if it is to work as law at all, if, in other words, it is to establish ordered relations between states—an extension of constitutional law to a wider political sphere. It must reveal the constitution of the world of states.

As such, it has undoubtedly laid the foundations of a greater order. In the course of ages certain principles concerning the rights of a sovereign state in respect of others, such as treaty-rights ; concerning the recognized modes of acquiring territory ; concerning the high seas, coastal waters, and the great international waterways or straits ; concerning jurisdiction over nationals abroad ; concerning diplomatic and other agencies of communication—have been evolved and are accepted as governing the conduct of states in normal times. They constitute a foundation on which a large number of specific agreements have been built, facilitating the multifarious intercourse and commerce that knit the peoples of the earth, and in recent times asserting certain minimum standards necessary to prevent obvious dangers to the health and efficiency of the working population of all civilized countries. Here is an international order in the making, gradually adapting itself to the needs of an international society. Here, as always, society comes before the state. The state, obsessed with the thought of its jealous sovereignty, timorous with the fear of abdicating its historic claims of self-sufficiency, reluctantly and belatedly conforms, as in the end it always must, to the demands which the evolution of society imposes upon it.

We have said nothing of that part of international law—still ostensibly the greater bulk of it—which pretends to regulate not peace but war. That more labour should have been expended on rules of war than on rules of peace is significant of that false ideal of sovereignty and of inter-state relationship which has retarded the whole development of international law. The idea that war, the sheer supersession of law by force, should have a law of its own, is absurd in principle and disproved in practice. Mere force creates no rights and acknowledges none. War is not a game of chess between belligerents. It is a struggle of life and death, and its means are the agencies of destruction. Considerations of humanity forbid useless destruction, destruction which does not serve the ends of victory. But who can frame rules to determine the limits beyond which, in time of war, destruction ceases to be effective? And within these limits it is adding a new irrationality to war to discriminate between permissible and non-permissible agencies. If poison-gas is more effective than high explosives, on what grounds should a belligerent refrain from employing it? Even if we appeal to humanity, shall we not be answered that the greatest humanity lies in the more speedy victory or the prevention of the disasters of defeat? War cannot afford these nice discriminations, especially modern war in which the non-military population is engaged directly or indirectly in the conflict, making munitions or taking the places of the soldiers in the necessary tasks of civil life. Apart from certain rules regarding the declaration of hostilities, communications with the enemy, truces and armistices— conditions, that is, which do not belong to the actual conduct of warfare ; apart also from a few rules regarding the care of the sick and wounded and the treatment of prisoners of war ; the bulk of the ' law of war ' is not only irrational but is so constantly violated that it has no claim to be called law at all. It is totally different from the ' law of peace ', which does actually, in spite of its occasional failure, regulate the conduct of states.

If we understand the foundations of constitutional law, we have no difficulty in perceiving the genuine sanctions which in part already belong, and in full may yet be attached, to international law. The sanction of all law goes back to public opinion. If we consider political law, we shall see that there are certain agencies of definition and enforcement which are absent in the case of constitutional law. Hitherto international law has lacked not only these agencies but also the unity of opinion. Were the latter achieved, the former, in so far as they might be necessary, would follow.

The two great obstacles to this development have been

the accepted theory of national sovereignty and the principle of territorial possession. The obstacles, in other words, lie primarily in the prejudices of public opinion and not in objective conditions. The theory of sovereignty reflects the ideal of the self-sufficient nation-state, the final embodiment of authority and power whose imperious will may own moral obligations but is unbound by any other law save that which it makes itself. Its majesty brooks no limitations from without. Supreme in its own range, it surrenders nothing of its proud claims when it deals with other states. It belongs to no brotherhood of states. Fantastically it asserts itself to be ' the guardian of a whole moral world, but not a factor within an organized moral world '. So overweening is this state-philosophy that it refuses to admit even that a state can contravene the laws of morality. If the state kills, it is never murder.[1]

This doctrine, as we shall show in a later chapter, is false to the facts. It rests on the wrong view that there is no society except within the limits of each state. But the existence of international society is beyond dispute. Now, so far as society extends so far must some form of order extend. No one state can assure that order. States do in part recognize their function within a common system, and international law is the result. The idea that any one state can assure this international system is obsolete. The idea that any one state can assert its sovereignty against it is already condemned by public opinion. The doctrine of the absolute state has been

---

[1] So Bosanquet, *Philosophical Theory of the State*, ch. xi. For searching criticisms of this doctrine *see* ' Proceedings of the Aristotelian Society,' New Series, vol. xvi, *The Nature of the State in view of its External Relations*.

dethroned so far as the internal operations of government are concerned. It has been undermined in respect of external relations, although it is still seated upon the throne. If public opinion further liberates itself from a tradition no longer consistent with the facts of the case, there would be no inherent difficulty to prevent the bestowal upon international law of a sanction which the most bigoted philosopher might no doubt explain away, but which he could no longer deny outright.[1]

The other obstacle to the development of international law is the principle that states are ultimate owners of the territories which they organize. The earth is regarded as parcelled out between a number of political landlords. Each is the master of his own domain and everything within the domain is his usufruct. Such a conception leaves to international law little beyond questions of frontiers and transgressions. It is in part a heritage from feudalism, revived however by the modern development of the colonial system. A state may be said to own colonies, unsettled or undeveloped lands, when it can dispose of these at its will, when it reserves to its own nationals the rights of exploitation and of trade, when it lays effective claim to a territory not yet distributed out to individual owners, or when it holds sway over a country occupied by native races whose title to possession is subject to its suzerain control. But these are temporary situations which disappear in the process of development. At one time it could be said that England, i.e. the English state, ' owned ' Canada, i.e. the territory of Canada, but the statement is no

[1] Cf. Bosanquet's curious dialectic in ' Proceedings of the Aristotelian Society,' New Series, vol. xvii, *The Function of the State in Promoting the Unity of Mankind.*

longer true. It is very doubtful whether England can be properly said to ' own ' India, though for a different reason. Moreover it is a confusion to say that the English state owns England itself. The state has the right of ' eminent domain ', in the sense that it can take over the land or other property of the inhabitants on grounds of public advantage or necessity.[1] Even so, it is little more than the right to acquire property on reasonable terms, which is very different from prior ownership. When the political settlement of the earth is complete—a process already far advanced—territorial ownership in any strict sense can no longer be predicated of states. After the process of settlement a state can no longer sell to another a part of the territory over which it exercises jurisdiction, as Napoleon sold Louisiana to the United States.

The reason of course is that territory cannot in reality be doubly owned, both by its inhabitants and by the state. All that the state can eventually possess, apart from the equipment requisite for its public services, is a right of control within a given territory, a right vested in the state by, and as an organ of, the community. The recognition of this fact would remove a serious obstacle to the range and efficacy of international law. Exclusive and absolute property-owners, like strong men armed, may be conceived as standing apart from any common system of law, but agencies existing for the express purpose of assuring the external conditions of well-being cannot, in a world made one by a thousand links of civilization, fulfil their tasks unless they unite to ratify

---

[1] This right may itself be circumscribed, as it is under the Constitution of the United States and in terms of the decisions handed down by the Federal and State Courts. In England the rubric of ' eminent domain ' is less familiar and the power of the state over property is less defined, but the active principle is similar.

for one another the order which each also seeks to establish for itself.

International law requires for its fulfilment an international court, not merely for the jurisdiction of disputes, but as a rallying-point for international public opinion. A great advance has been made in this direction by the establishment, through the League of Nations, of a permanent Court of International Justice, with elected judges appointed for a considerable term of years. This is a marked development as compared with the earlier Hague Court of Arbitration which merely made provision for an *ad hoc* tribunal selected from a panel after the fashion generally adopted in cases of industrial arbitration. A standing court has far greater potentialities. Its permanence will enable it to establish a tradition and, given the support of public opinion, to extend its influence until resort to this tribunal becomes the unquestioned mode of procedure in the case of inter-state disputes.

What has hitherto been lacking is not the law but the court. Under the Statute establishing the Court of International Justice the sources of law are specified as being (*a*) international conventions, (*b*) international custom, (*c*) ' the general principles of law recognized by civilized nations ', and (*d*) ' judicial decisions and the teachings of the most highly qualified publicists of the various nations, as subsidiary means for the determination of rules of law '. But none of these sources is so binding as to prevent the court from applying, by agreement between the litigants, the principles of equity. The principles of international law are fundamentally the same as those of national law. The former, like the latter, must grow and develop in response to the spirit of each age and the changing conditions of society.

In conclusion, we must again insist that the only support and sanction necessary for the effective operation of international law is a broad-based public opinion. A court is a definite public institution around which opinion must rally. One great difficulty has been the absence of any international institutions of a public character. The diplomatic service by its very nature is withdrawn from the impact of public opinion. While the internal affairs of the state have become the direct concern of its citizens, its external affairs have been conducted by an agency entirely withdrawn from the influence of the ultimate sovereign. In its seclusion it has held fast to traditions alien to those which inspire the modern state. Such unexpected revelations of diplomatic ideals and methods as have resulted from the recent rude violations of the secrecy of foreign office archives offer a marked contrast to the ideals and methods which are operative within at least the more democratic states. The state in its internal regulation and the state in its external dealings have constituted a sort of double personality. The guardian of order within becomes the enemy of order without the state. This condition remains in so far as international law is ineffective. The character of the state achieves unity only in so far as everywhere it works through and is subject to law.

There is no question here of the establishment of a dead level of uniformity, such as many people foolishly envisage when they think of a universal reign of law. Law creates no such level within the state, and is still less likely to create it between states. Law as it finds its true function restrains the oppressive manifestations of that mere force which is a substitute for and often an enemy of intrinsic strength. In the liberty created by the order of law, between as within states, the genuine forces that animate civilization can alone find their fulfilment. Order is the foundation on which life builds, and order is precarious and hollow until international law is assured.

APPENDIX TO CHAPTER VIII

CLASSIFICATION OF THE TYPES OF POLITICAL LAW

POLITICAL LAW

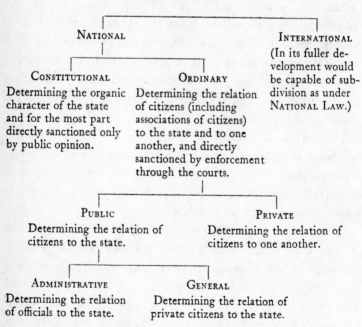

NATIONAL

CONSTITUTIONAL
Determining the organic character of the state and for the most part directly sanctioned only by public opinion.

ORDINARY
Determining the relation of citizens (including associations of citizens) to the state and to one another, and directly sanctioned by enforcement through the courts.

INTERNATIONAL
(In its fuller development would be capable of subdivision as under NATIONAL LAW.)

PUBLIC
Determining the relation of citizens to the state.

PRIVATE
Determining the relation of citizens to one another.

ADMINISTRATIVE
Determining the relation of officials to the state.

GENERAL
Determining the relation of private citizens to the state.

IX

POLITICAL GOVERNMENT AND THE ECONOMIC ORDER

I. ECONOMIC AND POLITICAL POWER

Now that the state has withdrawn from the control of religion, now that it has in general begun to refrain from acting as the arbiter of moral issues, the crucial question of politics concerns its relation to the economic order. So long as the focus of political power was also the focus of economic power, this question had little practical importance ; but we have pointed out that in the modern evolution of the state the two have grown not only distinct but in some measure separate. Yet, though separate, neither can leave the other alone. This struggle of power is very different from the medieval struggle of the ' spiritual ' and the ' secular ' sword. That issue was ended when each found its proper and exclusive field. Here no such solution is possible. Each acts and reacts incessantly upon the other, and must always continue to do so. Political government has lost its ancient finality. Economic power in turn asserts its sovereign claims. ' Government of your country ! ' cries the armament-maker with dramatic simplicity. ' Be off with you, my boy, and play with your caucuses and leading articles and historic parties and great leaders and burning questions and the rest of your toys. *I* am going back to

my counting-house to pay the piper and call the tune.'[1]
If this is a contrary exaggeration it is at least significant
of the spirit of the modern age. There have been, for
instance, certain flagrant cases where a government has
found itself paralysed by the action of an economic
organization. It has passed, say, a law prohibiting strikes,
and when strikes took place it has been powerless to
enforce the law. Or the government has capitulated to
economic pressure, such as a strike of railwaymen or
miners, and enacted legislation which they and not it
desired. Or it has yielded to the less overt demands of
a strong group of capitalists and framed its policy in
accordance with their wishes.[2] Or it has been impeded
by the economic resistance of a politically powerless
community, such as the Indian *swaraj*. Or again it has
confessed the impotence of its proper political weapon
by entering into alliance with one economic power as
a means of combating another.

Political power is formally superior. It can formally
decree the conditions and limits of economic power. If
other methods fail, it can take over the reins of direct
control or even ' nationalize ' any part of the economic
structure. But here too the form of power misleads.
Political authority rests on a unity of will which limits
its effective range, and it is encumbered by the fact that
any action which alienates any section of public opinion
weakens the hold of the government. With the cross-
divisions of interests, particularly economic interests,
which occur in our present society, any drastic legislation

---

[1] Shaw, *Major Barbara*, Act III.
[2] Witness the influence of the Comité des Forges of France in the
determination of reparations policy, in respect, e.g. of the deliveries
of coke.

is a precarious proceeding. All governments depend simply on a margin of strength, represented by the balance of effective opinion in their favour. An act which reduces this margin weakens its authority entirely out of proportion to the turnover of opinion. Moreover, governmental action within the state is overt and subject to all the risks of an extended publicity, greatly enhanced as they are by the fact that it is the business of an organized opposition to present that action in the least favourable light. Again, the last resort of political power is coercion, coercion of an external and physical character, and we have already shown the narrowing range of mere enforcement. We need only reflect on the general failure of systems of compulsory arbitration in the case of industrial disputes, even when a preponderant public opinion supported them, to realize the limits of state control. The struggle of the United States Government with monopolistic trusts offers another significant illustration, the more so because the economic power of the latter was applied, not merely to resist the political power, but to weaken it from within. Economic power has a singleness and concentration of aim which political power can rarely achieve.

The syndicalists go so far as to pretend that economic power can afford to ignore altogether that of the state. This also is a false extreme. We must not minimize the potency of the state. The fierce resistance which economic interests raise to certain of its activities, no less than their eagerness to capture the state for their own ends, witnesses to its proper and peculiar might. The power that alone ordains universal conditions need never fear to be dispossessed. But economic power also has its peculiar advantage. Economic power means direct control over the income, the very means of livelihood, of those subject to it. It means direct control over material resources, over employment, over markets, over the supply of credit, over price, over competition. It means the power of demand, based on the control of supply. It is hierarchical, emanating from and creating inequality. Its foundations lie in those conditions of life and environment which render men unequal and different, whereas the state discovers its foundations in those no less eternal conditions which evoke the claim of equality.

Economic power is swift and untrammelled, spontaneous and endlessly variable. Political power is slower and more rigid, amenable indeed to social change, but so broad-based and tradition-bound that it responds only to movements on a great scale which have already pervaded the life of the community. The economic order feels the impact of every social change before it touches the political. Political power must act upon the whole community, if it acts at all. Economic power can act at the nearest centre and turn wherever it will. Political power has determinate frontiers, economic power has the freedom of the world. The economic network covers the earth with its unbroken strands, woven most thickly where civilization is most advanced. The state, by tariff regulations, embargoes, and other devices, impedes this ceaseless weaving, which if left alone proceeds with little regard for the rigid lines drawn between one state and another. Here we have a good illustration of the difference between economic and political power, the former acting freely in every direction, the latter imposing one determinate mode of unity and separation. Economic power is protean and multi-centred, whereas political power is stolid and centralized.

It follows that political frontiers are never conterminous with economic ones, if indeed we can speak of economic frontiers at all. By means of tariff-regulations the state often seeks to circumscribe economic activities as far as possible within its own political bounds, but its success at best is very partial and even so is achieved at the cost of certain economic interests within its territory. If it benefits, say, the steel-makers, it injures, say, the ship-building industry. If it benefits certain industrialists, it injures the agriculturists, or vice versa. If it aids the home manufacturer, it hurts the importer and the exporter. If it aids the producers, it hurts the consumers. The intrinsic character of economic power is such that it cannot by any manipulation of control be made to coincide with political power. This fact becomes increasingly obvious as the prosperity of a country grows. For on the one hand its people draw more and more upon the resources of the whole world, and on the other they invest their surplus wealth in the development of other countries than their own. The partnership of citizens becomes distinct from the partnership of financiers or shareholders or business men, for the latter ceases to be confined within the circle of the former. This is one aspect of that vast differentiation of interests which the state has been so reluctant to admit. The ancient tradition of the identity of the two spheres is still strong enough to work great damage upon both. Men trained in the political notions of a bygone age and supported by the prejudices of the hour can still, in the name of the exclusive and sovereign state, cut through the arteries of economic life which binds each to the other. The treaty of Versailles offers a sufficient illustration.

There can never, of course, be any such demarcation

of sphere as will assign economic concerns to economic associations and political concerns to the state. The solution arrived at in the problem of church and state is quite impossible here. We must remember that economic and political power are two distinct means of achieving the same ends. They are both agencies to ends beyond themselves; they are alike preconditions of human welfare. They overlap and intersect. They are alike external and secondary means. They are alike universal means, because nothing that men seek can be attained without economic power and nothing that men seek can be attained without political power. All other objects that men pursue offer direct satisfaction as well as indirect. But economic and political agencies exist only for their results. They are solely instruments, whose service lies entirely outside themselves. The family, the church, the club, all the associations of common living or of friendship or of culture, bear their fruits within themselves; but the state and the economic order are mechanisms only, eternally necessary because of the eternal necessities which lie between men and the objects of their desire. For that reason we think of them primarily in terms of power.

For the same reason neither of them can ever be separate from the other. The state cannot abandon the economic field, because within it some forms of universal regulation, such as only law can secure, are desirable and even necessary. The extremest advocate of *laissez-faire* would admit, for example, that it is expedient for the state to establish and assure a legal currency. Nearly every one would admit that certain economic services of a universal character are best monopolized by the state or its subdivisions such as county or municipality.

We might instance the postal service or the water-supply. The lines we draw must be determined by considerations of competence, not by a sheer demarcation of interests. There is little doubt, for example, that no agency is so well fitted as the state to collect and publish all manner of statistical information concerning economic conditions. On the other hand, there is little doubt that the state is wholly unfitted to conduct the business of retail selling. Where common standards are socially desirable, and can be the successful subjects of legislation, there is the place for the regulation of the state. Where individual enterprise and experiment are socially desirable, there the state should refrain from regulation. Since both common standards and the enterprise of individuals are valuable things in every economic sphere, the function of the state is not constitutive but regulative. In other words, the state properly intervenes, not to conduct the economic business of the country, but to uphold social standards, to prevent exploitation and manifest injustice, to remove the needless hazards of the economic struggle, to assure and advance the general interest against the carelessness or selfishness of particular groups, to control monopolies so that the public may be protected against their exactions, to see that the future well-being of the country is not jeopardized by the pursuit of immediate gains. The range of state-action is not to be defined by any eternal criterion. It must vary with the conditions, with the need for it and with its own capacity. There is hardly any subject which men are less willing to consider calmly and clearly than this. Their fears or their hopes are so bound up with the action or inaction of the state that they substitute sweeping denials or passionate promises for reasoned judgements. Nevertheless the state is learning, as its successes and its failures are slowly revealed through the mists of prejudice, here also to find its sphere.

The great internal struggles of the modern state have centred round just this question, what the extent and character of its control of, or participation in, the economic order should be, and out of these struggles have come its chief developments in recent times. One of the main issues has been that of the protective tariff. A protective tariff makes a double appeal, first to the general spirit of nationalism, since it seeks to restore the unity of the political and the economic area, then to the particular interests which by its aid are sheltered in the home market from foreign competition. But it is resisted by the great economic influences which stimulate the fruitful extension of the division of labour over all the earth and which care nothing for the rigorous lines which sever state from state. Another vital issue concerns the function of the state in establishing and upholding conditions and standards of living against the competitive stress of modern industrial life. The small isolated family of our society has lost the support of the coherent kin-group. The instinctive solidarity of the older community no longer comes to the aid of the dispossessed and the weak. New hazards have entered together with new opportunities. Accident, disability, unemployment, often exploitation, menace the livelihood of the industrial masses. Against these they organize, creating a new form of economic power. But they also appeal to the state, and the state has moved through conflict to new functions of control.

We should in this connexion always remember that economic power rides through inequality to new inequality; that its methods of competition and monopoly and bargaining are methods which set the interest of one against that of another, the relative gain of one against the relative loss of another; that the economic order is also an arena of struggle, however mitigated by co-operation within it. In this struggle the common interest may suffer grievous hurt. The weaker are driven to the wall and are subjected to privation and oppression, which are evil not only for themselves and for their families, but for the whole of society. But the state stands for the common interest. Its broader foundations are the likenesses, not the differences, of men. It gives men citizenship, which is a common possession. It assumes the role of protector, and in so far as it is true to this great office it tempers for the common good the inequalities and the perils of economic struggle. That such action is desirable and that it can succeed, the history of industrial legislation in the last hundred years sufficiently reveals.

In its external relations the state most obviously makes political power the minister of directly economic aims. The sheer political ends of extended sovereignty and dynastic or nationalistic prestige make effective appeal no longer so much in themselves, but as a means to economic advantage. The ambition for colonies and protectorates and mandates and spheres of influence is itself motived mainly by the desire for controlled markets or new sources of raw materials or natural products. Between independent states most treaties and conventions are forms of economic bargaining, dealing with tariff concessions, trading facilities, and similar advantages. The state has of course a peculiar control over the economic relations between its members and those of other states, a control which increases with the growth of economic internationalism. Thus there has developed between countries an elaborate nexus of debts and credits. Sometimes a state itself borrows or lends abroad, but more commonly the borrowing is on account of smaller public bodies or of private corporations, and nearly always the transaction takes place through banking houses which place the loan with private creditors. Nevertheless the government of the lending country exercises direct or indirect control over these foreign loans. Unless it assents the transaction will not take place, for the financial houses, in case of doubt, find it expedient, even if not obligatory, to consult the foreign office. For long periods, for example, the English money market was closed against Russian loans, because of the attitude of the English government. The control over foreign loans puts a formidable instrument of policy in the hands of the governments of the more wealthy countries.

If the state cannot leave the economic order to its own devices, still less is it possible for economic forces to ignore the state. They may proclaim ever so loudly the principles of *laissez-faire*, but when they cry, ' Let us alone to pursue our aims ', they do not address to themselves the reciprocal of that command, they do not promise in turn to cease exerting influence on the government of the state. In the first place, the state must raise taxes, and the manner as well as the amount of taxation is a lively concern of all economic interests. All forms of taxation, no matter what principle of fairness or equity is invoked, affect the distribution of wealth ; some forms, particularly the tariff, combine the raising of revenue with a definite economic policy. But in fact, every action of the state has economic consequences, and economic interests are always at work seeking to determine its action. The very fact that economic interests are opposed and unequal causes them to appeal to the state for their respective reinforcement. Whether it be wage-earners striving for better conditions of labour, or employers resisting trade-unionism, whether it be producers forming a 'combine' or consumers opposing high prices, whether it be capitalists attacking socialism or socialists attacking capitalism, they all, whatever their protestations, are anxious to control the great engine of the state. This is abundantly evident in the alinement and activity of political parties. Differences of economic interest and status are the chief determinants of party differences. The great cleavages of modern society are economic, not racial or cultural, and from them political parties derive their vitality, their permanence, almost their very being.

What gives its peculiar quality to the modern state, perhaps more than anything else, is the fact that the centres and areas of economic power do not coincide with those of political power. Democracy gives to the working classes a preponderant voting power, but it does not thereby confer upon them, as was hoped by its protagonists, and dreaded by its opponents, a similar degree of economic power. Political strength may be associated with economic weakness. The opposite condition may also, though more rarely, be found. Strong economic interests may in certain situations fail to exercise control over public opinion, and may in fact alienate it instead. The economic strength of the great monopolistic industries of the United States could not prevent the passage of legislation against monopolies. But even so they could evade what they could not resist. It is only under the conditions of a prodigious revolution, such as the Soviet rising, that political power can trample economic power under its foot, and then at an enormous cost. Economic power has many weapons and political power has few. Political power must fight in the open, economic power has the advantage of secrecy. Economic power, once established, has a single and definite aim, political power is composite and easily divided. Economic power can scarcely be corrupted, because what it seeks it seeks only for itself, because also there are scarcely any means of corruption but its own. But political power at all stages, whether belonging to a newspaper or a party or a government, is subject to the constant and sometimes insidious influence of wealth.

Yet the two powers never coincide. Wealth may buy and control the organs of opinion, but the sense of divergent interest will survive and find expression. On the other hand, the growing power of organized labour, in some vital industry such as transportation or mining, may compel an unsympathetic government to yield to its desires, but the legal enactment proves too rigid for the changing situation or may be defeated by the more subtle devices of capital.[1] Moreover, the political structure responds only after a time-interval to the economic process. Great political changes are generally achieved all at once or by sudden steps—they are there-

[1] It is significant that the most formidable exercise of the economic power of labour, the general strike, has never so far succeeded when the issue was an economic one. We might instance the general strike of 1903 in Holland and of 1909 in Sweden, and the semi-general strike of 1913 in New Zealand. It has occasionally achieved some success when the issue was political, as the general strike of 1893 in Belgium for universal suffrage or that in Germany at the time of the Kapp *Putsch*.

fore harder to bring about than economic changes.
The latter may come gradually, even imperceptibly,
whereas political changes take place, in the main,
through the deliberate and concerted resolution of
a group large enough and strong enough to control
the state.

II

THE STATE AND THE ECONOMIC LIFE: RETROSPECT AND PROSPECT

The demarcation of the economic from the political
order was part of a great movement of social liberation.
In the historical process the pressure of authority over
the thoughts and activities of men was relaxed. They
learned to think thoughts which were not the thoughts
of all the tribe. They learned to act in ways which
were not the expression of binding customs. Of this
liberation one great aspect was their deliverance from
the sheer subjection and immobility imposed by a life
wholly dependent on the soil, on the immediate products
of the small area which each family or each group cultivated or ranged over. In old times trade brought this
liberation for some, and the fruits of conquest or extortion
bestowed it upon others. But it was only as industrial
capital developed that the economic life began to claim
a real autonomy. Capital was mobile. Its ownership
was not, like that of land, the concomitant and direct
consequence of political power. It was created by the
enterprise and inventiveness of individuals or groups.
The restless energy of capitalism broke the moulds of
custom. It contained a potentiality of extension and
reproduction unknown in previous economic stages. In

this sense the words of Marx are true that 'capital is a live monster that is fruitful and multiplies'. The value of the instruments of production came to surpass that of the land, as well as that of the current stocks of goods to which they were applied.[1] Thus was born an economic might which overthrew the ancient unity of power.

Formerly there were struggles *within* the political system as changing conditions altered the distribution of wealth. The new wealth of commerce claimed to share authority with the old wealth of land. The middle classes, gaining economic opportunity, sought political privileges. The money-power of the commons was a lever for their political elevation. The character of the state adjusted itself to the impact of economic forces. Oligarchy broadened to incorporate within itself the *nouveaux riches* or was transformed when a subordinate class organized its economic strength. But these struggles in themselves involved no new principle. The issue was rather one of the constitution of the governing classes, of the admission and absorption into them of new elements. The result of the conflict was to assure and re-establish the unity of political and economic dominance. This unity always characterized the class-state. In it the classes that were subordinate politically were also subordinate economically. The governing classes were also economic classes, as under feudalism. Even the estate of the clergy, in so far as it participated in government, had the distinct attributes of a class economically powerful.[2] The hierarchy of estates, the nobility higher and lower, the clergy, the propertied

[1] Cf. Marshall, *Industry and Trade*, I. iv. 3.
[2] Cf. Beard, *Economic Basis of Politics*, ii.

burgesses, represented degrees of economic power, below which came the propertyless masses, the peasants, and the proletariate.

The onset of modern capitalism brought a new condition. So long as trade and finance remained the chief sources of wealth apart from land, the class which was thereby enriched still sought power and prestige through political avenues. Thus the ambition of the English merchants of the seventeenth and eighteenth centuries was to buy land, to acquire the status of a ' gentleman ', and to establish relations, matrimonial and social, with the dominant landed classes. ' The merchants could only obtain political power and social position by becoming landowners.' [1] But industrial capitalism brought changes too vast and too decisive for the ancient order. The owners of cotton-factories and steel-mills did not need to knock at the doors of power—they were already inside. Large populations depended directly for their livelihood on the processes which they controlled. Power, said Harrington in his *Oceana*, goes with ownership. Assuredly it goes with the ownership of the means of living, and the industrial revolution meant that ever-increasing multitudes came to depend far more on the instruments of capital than on the land.

Why then did not the capitalists simply take over the political role of the landowners and restore in this way the ancient unity of power ? There were two reasons, both witnessing to that great social differentiation which accompanied the capitalistic revolution. In the first place the landed class had a unity of interest, a solidarity, which the capitalist classes did not enjoy. The economic differentiation which accompanied the rise of the

[1] Toynbee, *The Industrial Revolution*, v.

capitalists created oppositions of interest within their ranks. Competition and the struggle for monopoly divided them. The interest of the owners of raw materials was disparate from that of the manufacturers. The interest of the trader and the shipper was at variance with that of the home-producer. The new power of finance sought control over the power of industry. The inequalities of the economic order grew more varied and more confusing. It was relatively easy for a land-owning class to agree on political policy, say on a tariff, but it was far harder to unify the political demands of capital. Moreover, the new division of labour gave to the economically subject classes an opportunity to assert themselves which they never possessed before. They learned the potentiality of organization. Always the world had depended on their toil. Now they made this dependence an effective economic weapon against the owners of capital. Governments might pass Acts against combination of workers, but they could not prevent the spread of ideas among a compact proletariate nor the concerted withdrawal from work which new forms of organization made possible. For the first time in history a type of economic power arose which was divorced from the ownership or the control of property. The industrial revolution had taken from the workers, when the machine was substituted for the tool, the ownership of the instruments and materials with which they worked. But in return it gave them this potent immaterial weapon, a power that not only did not depend on property but in fact was the more untrammelled because of its very detachment from ownership.

The existence of this new power greatly modified the attitude and the action of government. The capitalists did not become a governing class in the sense in which the landowners had been. They exerted of course a strong influence on government, but they were not, as by a kind of natural right, the rulers of the state. Their property-power was not spontaneously translated into political power. They had either to fight against, or ally themselves with, the classes which owned little or no property. Government was thus a resultant or a compromise. The assurance of the old class-structure was lost. But in consequence the claims of the common welfare became audible through the clash of interests. In the old days the landlords had generally been able not only to protect their special interests but freely to extend them, as in the early enclosures. Similarly, the guilds had been perfectly able to dominate their markets and control their crafts for their particular purposes. Now each interest had to plead its cause before the greater tribunal of the electorate, and whatever its motives, must present its aims and win its ends in the name of the common good.

This much at least can be said of democracy, that it imposes on even the most powerful interests the necessity of appealing for the support of the public. There is no longer any *direct* identification between government and wealth or government and social prestige. Consequently the class-structure of society loses its definition and rigidity. Social and economic superiority must struggle, and may struggle in vain, for a corresponding political advantage. In the earlier stages of this development, for example in the age of Walpole, wealth was able to buy political power, but the further extension of the suffrage defeated this method. In any case it could not compete against the promises of the demagogue and the rewards of service which he could offer to his supporters—though these devices in turn proved of comparatively little avail except where public opinion was grossly unenlightened. Generally speaking, the only way to political power in the modern state has become the persuasion of the public. To this end wealth too devotes itself, its chief weapon being its ability to buy and control great organs of opinion. But its efficacy in this respect may easily be exaggerated. Opinion forms spontaneously and has many modes of expression. The great organs of opinion, particularly the great newspapers, may exploit the prejudices of the people but they cannot run counter to them. They are expensive instruments and depend entirely for their success on the support of those to whom they address themselves. A body of opinion creates a newspaper rather than a newspaper a body of opinion. The press can confirm and strengthen trends of opinion already formed. In matters concerning which the source of information is exclusive and privileged, such as foreign relations, it is particularly effective. For this reason governments are apt to cultivate the press especially in the exposition of their foreign policy.[1] But great movements of opinion rise and grow in seeming independence of the efforts to control or repress them. The rise of socialism in Europe offers abundant illustration. Public opinion is in the last resort the expression of the character of the public.

One consequence is that capital, for all its economic

[1] Thus in 1924 the French Premier Poincaré, according to press dispatches dated 27th Nov. of that year, asked for a credit of six million francs as a secret fund for the dissemination of French news abroad. The Iswolski correspondence throws a somewhat lurid light on the uses to which secret propagandist funds may be devoted.

power, has had to assume a defensive attitude in politics. It has been fighting to retain the advantages of economic superiority against the pressure of the classes who seek to diminish it by legislation. There are weaknesses in its legal foundations, and about these the struggle centres. Thus the stability of capitalism depends on the inheritance of wealth, and the state by its death duties and succession duties has accepted a principle which endangers that stability. There are many who urge that the state should proceed much farther in this direction, advocating for example the abolition of the right of inheritance over all except a moderate amount of property, with special consideration for direct heirs.[1] The state's taxing power in general is an object of fear to capitalism. The business of the state has assumed vast proportions, and in addition it has contracted enormous debts, though mostly as a result of the wealth-destroying operations of war. On both accounts it has been compelled to extend the range of taxation. Inevitably this process of taxation has become an engine of social control, especially as the need of income has driven the state to graded, selective, and finally progressive taxation.[2] Capitalism opposes the extension of the business of the state, especially in the sphere of 'social legislation', opposes taxation as a means of achieving social change, and particularly opposes what it regards as the discriminating legislation which falls more heavily on the wealthier classes. Issues are thereby raised of the gravest importance for the future direction of the state.

[1] Cf. e.g., Dalton, *Inequality of Income*, Pt. IV.

[2] The term 'progressive' is used in the technical sense, referring to taxation, such as the supertax on incomes, which exacts more than a proportional share from wealth of progressively larger amounts.

Capitalistic power, faced with these and other menaces from without, has sought to consolidate itself from within. To this end it has developed the corporate form of organization. We cannot here do more than refer to the remarkable achievements of this system of control. It has enabled the active capitalist to direct far more capital than he owns, while giving to a wide circle of investors a stabilizing interest in the great concentrations thus effected. It has separated financial control from technical management, thus bestowing greater power on capital as such and permitting it to combine and unify its operations over diverse regions of industry, trade, and commerce. It has enabled the strong and highly centralized agencies of banking, investment, insurance, and other forms of finance to determine, through interlocking directorates and other devices, the policies of business.[1] It has transmuted into present capital the mere prospect of earning power and the invisible assets of the 'going concern', so that the very favour and the custom of the public, as well as the charters and franchises once granted by the state, are turned into the substantial gains of the captains of industry, by the same process which makes them the 'vested interests' of a far wider circle. Above all, it has created an impersonal entity, anonymous and elusive, self-perpetuating and potentially immortal, under the form of which the real owners of economic power can achieve a security and permanence of control unknown in the world before. Thus the central power of capital, grown more mobile and more pervasive, dominates and

---

[1] Cf. the report of the Pujo Committee as to conditions in the U. S., popularly presented by Brandeis in *Other People's Money*. But Mr. Veblen may be right in holding that the 'massive interests' need no longer to depend on formal devices of this sort. See his *Absentee Ownership*, ch. xii.

directs for its own purposes the productive activities of the community.

The fluctuating eccentricity of economic and political powers could not be better illustrated than by the resulting situation. The growth of the economic corporation has killed the principle of *laissez-faire*. Its might for good and evil is too great to be 'let alone'. It cannot refrain from influencing the policies of the state, nor can the state, without denying its *raison d'être*, the common interest of its members, refrain from the task of regulation. The consumer appeals to the state for protection against monopoly, the worker demands safeguards for labour, the small business man cries out against 'unfair competition', while 'big business' seeks tariffs against the foreigner. The state, feeling the constant impact of opposing economic forces, cannot stand still. It must act as the trend of public opinion directs. In general it must, in the measure of its democratization, act as a moderating influence to temper the inequalities which form the essential condition of economic power.

It should be observed that the executive and judicial functions of the state are thereby greatly extended in comparison with the legislative. Sometimes the modern state assumes entire control over railroads, telephones, telegraphs, and other 'public utilities', but even when it shrinks from that step it sets up commissions and boards to undertake the work of regulation. These commissions and boards are endowed with very considerable powers of investigation and supervision, having generally, under the conditions provided by law, the right of controlling standards of service, rates, and other charges, and the issuance of securities by the corporations concerned. One of the most illuminating conflicts of economic and political power is being waged upon the question of the composition and the authority of political commissions appointed to supervise the greater and more monopolistic corporations of the economic world. Thus, of one of the most recently developed monopolies, that providing the supply of electricity, the Governor of Pennsylvania has gone so far as to say : ' As Pennsylvania and the Nation deal with electric power, so shall we and our descendants be free men, masters of our own destinies and our own souls, or we shall be the helpless servants of the most widespread, far-reaching and penetrating monopoly ever known. Either we must control electric power, or its masters and owners will control us.' [1] It should again be observed that the passage of certain acts of ' social legislation ', such as health-insurance Acts, workmen's compensation Acts, unemployment Acts, and so forth, itself necessitates the establishment of permanent boards of administration, new semi-detached sub-departments of the executive possessed of considerable discretionary power. These boards and commissions form as it were a series of strategic political outposts within the economic field.

There is another aspect of the eccentricity of political and economic power which deserves especial comment. Traditional ideas are apt to linger in the sphere of international relations when elsewhere they have been discarded. It is so in regard to this question. It is still a prevalent view that political power carries with it, in the relations between states, a corresponding economic advantage. But political power in its external aspect is

[1] Governor Pinchot's Message of Transmittal introducing the Report of the Giant Power Survey Board, 1925.

a costly parade of force, imposing a heavy burden on the country which becomes an additional tax on its productivity and a clog on the competitive strength of its industries. The chief argument for the association of political and economic power turns, however, on the advantage of imperialistic dominion. It is claimed that political ownership is equivalent to economic usufruct. This argument, as we have already seen, can apply only to what may be strictly termed ' colonies ' or dependent possessions. As soon as a former ' colony ' becomes autonomous, like Australia or Canada, it consults its own economic interests with relatively little consideration for political ties. The imports of Canada from the United States are thrice as great as from the whole of the British Empire.[1] If on the other hand we turn to the true ' colonies ' we find that the economic advantage of political possession, save for a few favoured concessionaries, is greatly exaggerated in the general conception. According to the trade statistics of the year before the war, ' if the United Kingdom were able to reserve the whole of its tropical African possessions as a market for its manufactures, and as a source of raw materials for its industries, the whole of these possessions would only have provided a market for two per cent. of British exports, and would have furnished only two per cent. of British imports. But no country, of course, has ever succeeded in such a monopolistic exploitation of its possessions, and in actual fact these British African possessions furnished a market for only one per cent. of British exports and provided less than one per cent. of British imports. Their

---

[1] Thus for the twelve months ending February 1924 the imports from the British Empire were valued at 198 millions of dollars as compared with imports of 604 millions from the United States.

economic importance to British trade and industry was about the same as that of Chile ; as a market for British manufactures the Argentine Republic was nearly three times more important and as a source of British imports was six times more important.' [1] And the Argentine has imposed on Britain no costs of acquisition or ownership.

In conclusion, we may seek to estimate, very tentatively, the trend of development to which the revealed character of these respective powers commits the modern state. There are some thinkers who envisage a re-unification of the economic with the political focus. This is the attitude of the state socialists, and also, under a different formula, of the guild socialists. Our whole argument makes for the contrary conclusion, endeavouring to show that the demarcation of economic and political powers is part of the general process of social evolution. The conflicts of economic and political power lead some thinkers to postulate a unity of authority which will remove them, just as the conflicts of religious and political claims led men to the doctrine of theocracy or to the opposite theory of Erastianism. But the problems of differentiation are never solved that way. Not identity, but harmony, must be the solution, where a solution is possible. It is interesting to note that Sovietism in its original form was also a programme of economic and political unification, but the necessities of the crisis, even in a relatively undeveloped society, prevented its consummation.

How far indeed the two powers can be harmonized is one of the most difficult and most fascinating of questions. The answer will depend mostly upon the

[1] Leonard Woolf, *Economic Imperialism* (Swarthmore International Handbooks), ch. ii.

direction of economic development. The economic system is very far from having attained an equilibrium comparable to that of the state. It is beset by sheer internal conflicts and particularly by the great cleavage of labour and capital. If the rise of the standard of living in industrial countries which characterized the eighty or more years prior to the war should continue, it will tend to lessen that cleavage. The working man who is able to save and establish a reserve fund, however small, is drawn in a measure into the same system which includes the great capitalist and generally becomes no less opposed than the latter to radical economic change. This is well illustrated by the situation in the United States. If then the fruits of the industry of generations should no more be wasted by war, there is a reasonable likelihood, especially in view of the spread of ' birth-control ', that with the reduction of poverty the economic order will achieve a greater integration.

The operation of the state tends in the same direction. Ever since the political enfranchisement of the working classes the net result of its economic activity has been the gradual establishment of minimum standards, in the form of insurance against ill-health, accident, and unemployment, minimum wage measures, family allowances, old age pensions, the prohibition of child-labour, the regulation of hours and working conditions. Were the economic order more integrated a greater part of this control would be assumed directly by the economic agencies themselves, leaving to the state not so much the determination of such standards as their protection and co-ordination.[1] In any event the trend is clear. The steps

[1] Thus the Report of the Whitley Committee, envisaging a greater economic integration through industrial councils, went so far as to say:

which have been taken in this direction can scarcely be retraced. The community, as well as the classes directly benefited, come to realize the importance of measures which assure its members from the waste and degradation and blind revolt of economic helplessness. The state has finally taken stand as the great protector of the commonwealth. Once a reasonable minimum is assured to all the members of the community, such that none shall suffer from the mere lack of the bare physical necessities of nutrition, shelter, warmth, and health, society itself takes on a new and fuller meaning. Above that margin the economic arena is freed from the worst of its social perils without losing its potentialities of social benefit. When men are striving to save themselves from drowning it is a very different thing from the contest of swimmers to win a prize. An advancing civilization is consistent with, and may in fact depend upon, the struggle for the material prizes of life, but it is not consistent with the struggle for life itself.

The state safeguards the economic arena, but does not and cannot destroy it. Its activity, as for example in the control of monopoly, is to protect the contestants, whether from one another or from external dangers. Here, as everywhere else, its business is that of protection, of order, and of furtherance of the common interest within the limits of its means. But because the economic power both creates and rests on inequality its task is here more difficult and perhaps greater than in any other sphere.

' It appears to us that it may be desirable at some later stage for the state to give the sanction of law to agreements made by the councils, but the initiative in this direction should come from the councils themselves.'

BOOK THREE

FORMS AND INSTITUTIONS

X

FORMATION AND DISSOLUTION

I. THE RISE AND FALL OF STATES

In this chapter we must seek to interpret the impressive historical fact that states begin and end. Most of the states of the modern world are only a few centuries old, while the few that have seemingly persisted from an earlier epoch have so changed their institutions and frontiers that they have only in name endured. Even in our own day new states, like Czechoslovakia, have come into being. Sometimes a state has perished and, like Poland, been re-created. But what survives of the smaller states or the one empire of the Middle Ages? And if we go back farther in historical retrospect we see a long series of ancient empires which rose on the ruins of their predecessors and themselves utterly passed away. 'Sceptre and crown must tumble down'—such is the reflection which history urges upon us. How must we understand this mortality of states? How do they come into being? And why do they disappear?

The births of particular states admit of sufficiently simple explanation. The old writers distinguished between ' commonwealths by institution ' and ' commonwealths by acquisition ', indicating the fact that some states are born in peace and others in war. We have seen that the state emerges naturally within society, gradually taking on its specific form and character. This is the original birth of the state—all else is but re-birth or re-formation. When a new country is occupied or peopled a new state in some sense may be created, but its members have carried with them from older states the pre-formed character of citizenship. No state is ever born without a long preparation, though it may seem to come to birth in an hour. This is true also of the states which are delivered by war. A subject people may throw off the yoke and triumph into statehood, but it must have cherished long traditions or aspirations of political independence and in the meantime have been, even as subject, participant in the life of the state. An established state may itself create or liberate another, but only on similar conditions. Likewise every state that holds alien peoples subject to itself is preparing, however reluctantly, the way for their political renaissance. It keeps alive the discipline of law and the sense of organization while it intensifies, by its alien presence, the spirit of unity, and the desire for autonomy. This fact has been perceived by modern empires more clearly than by ancient ones, and they have learned in large measure to preserve their bounds by moderating and finally relinquishing their claims of dominion. Empire has always been the fertile mother of new states, but in ancient times the children often rent the parent. The great anxiety of modern empire is to prevent such disruption, and to discover how far it can retain its suzerainty without provoking rebellion and its own downfall. This, for example, is the present attitude of the British Empire to India.

New states may arise from the partition or unification of old states. England and Scotland became the state of Great Britain. The United Kingdom was again partitioned when the Irish Free State was formed. Norway and Sweden became separated, and Belgium and Holland, while the states of Germany were united. Conquest and dynastic union were the chief agencies of the older world in the creation of larger states, just as the internal disturbances of power and dynastic quarrels were the causes of disruption. Then nationality entered as the solvent of established power-systems. The demand for self-government is realized sometimes in division, sometimes in union, or else is resisted by an established dominion which unites or holds apart. These are, in the modern world, two forces which determine the secondary formation or re-formation of states, the essential spirit of nationhood seeking full incarnation within a state and the coercive sovereignty which resists it. When the force of nationality is spent or has succeeded, another principle may become effective, that which underlies federation. As a determinant of federation nationality is less influential and is liable to be overlaid or superseded by the sense of more concrete interests. For the peculiarity of federation in this regard is that if the federal union is based on nationality, the participant states are generally demarcated on some other principle, whereas if the participant states are nationally determined, the inclusive union generally transcends nationality. It would be absurd to speak of the nationality of Ontario or Massachusetts or South Australia or Würtemberg or Bern, just as on the other hand it would be absurd to attribute nationality to the whole of the British Empire. Thus federation has a peculiar function in mitigating the extremities of nationalism, since it alone seems to permit of the free formation of states on a non-nationalistic basis.

New states occasionally arise through secession, as distinct from nationalistic revolt, from older states. Secession within the body of the larger state has rarely succeeded. One of the most remarkable attempts was the economic secession of the Roman plebs, on two occasions in the early history of Rome. The economic secession of the Southern States of the American Union was based on the right of sovereignty resident in the members of federation. Various 'colonies' of the ancient and the modern world have arisen as secessions inspired by religious or class differences. In such cases the seceders have sought a new home, like the Pilgrim Fathers or the Mormons, where they could live freely the kind of life denied them in their former state.

It will be seen that the same causes which have been operative in the secondary formation of new states account also for the dissolution of old ones. The primary cause of formation lies beyond all these. The state, as distinct from any particular form of state, is born of a social process which slowly shapes a definite organization to its appropriate functions. This is, we may say, the natural birth of the state. Is there then, we are tempted to ask, a corresponding process which we may call its natural death? Just as, beyond the secondary causes of formation there lies a single cause of its being, does there lie, beyond the secondary causes of dissolution, a single and inevitable principle of its mortality?

To this question many thinkers have answered, Yes. They have not been content to enumerate the catastrophic consequences of war and invasion, the break-up of empires through changes in the distribution of power or through the pressure of new-grown external forces. It has not been enough for them that under dynastic conditions a state may crumble from the loss of economic strength, when old lands grow dessicated, when the channels of trade are changed, when populations are reduced by disease or war or famine, or when the wanton pride or arrogant stupidity of government or the folly of the people wastes its resources. The accidents of history, they say, do not account for the common mortality of states any more than the accidents of life explain the mortality of men. There is a deeper cause, innate in the being of the state. It too has a destined course of life which ends in death.

This is part of that mystical interpretation of the state which we have already had occasion to criticize. It applies to the state a conception of life which could be relevant only to society, and which is false even for society. I have elsewhere sought to show that society is not subject to the rhythm of organic life.[1] Here we shall follow another road. Once more we must point out a difference between the state and society. The state is a structure, and a structure may collapse and disappear. Like any other organization, it may break in pieces, destroyed from within or from without. Such destruction quite obviously does not imply the destruction of society. The community of Poland remained when the Polish state was crushed. The communities of Rome survived when the vast shell of the empire was annihilated. We lose the sense of the continuity of history if we regard the rise and fall of principalities and powers as the beginning and end of communities and cultures.

The succession of ancient empires did not represent so many fresh starts in the history of mankind. Often it made little difference to the life and custom of the people

[1] *Community*, Bk III, ch. ii.

whether an imperial power flourished or fell. They lived and suffered and died; they followed the ways of their fathers; they dreamed and struggled, unresponsive to the dynastic ambitions which raged above and about them. It is, in truth, the destiny of *empire* to perish. That which lives by power must fall by power. Empire falls not because it has fulfilled an organic cycle from youth to age, but because it rests on a precarious conjuncture of force whose very employment begets resistance, and because the shifting of power is inevitable in the changing conditions of human affairs. Empire begins and ends in catastrophe, first the catastrophe of the vanquished and last the catastrophe of the victors. This simple law of power should not be erected into a principle of the mortality of states..

The distinction between life and organization finds its sharpest expression in the sphere of the state. In the state we have the greatest and perhaps the most permanent expression of conscious organization. The ends men seek are defined by the very modes established for their attainment, and the state becomes a vast agency of direction and control. Unwittingly men come to think of the agency as though it existed for its own sake or held within its mere form the worth of the ideal which created it. But this idolatry ends in revulsion. Its mere creations cannot take the place of the creative spirit. The form decays and can be renewed only from without. There is a disharmony between the form and the spirit, the institution and the life. The new life of the successive (and continuous) generations breaks and remakes the institutional moulds. Where it fails to do so life itself decays. But never is the organization adequate for the things men seek by means of it, and its transformations witness to the persistence more than to the change of human ideals. Society, in a word, is more continuous than the state. This is a truth which deserves a fuller explanation, for it illuminates our argument concerning the nature and the service of the state.

II

CIVILIZATION AND CULTURE

Society has an inner environment which it makes, besides the outer which it only moulds. The former consists in the whole apparatus of custom and institution, the complex and multiform mechanism of order, the devices and instruments by which nature is controlled, the modes of expression and communication, the comforts, refinements, and luxuries which determine standards of living, and the economic system through which they are produced and distributed. It includes all that human intelligence and art have wrought to make the world a home for the human spirit. It includes alike the technological and the institutional equipment, parliaments and telephone exchanges, corporation charters and railroads, insurance agencies and automobiles. This whole apparatus of life we shall here call civilization. It is obvious that the political system belongs to this region and constitutes one great division of it.

From civilization we must distinguish culture as its animating and creating spirit. Civilization is the instrument, the body, even the garment of culture. Civilization expresses itself in politics, in economics, in technology, while culture expresses itself in art, in literature, in religion, in morals. Our culture is what we are, our civilization is what we use. There is a technique of culture, but the culture itself is not technique. Culture is the fulfilment of life, revealed in the things we want in themselves, and not in their results. No one wants banking systems and factories and ballot-boxes for any intrinsic significance they possess. If we could attain the products without the process we would gladly dispense with the latter. But the objects of culture have a direct significance. It is the difference between the mode of achieving and the thing achieved, between the way of living and the life led. The interest in technique is derivative, though like any other it may come to engross the mind, but the interest in culture is primary.

There is a great difference between an object of civilization and a work of culture. An institutional or technical achievement raises, so to speak, the level of civilization. It is an improvement on the past. Once the spinning-machine or the railway-locomotive or the typewriter is discovered, men go on developing it. Civilization is cumulative. The new model betters the old, and renders it obsolete. The achievement perpetuates itself and is the basis of further achievement. Civilization is rightly described as a ' march ', for each step leads to another and is always forward. Great historical catastrophes can interrupt this cumulation, but nothing seems able to break it altogether. It is a poor age indeed that does not add some stones to this rising edifice of civilization. But culture is not cumulative. It has to be won afresh by each new generation. It is not a simple inheritance like civilization. It is true that here too past attainment is the basis of present achievement, but there is no surety that the present will equal, still less that it will improve on, the past. The heights reached by Greek art and Greek drama are not held by succeeding ages. The achievement of Dante or of Shakespeare is not equalled by those who follow them. What Archimedes or Galileo or Newton discovered is the basis of further discovery that exceeds any of theirs, but what Sophocles or Michael Angelo or Milton expressed is not expressed better or more fully by others who have their works before them. We do not deny that there is advance in culture also, but it is no steady advance. It is variable and seems capricious, subject to retreats and setbacks.

The reason thereof suggests another difference between civilization and culture. Culture must always be won afresh, because it is a direct expression of the human spirit. In a very real sense a musician composes only for musicians and an artist paints only for artists. A poet can write only for those who have themselves the poetic quality. Every work of art implies at least two artists, he who creates and he who understands, and so with all the achievements of culture. Cultural expression is communication between likes and is possible only by reason of their likeness. The work of the artist is only for other artists, but the work of the engineer is not for other engineers. The bridge-builder does not construct for other bridge-builders, but for those who themselves may appreciate nothing of his skill. Millions may use a technical invention without the least understanding of it. Devices for use are in fact the more perfect the less understanding they require, and the aim of the inventor is to make his invention, in the American phrase, ' fool-proof '. We would get an entirely false conception of the intelligence and capacity of our age, and an entirely false standard of comparison between it and other ages, if we judged it by its institutions and its technical equipment. Our estimate would be much more just if we judged it by the books men read and write, by the ideals they cherish, by the pleasures they pursue, by the religions which they practise, by all the things they really care about and think about.

It follows that one people can borrow civilization from another people in a way in which culture cannot be borrowed. Technical devices can be transplanted without change. Institutional devices, being more nearly related to the form of culture which they serve, undergo some change when they are borrowed. The barbarian can learn more easily to use the rifle than the ballot-box. The institutions of Western democracy do not accommodate themselves without strain to the social life of the Orient or even of South America. Nevertheless they are transferable to a degree, and have in fact been adopted in many countries to which they were not native. But a culture cannot be adopted. A culture may be assimilated gradually, by peoples who are ready for it and who are brought into constant contact with it, but even so they inevitably change it in making it their own. When extraneous considerations lead to the nominal acceptance of an alien culture it becomes a travesty or an empty form. The extraordinary transmogrifications of Christianity in the course of two thousand years, involving not merely the restatement but often the rejection of its original principles, offer a splendid illustration of the truth that a culture cannot be ' adopted '. The culture of a people expresses their character and can express nothing else. Hence civilization is far more pervasive than culture. Japan can speedily adopt the civilization of the West, but it neither can nor cares to adopt its culture. Of course we must not imply that the two factors are entirely separate. Civilization, whether native or adopted, is a kind of social environment, and human beings respond in similar ways to similar conditions. Civilization and culture necessarily react on one another. Nevertheless it seems clear that cultures can remain distinctive within the form of a common civilization. Given the means of communication, it is inevitable that civilization should become, in its larger aspects, one and universal. But under this seeming uniformity of life great cultural differences remain, both within and between the peoples of the earth.

One further distinction can now be made. We have pointed out that civilization, in contrast to culture, is cumulative. This is true in another sense also. Means can be massed into great engines of power. Systems can be extended into vaster systems. But culture resists the mechanics of addition and multiplication. I have elsewhere expressed this truth as follows: 'We can add the wealth of a group or a nation and get some kind of a total. We can add its man-power and get a total. But we cannot make a sum of its health or its habits or its culture. A thousand weak purposes cannot be rolled into one strong purpose as a thousand weak units of force are joined into one strong force. We cannot add wisdom as we can add wealth. A thousand mediocrities do not sum up into one genius.'[1]

We can now consider afresh the significance of the rise and fall of states, in relation to the society within which these phenomena occur. The state is not only the greatest structure of civilization, it is the framework which gives cohesion to all the rest. But its relation to

[1] *Elements of Social Science*, ch. i.

culture is not so indissoluble that the fall of a state must involve the end of a culture. The political structure may be overthrown while the life endures, finding shelter in other though less adequate structures, in the family, in the complex of custom and local organization, awaiting the time when again it can reaffirm its nature through the state.

Here we are face to face with the final and fascinating question : What lives and what dies in history ? In that multitudinous record, so full of confusion and change, in which time seems to devour all its children, what abides of the doings and sufferings of men ? Beyond the drums and tramplings of a thousand conquests, beyond the wreck of empires and the slow crumblings of ancient creeds, is there anything that has survived, nay, that from the first has been formed and fashioned by the very process of the ages ? If all is flux, what is it that flows ? If all is change, is there at least direction in the change ?

The continuity of life is not the continuity of its institutions. Organizations are renewed from without, they are reformed, or scrapped and replaced. Society is renewed from within. It has the continuity of the living flesh which is subtly restored, in an imperceptible process, by new elements of life. If we look at the institutions alone, or if we identify society with the state, history becomes episodic and discontinuous. We think of the rise and fall of civilizations as though each were an isolated development, completed in birth and death. We apply to them that inveterate analogy of the closed organism, which runs its course from the nothingness of pre-existence to the annihilation of dissolution. We think peoples must pass away like the generations.

But peoples do not pass away, they are renewed in

endless change. They know neither birth nor death. They own a conditional immortality, for the present must for ever abandon the dead of its own past. A people has no identity, only continuity. Self-sameness is impossible to anything that lives. A people is, as it were, a web of society woven by stock and environment, and variegated by event and experience. The pattern grows and changes, for the loom is never at rest. The web narrows and widens, and it is vain to look for the repetition of historic forms. The threads mingle and part, intermixed beyond recognition. Nothing remains the same, except the unknown materials of life from which the threads are spun.

The continuity of life triumphs over outworn creeds and dead institutions. It is deeper than the historic unions with which we fondly identify our present social groups. The England of Elizabeth offers no real inspiration, in spite of historic pride, to the Englishman of to-day. What in fact survives of it? Family portraits and entailed estates, such as remain, do not assure the oneness of the most exclusive groups with their own past, for each generation is a fresh intermixture and eternally variant. Institutions have been remade out of all semblance to their ancient forms. The English environment endures, but how vastly different! The English stock endures, but with such a reblending of old elements and such a recruiting of new ones that it must have undergone an incalculable change. New standards, new opportunities, new beliefs, new problems, make our world to-day wholly foreign to that world of only a dozen generations back. A few monuments of culture survive which still have significance for our age, a few poems and plays and buildings and pictures, but they live because they expressed something that seems universal, that belongs to humanity itself.

Yet the new life of to-day is wholly sprung from the life of the past. New peoples and old peoples alike, they are but different derivations of stocks that go back to the dawn of the earth. No people is biologically younger or older than another. What is young is the union that historical forces have brought into being. What is new is the opportunity that utterly inextricable conditions of heredity and environment have wrought. If a people has no beginning nor end, neither has it eternity. A nation is a conjuncture, a social harmony. When it attains a certain development, its members grow conscious of it and seek to give it assurance within a state. But what they are really conscious of, aside from vain dreams of racial purity and scarcely less vain traditions of historic identity, is a common culture realized in the present. And we have seen that this culture is always changing, that it exhibits vast differences within the limits of the single nation, and that its only enduring expressions are those which transcend nationality.

These considerations run contrary to an old and still prevalent doctrine, that human societies, like human beings, pass through determinate stages of existence from birth to death. The rise and fall of a state, on that view, would be the beginning and the end of a rhythmic social process. Every community and every culture would pass through characteristic age-periods. Each would have, as one recent advocate of the doctrine repeats, ' its childhood, its youth, its manhood, and its old age '.[1] History would reveal not the growth of one civilization or culture but a discrete succession, each in

---

[1] Spengler, *Untergang des Abendlandes*, vol. i, ch. ii.

its turn fulfilling its proper destiny. A curious elaboration of this cyclic conception is given by Spengler, who professes to reveal the spring, summer, autumn, and winter of cultures and peoples.[1] He exhibits in parallel columns the distinctive traits of each stage in four grand instances, which he names the Indian, the Classical, the Arabian, and the Western cultures. All four, including the last which is that of contemporary Europe, have completed, or are in the last stage of, their career. Further development is closed so far as they are concerned. The only future is for new cultures which may lie in the womb of time, when the ' world's great age begins anew '.

This latest interpretation of an ancient fatalism deserves analysis, since it flatly contradicts the conception of civilization and culture, and of the relationship of society and state, which we have been advocating. According to our author, the spring time of culture is the awakening of a ' dream-heavy ' consciousness, expressed in mythological fantasy. These myths and legends, instinctive renderings of man's sense of oneness with nature, are the material of that mystical construction of experience whose product is the Rig-veda, the Hellenic cosmogony, the writings of the Christian fathers, and, for the Western culture, the ' Divine Comedy ' of Dante and the ' Summa ' of Aquinas.

Meanwhile the town with its sharp, if narrow, intelligence arises, and its spirit begins to overcome the instinctive life of the country. The world-view of the spring time is subjected to critical restatement. Men begin to reason, to develop abstract thought. It is, as it were, a ripening of culture. The inquiring mind,

[1] *Op. cit.*, vol. i.

still confident in itself, seeks new methods, new instruments of interpretation. The world widens to new horizons. It is the age of exploration, the age, in the West, of Galileo and Descartes and Bacon. This is the summer time that imperceptibly passes into autumn. The spirit of the great city, the metropolis, gathers strength. The social life is detached from the life of nature. To the philosopher the former appears a convention, not rooted in necessity. This is the age of ' illumination ', the age of the Greek sophists, or the age of Locke and Rousseau and Voltaire. But autumn also brings its fruits. Ere the disintegrating forces have their way, great synthetic philosophies, based on the conviction of the unity and intelligibility of the universe, are brought to fulfilment, and we have the comprehensive thought-structures of Plato and Aristotle, or of Avicenna, or of Kant and Hegel.

Then comes winter. The unity of thought cannot withstand the critical intelligence, nor the unity of society the assaults of individualism. The great social moulds are broken. No longer does religious faith or native tradition maintain the solidarity of life. It is the age of the world city, the age of cosmopolitanism. With individualism grows its counterpart of radicalism or socialism. The last great unity of the nation is thereby disintegrated, and there is nothing to take its place. In the Greek world it is the age of the Cynics, Cyrenaics, and Stoics ; in our Western world the age of Schopenhauer and Nietzsche and Wagner and Ibsen. The time of building is at an end, and men live in the ruins of the traditions they have overthrown. When this happens, the culture has run its course. Its life is dissipated. The centrifugal forces have triumphed.

The doctrine thus briefly sketched is impressive, and its author reinforces it with a wealth of historical illustration. But neither the seasonal nor the organic analogy has historical validity. It is very possible to argue, with Comte, that human culture, *taken as a whole*, evolves through definite stages. But to maintain that each culture is a closed or closing circle, self-complete and predestinate, is surely vain. The spectacle of fallen empires need not blind us to the broader march of human civilization or the less secure but less predictable advance of culture. To mark off distinct cultures from birth to death, from spring to winter, is a very arbitrary proceeding. How can we show that the Homeric culture represents a beginning and not, as many scholars think, a culmination? How can we show that the Indian culture has fulfilled its course? Why should the Greek sophists belong to the time of fruition (along with Plato and Aristotle) while the stoics belong to the winter of the age? Why should the absence of a religious-metaphysical point of view and the presence of a purely ethical one denote the close of the circle, when the Chinese culture, for example, has exhibited these characteristics at least from the time of the radical Lao-tse and the ethical Confucius, some twenty-five centuries ago?

There does seem to be in the course of human history a process from the stage of the small kin-group to that of the world-city. In this process at least, civilization and culture have gone hand in hand. There does seem to be a general direction from the stage of dim legend to that of reasoned belief and scientific thought. There is much to support Comte's bold generalization that humanity moves from what he named a theological to a positive world-understanding. This process is undoubtedly associated with the growth of city life, whose influence profoundly modifies the spirit as well as the forms of society. We can thus trace a certain evolution not merely of *a* society, but of society ; not merely of *a* state, but of the state. Humanity falls into groups and divisions, but it is still humanity. The bulk of the apparatus of civilization is a means to its common wants, and being transferable it is gradually extended over all the earth, by agencies which themselves are a part of civilization. Civilization becomes in ever greater degree world-civilization, and is thus saved from a danger to which civilization in the past was subject, that of being submerged by waves of outer barbarism. If it is to be destroyed at all, it can only be, so long as the resources of the earth endure, from within itself ; and the character of civilization, as we have shown, is such that this could not occur without a catastrophic and unparalleled regression of humanity. So far as civilization is concerned, there is no completion of a cycle, no new beginning. *Vestigia nulla retrorsum*—there is no way back. If the road leads from the peasant-community to the world-city, there is no return to the conditions of the peasant-community. The stage of the world-city has come to stay, because it depends on technological advances which are a permanent possession of mankind.

Culture, on the other hand, is less stable, less secure. It rises and recedes, and no study of the conditions of its civilization seems to explain its course. We cannot tell why it rose to a remarkable height in a particular age or why the height once gained is lost. Here we are in the region of unknown mutability. We can point to conditions which favour or hinder its advance, but these do not account for its vigour, or failure. It is, for our present knowledge, too much like the wind that blows where it lists. It is the supreme instance of that variability which belongs to life. Culture cannot stand still. Even to endure it must change, it must seek new ways of expression. Culture is creation and it never ceases while life renews itself in the generations. Incessantly it seeks new modes, new outlets, new interpretations.

In this search, with its success and failure, we are farther than ever from the rounding curve of fulfilment and completed destiny. The hills and valleys stretch back to an unknown horizon and the mists of the future hide a new succession to which the imagination can assign no limit. The widening of our time-span through astronomy, geology, biology, and anthropology has delivered our thought from the mean little cage of Biblical time. This expansion should change our response to the events of our own short hour. A moment's doings in its history cannot ' ruin a civilization ' or ' inaugurate a new era for mankind '. Our too near-sighted hopes and fears construct for us new prisons within which we vainly pen the culture and the civilization that not our age but humanity itself has made from the beginning until now.

In this process man has fashioned many instruments. Some he has discarded, others he finds more and more potent and serviceable as he learns to understand them better. To the latter order belongs the state.

XI

THE FORMS OF THE STATE

I. HISTORICAL AND CONTEMPORARY TYPES OF STATE

THE first part of this work is devoted to an account of the general evolution of the state-type. We have tried to show that the political form of association gradually emerged out of an undifferentiated social structure, and took on those specific characters which distinguish the state from the community as well as from other forms of association. We have represented the process as one in which a single and unique form, properly called the state, has developed its characteristics, passing through various imperfect (because incompletely differentiated) forms such as the Hellenic polity and the feudal organization. We regard these as transitional forms rather than distinct state-types. Perhaps they should not be included within a classification of states any more than *pithecanthropus* is to be included among the races of men. But no doubt there is variety in the product of evolution as well as in the process. The single and unique state-association has many distinctive forms. Where we should draw the line between transitional developments on the one hand and properly constituted states on the other is a needless and perhaps impossible inquiry. The differentiation of the state out of the non-state passes imperceptibly into the evolution of the state within itself. In the latter process can we again distinguish rudimentary and immature forms of state from types which we may regard as more highly developed? Can we range, for example, dynasty and theocracy in the one group, and modern democracies in the other?

A doubt may be raised as to the reality of the democratic character attached to the early tribe and other primitive communities. At any rate, in so far as they were democratic, it was as communities and not as states. The political order seems always to have been first achieved through the domination of a class or caste or family to which the rest of the community was directly and ostensibly subject. The early state is strictly a class-state. The order it imposed was based on the distinction between the king, the priest, and the nobility on the one hand and the tribute-paying and service-rendering commonalty on the other. This was inevitable under the conditions of primitive life, where the herd instinct was confirmed by rigorous custom, where ignorance bred the spirit of superstitious subjection to unknown powers and to their human ' interpreters ', and where the weakness and uncertainty of life required a rallying point in undisputed power. The transformation and dilution of that power we have already traced. The state passed from the form of traditional subordination to that of conscious institution. Undeveloped power became hereditary right, which became responsible and finally elective authority. The end, if not the beginning, is some form of democracy, if we understand by democracy not necessarily the rule of the many but the active functioning of the general will, giving direct support, and not merely passive acquiescence, to a government chosen by itself.

If we are right in our interpretation of the state as an organ of community, we must regard all states in which the general will is not active as imperfect forms. This view seems to be confirmed by a study of the historical process, for it appears to be true that, in spite of reversions, the main trend of the state, *after it has finally emerged as a state*, is toward democracy.

This view is not infrequently challenged. Spengler, to take one of the most thoroughgoing of its recent opponents, declares that democracy is 'superficial and unhistorical' as contrasted with hereditary dynasty or the class-state. It is perhaps idle to deny the historicity of the outcome of any historical process. Nor is the charge of superficiality confirmed by the crucial test, that of the great crisis. We may assume that the more stable form is also the best founded, and we have seen, in our discussion of political revolutions, that democracy abides the crisis more surely than dynasty. The form of *political* equality, among peoples who are ripe for it, is not superficial, nor is it easily overthrown. No institutions are secure, but those which rest on the sustaining power of the conscious co-operation and participation of the community are the strongest. A people can overthrow every form of government but its own—then it finds no alternative. A republic may be destroyed from without, but it is as nearly invincible from within as anything human. Every crisis has the effect of thrusting into the general consciousness a picture of the order within which it occurs. If there is any habit of conscious rationalized support underlying this order that sudden revelation is so much less disturbing. Thus democracy has the most subversive of all social forces, the consciousness of itself, already on its side. In every other form of state but conscious democracy the roots of government become detachable from the trunk of the tree. Customary or traditional authority may suffice for the time when custom can follow its quiet path, but when custom-shaking events occur, as inevitably in times of crisis, it is seen that custom is not itself the deepest thing but only its crust, that age alone is not strength, that faiths are neither sure nor inviolate because they are dim, that the instincts of life are never fully translated into the institutions of men. The form of democracy admits more freely of retranslation than other forms, and therefore it seems capable of a more permanent and a more stable development.

Furthermore, unless the general will is active in the determination of government, the state necessarily assumes, in the eyes of the majority of its members, the aspect of a power-system rather than of a welfare-system. The holders of irresponsible power may profess the general welfare, but such profession is generally a matter of policy rather than of conviction, and in any event gains little credence. Now the conception of a power-system is not an ultimate one, as the conception of a welfare-system must be. Power is an instrument and welfare a goal. The ultimate contrast is therefore between a system maintained for the welfare of a class and one maintained for the welfare of the whole. Every advance in education or even in the ability of the many to organize, to express, or to communicate their ideas, is thus a menace to the power-system. The power-state requires stability above all things, but that is what its power can least achieve, for the operative forces of civilization are mainly beyond the reach of the political arm. We must remember in this connexion that the *social* order (which comprehends the order of custom, morality, kinship, and religion) is never force-determined, even where the *political* order is flagrantly coercive—in fact that a coercive political order could not exist save as superimposed on a social order which expressed the innate attitudes of the community. No despotism, as Green pointed out, can touch this underlying order save at the risk of its overthrow. There is always therefore a latent contrast between the power-system and its own social conditions. This contrast is emphasized and brought to consciousness by the influences which we include under the term ' civilization '. Thus we conclude that the slower processes of social change no less than the catastrophic shock of the social crisis reveal the instability and the inadequacy of the dynastic or class-state as compared with the democracy.

We have dwelt on this point in order to justify the classification of states which we now proceed to make. Our object in this chapter is to classify and to characterize the various forms of state. We can now distinguish two main types of state as follows : (*a*) dynastic states, i. e. states in which there is no general will co-extensive with the community embraced within the state, or in which the general will is merely acquiescent or subservient ; (*b*) democratic states, in which the general will is inclusive of the community as a whole or of at least the greater portion of the community, and is the conscious, direct, and active support of the form of government.

Under (*a*) we include the class-controlled state, the empire, and also all those states, even though termed ' democracies ', in which the government is constituted by a privileged portion of the total community. We would include the Greek commonwealths in this category.

Their citizens, although they achieved a democratic relation to government, in reality formed a ruling caste, and therefore from the point of view of the whole community, these states, even at their fullest development, were oligarchical. No matter how complete the civic equality existing within a limited group, the state remains dynastic if it excludes a considerable portion of the community which it regulates. The necessity for the habitual use of coercion over residents whose will is no part of the general will makes the state essentially a force-system. It is founded on force and its policies are inevitably exploitative.

Under (b) we include only the forms of modern democracy. Democracy, it is true, is a matter of degree, and lines are hard to draw here as elsewhere. But we would not, for example, refuse the title of democracy to a state because it leaves its women members politically unenfranchised, since women do not form a class politically distinct and may be regarded, though the view is of course inadequate, as represented indirectly through the male members of the family. Nor again would we deny the title of democracy to states which limit citizenship in terms of qualifications which can reasonably be considered as implying a minimum personal fitness for the discharge of civic responsibilities. Nor need we raise here the question of the reality of democratic control as it is affected by social and economic considerations which influence the ' will of the people '. So long as the legislative sovereignty is formally determined by the exercise of the general will, no matter what influences impinge upon the latter, we shall call the state a democracy. In this chapter we are concerned with distinctions of form.

FORMS OF THE DYNASTIC STATE

In the dynastic state the aspect of power or coercion is necessarily dominant, though it may be obscured by the influence of a tradition and a religion consonant with the subjection of the many to the few. Under dynastic conditions the state has a peculiar character, since it does not even ostensibly make the welfare of the whole its object. It requires therefore the support of all available psychological influences which impress the mass of men with the sense of its own majesty and of their inferiority. To this end it idealizes power and encourages that form of emotional loyalty in the subjects which finds its unsubstantial reward in the reflection of the glory and might of their rulers. It esteems military distinction as the prize of life and inculcates the virtues of courage, discipline, and sacrifice. It identifies ' king and country ' in its programme of conquest, and poses as the champion and deliverer of the commonwealth from the perils which its own warlike policy entails. It elevates distinctions of class and birth so as to draw a nearly impassable gulf between the base and the noble. It appropriates, in the form of rents and taxes, the surplus accruing to the toil of the base, so combining economic and political power and depriving the subject class of the two external conditions of opportunity. So drastic a system of subjection, through which all civilized peoples seem to have passed, could scarcely have upheld itself against the opposing interests of the suppressed, were it not for its kinship and alliance with religious systems inculcating submission and reverence, and providing an appropriate background for political dynasty by their insistence on the all-power of jealous and exacting deities and on the duty of submission to their will as interpreted by the priesthood. Such religions, the natural response of imaginative ignorance to the phenomena of a mysterious and baffling world, have always been associated with the class-rule of the dynastic state.

All dynasties are oligarchies. It has been customary to classify monarchy and oligarchy as two distinctive forms of the state, but the distinction rests on secondary differences. Of all the terms designating political forms, none are more confusing than those which denote numerical factors. Monarchy ought strictly to signify the rule of one, as distinct from oligarchy, or the rule of the few. But it is characteristic of most oligarchies that they possess titular or monarchical heads, and on the other hand no government is ever a mere monarchy. If there is a single seemingly supreme ruler he inevitably rests his power on the active support of an associated class. He rules in its interest no less than with its co-operation. He nearly always has a council of advisers who represent the class. He may indeed claim, like Wilhelm II, to rule ' by the grace of God alone ', but it is necessary that a privileged group should find its interest quite compatible with the exercise of the power so claimed. It is true that disputes may arise within the class which suggest a conflict between monarchy and nobility, as between King John and his barons, but in reality they are divisions within the oligarchy, between a court party and a dissident faction. All monarchies are forms of oligarchy, though all oligarchies are not monarchical.[1] An oligarchy may be directed by a council

[1] In certain primitive societies the chief or king is raised to such a mystic eminence above *all* his subjects that it is possible to accept

without a single pre-eminent ruler or monarch, though this is generally due to a survival of 'city-state' conditions, as in the case of the senate and magistracy of 'republican' Rome. We can therefore classify oligarchies as monarchical or conciliar.

The monarchical oligarchy is generally either hereditary or elective. Not infrequently it assumes at first an elective form (the power of election being in the hands of the dominant class), and later becomes stabilized under the hereditary form. The elective monarchy of Poland is usually regarded as one of the weaknesses of its curious constitution. The history of imperial Rome shows remarkable fluctuations between the two principles. At first formally elective, the imperial power remained for a long time within an imperial family, but never was fully established as an hereditary right and finally became subject to the capricious acclamation of the legions. The hereditary form has the great advantage of ensuring that stability which is an essential condition of the dynastic state. It instils that mystic reverence of power which is divorced from the contemplation of its achievements, and so more than compensates for the weakness and folly of the heirs of power. Under the conditions suitable to oligarchy the incompetence of the hereditary sovereign merely affirms the real power of the ruling class.

Besides the regular forms of hereditary and elective monarchy we must add certain abnormal forms which are the result of political upheavals. A monarch may be established as the result of a *coup d'état*, and in ancient oligarchies even a 'palace-revolution' might determine literally the term 'monarchy', but such a condition cannot occur in any organized or modern state.

the succession. But a ruler so enthroned always held a precarious position unless he could found a dynasty or regularize his own appointment under some mode of election. Another abnormal form is the dictatorship where the monarchy is ostensibly a temporary expedient adopted to meet a critical situation. Such was the theory of the Roman dictatorship, and in modern times certain rulers, such as Cromwell, have governed as 'saviours' of the state. A dictatorship may have a constitutional character, as at Rome ; more often it rests on the control of armed force.

We pass next from monarchical to conciliar oligarchy. This is the rarer form, being less apt to secure the stability of government which oligarchy demands. It was of course characteristic of the city-state where government was of the nature of a political magistracy. It is found occasionally under primitive conditions, where a council of elders or of tribal chiefs holds sway. But in its pure form it is unknown under modern conditions. What we do find is a mixture of the monarchical and conciliar forms, the titular monarch or ruler being in part dependent on a council which is not advisory but a definite participant in sovereignty. The council may be either representative or inclusive of the privileged class. In structure it may be either simple or hierarchical. In other words the members of the council may have equal political rights or they may be graded. The Polish system with its *liberum veto* is an example of the former type. The feudal constitution elsewhere is an outstanding example of the latter. Another example is found in what is called theocracy. We do not distinguish theocracy as a separate form from oligarchy, since the difference lies not in the structure but in the derivation of control. Pure theocracy is however a rare thing. That which is not infrequent in oligarchic states is a combination of theocratic with other forms of authority, sometimes fused into a unity, sometimes creating a duality of power. Examples are the Egyptian dynasties and many Eastern empires of the past, the Holy Roman Empire and in fact most medieval states before the Renaissance, and the Turkish empire before the separation and finally the abolition of the Caliphate.

Conciliar oligarchy may also be classified on the same basis as unitary; in other words the council may be hereditary or elective or it may constitute a dictatorship. We should characterize the soviet government of Russia as of the last-mentioned type. Nominally it is a ' dictatorship of the proletariat ', which means in effect the dictatorship of a small group based on proletarian support. It is a unique form, being a class-limited oligarchy which, unlike all other oligarchies, limits citizenship not from above, in the socio-economic sense, but from below. It is a form that could arise only in an oligarchical state, when a strongly oligarchical structure is so completely and suddenly overthrown that certain hitherto subject elements become dominant and apply the methods of their former masters.

Passing from unitary to composite forms of oligarchy we may include the larger feudal states in the latter category. But the characteristic form of composite oligarchy is empire. We have already pointed out the broad distinction between land-empire and sea-empire. The former embraces an extensive and usually continuous territory of heterogeneous peoples held together by the prestige and military organization attached to a ruling family or caste. The subjects of the dynastic empire are not consciously united as a nation or people, nor do they comprise an effective community, though usually, as in the case of the Chinese dynasties (Ts'in, Han, Ming, Manchu), there is, due to earlier migrations, invasions, and conquests, some degree of common culture and some intermixture, without which the necessary sentiment of dynastic respect and submission could not exist. This dynasty is, however, first established by the genius of a conqueror, such as, for China, Han, Genghing Khan, Kublai Khan, or by the matrimonial alliances—*tu, felix Austria, nube*—or other compacts of the ruling families of smaller dynastic states. The area of dynastic government is generally divided along geographical or ethnographical lines into ' provinces ', to which the central government is quite external. They have their own organization with which the dynasty has little or no concern, regarding them as it does mainly from the point of view of financial and military contribution and therefore leaving to the provincial ruler, apart from his quota of revenue and arms, a more or less arbitrary power.

The weaknesses of such a dynastic form, apart from the disputes over succession which the hereditary transmission of authority to incapable descendants is apt to breed, lies in the centrifugal tendencies of the provinces, bound to the central government by no adequate unifying principle, receiving no sustenance in return for their contributions to it, and subjected constantly to the heavy and wasteful extortions which the tribute-collecting system promotes. In consequence the whole dynastic structure is often endangered, and at times broken, while the focus of empire is liable to be transferred, after devastating struggles, from one centre and one family to another.

The second main form of empire, the maritime, presents interesting differences of structure. It is, racially and culturally, much less homogeneous than the land empire. It can include peoples of entirely distinct levels and types of civilization, and from the power-standpoint this is an element of security, for its subject peoples are less likely and less able to unite against it. It does not need the art of politics in order to ' divide and rule ', for the seas on which its power rests have already divided its elements. Its power is more swift and more sure, and less liable to insidious encroachments from within. The form of the central government is of less moment to it. A democracy may govern a sea-empire, though not without undergoing some un-democratic changes, but a democracy could scarcely rule a land-empire. Sea-power demânds a less militaristic discipline than land-power, for it is more concentrated and less dependent on numbers and armed men. Further-more the maritime empire derives its gains of dominance through commercial advantage and trading concession rather than through fiscal enforcement, and the economic method has an aspect of mutuality which is lacking to the political. It is also more adaptable to changing conditions. Athens treated her short-lived empire according to the territorial principle of enforced levies. Spain treated her empire as sheer ' possession ', exploiting and confiscating its resources. The modern colonial empire changed its policy gradually. Even in its origins it differed from earlier empires by the dominance of varied economic motives, the colony being founded as a means of maintaining commerce within the control of the home country, as a source of raw materials and precious metals, as a market for wares, and as an outlet for surplus population. As the colony developed it demanded a greater autonomy than was compatible with such control over its economic life. Hence arose friction between the colonial and the imperial authorities, and the disastrous failure of Grenville's policy wrote the end of a chapter. So the whole tendency of the colonial empire was towards a less imperial form. In those regions which its own nationals had effectively colonized, it relinquished in large part the claim of centralized control, seeking instead co-operative union and economic privilege. Here empire passes into a sort of permanent alliance or confederation. In those regions where climatic conditions together with the presence of an alien civilization prevented effective colonization it established, in place of the ancient domination, some form of suzerainty from which it might derive both economic advantage and military strength. Only in regions where it ruled native races of a much less advanced civilization did it retain, and even there in a modified form, the older methods of exploitation.

III

FORMS OF THE DEMOCRATIC STATE

The study of the character and development of democratic forms will mainly occupy us in the following chapters. Here we shall consider only those major differences on the basis of which we can relate the numerous varieties of democracy under a few general categories. Practically all modern states are, in terms, of the definition already given, to be classed as democracies, but no two are quite alike in character. Democracy is in part a matter of degree, in part a matter of the particular mechanism through which the general will is expressed.

The oldest distinction within the democratic form is that between direct and indirect democracy, according as the body of citizens does or does not actually legislate. In the former case there is a coalescence of the ultimate and the legislative sovereignty. Direct democracy, which Rousseau regarded as the only true form of the state, is in fact of very little significance. It may even be said to be contrary to the genius of democracy. We have pointed out that the so-called direct democracies of the ancient city-state were not democracies at all, but egalitarian oligarchies in which a ruling class of citizens shared the rights and spoils of political control. These tense and unstable experiments, highly significant as they are for the evolution of the state, offer no exception to the principle that democracy is a modern form. There was no solidarity in these states, no such identification of collective and individual interest as makes possible a system of political representation. The general will was insecure as well as partial. Democracy requires a degree of solidarity which enables the few to act for the many, because the many have confidence in, as well as control over, the few. Otherwise there is little proof that a common interest binds the state. We do find a few obscure ' direct democracies ' in the modern world, particularly in certain small mountain cantons of Switzerland. But they belong to undifferentiated rural communities where a lingering patriarchal principle gives cohesion to the common life.

The representative principle belongs to the very being of democracy. It is true that certain institutions for the direct expression of the popular will in legislation exist in some modern states. These however—the referendum and the initiative—are not continuous agencies of legislation, but constitutional means, employed on specific occasions for the determination of some vexed question. If they were continually in operation they would destroy the responsibility of government, without which a democracy cannot operate. Moreover as we shall see later, every democracy requires and develops a party-system, and the referendum and initiative are of little avail in respect of questions on which party-lines are already formed. The referendum is practicable only where important issues arise which cross the lines of party and yet demand settlement—such as the issue of ' prohibition' in certain states.[1] In such cases the referendum may be appealed to without disturbing the stability and responsibility of government, and in fact may be regarded by all parties as a welcome means of relieving them from the necessity of a disintegrating choice. As for the initiative, which is a peculiarly Swiss institution, devised in a federal state of numerous small political sections and united out of elements distinctly heterogeneous in language, race, and religion, its value, outside of the exceptional conditions within which it arose, is open to

[1] We should of course distinguish the employment of the referendum in the original establishment or the amendment of a constitution from its employment in respect of legislative acts. In the former case it is a device for eliciting the general will, not an instrument of government at all but a means of creating the constitution within which government shall act. So employed it is in fact the obvious mode of expression of the general will and does not properly present an alternative to the established forms of legislation. Here however a confusion is apt to occur if mere legislative enactments are illogically treated as if they were constitutional amendments, as in the case of the eighteenth amendment of the American constitution.

grave doubts. It is practically a city-state device, and it is significant that it is only in a few states with small populations, such as Oregon and Colorado, that its regular use has developed. In a large state, unless employed very rarely, it would probably become an additional and vexatious piece of legislative machinery under the control of irresponsible politicians. It is also noteworthy that ' the demand has generally been loudest where the reliance upon the integrity and capacity of the representatives has been least.[1]

Some form of representation is found in every modern democracy, and the simplest mode of classifying democracies is according to the form and range of the representative principle. The common feature of all such states is that the main legislative assembly is based on representation. The two extreme types are (a) states wherein the central government, including both legislative houses and the head of the executive, wholly depends on the result of representative election—this being the system of which the United States is the outstanding example ; and (b) states wherein only the ' house of commons ' is directly representative, while there exists a non-representative ' upper house ', a ministerial head not determined by the electoral system, and a permanent titular chief of the state. Of the latter class the British Constitution is to-day the most notable remaining instance. Between these formal extremes there is found a great diversity of types which renders

[1] Lowell, *Public Opinion and Popular Government*, p. 103. The exceptional employment of the initiative, to decide a conflict between the legislative and executive branches, as in Esthonia, or to determine a question of boundaries within a federation, as contemplated in the new constitution of Germany, or to remove some constitutional deadlock, is an entirely different matter.

classification very difficult. The selection of the 'second chamber' may be determined by heredity or election or nomination or any combination of these principles, while a few states abjure a second chamber altogether. The choice of chief executive may depend, directly or indirectly, on the popular vote or on the decision of the national assembly or legislative body. The ministry may be dependent on or independent of the party in control of legislation. It would complicate overmuch our classification if we considered the numerous variety of forms which arise in fact from the admixture of these methods. They depend on historical conditions peculiar to the states so differentiated and have often little relation to the degree of democratic development. The form is here misleading unless we look beyond it to the substance. To appreciate the character of a democracy we must consider for example whether the second chamber is effective or ineffective, not merely whether it is or is not representative ; and whether the head of the executive has considerable or inconsiderable power, not merely whether his office is hereditary or elective. Perhaps the most important distinctions are those between 'limited monarchy' and 'republic', according as the titular leadership is hereditary or otherwise, and between the 'parliamentary' and the 'congressional' system, according as the executive depends or does not depend on legislative support. The latter distinction we shall consider in the next chapter. The former distinction has in the course of political evolution lost much of its erstwhile sharpness. Democracy is inconsistent with any hereditary transmission of political authority, but a titular monarch may remain as a traditional relic, or as a symbol of unity, generally also as a focus of social or class prestige, long after the state has evolved an elaborate array of democratic institutions. The distinction between 'limited monarchy', however 'limited', and 'republic', nevertheless retains significance, for the psychological effect of the extrinsic social prestige of monarchy, even where bereft of political power, makes for conservatism and the confirmation of certain characters of the class-state, such as gradations of rank and honour.[1]

Democracy, like oligarchy, may be unitary or composite. A composite state involves the union under one government of a number of political entities, retaining separate administrations. In the form of empire the components do not create the common government. In the form of federation the components both retain a degree of sovereignty and together constitute the sovereign power which upholds the federal union. There is a general will as broad as the federation (except in a time of civil war), whereas empire rests on a far narrower basis of will. Federation differs from a mere league or alliance in that the comprehensive union which it forms is itself a true state, and not only the consentient and revocable act of a group of independent governments. It distinctly limits, though it does not abrogate, the sovereignty of the components.

There are leagues or unions of states which seem to fall somewhere between the mere alliance and the federation. They differ from the alliance in having a form of common government, so that they act through a single recognized authority in matters affecting the

---

[1] Constitutional monarchy, said M. de Laveleye, is the most 'delicate' of the forms of government, 'mais ce régime excellent exige de la part du souverain ou une indifférence complète ou un tact supérieur' (*Essai sur les Formes de Gouvernement*).

whole and especially in respect of external relations. They differ from federation in that this common government deals only with the constituent states and not directly with their individual citizens. Of such a type was the American Confederation whose articles were drawn up by the Continental Congress in 1777, a loose and ill-adapted unity without coercive authority, whether over the states or over individuals, to carry out its decisions. A much more remarkable and intricate type is that found in the British ' Commonwealth of Nations ', formed through the devolution of a colonial empire. Its external unity is assured through the existence of a single ' foreign office ', which acts on behalf of the whole ' empire '. The component states however autonomous, possess no international status except as members of that empire.[1] Its internal unity, on the other hand, is scarcely formal or constitutional at all, depending in part on tradition and sentiment, on common factors of nationality, and in part on specific arrangements and undertakings between the home country and the various dominions. The constitution of the ' League of Nations ' is yet too rudimentary for classification, but if it develops its character it will probably fall within this class. Its effective working involves a new type of ' confederation ', in which the member-states must confer limited powers on a super-state in respect of decisions affecting the relation of one to the other, and in which the individual citizens do not, as in a federation proper, owe a direct allegiance to the international government constituted by the particular states to which they belong.[2]

[1] On this interesting and difficult point, see Kennedy, *Constitution of Canada*, ch. xxv.

[2] This was in effect the type of federal union achieved by the old

Confederations of these types should probably be classed as actual states and not as mere alliances. The theoretical difficulty of attributing sovereignty to such unions as corporate wholes is met by the broader interpretation of sovereignty with which we have elsewhere dealt.

The distinctive feature of federation is the formal division of sovereign powers between the constituent or part-states and the larger state which they together compose. The citizen of each constituent state within the federation owes a double but not a conflicting political allegiance. He is a citizen of Ohio as well as of the United States or of Bavaria as well as of the Reich. This duality is made formally possible by a written constitution which demarcates the competence alike of the constituent state and of the federation. It assigns, say, the control of education or of criminal law to the part-states, and over those domains any action of the federal sovereign is thereby *ultra vires*. On the other hand it assigns, say, the control of the currency or of tariffs or of external affairs to the federal state, and over these domains any action of the constituent states is *ultra vires*. In respect of certain subjects concurrent legislation may be admitted, so that the governments of the constituent states share with the government of the union the control of legislation and administration. The true conception of this complicated system is attained when we attribute to the ' general will ' the act of synthesis and the form of unity which reconciles the division of sovereign powers. As we have shown elsewhere, it is futile to look in a true federation

Achaean League, although the citizens of the component states were nominally empowered to vote in the national assembly of the ' League '.

for some ultimate unity on the level of the legislative sovereignty. The written constitution is the expression or embodiment of a will more fundamental than any which is exercised by either the federal state or the constituent states.

The form of federation differs markedly in the various cases.[1] It has a distinctive character in Germany, in the Swiss Confederation, in Australia, in Canada, and in the United States. The division of sovereign powers varies in such a way as to make generalization very difficult, and in some cases, as in the German Confederation of 1871–1918 and the Swiss Confederation established 1874, even certain rights of entering into external relations may be retained by the constituent states. These latter must however be regarded as mere exceptions to or very partial limitations of the general principle. Substantially the federal state as a unity controls all the relations of the constituent states with external powers, and invariably it has the exclusive right of war and peace. Apart from that principle there is no necessary allocation of functions between the constituent states and the union, though considerations of expedience and convenience suggest that, as usually happens, the control of armed forces, of immigration and naturalization, of coinage, and of the agencies of intercommunication, should be vested in the federal authority.

In some federations the powers and functions of the constituent states may be viewed as subordinate in importance to those exercised by the union. This happens in Canada where the undefined or residual powers of sovereignty rest with the Dominion, where

[1] For an account of these differences see Newton, *Federal and Unified Constitutions*, and Smith, *Federation in North America*.

the Dominion is vested with the general right ' to make laws for the peace, order, and good government of Canada in relation to all matters not coming within the classes of subjects by this act assigned exclusively to the legislatives of the provinces ', and where above all the Dominion has the general right to disallow any provincial legislation whatever which it deems to be injurious to the welfare of the country as a whole. Formally, the United States stands at the other extreme, since, as expressly stated in the Tenth Amendment, ' the powers not delegated to the United States by the Constitution, nor prohibited to it by the states, are reserved to the states respectively, and to the people.' Such formal limitations tend however to be obscured by the logic of the federal state, which through governmental boards and commissions, through the allocation of federal funds on condition of co-operation by the states in general projects, and through the growing prestige of the greater and central organization, extends its activity more and more widely over the fields of inter-state concerns. Federalism, like democracy itself, is a matter of degree, but the general tendency is towards a stronger unity. This is inevitable, provided the federation is one that really meets the approval of the states so joined. For it evokes contacts and closer communications, and removes the invisible as well as the visible barriers of alienism erected by separate sovereignties. New threads of relationship are freely spun across the consentient states. The universal character of many human interests is liberated and recognized. Within the close federation the absence of customs barriers alone is a most potent factor in liberating the common spirit, for travellers are not confronted with the abrupt and uncomfortable reminder that an invisible line divides land from land. Common facilities of all kinds co-operate with common laws and common standards. A federation once formed on a sound basis is the beginning of a continuous process of integration. It by no means follows that the autonomy of the constituent states will ultimately disappear. Interests that are best served by a common government will tend towards centralization while particularist interests will assert the nearer autonomy. Similarly in the unitary state the logic of interests creates at once centralization and decentralization, so that from both directions the federal and the unitary state approximate in character to one another.

The great advantage of federation lies in the fact that it permits, without undue or enforced centralization, the recognition and establishment of common interests. An excellent illustration is found if we contrast the situation existing between two states of the American union, say New York State and Virginia, with that existing between an American state and its immediate neighbour across the international line, say New York State and Ontario, or Washington and British Columbia. In the latter situation all the demographic characters, the conditions of climate, territory, population, and social development, are very similar, whereas in the former they are more diverse. But the facilities of intercourse and the free development of common interests within the federal union quite spontaneously create an operative sense of solidarity which political barriers and separate political affiliations prevent under conditions otherwise far more favourable.

We may now proceed to give a conspectus of the forms of the state, remembering at the same time that states, like other social forms, are not explicitly and finally marked off into genera and species. The types pass almost imperceptibly into one another, both historically and in the present. Social types have not the comparative fixity of organic forms. There are instead a few distinctive principles of formation which are embodied, scarcely ever completely, scarcely ever without admixture, in historical and contemporary states.

FORMS OF THE STATE

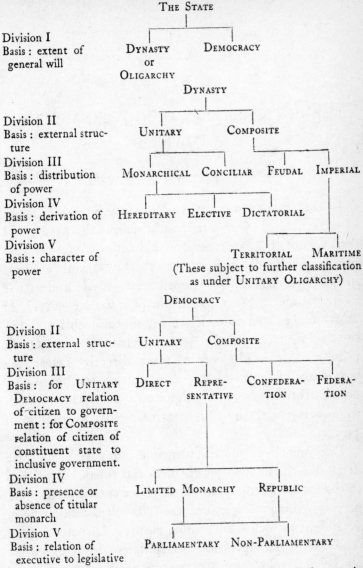

THE STATE

Division I
Basis : extent of general will

DYNASTY or OLIGARCHY — DEMOCRACY

DYNASTY

Division II
Basis : external structure

UNITARY — COMPOSITE

Division III
Basis : distribution of power

MONARCHICAL — CONCILIAR — FEUDAL — IMPERIAL

Division IV
Basis : derivation of power

HEREDITARY — ELECTIVE — DICTATORIAL

Division V
Basis : character of power

TERRITORIAL — MARITIME
(These subject to further classification as under UNITARY OLIGARCHY)

DEMOCRACY

Division II
Basis : external structure

UNITARY — COMPOSITE

Division III
Basis : for UNITARY DEMOCRACY relation of citizen to government : for COMPOSITE relation of citizen of constituent state to inclusive government.

DIRECT — REPRESENTATIVE — CONFEDERATION — FEDERATION

Division IV
Basis : presence or absence of titular monarch

LIMITED MONARCHY — REPUBLIC

Division V
Basis : relation of executive to legislative

PARLIAMENTARY — NON-PARLIAMENTARY

In respect of composite states the term DEMOCRACY refers to the relation of the constituent states, not of the citizens, to the inclusive union. If that relation is a free one it is classified as DEMOCRACY, whatever the internal character of the constituents.

XII

THE ARTICULATION OF GOVERNMENTAL POWER

I. THE DIVISION OF POWERS

In this work we are not concerned with the mechanics of government. Our task is to bring out the nature and direction of the state, and it would suffer confusion were we to involve it in a survey of the variant political institutions which have been elaborated under the historical and present conditions of different states. It must suffice, therefore, if we examine, in this and the succeeding chapter, the general character of certain primary institutions which most directly reveal the moulding influences of the community. In this respect no institutions are more significant than those which we associate with the famous principle of the division of powers.

This was no primordial principle, born with the state itself, like the distinction of rulers and ruled. It belongs to the modern democratic state. No dynastic state could proclaim this principle, because it involves a doctrine of sovereignty which is alien to its nature. It requires more than the mere separation of legislative from executive power, it implies also a certain priority of the former, and this the dynastic state could never admit. Nor could it arise under the magisterial system of the ancient city-state. A magistracy works on too small a scale to separate the legislative from the executive function.[1] The effective distinction of the legislative function from all others depends ultimately upon the distinction between the authority of the law and that of the law-maker. If law is universal, the expressed will of the state as a whole, it must be saved from the dangers of its dependence on the wills of those who at any time are empowered to act in the name of the state, to modify and to interpret and to execute it. It was the root-idea of Montesquieu, the great promulgator of this doctrine, that the assurance of law was to be found in the separate embodiment of the various functions connected with the law. In his own simple terms, ' from the very nature of things power should be a check to power ',[2] if liberty—or law itself—is to endure.

The division of governmental functions into distinct types, and usually into three, is ancient enough, and may be traced back to that fountain-head of political analysis, the *Politics* of Aristotle.[3] There were also, before Montesquieu, thinkers who emphasized the distinction as having practical importance, notably Locke. But the author of *L'Esprit des Lois* went a step further. To him the important thing was not the analysis of functions, but the principle of their embodiment in separate organs. For him this was above all else a practical recipe for political liberty, the philosophical implications of which he scarcely examined or even realized. The trinity of powers conceived by him, ' legislative ', ' executive ', and

---

[1] It is interesting to note that the Soviet system, resting on the conciliar or magisterial idea, also fails to demarcate these functions. Cf. Bonn, *Die Auflösung des modernen Staats*, p. 28.

[2] *L'Esprit des Lois*, XI. iv.   [3] *Politics*, IV. xiv.

'judicial', *ought* to be, *must* be, separately embodied, that is, exercised by different men or groups. It is the doctrine which was stated in forthright terms in the constitution of certain states of the American union, such as Virginia and Massachusetts. It was also proclaimed as part of the very meaning of the state by the French Revolutionary Assembly when it laid down the dogma that 'every society in which the separation of powers is not determined has no constitution'.

This doctrine, so perceptual and so simple-sounding, nevertheless raises some of the profoundest questions of political theory. Can we speak at all of distinct political *powers* ? Are we thinking of mere aspects or manifestations of a single indivisible sovereignty, and if so how can they be separate in their 'embodiment' ? Are the 'powers' merely activities or functions connected with government which may be exercised through separate *organs* that remain nevertheless within the unity of the political 'organism' ? Should we distinguish between 'powers' and 'functions', and say with Hauriou [1] that, while the functions may be combined in practice, the powers are in the nature of things separate 'provinces of will' underived from one another, and inalienably distinct ?

The distinction of organ and function is clear enough. Parliament may be described as a political organ, whose function is to legislate. A ministry is a political organ whose function is executive. The Cabinet is an organ which combines legislative with executive functions. A court of law is an organ with a judicial function. And so forth. This distinction is merely embarrassed if we follow M. Hauriou and others in their insistence on

[1] *Principes de droit public* (2ᵉ ed. Paris, 1916).

a further distinction between functions and powers.
Wherever a function is performed there is of course
a power to perform that function. Wherever there is
an activity there is a potentiality in respect of it. The
function of the eye is to see—does it help our study of
that function to discover, behind the function of seeing,
an entity we call the power of vision? We cannot
study powers except as active, except as functioning.
For the purpose of this discussion the distinction of
function and power involves a 'needless multiplication
of entities'. Our problem (like Montesquieu's, though
he spoke of 'powers') concerns the nature of political
functions, the lines of division between them, together
with the possibility and the desirability of their fulfilment
through separate organs.

What in the first place are the irreducible types of
governmental functions? What, in other words, are
the essential ways in which all governments must carry
on their work? Since a government does not act on its
own behalf or in its own right but always in the name of
the state, since also its primary task is the maintenance
of a general order within society, it must act according
to established rules or laws. In so far as it adds to, amends,
or abrogates any of these laws it must, for the same reason,
conform to established principles of law-making. Finally,
it may be empowered to amend even these principles of
law-making, but always according to already established
modes—or this constitution-making power may be with-
held from it by the constitution itself. In so far as
government lays down rules, whether legal or constitutional, it is exercising the legislative function. This is
the fundamental function of government. In the developed state all other activities of government are

expressly referable to an authority assigned by law. The legislative function is therefore logically supreme.

We might indeed carry analysis further and distinguish two functions of legislation, one relative to the constitution and the other relative to the code of ordinary law, and as we have seen these functions may be exercised by the same or by different organizations within the state. In some states we find a still further differentiation of functions. This is notably the case in the United States, where a constitution-amending body may at any time be called into being under conditions prescribed in the constitution itself, while on the other hand a regular organ of the state, the Supreme Court, is assigned the right of deciding on the constitutionality of ordinary laws.

Reserving for later consideration the peculiar problem created by the relation of law-making power and constitution-making power, we may meanwhile conclude that the regular functions of government fall into two main divisions, one concerned with acts of legislation and the other with acts which are requisite for carrying legislation into effect. This classification does not properly include acts of government which are not directly or indirectly dependent on legislative power, such as the acts of an oligarchical ' executive ' or absolute monarch. Such acts belong particularly to the sphere of foreign relations, treaty-making, war and peace, and foreign policy in general, and it is significant that Locke made the ' federative ' function which deals with these matters one of his three ' powers ' of government. In fact his classification, distinguishing the legislative, the executive, and the federative powers, was at least as logical for his age as the later Montesquieuan classification which replaced it. Even in the most modern democracy the power of the foreign office can only by a stretch of language be named ' executive ', so independent does it still generally remain of the processes and forms of legislation. As democracy develops it claims that Parliament shall exercise greater control over this most important sphere, and in so far as its control grows effective the department of foreign affairs approximates to a true executive department.[1] We may say then that in a complete democracy, though there alone, the twofold division set out above includes all the regular activities of government.

It is characteristic of oligarchy that the executive or administrative authority dominates the legislative, just as the contrary relationship is a principle of democracy. But in the development of oligarchy, as well as in that of democracy, a further distinction of functions appears. The judicial application of the law may be vested in the people or their agents, while the execution of it belongs to a narrower class. Thus ' in the Germanic States the interpretation of the law, *Rechtsprechung*, with the adjudication of wrongs to property and torts, remained in the hands of the people long after the execution of judgements and sentences (the administration of justice) had passed over to the King and his servants '.[2] In the broadest sense the judicial function is part of the administration of law, but the historical process has demarcated the executive from the judicature, and since in fact the latter is peculiarly isolable from the business

---

[1] It may in fact be maintained that treaty-making is properly a form of legislation. Thus under the American Constitution a treaty duly ratified by the Senate and entering into force becomes *ipso facto* a portion of the law of the land (cf. Oakes and Mowat, *The Great European Treaties of the Nineteenth Century*, p. 5).

[2] Redlich and Hirst, *Local Government in England*, Bk. II, Pt. VII.

both of the legislature and of the ministries we arrive at the accepted division of powers into three.

What then of the claim that these functions should be embodied in separate organs of government, each acting as a check on the other ? We should note in the first place that the functions are not co-ordinate or equal. The judicial function, although its range is much wider than the interpretation and application of legal enactment, is obviously subordinate to the legislative. And in the growth of modern democracy the executive has been gradually reduced from a superior or co-ordinate power to one which is subject to legislative control. This subjection is an essential condition of all ' responsible ' government, without which democracy cannot exist. Thus in the process by which colonies become self-governing states, a first necessity was the substitution of an executive dependent on the legislature of the colony for one appointed by an outside government.[1] Similarly, the internal transition from oligarchy to democracy and the abolition of kingship or its reduction to ' constitutional monarchy ' was realized through the development of a representative legislature which gained authority over the ministers of state.[2] If then the functions are to be separately embodied it is not because they are or should be equal in authority. Nor can they equally act as a check upon one another. The judicature, for example, can scarcely check the legislature at all.[3]

When Montesquieu wrote, the other powers were not

---

[1] Cf. Kennedy, *The Constitution of Canada*, cc. xii, xv, and xvi.

[2] Cf. Adams, *The Origin of the English Constitution*, ch. iv.

[3] The Supreme Court of the United States does not check congress in its judicial function, but as exercising powers of an entirely different character. See Bk. IV, ch. xvi, § ii.

properly subordinated to the legislative. That all the activities of government should be determined by law proved to be a more important safeguard of liberty than his own prescription. The immediate object of his prescription was to insure the purity of law against the temptations of personal power. He could offer only this mechanical device of separation, which has its own place, particularly as applied to the judicature, but which is of minor importance compared with the greater principle of democracy, the attachment of responsibility to power by a vigilant electorate.

The absolute separation of powers prescribed by Montesquieu is obviously impossible. Every legislature performs some executive duties and as the chief and sometimes the only representative organ, being directly responsible to the citizens, it raises and discusses questions relative to the conduct of the executive and the judicature. Moreover the line between legislative enactment and executive or judicial decision is never hard-and-fast. Ministerial ordinances or decrees have been a formidable substitute for legislation and, as in Austria and Prussia under the old constitutions, have been a bulwark of oligarchy against the control of the popularly elected house. There is even to-day no clear line to demarcate the proper objects of legislation from those of executive or even of judicial decision. In the English parliament it is a matter of discretion whether certain measures are introduced as ' public bills ' or ' private bills ', the former being regarded as of a true legislative character, whereas the latter are matters of local government over which parliament exercises an administrative control. In Canada, to take an extreme example, a divorce can be secured in certain provinces only through a formal act of the Federal parliament, although almost anywhere else it is simply a matter for the courts. The chief reason why the legislature should not seek to undertake the regular work of the executive and the judicature is to-day not so much the danger to liberty as the loss of efficiency which their union involves. The business of legislation falls to a representative body which is inevitably un-specialized as well as being of considerable size. It is therefore unadapted to the specialized tasks of the executive. It is wholly unfitted to do the work of the judicature, because it is subject to the influences of every-day politics, because its organization as well as its temper is out of accord with the judicial spirit, and because its members are not chosen for their capacity or training as judges.

Perhaps the real problem of the ' division of powers ' is so to articulate these functions that responsibility shall not be divorced from efficiency. Responsibility implies representation, efficiency demands expert knowledge ; the two can scarcely be united in a single organ of government. If the representative principle is applied to administrators and judges, as is the tendency in the United States, we have the strange result that offices demanding the highest expert qualifications are at the mercy of the popular appeal, a situation that would be ruinous to the affairs of the most ordinary business. Besides, under such a system there is no guarantee of co-operation and harmony between the legislature and the executive. The latter is not responsible to, nor dependent upon, the former. There is isolation and disharmony.[1] What is needed, in fact, is not the separa-

---

[1] Cf. Woodrow Wilson, *The State* : ' Under our system we have isolation *plus* irresponsibility—isolation and *therefore* irresponsibility.'

tion of functions but their proper articulation, in conformity with the first principle of democracy, that all government is a trust delegated and controlled by the governed.

Every modern state both distinguishes and seeks in some degree to articulate the three accepted functions of government. The methods adopted differ in important respects. As regards the relation of the judicature to the other functions, the form of articulation is usually simple, being mainly a matter of the mode by which courts are constituted and judges appointed. Judges may be appointed by the executive or by the legislature or may be directly elected by the people, the usual method being some form of nomination by the executive. The merits of the various systems cannot be discussed here nor need we consider the problem raised by the fact that some states have special administrative courts to which the executive is subject while others have not. It must suffice to remark that the business of judging both demands and admits an unusual independence, on the part of the judge, from the engrossments and fortunes of party politics. He sits apart, to interpret and to pronounce, and the limits of his function are set for him, not by the policies of the hour but by the spirit of the code and of a great profession trained in its study. An ultimate safeguard is even here necessary. None can be entrusted with power without some guarantee against its abuse. A judge, within the limits of his jurisdiction, can be a petty and irascible tyrant. But the right of appeal is a restraining influence, and in the last resort the judge may be made subject to the general power of government, exercised through the legislature or through the combined action of legislature and executive. This final guarantee can be secured in such a way that political expediency is not suffered to touch the authority or effect the status of the appointed judge.

The relation of executive and legislature is necessarily more intimate and more continuous. Of all devices to secure this very important contact the 'cabinet system' seems the most effective, the 'knuckle joint', in Bagehot's famous phrase, where the two functions coalesce. There is little doubt as to the advantage of this system in all states where the chief executive is not directly constituted through popular election. There it proves a means of assuring responsibility no less than of maintaining the harmony of government. Without it there is no assurance of the supremacy of the legislature, a desideratum which is in accordance with our principle that the making of law is the primary business of the state. It makes parliament the focus of government so that the ultimate sovereign, by direct control of parliament, can without an elaborate constitutional machinery control the whole conduct of the state. The cabinet may in fact dominate parliament, but since parliament has always the right and the power to control the cabinet, all that is necessary to avoid this danger is the public recognition of it. The weakness, so far as it exists, lies not in the system but in the passivity of the popular will—and no system can be stronger than its own supports. On the other hand, where the executive is not directly related to the legislature, where, as in the United States, it is not formally subject to legislative control, the respective functions of the two, must be elaborately prescribed by the constitution.[1] This method is much less flexible than the cabinet system. The machinery of the state is not unified

[1] Cf. Goodnow, *Principles of Constitutional Government*, ch. x.

within itself. The law-making power has not the clear supremacy which our understanding of the nature of law properly assigns to it. The executive acts in awkward independence, or exerts an influence over the legislature which cannot easily be reconciled with the principle of democracy.

Where there is a single focus of government, as under the cabinet system, the responsibility of government as a whole to the ultimate sovereign is formally assured. Where there is more than one focus, as under the former German system or the Presidential system of the United States, the onus of co-ordination is thrown back on a constitutional device which responds far less freely to the changing conditions of government and the movements of the popular will. In fact, the latter method raises in a peculiar measure the problem which in some measure arises in all modern states, the problem of sovereignty as it is set by the system of checks and balances through which one organ of government limits and controls the action of another. To this question we now turn.

II

CHECKS AND BALANCES WITHIN A SYSTEM OF GOVERNMENT

Practically all modern states have provided some form of check upon the free action of their own representatives. In none of them is a single legislative body absolutely untrammelled, so that its will shall prevail without possible stay or question. If we leave out of account the special circumstances created by an independent executive, there remain three modes in which the legislature is or may be restricted in its power to make or change the law. The first of these is a written constitution which the legislature is not competent, in its normal activity, to alter. The second is the presence of two houses of legislation, each of which must ratify the acts of the other before they can assume the form of laws. The third is the direct intervention of the electorate itself not now to choose its representatives, but actually to legislate, to initiate acts or to ratify or veto acts emanating from the legislature. All these modes are significant for the study of the nature of sovereignty.

The limitations set by a written constitution are very various in degree and kind. In some cases, as in Italy, the constitution is amenable to the same process of amendment or repeal as ordinary laws : in others, as in France, the legislature, in a special form of convocation, is formally competent to amend : in others, as in Belgium, amendment requires a two-thirds majority of both houses after a special election for the purpose of revision ; while in certain cases, and pre-eminently in the United States, the constitution is set above the power of the legislature altogether, and can be amended only by an elaborate and difficult process intended to secure that no change shall take place without a strong preponderance of opinion in its favour. The recognition of a constitution or fundamental law of the state—whether written or unwritten—sets a certain *moral* limitation to the power of the legislature even where no expressed difficulty is placed in the way of amendment. The legislature is not likely to modify it except under strong impulsion. But where the constitution itself makes amendment difficult, by requiring, say, a two-thirds or three-fourths majority vote as a condition, a peculiar problem is raised. It may be argued that what the constitution does is to insure that public opinion is very definitely in favour of any proposed change before it can be translated into law. But it does more than this. It gives a veto power against change to a minority. If then all government rests on the will of the people, on what will does a system rest which confers on the minority a right to veto the will of the majority? It may be that the majority will acquiesce in, or even approve of, a limitation of this kind, but how can we be sure when by a past act it is deprived of present power? Does not a constitution of so rigorous a character bind the living will of the state in the present? If we say, with Austin, that the sovereign in the United States is a three-fourths majority of the states, are we not really saying that a one-fourth minority is supreme? Have we not here an example of what happens wherever men try to assure a more-than-majority will? The endeavour ends in their enthroning a minority-will, just so much the less as men seek to attain the more.

That the sovereign cannot curb its own sovereignty, that its past act cannot restrain its present exercise save as it wills to recognize and reaffirm that act, is a maxim accepted by the jurisprudence of at least such states as are not held within the framework of an iron constitution. This, in fact, is the only logical position. What a majority decides a majority can rescind—that is the logic of sovereignty—but it does not follow that what a three-fourths majority decides *should* require a three-fourths majority to rescind, or in other words only a one-fourth minority to maintain. A constitutional rule of this nature, even if unanimously adopted on some historical occasion, may put an unnecessary and unreasonable strain on the general will itself, by restricting the liberty of the true determinant of policy, the ultimate sovereignty. There are in fact many historical cases where a government has proclaimed a rule or a guarantee as binding for all time, only to have the pledge of perpetuity itself rescinded at some later date. The power to bind is logically the power to loose. Even if government, through the legislature or the courts, reaffirms its original pledge, as Chief Justice Marshall did in the famous Dartmouth College case, it is a new act of sovereignty and might have been a retractation instead of a confirmation of the pledge. It may be maintained that this doctrine strikes at the sanctity of every contract made or guaranteed by the state. But the answer is surely that here we are thrown back on an ultimate moral principle. The state is morally bound to fulfil its contracts and pledges, not blindly for all time—for that is not the nature of moral obligation—but as it perceives the whole of the issue involved. It is within such limits morally bound, but how can it be legally bound? To maintain that it is involves a misunderstanding of the source and sanction of law. Nor can we accept the simple solution that a state *should* observe in perpetuity all the guarantees which past governments have sought to make perpetual, for that would be to ' allow their mistakes of fact, their legal misconceptions, their economic obtuseness, their partisan passions and prejudices, to reach down through the decades and make law for us in regard to some of our most vital interests '.[1]

In a federal state there is of course an additional problem of sovereignty. Here a written constitution is necessary to define the respective powers of the federal

---

[1] Jesse F. Orton, on ' The Dartmouth College Case ', in the *Independent*, August 1909, quoted by Orth, *The Relation of Government to Property and Industry*.

state and of its constituent states, but what is the will which determines, and may on occasion revise, the allotment of powers? Here we cannot simply appeal to the principle of majority, whether it be a majority of the federal state as such or a majority of the constituents regarded as units. For in a true federation each constituent has *ex hypothesi* a certain autonomy, recognized in the articles of union. This would seem to imply that no change of its relation to the whole or to the others can legitimately be forced upon it by a majority outside itself, or, more strictly, that, *apart from the conditions it has accepted in entering the federation or at any later time*, it remains in the position of a free state. The fact that a state resigns certain powers should not logically prejudice the powers that it retains. Its tenacity in respect of these powers may impede the development of the federal state of which it is a member and may seriously interfere with projects of a national character. But this is a difficulty inherent in the very form of federation.

A deeper problem lies hidden in the most important limitation on which we have insisted above—' apart from the conditions it has accepted in entering the federation or at any later time '. A constituent state, for example, is bound by the federal constitution to which it has agreed, including the form of an amendment therein prescribed. But it is bound only in so far as the sovereignty it retains is not affected against its will. Up to that point the constitution is a fundamental law, beyond it the constitution is still only a treaty between states. This conclusion is in accord with the spirit and purpose of federation. Otherwise there would be no permanent significance in the general clause defining sovereign powers which is found in federal constitutions, such as the Tenth Amendment of the American Constitution or Articles 3 and 5 of the Swiss Federal Constitution.[1] It is reasonable to regard such a clause as not itself amenable to amendment by a majority vote, being itself the precondition of the federation. A federal state is one with a specifically limited sovereignty, the limits being set by the reserved sovereignty of its constituents. The conception of a sovereignty so limited is hard to reconcile with the older theories of sovereign powers, but it is perfectly consistent with a realistic interpretation of the state, as we shall show more fully at a later stage. The sovereignty of the federal state is no less real for being limited. It too rests on a general will which may grow stronger and broader with the process of time. In this will, the will of its members for the federal state as a whole, is alone found the guarantee of its permanence and unity. The federal state, by a wise respect for the sovereign powers retained by its constituents, cannot only prevent disruption but can confirm and strengthen its own integrity. The sense of its common citizenship is fortified by the community of interests which are fostered within it. Custom and precedent will work continuously in its favour. A national spirit will develop which will lay less stress on the autonomy of the constituents, which will neither seek nor need to abrogate that autonomy because with a deepening sense of common

[1] Art. 3 reads : ' The Cantons are sovereign in so far as their sovereignty is not limited by the Federal Constitution, and as such they exercise all the rights which are not delegated to the federal power.' Art. 5 reads : ' The Confederation guarantees to the Cantons their territory, their sovereignty within the limits fixed by Art. 3, their constitutions, the liberty and rights of the people, the constitutional rights of citizens together with the rights and attributions which the people has conferred on the authorities.'

purpose it will find its proper place. The original acceptance by each member-state of the conditions of federation will be transformed into its permanent devotion to the union, and the oppositions of interest and policy will cause no deeper division than occurs in unitary states. Under such conditions the member-states may still maintain their state-rights as formally defined, or, as in the case of South Africa, they may move towards a full legislative union in which the general will is so integrated that it can dispense with the hard and fast limits of the federal demarcation of powers.[1]

We turn to the second mode by which the action of a legislative assembly may be limited or checked. In nearly all modern states, if we omit certain member-states within a federal system, there are two legislative houses. All of the new post-war constitutions, excepting those of Finland, Esthonia, and Jugoslavia, have adopted this system. In times of upheaval and transition three great states have experimented with a unicameral legislature, England in the time of Cromwell, France in the period of Revolution, and America before the establishment of the Constitution, but each returned to the bicameral principles. It would seem therefore as if there were strong motives impelling the state to set up two legislative houses neither of which can make its will effective as law without the consent of the other.

Yet when we ask just what their motives are the answer is none too clear. It is most commonly asserted

---

[1] The process of integration makes it sometimes hard to say whether a once federal state is still entitled to be called a federation. Is the German Reich under its post-war constitution really a federation? It is highly doubtful. See e. g., McBain and Rogers, *The New Constitution of Europe*, ch. iv.

that the reason for the existence of a second chamber is the need felt for some check against the danger of hasty or ill-considered legislation by the first. If this reason justifies the fact it does not at any rate explain the origin of the bicameral system. It originated from the caste divisions of society, the upper classes retaining an organ of government while the growth of democracy fashioned a representative assembly. The later-born federal states found the general principle convenient, a second house providing a means whereby the member-states might, as unities, be more distinctly represented. Thus the principle came to be regarded as one of those universal characters of government whose mere existence is taken for granted. Most discussions turned more on the question how a second chamber should be constituted than on the prior question whether a second chamber should exist and on what grounds. Nor was much consideration given to the problem of sovereignty which is involved in the fact of a double legislature. The staunchest upholders of the doctrine of the 'one and indivisible' sovereign approved a system of two houses so far from being unified that they were sometimes acutely divided.

If we could literally accept the nomenclature which distinguishes the houses as 'upper' and 'lower' the theoretical difficulty might be solved. For then the relation between them might be analogous to that between a lower court and a court of appeal, involving no true conflicts of authority. But this relation no longer holds in the modern state.[1] With the growth of democracy the once lower house has generally become dominant and in no one instance does it regard itself as inferior.

[1] Cf. McBain and Rogers, *op. cit.*, ch. iii.

The tendency has been, except in certain federal states, rather to subordinate the second chamber. It is usually less ' popular ', less representative of and less responsive to the changes of public opinion. The second chamber has in fact become subject to a peculiar dilemma. Unless it is constituted on a broad representative principle it lacks the authority which derives from the support of public opinion ; if it is so constituted it tends to be a duplicate of the first house and lacks a *raison d'être*. In some recent constitutions, as in that of the Irish Free State, much ingenuity has been expended to devise for the second house a basis of representation which shall be different from that of the first house without forfeiting the claim of the former to rest on the popular will.[1] Whether the problem so stated is in fact soluble still remains open to doubt.

It is possible to have a system of two houses equal in authority, so that each has an equal veto on the legislative acts of the other. It is possible, but it has extremely awkward consequences. A formal deadlock may be avoided by some form of joint committee, as in France, Sweden, and other countries, but unless the two houses are equally supported by public opinion— a situation which it seems almost impossible to maintain— on any crucial measure the will of the more representative house must in time prevail. A further difficulty lies in the relation of the executive to the two houses. No

[1] The Constitution of the Irish Free State provides that the Senate shall be elected by proportional representation, the whole state forming for the purpose a single constituency, from a list of candidates nominated by the Dail and the Senate itself ' on the grounds that they have done honour to the nation by reason of useful public service or that, because of special qualifications or attainments, they represent important aspects of the nation's life '. (See Articles 30–4 of the Constitution.)

system of ministerial responsibility to the legislature can work if that responsibility is itself divided. If a ministry and the ' upper house ' can join forces against the ' lower house ', the basis of responsible government is insecure. There is here a strong argument for the English system which makes the ministry directly responsible to the House of Commons, while at the same time assigning it the power of dissolving parliament. The working of the cabinet system seems to imply the supremacy of the ' lower house '. In a democratic state it is the only way to secure the unity of government. It is significant that the recently established constitutions of Europe, created under the impulse of the democratic spirit, have in every case sought to secure, both that the ministry shall be responsible to parliament and also that the second chamber shall be subordinate to the first.[1]

Unless the question of priority is determined it is obviously impossible to arrive at any conclusions regarding the relative functions of the two houses. There are such great discrepancies in the degree and kind of power exercised by the second chambers of various states that a mere induction is of little value. Nor does the formal right of the second house to control legislation avail as a criterion of its actual power. Much depends on the prestige which public opinion bestows, the support accorded by the final source of power, as the House of Lords realized in its famous conflicts with the Commons. A weak second chamber, like the Canadian Senate, whose members are appointed on a life tenure by the cabinet, may have ample powers according to the letter of the constitution, but may prove relatively ineffective. A strong second chamber, like the American Senate, can

[1] McBain and Rogers, *op. cit.*, ch. iii.

with impunity exert a degree of authority which would cause a constitutional crisis, if attempted by other Senates formally as free.[1]

There is a general, though not universal, acceptance of certain principles regarding the relation of the second chamber to the first. It is generally agreed that, both to maintain the unity of government and to assure the claims of democracy, the second chamber should not exercise powers equal to those of the first, either in scope or in finality. It is generally agreed that the initiation of money bills should belong to the lower house, and that it should have greater control in respect of these. It is also generally agreed that the executive should be, at least in countries where the cabinet system prevails, directly related to the lower house, rather than to the upper.[2] These agreements, in so far as they represent the practice of modern states, make possible an articulated and unified form of government.

What then, if we accept these principles, are the proper functions of the second chamber ? It is commonly said,

[1] For example, ' in 1909 the Tariff Bill, when returned from the Senate (of the United States), carried eight hundred and forty-seven amendments ' (Senator Lodge in *The Political Quarterly*, February 1914).

[2] It has repeatedly been maintained that in a true federation there must be two houses of approximately equal power, the upper chamber being the guardian of the federal principle, and that therefore the cabinet system is alien to this form of government. This was strongly maintained by certain representatives, notably Sir R. C. Baker, during the passage of the Commonwealth of Australia Bill. (See Official Report of the National Australasian Convention, Adelaide, 1897, pp. 27–31, and Debates of the Australasian Federal Convention, Second Division, Sydney, 1897, pp. 782 ff.) But the experience of Australia, and we may add that of Canada also, shows that the cabinet system is quite workable within a federation.

that the true business of the second chamber is to act as a revising body and as 'a check on hasty legislation'. As for the former function we should distinguish the situation created by cabinet government from that which exists in states in which the executive is independent of the legislature. In the former parliament has at its service a responsible ministry and therewith a permanent body of experts in the drafting of laws. It does not, or should not, need to depend on a second chamber for mere technical revision, though this function may be appropriate where such conditions are lacking. As for the claim that a second chamber is a useful check on the precipitancy of the first, it is practically equivalent to saying that the second chamber, because of its less representative character, tends to be more conservative than the first. The statement is doubtless true, but it would be unfortunate if we had to seek the justification for any political institution in the fact that it favours one rather than the other of the great antitheses of public opinion. On this subject there is wisdom in the words of Mill : ' I attach little weight to the argument oftenest heard for having two Chambers—to prevent precipitancy and compel a second deliberation ; for it must be a very ill-constituted representative assembly in which the established forms of business do not require many more than two deliberations. The consideration which tells most, in my judgement, in favour of two Chambers (and this I do regard as of some moment) is the evil effect produced upon the mind of any holder of power, whether an individual or an assembly, by the consciousness of having only themselves to consult. It is important that no set of persons should be able, even temporarily, to make their *sic volo* prevail, without asking any one else for his consent '.[1] Perhaps this is the final argument, and were it possible to devise a second chamber which would not, by its very constitution, incline towards one rather than the other of the great traditional parties, the argument might pass unchallenged.

But this is a desideratum which it is perhaps beyond human ingenuity to achieve. Consequently the powers of the second chamber in many countries have been subject to the attack of the party which it is presumed least to favour. The result has been the weakening of its powers, since in the case of a conflict with the lower house it cannot appeal to a party, it must appeal to the country. This has led to a new theory of its chief function, as being 'the interposition of so much delay (and no more) in the passing of a bill into law as may be needed to enable the opinion of the nation to be adequately expressed upon it.[2] So functioning, the other house is at least secure in its supports, offering to safe-guard instead of to oppose that will of the state which has already learned that it can and must prevail.

There remains for consideration a set of institutions which give the ultimate sovereign, instead of its representative assembly alone, the direct function of legislation. These are the initiative and the referendum.[3] They represent movements in the modern state towards direct

[1] *Representative Government*, ch. xiii.

[2] *Conference on the Reform of the Second Chamber : Letter from Viscount Bryce to the Prime Minister*, 1918. Cmd. 9038. By the constitution of the Irish Free State a three-fifths majority of the Senate may cause a bill to be submitted to referendum.

[3] With these is sometimes associated the ' recall ', a device intended to give the electorate a direct control over the executive or judicature, through the right to recall public officials, or compel them to submit on petition to the test of re-election.

democracy. They imply that the principle of representation is not adequate to provide the true expression of the popular will, or else that there are certain spheres of legislation, pre-eminently the constitution or fundamental laws, over which no representative assembly should be supreme. We should distinguish the application of these devices to constitutional amendment from their employment in the making or the unmaking of the ordinary laws. In the former case they may serve to emphasize and give a special sanction to the constitution, without involving the logical and practical defects of the systems which require a more-than-majority will for its amendment. We have pointed out that the formal attempt to institute a mightier will than the majority defeats its purpose by assigning to that extent the right of sovereign decision to the minority. The use of the referendum in its simple form permits the ultimate sovereign to decide directly, isolating so far as possible the single constitutional question from all the cross-issues which complicate the decision of a representative assembly. It is still the majority that must decide, but under conditions of direct responsibility which give a signal importance to their choice. Thus the law of the constitution may, without confusion or impediment, be distinguished and set apart from the ordinary laws of the state.

This distinction is to a certain extent borne out by the practice of modern states. In Switzerland, the home of these devices, the referendum is obligatory in respect of constitutional questions, while in respect of others it is ' facultative '. In the United States it came into prominence chiefly in the process of constitution-making. In Australia it has been adopted federally for the determination of constitutional issues. This is also the direction which has been followed in the recently established constitutions of Europe. In the new Germany, for example, these devices are admitted, though under stringently determined conditions, as a means of amending the constitution.[1]

The situation is quite different when the initiative and the referendum are made instruments for the enactment or repeal of ordinary laws. Given a truly representative parliament, it is hard to see the need or the advantage of the loose legislative competition of the electorate, nor do the results of direct legislation afford any convincing evidence that the system awakens in the people a deeper interest in politics or a greater sense of responsibility. The idea of direct democracy seems to belong to the city-community, whence it was taken and preached by Rousseau without regard for the extent and the complexity of modern societies. Even to-day it is in vogue chiefly in the small communes of Switzerland and in the less complex and less populous states of the American Union, such as Oregon and Arizona. In so far as it is prompted by distrust of the control of professional politicians the true remedy would seem to be the greater education of the democracy itself, as a result of which it can be more adequately and faithfully represented. Resort to the referendum may be justified as a means of deciding with respect to legislation on which the two houses are not in accord, as provided in the constitution of the Irish Free State. There may be a place for the referendum and perhaps even for the initiative in the determination of those relatively rare issues which cut across the lines of party representation, such as in some

[1] Constitution of August 1919, Art. 76.

states the question of 'temperance' legislation, but even here the simpler and less confusing method is that of the *plébiscite*, whereby the constituted government may ascertain the opinion of the community on a disputed issue while remaining free to decide the form and degree of legislation which this expression of opinion renders desirable. Thus the responsibility of the legislature remains unbroken.

Our survey of the various checks and balances of government has shown the necessity for a unified and articulated system, in which responsibility is itself not divided with the division of powers. It is suggested that no more in the state than in any other association should there be organs of equal validity for the doing of the same things. Functions should be differentiated, not duplicated, if unity is to be attained and the responsibility of a government to the ultimate sovereign is to be focussed and secured. A brief study of the relation of local and regional authorities to the national government will reveal a further aspect of this principle.

III

CENTRAL AND LOCAL GOVERNMENT

If we think only of the relation between a central government and the whole body of citizens we shall have a most inadequate idea of the remarkable and exceedingly complex order established within the modern state. The state is far from being simply the organization of a people or nation conceived of as a whole. Whatever the basis of its unity it is a territorial organization. There are certain great interests which are the common concern of all citizens ; there are others, perhaps not at all less important for the welfare of those who share them, which are defined by the special conditions of a locality or district, due to its geographical character, to its economic activities, to the particular distribution of population within it, to the historical process which has given it a form and a social setting of its own, and most of all to the sheer fact that certain human needs are best provided for within the local areas in which they find conscious expression. Thus besides the central government there exists a complicated array of local authorities. Together they form the vast machinery of state, and the relation of the one to the other creates a highly significant task of political articulation.

To discuss in any detail the various modes of this relationship in different states is here impossible nor in any case would they yield their meaning without an historical survey of the whole process by which small independent communities become merged in larger ones, leading to successive movements of centralization and decentralization according to the tenacity of local traditions and the strength of the nation-making impulse. We must be content to offer some general observations on the problems of articulation which this rich historical material presents.

We may distinguish, in respect of their range or area, three types of function which the state seeks to fulfil. In the first place there are certain functions which are assigned exclusively to central governments. Obviously, such functions as treaty-making and other dealings with foreign states, military and naval measures, certain forms of taxation including tariffs, and legislation determining the general rights and duties of citizens, belong to this class. Furthermore, all matters which are not peculiarly associated with one particular locality belong naturally to the central authority. The state may require local agencies for its work of administration, such as taxing officials, but these are appointed and controlled by a central department. The locality itself has no voice in the matter merely because these activities of government are carried on within it.

In the second place, there are functions which have a universal character but which for their efficient fulfilment, or on other grounds, may require the co-operation of local authorities, acting within a system controlled by the central government. We may think of the administration of justice, police protection, the care of the poor, sanitary regulation, and various other activities. In so far as local authorities, authorities, that is, appointed or controlled by the citizens of the locality, participate in these activities we have a system of devolution. The localities undertake the responsibility of applying within their own areas the general regulations laid down by the central government. There is a special reason for such devolution where the costs of administration can also be localized and thus placed as a burden on those who receive the corresponding services. Devolution saves the central government from the otherwise overwhelming task of detailed administration and liberates the state from the dangers of a rigid bureaucratic control.

Lastly, there are functions which are of peculiar concern of the locality. The water-supply of a town or city, for example, is not part of a general system for a provision of water throughout the area of a state, in the sense in which the administration of justice in a locality is part of a general system. The former is a closed system complete in itself. This happens also with many services which are classed as ' public utilities ', such as tramway- or omnibus-transport. It seems reasonable that over such services the locality should have direct and fairly complete control. The locality is best able to appreciate and provide for its particular needs. There is, no doubt, a wider interest involved, for no locality lives to itself, and the wider interest may demand that the state as a whole should exercise a measure of supervision, requiring the locality to obtain its authorization before undertaking new projects and laying down certain principles with which localities must comply. In England, for example, new projects must be assented to by parliament under the form of ' private bills ' while a department of the central government, the Ministry of Health, possesses certain advisory and supervisory powers in respect of local finance, poor law administration, and public health regulation.

It is not possible to draw sharp lines between the functions just enumerated. Local interests merge into national interests in variant degrees. It is clearly desirable that in matters which concern it most intimately the locality should so far as possible be entrusted with control, but because of the wider public interest involved this control can never be absolute. The classification of functions we have just made reveals at least the logic of articulation. The problem is to assure at once the reality and the responsibility of local government. Modern states differ very widely in their answers to this problem. The extreme centralization of the Napoleonic state has everywhere been discarded. In some states, as in present-day France, in Belgium, in Italy, and in Holland, the central government exercises a degree of direct administration over the localities through its own officials appointed, like the French prefect, for that purpose, while at the same time locally elected councils have been developed with real powers of their own. In Prussia the central government is concerned with the appointment of professional technicians for the public service of localities, but these, unlike the French prefects, are wholly under the direction of the local councils. In England, on the other hand, and generally in Anglo-Saxon countries, the central government is not actively represented in the conduct of local affairs. The organ of local government is exclusively local, acting freely within the range of authority by law assigned to it. So long as it fulfils its functions and does not overstep its limits, its autonomy is secure.

It is not unimportant to observe that the autonomy of local government rarely causes any serious conflict on the general issue of state-sovereignty. The sovereignty of the state is as it were taken for granted, and the degree and range of power exercised by municipalities and other local authorities can thus be made matters of adjustment and of discretion. In this field the practical problem takes precedence. It is a question of apportioning powers and areas of power. When men look primarily at the interests to be served, not at abstract claims of right or titles to power, the greatest obstacles to the articulation of power are removed, and in the relation of local to central government the obstinate and jealous traditions of sovereignty have in a measure lost their hold. It does not follow that the relation of central to local government is adequately solved. It is an exceedingly complicated question, but, because it is a practical one, it can be more easily considered and met on its merits. Whereas the great difficulty of, say, the international problems of authority, is just that men are not ready to consider them on their merits, so obsessed are they by abstract claims.

What renders the question of local government so intricate is the way in which industrial development, involving the growth of urban areas and the improvement of communications, has knit up into one web the whole social life of great communities. There is no circle of isolation around localities as in the ancient days. The city spreads its extending fringe and its satellite-settlements far into the *hinterland*, so that not only is the line between town and country often lost, but also the line between city and city disappears in a great 'conurbation'.[1] Different demarcations are rendered necessary for different services, while at the same time whole regions require some common control, alike for their present needs and for future development. Thus there has risen a demand for what is termed ' regionalism ', the merging for certain purposes of larger areas within a common government.[2] The general principle is easily stated, that the range of common control should be the range of effective service, but in the rapidly moving world of to-day, with the constant changes imposed by technical advance, the application of it lags behind.

[1] Perhaps the most remarkable instance of this may be seen in the war-ruined area of French Flanders.

[2] Cf. Cole, *The Future of Local Government*.

XIII

THE PARTY SYSTEM

I. EVOLUTION OF PARTY

WE may define a political party as an association organized in support of some principle or policy which by constitutional means it endeavours to make the determinant of government. Without such party organization there can be no unified statement of principle, no orderly evolution of policy, no regular resort to the constitutional device of parliamentary elections, nor of course any of the recognized institutions by means of which a party seeks to gain or to maintain power. Without party organization there may be factions and cabals, there may be appeals and petitions to government, or again those leagues and covenants, 'agreements of the people', manifestoes and protests which flourished before the days of party control. But a political party seeks to do more than influence or support the government, it seeks to make it. It implies therefore some kind of parliamentary system on the one hand, and on the other a recognized electorate by whose vote, at stated intervals or on special occasions, the legislature is created. The primary business of a party is to influence an electorate which in turn has the right of determining government.

The party-system implies an elective, and therefore representative, government, and could not develop until this was finally secured. So long, for example, as the issue of sovereignty lay between parliament and king, the crucial question was, Who shall govern? But the real divisions between parties depend on their answer to the question, What policy shall government be instituted to follow? When policy comes to be determined by parliament, it divides within itself on political issues. Parties form themselves within parliament before the party-system is established in the country. But parliamentary majorities cannot rule by divine right, they must be maintained and sanctioned by public opinion. That opinion must express itself in organized form, and so parties grow up within the state.

The lateness of the development of parties, as we have defined them, is at first sight surprising. For a considerable time parties remained rudimentary and, like the earlier ' associations ', extra-constitutional. They were generally regarded as factions or schisms, the dangerous disturbers of established loyalties. In the American Constitution the existence of political parties is quite ignored, and the adoption of the collegiate system for the election of president is significant in this regard. Madison shared the common opinion that the influence of parties was detrimental,[1] and no one seemed to recognize that party-organizations are absolutely necessary for the working of a democratic government. Bluntschli, writing as late as 1875, does not include in his comprehensive *Theory of the State* any reference to party government. It was only when the logic of parliamentary government brought it about that a dispute between the ministry and the representatives was decided by an appeal to the

[1] See Morrow's Introduction to Morse, *Parties and Party Leaders*, p. xxix.

country, involving the retirement of the ministry if defeated (the first clear case being that of Peel in 1835), or when an unpopular government found it expedient to resign, that the importance of parties emerged, and they began to assume a new status. So there came the elaboration of party machinery, such as that established by the famous Birmingham 'Caucus' of 1867.

Party is the only means by which the ultimate political sovereign, which we saw to be at most a fluctuating majority, can definitely control government. It may be maintained that in the democratic periods of Greece and Rome there were elective and controlled governments without a party system. We can perhaps distinguish the beginnings of party in the city-state, as for example in the Athens of Pericles and the Rome of the Gracchi. Its development, however, and therewith the orderly control of government, was prevented partly by the lack of a true representative system, and partly by the limitations of citizenship. Party attains fruition only in democracy. Otherwise the right of election, as itself a guarded privilege, is fulfilled in the spirit of class and not of party, and the control of government becomes the prize of factional strife, not the result of an orderly appeal. The ancient 'democracies' were still, even in form, class-states, and therefore the decisive changes of government were brought about by revolution rather than by party victories. The famous eighty-second chapter of the third book of Thucydides affords the most lurid commentary on the violent dissensions of the class-state which could not without disruption admit the principle of democracy, and if further proof were needed it is furnished by the course of events at Rome from the days of Gracchus to the establishment of Caesarism.

The quarrelsome medieval cities were divided ostensibly over political principles, but the struggles of Guelfs and Ghibellines were factional wars in which the very meaning of the cause was forgotten. Owing to the lack of constitutional appeal issues originating in real political differences degenerated into partisan conflicts as empty of true significance as those between the big-endians and the little-endians. So futile were such struggles that sometimes historians can no longer decide, as in the instance of the Dutch conflicts of the 'Hooks' and the 'Codfish', which of two groups stood for one or the other principle.

Without the party-system, we may conclude, the *coup d'état*, the *putsch*, or revolution, are the only methods of securing a change of government. Without it, the government in power is controlled only by the pressure of custom, which itself is weakest in times of crisis ; by the desire for popularity, which is easily overborne by the ambitions of despotism ; by the consideration, too insecure to allay the just fears of the subjects, of the advantage to itself of a contented prosperous people ; and beyond that by the fear of revolution. Without the party-system the state has no elasticity, no true self-determination. Without it government is rigid and irresponsive, conceived in terms of mastery rather than of service. The state under such conditions is either a closed system of arbitrary domination or else the battlefield of contending factions. The party system is based on the contrary theory that men are rational beings, in so far at least that they admit principle to be a better ground of government than force, persuasion more desirable than compulsion, and the conflict of ideas more creative than the clash of arms. The keys of the very stronghold of coercive might, the masterful state itself, are handed over to those who can convince by the force of their appeal. Here then is the great triumph of the party-system, which its own defects or shortcomings should not be suffered to obscure.

The party-system was in particular the mechanism by which the class-state was transformed into the nation-state. We have seen that all states at one stage of development are class-states, controlled by and in the interest of the dominant classes to which the rest of the population is subject. The decisive distinction is between the classes and the masses, the classes in this signification being generally two, the nobility and the clergy. The nobility has two primary sources of authority, the ownership of land and leadership in war, together with one secondary source, the prestige of birth and station. The authority of the priesthood rests on a different prestige, the prestige of culture, a spiritual dominance, which of course took a grosser character in proportion to the ignorance of the subject population. Government under such conditions is not created and directed by the changing balance of opinion. The opinion of the subject orders has little to do with the policy of the state. The ruling classes rule together in perpetuity, because they depend on tradition and not on opinion. Class-rule is in this respect at the opposite extreme from party-rule. Party-rule implies the alternation of power, a system of succession which gives each its opportunity. Class-rule implies sheer fixity, claiming inviolate right.

Party begins as a protest against such claims. Its origins are found in those social changes which disturb the prestige or the power of the established classes, pre-eminently in those influences which have worked so constantly in the evolution of society, the new wealth of trade and commerce and the concomitant growth of cities. When the power derived from these influences is great enough to challenge the prestige of the ruling classes, the time is ripe for the formation of political parties. The original, as it were the 'natural', party is that organized in protest against privilege and class, the party of the 'bourgeois' liberal. But it can take form only after the old order is already undermined, so that it has conceded the rights of citizenship to the 'protestants'. The party-system implies a mutual recognition of rights which the class-system abhors and which it yields only with vast reluctance. The unprivileged must first be enfranchised before they can form a political party. When that stage is revealed, the hitherto ruling class must also, contrary to its instincts, organize in the form of a party. This is contrary to its instincts, because a party must make its appeal in the name of principle, and not of tradition, because it must appeal to the 'people', and employ the weapons and slogans of publicity. The ruling class ceases to have the mere privilege of ruling, and must stand or fall in respect of issues and on a ground not chosen by itself.

So political parties, though first organized in terms of class, are driven by the logic of the system to new positions. The 'appeal to the people' necessarily obscures and modifies the claims of class-interest. Besides, under the new conditions the psychological as well as the economic solidarity of the old class-system is broken, in ways which we must presently point out. The strife of parties comes to have a significance very different from that of the struggle of classes.

The original opposition is that between the party of the commercial and urban interests and the counter-formed party of the landed interests. In England the Whig and Tory parties were divided along these lines, the Tories being the 'country gentlemen' and their supporters and dependants, the Whigs the 'moneyed men', the new capitalists and their allies, led by certain ennobled families which had come to power and influence through trade or participation in those anti-feudal expropriations which had been made at the expense of the great landlords or the church. All over Europe similar developments occurred sooner or later, the conservative party, the representative of the landed interest, resisting the democratizing trend to which the liberals, the party of the *bourgeoisie*, was pledged. On the general issue the conservatives supported a losing cause, and the tide of political change swept far past the positions adopted by the liberals themselves. Most of the *constitutional* demands of the more radical groups of the earlier nineteenth century, such as the Chartists, came in time to be accepted. But at each stage, after each victory or defeat, the opposing parties adopted a new front. No party can rest on its past. It must always find new issues or revive old ones. It must adapt its fundamental principle or interest so that it will make its appeal effective in the current state of public opinion. The conservatives are at least as ready as the liberals—and perhaps much more so than the radicals—to adopt new weapons and to restate their appeal. But in the process the older identification of class and party is to some extent obliterated.

When a hitherto dominant class loses its *point d'appui*, the right to govern, it loses its integrity. It is readier to ally itself with a new-risen class, to share the advantage of new wealth, especially when, as happened to the feudal governing class, its own source of wealth shrinks either absolutely or in comparison with others. Apart from the right to govern, a class possesses only an obscure uncertain unity. Ancient prestige can scarcely maintain itself against new riches. In modern civilization the distinction of classes has become mainly economic. The chief characteristics of social groups are correlated with income and occupation. Whether we take such external evidences as 'vital statistics' (fertility and mortality rates, and age at marriage [1]), or consider customs and cultural conditions, we must classify the population of a country mainly in terms of relative wealth.

The unity of such income-classes is much less static and less compact than that of the ancient classes of birth and privilege. There are no strict dividing lines, no insignia of distinction, no established orders. Thus in the United States and in Canada the government may not confer or recommend titular rank, because such action would offend the general sentiment against distinctive classes. Income-classes shade into one another, and within themselves they have no determinate solidarity of interest. Karl Marx, interpreting, after his wont, modern situations in medieval conceptions, exaggerated the unity of class-feeling and of class-interest which characterizes either side of what is undoubtedly the greatest division within modern society, that between capitalists and wage-earners. In the first place, it is not a dichotomy of society. It ignores particularly the intermediate positions occupied by the new 'middle classes', the professional groups, the civil service, the technicians, the small

[1] See, for example, the remarkable Report on Fertility of Marriage, Pt. II (Census of England and Wales, 1911).

traders, the farmers. In the second place, it assumes an identity of interest among the capitalists, standing sheer against the identity of interest of the wage-earners. But there are serious oppositions of interest between capitalists, and likewise between groups of wage-earners. This is manifest in every political issue. Shall we put a heavy tax on ' luxury goods ' ? The workers engaged in their manufacture protest, no less than the consumers of these goods. Shall we freely admit immigrant workers ? The native workers protest. Shall we lower tariffs to make goods cheaper for the workers ? As producers of particular goods they join in opposition with the capitalist manufacturers. A completely common interest of either side against the other could exist only in the constraint of slavery. Wherever competition of any kind enters in the solidarity is crossed and broken. The interest of the importer is at variance with that of the home manufacturer. The interest of the working farmer does not coincide with that of the industrial wage-earner—witness the abortive attempts in the United States and elsewhere to form a party combination of the two. On the other hand, even the opposition between profits and wages is limited and subject to a common interest. Periods of prosperity benefit both capitalist and worker, and in periods of adversity they suffer together.[1] These considerations enable us to understand why party, though originating from class, assumes a character much more in harmony with the development of a national life.

The further evolution of the party-system is associated with the development of those agencies of communication which have brought all classes and all parts of the country into immediate contact with the trend of events and the

[1] Cf. Layton, *Introduction to the Study of Prices.*

movement of opinion. Of these agencies the most important, which utilizes all the rest, is the press. The press is more than a vehicle of news, it is an ' organ of publicity ', seeking to influence as well as to register opinion. It is not only a means of information but also a great bulwark of prejudice and instrument for its exploitation. Inevitably it links itself with party. Inevitably, because its modes of influence are so powerful and so pervasive, because by selection, repression, and suggestion it can be so potent a champion of whatever cause it espouses. But again there are limits to its power. It vastly enlarges the range and enhances the activity of party, but it does not normally control it. Governments have been elected, such as the Ramsay Macdonald government in Britain, in spite of the attacks of a large majority of the press. A party-controlled newspaper always speaks with the same voice. Its automatic deliverances tend to be discounted. An opposition press is created by the interests which it attacks and as vehemently accentuates the views of the other side. Above all, the press depends on its circulation, and its financial success is in proportion to its popularity. It is true that its popular appeal depends considerably on devices and services which are altogether apart from the particular political views which it supports. But if it adopts an attitude to which any portion of its readers object, it at once suffers—witness the outcry against the *Daily Mail* when it attacked Lord Kitchener—and if it persists in this attitude it may stake its very existence. Nor can any financial support from outside sources compensate for the loss of popularity. Occasionally a powerful press-syndicate can attack the policy alike of government and opposition, as the Rothermere press attacked both the George and Baldwin parties in respect of their Ruhr policy, but only if it believes that there is in the country a strong body of sympathy for its views. The press, for all its influence, is utterly dependent on the goodwill of its readers. It radiates the influence of party into every corner of the land, and thus gives it a broader and more national character. But apart from that the most it can do is to evoke—and to exaggerate—the existing trends of opinion. These are its true services in the evolution of the party-system.

II

THE ALINEMENT OF PARTY

We shall show that political parties, apart from aberrations due to special circumstances, fall regularly along a single alinement, whether the two-party or the multiple-party system prevails. This fact indicates the antithetical or 'polar' character of the party. It is the political form of the great alternative which everywhere presents itself in human activity. One man stays at home and another prefers to explore; one seeks safety and another adventure; one looks to the past and another to the future; one cherishes the appointed order and another is more conscious of its defects. In nearly every man is the potentiality of either attitude, but, in the language of the biologists, one is dominant and the other recessive. Much depends on circumstances and training. Wealth and birth and privilege obviously make for conservatism; poverty and lack of opportunity urge in the opposite direction. The sense of superiority makes men conservative; the sense of potential superiority makes them radical. The conservative builds on the pride of race and the ' organic ' unity of the nation. He believes in the slow evolution of precedent and in the wisdom of time. He feels that neither nature nor human history goes by leaps. The radical, impatient of time, would make history move in the present. For him the great unity is humanity, not his nation. He is impressed with the power of environment and therefore would change it. The fact that an order is established does not dispose him to accept its finality. The radical is a critic of social conditions ; the conservative is a critic of social theories.[1]

Such is the general antithesis on which party rests. But a thousand nearer circumstances determine men one way or the other. The active and daring intelligence tends in one direction, the passive and timid mind in the other. Sharp disappointments lead to revulsions from either side. Youth is less conservative than age. Pride and self-interest lead the fortunate one way and the unfortunate another. The radical may grow conservative in his radicalism and the conservative, though more rarely, become liberal under the aegis of his conservatism. Economic interest as it is affected by the attitude of either party leads many to espouse this side or that. And there are many also in whom the opposing instincts are so well balanced or so undeveloped that they are easily led to the opposite side in conscious or unconscious protests against the errors or misfortunes or mere dominance of the party in power. These are they who make party government so insecure for the party, and, perhaps, so safe for the nation.

[1] Of the various studies which throw light on these opposing attitudes special mention may be made of Kent, *The English Radicals*, and Feiling, *History of the Tory Party*, 1640-1714.

For there are dangerous tendencies to which the special genius of each party inclines it. The conservative party has been historically the party of privilege, and still tends to appeal to wealth. It is apt to minimize the significance of new social movements, and when seemingly secure of power to grow reactionary and frustrate developments which the times demand—witness the action of the English tories in rejecting electoral reform in 1693 and 1785. But as democracy extends, this hardening spirit of conservatism is inevitably modified. For now every party must profess what Jefferson called the ' cherishment of the people '. The party of the right must with outer illogicality appeal to numbers. Their leaders must adopt the methods of democracy, and we have such phenomena as the extension of the suffrage by the conservatives under Disraeli and the enfranchisement of the freedmen by the republicans. In fact this necessity drives all states in which party government prevails towards the complete form of democracy.

The party of the left, on the other hand, is exposed to an opposite danger. Its natural appeal is to numbers, but when it attains power it is subject to strong influences which are out of accord with its democratic pretensions. The ambitions of office, the sense of the practical difficulties which beset the fulfilment of programmes easily proclaimed while in opposition, and the pressure of particular interests, all tend to create a contradiction between the motives of government and its professed principles. Elements within the party grow discontented with its performance, and especially with its official leaders. There is division in its councils, and the party falls from power. The alternations of power and opposition are essential to the working of the party system, and help to protect the state from the menace and arrogance of power to which it is exposed under every other form of government.

These alternations, involving constant attack and counter-attack as each party discerns a ground of vantage over its opponents, require a single alinement along which the parties are ranged. There could, for example, be no proper issue between an ecclesiastical party and a protectionist party or between a prohibition party and a socialist party. There must be some dominant and comprehensive issue, overshadowing all cross issues, of a permanent character under its changing forms, and making a permanent appeal, though in different ways, to the whole people. This is implied in the common terminology by which parties are spoken of as belonging to the right or the left or the centre. These terms indicate opposing attitudes and policies in respect of a profound and abiding question.

Territorial or nationalistic parties do not conform to this principle. They do not range themselves along a true alinement. They do not appeal, on questions of policy, to the whole of a citizen body. They are still at the preliminary stage, where the question remains, Who shall govern the state? not, How shall it be governed? They do not provide for a regular alternation of government. There is no shifting of forces from one side to the other. Each party remains a solid and intransigeant *bloc*. If one is dominant, like the Magyar party in pre-war Hungary, it may have a practical monopoly of government. There is no proper opposition, no party, that is, which seeks to win over the members of the party in power by insisting on the failures and errors of the latter. We have under such conditions only a semblance of party, a constitutional form under which lurk divisions that disintegrate the state. Parties based strictly on class-distinctions would be equally disintegrating and equally alien to the spirit of the party system. To function properly each party must make a national appeal, on behalf of principles which it advocates as for the welfare of the whole.

What then is the profound and abiding question around which parties normally range themselves? Hume in his *Essays* distinguishes three kinds of parties (or factions, as he still regards them) : parties from interest, parties from principle, and parties from affection, and adds that ' parties from *principle*, especially abstract speculative principle, are known only to modern times, and are, perhaps, the most extraordinary and unaccountable phenomenon that has yet appeared in human affairs '.[1] But ' affection ' is more short-lived even than its objects, and ' interest ', since it must appeal to the people, always takes on at least the cloak of ' principle '. All real parties are professedly based on principle, and the same principle must at once consolidate each within itself and divide it from the rest. The root-principle involved seems to be indicated by the common names by which parties are everywhere designated, such as ' reactionary ', ' conservative ', ' liberal ', ' reformist ', ' progressive ', and ' radical '. It is the attitude towards the established order of things which fundamentally distinguishes party from party. The parties of the right desire the maintenance of the existing system or, where institutions have already been changed beyond their liking, the restoration of a traditional or historical *status quo ante*. They would adapt past institutions to present situations with the minimum of change, save for the abolition of changes

[1] Essay VIII.

which their opponents have brought about. The parties of the left have less reverence for institutions. They are ready to modify or reform them without scruple, and the extreme left would ' reform them altogether '.

But though these dispositions form the universal ground of party alinement, men do not consistently reveal a single attitude in respect of all questions. A man may be, like Gladstone, a conservative in religion and a liberal on constitutional issues. Or he may be, like Spencer, a radical in his general outlook and a conservative advocate of *laissez-faire* in economics. Or an individual's particular interest, say in respect to free trade or protection, may bring him into line with a party which does not represent his native disposition. Every age has its dominant problems, conditioned by the institutions of the age. In an age of ecclesiastical controversy parties divide on the relation of the state to religion. In the growing period of formal democracy parties are formed around constitutional questions. This was in fact the period from which our present parties have derived. We must recall that at that time, with the landed interests still in the ascendant, the focus of political power was striving to maintain itself as the focus also of economic power. Consequently the constitutional issue seemed all-important and divided the conservatives, such as the royalist tories, from the liberals, such as the anti-royalist whigs. Roughly speaking, we may say that in England the constitutional issue was dominant until about 1832, the form of government being crucial. Thereafter its importance declined, except when, as in the later struggle over the House of Lords, it arose as an incident within a newer issue. A similar development occurred in various European states. As they achieved the form of democracy the centre of party conflict shifted away from the constitutional issue. In the United States, owing to its federal character, the constitutional question had a special significance. Here the ' democratic party ' was first in the field, depending on the dissatisfaction of various groups with the nationalistic and somewhat aristocratic aspect of the federal government established after the ratification of the constitution. On the whole the federal government was true to the conservative and centralizing spirit of the constitution, but in being so it offended those tendencies towards democracy and state-sovereignty which the constitution was in large part devised to restrain. Thus the democratic party stood for state-rights as against federal sovereignty, professed a greater respect also for the ' rights of the individual ', as against such measures as the Alien and Sedition Laws, welcomed the easy admission of the immigrant to citizenship, and proclaimed hostility to privilege and ' vested interests ', such as the protective tariff might be deemed to create. But by this time the names ' democrat ' and ' republican ' have almost wholly lost their constitutional significance.

We may take this last example to show how a single party alinement is essential and how, once formed, it maintains itself throughout the changes caused by new problems and new divisions. Parties split up and re-form, but the old attitudes remain. In the United States a hitherto secondary issue grew dominant—the question of the restriction of slavery to the territory in which it had become established as an institution. No existing party could identify itself with the principle of restriction, neither the democratic with its southern affiliations, nor the whig party with its relaxing hold upon its earlier ideals and its record of compromise, nor yet the minor, transient, and sectional ' know-nothing ' and ' free-soil ' parties. A new party was called for by the supremacy of the issue, and the republican party came into being. Quickly the party alignment adapted itself to the new situation, the democrats ranging themselves as the proponents of the opposite principle. Unhappily, but inevitably, the line of party division now coincided with a territorial demarcation, and the worst perils of this condition were realized. The parties ceased to be national parties at all, became in fact something other than true parties appealing respectively to the whole country. The federal union was not strong enough to hold its integrity, and the civil war ensued. Thereafter party alinement moved gradually to new ground. Constitutional questions became less important, and the parties fell into conformity with the prevailing trend elsewhere. In a word, the dominant issue became a directly economic one.

In European countries this issue was more sharply defined. In America the pursuit of economic interests seemed less impeded by social and political barriers, and the sense of economic opportunity led men to rely less upon the state. Apart from the ever-present tariff question, in respect of which state-action was of course decisive, economic controversies ranged around transient and rather mechanical expedients advocated as remedies for particular ills or grievances, such as bi-metallism, cheap money, and anti-trust measures. When these were not in the foreground, the difference between the greater parties resolved itself largely into that between the ' ins ' and the ' outs ', the republicans being traditionally the more conservative of the two. But in Europe economic differences went deeper. There were large numbers, specially among the more recently enfranchised classes, who, beset by poverty, had no trust in the beneficence of the established economic system and desired to have it greatly revised or even abolished. All other differences, such as the former conflicts on constitutional or ecclesiastical questions, were for the most part politically subordinated to this now supreme issue. Only certain intransigeant nationalistic groups remained generally outside the new alinement. Its character may be simply exhibited in the table which follows, giving a comparative picture of party groupings in the modern state.

PARTY ALINEMENT IN THE MODERN STATE

	Extreme Left Communist Socialist. }	Left Radical Liberal. }	Right Conservative.	Extreme Right Reactionary.
Principles	Public or common ownership of means of production, with abolition of private rent, interest, and profits.	Public or common control, complete or partial, of the capitalistic system.	Maintenance of capitalism with minimum of political control except for protective tariff.	
Attitudes	Anti-imperialistic and pacifist. Revolutionary, Reformist. class-conscious.[1]		Imperialistic and nationalistic. Industrialist. Militarist, class-conscious.[1]	

It is scarcely necessary to add that these principles and attitudes shade into one another, and that while they characterize the groups as wholes they need not fully apply to all their members. It is also obvious that in the strategy of political warfare the names adopted by parties

---

[1] Class-consciousness occurs to some extent in every group, but it is here an attitude which definitely expresses itself in policies and methods.

may not conform to their principles. A party, for example, which is essentially conservative may call itself ' liberal ', or ' progressive ', like the *action liberale populaire* in France. Such terms as ' liberal ' and ' conservative ' are relative to one another, and do not connote absolute principles. The trend of opinion may move at one time and in one country towards the left, while elsewhere or at other times the movement is towards the right. There was, for example, a leftward movement in Europe since 1871 which was scarcely felt in America. And since the war there have been marked oscillations in various countries. The whole alinement shifts under the influence of general prosperity or adversity, or through those more subtle influences of mood and reaction, of optimism or disillusionment, which permeate communities. The distinction between parties, unlike that between castes, is one of ' more ' or ' less ', and in the evolution of opinion a group, while retaining its old name, may have adopted principles which formerly characterized its opponents. The opportunist policy of parties, in their efforts to retain or to regain power, such as that of Disraeli or of Bismarck towards labour, is a further cause of confusion between principles and names.

Our conspectus brings out the fact that a party represents not a homogeneous bloc of identical opinions, but a range of opinion which lies within rather vaguely determined limits. There is in each party also a right and a left wing, and under certain stresses there may be a fissure between them, so that the two may separate and form distinct organizations. We define a party by identity of organization, not of opinion. In a few countries the real issue, so far as the determination of government is concerned, remains with two major opposing parties, the others being politically too weak to make an effective bid for power. This situation has endured most conspicuously in the United States. Thus in the presidential election of 1920 there were six national parties in the field, but the decisive struggle lay between the republicans and the democrats. If either of those parties splits up or suffers an important secession, as did the republican party in 1912, it is felt to be an abnormal and transient situation. A similar condition characterized until recently the English party-system, and in fact it has been generally regarded as distinctive of the English-speaking world. But in England the advance of a new left-wing party has wrecked, for the time at least, the two-party principle. Generally, where the left wing has gained ground, it has at the same time broken up into separate party-organizations, and this is one reason for the development of the multiple-party system in continental Europe. This development raises a new problem of government to which we now turn.

III

MULTIPLE PARTIES AND THE MECHANISM OF GOVERNMENT

So long as the two-party system prevails the determination of government is simple and, except in times of peculiar crisis, automatic. When either party falls from power, the opposing party accedes to it. The leaders of the party which is out of office are the prospective leaders of the alternative government. The opposition is itself a part of the machinery of government. The recognition of this fact may go so far that the leader of the opposition becomes, as in Canada, a state official with a regular salary. There is, on the one hand, a concentration of authority, since the party in office is not dependent upon any other ; and there is, on the other hand, a concentration of responsibility and an easy means of enforcing it— by the return to power of the opposite party.

But this system involves a readiness of adjustment and compromise within the party organizations, and such a traditional devotion of the electorate to it that they will sacrifice their differences for the sake of a general cause. The two-party system puts definite limits on the political expression of public opinion. It is adapted to conditions where no profound changes of political institutions are demanded by any considerable body of citizens. Whenever either the extreme left or the extreme right commands a considerable following, it tends to become unworkable, because the more moderate elements of either party refuse to co-operate with it in a single organization. Moreover, it is apt to be embarrassed when new issues arise or new policies are advocated in respect of old issues. The essential problem of the two-party system is the maintenance of its integrity. The multiple-party system has no such problem. Under it groups can be freely organized, can unite and separate with every change of the situation. Opinion-groups, being liberated from a common organization, are able to formulate their doctrines without compromise. Compromise comes at a later stage, through the ever-present necessity which is imposed on all who would achieve political success, the necessity to act with a majority.

Under the multiple-party system no party can normally expect to have an absolute majority of its own. This fact profoundly alters not only the tactics of parties but also the whole mechanism of government. The government of the day depends on a coalition of groups, and is the result of bargains and agreements between them. It is a *bloc* government rather than a party one. The *bloc* may be formed by groups from either wing or from the centre. There are several alternative governments which may take the place of a government which suffers defeat, and it is often impossible to predict which shall be its successor. Thus the certainty of the two-party system, the clear-cut conflict for power, disappears. Governments tend to be less stable and to be shorter-lived. If they offend a group of their supporters, these do not feel the same obligation to continue their loyalty. They may even join with other groups outside the coalition to overthrow it. Governments are consequently more sensitive to changes in public opinion. There is less continuity of policy, especially if the executive depends on the support of parliament. Leaders and governments rise and fall with dramatic suddenness. They can seldom act with the assurance which the older system frequently bestows.

Whether these results of the multiple-party system are to be reckoned advantageous or disadvantageous is a question of too subjective a character to be considered here. Certainly the two-party system pays a price for the more stable government which it provides. The citizen has a narrower choice. The independent voters are faced with the dilemma that they must either accept the simple antithesis of two parties, or, rejecting it, make their votes of no avail, unless perhaps to aid indirectly that party to which they are the more opposed. The electoral institutions which normally (though not necessarily) accompany the two-party system place a heavy premium on conformity. The principle on which the permanent opposition to one another of two parties is based encourages in every way that blinder devotion which substitutes a kind of inherited emotional loyalty for intelligent choice. The political leader must also exhibit a more slavish devotion. He must accept the whole platform of one side, determined as it is by the narrowly astute considerations of party harmony and political success, and oppose the whole platform of the other. A leader with strong personality is likely to prove a menace and is often rejected. The mere politician finds a greater opportunity, the man whose chief concern is with what will work, will appeal, will triumph, who measures but does not add to the strength of a cause, whose tools are the convictions of others because he has none of his own. Under the multiple-party system the leader bargains more or less openly for support, under the two-party system he must silently accommodate himself to the common level on which all his supporters can meet.

Under such conditions the party 'machine', the secret-working group of professional politicians, gains authority. The two-party principle tends to establish strong vested interests in political opinion. This result occurs to some extent under all forms of party government, but it is obviously enhanced where there is a single and permanent contrast between the 'ins' and the 'outs'. Its grossest form is the 'spoils system', and it is not without significance that this system should have developed most flagrantly in the United States, where the two-party principle dominates more than anywhere else.[1] The dual principle hampers the free expression of political opinion, and consequently introduces, as various

[1] No doubt other causes have contributed, such as, socially, the indifference of many unassimilated immigrant voters and, constitutionally, the popular election of the president and of a large number of both executive and judicial officials.

writers have pointed out,[1] a certain artificiality into political groupings which affects both voters and leaders, making it easier for the party 'machine' to assume control.

We must not suppose that a state can deliberately choose which of these two systems it will adopt. It depends on the condition of public opinion, responsive to all the forces at work within the community. All states have begun with the simple dichotomy of parties, but the great majority have swung towards the multiple system. It is hard to maintain a single political line of division, especially when economic issues become prominent. A variety of attitudes and of policies is possible, and it is natural that they should seek to be expressed through separate organizations. Cross-divisions are also bound to occur, for all the interests of men do not cohere in one complex by an eternal necessity. What is necessary is the single alinement, not the single division. The very fact that parties appeal to a whole country indicates that they seek support from people in all situations and circumstances. Even where the dual system prevails it is subject to the assaults of 'third parties', and a moderate strengthening of any of these would be sufficient to disrupt it for the time being. The strength of the two-party system lies in the fact that it provides a clear contest which assumes a simple issue. But the issue may refuse to remain so simple.

In any event the advantages and disadvantages of either system are relative to the intelligence and culture of the community. The essential thing is that government should rest on as broad a basis of opinion as possible, maintaining, in spite of its party character, the unity of a whole people.

[1] Cf. Sidgwick, *Elements of Politics*, ch. xxix.

BOOK FOUR

THEORIES AND INTERPRETATIONS

XIV

THE EVOLUTION OF MODERN THEORIES OF THE STATE

I. INTRODUCTION: THE INITIAL DIFFICULTY OF ALL SOCIAL THEORY

THE sociologist, seeking to interpret the state or the economic system or any part of the social scheme, is faced with a peculiar though obvious difficulty, the difficulty of reconciling an objective or scientific understanding of its character with the necessary appreciation of its ethical value. The latter is necessary because without it there is no meaning, no *raison d'être*, of the social structure; the former is equally necessary because without it there is no foundation, no validity in its values. The state is an agency of human purpose, and its character changes as it is directed more to the interests of this or that class within the community, as it serves more this or that set of aims, as its area of purpose narrows or widens. The political thinker finds it exceedingly hard to avoid those arbitrary and subjective interpretations which accord with his own ethical tradition. It is impossible for him, treating as he must of purposes achieved or suppressed in the variant forms of state, dealing as he must with the motives which inspire the formation and development of political institutions, estimating as he must the consequences in human life of each type of organization and control, to achieve the objectivity of the physical scientist who is concerned only with the objective.

Nor can we by evoking the concept of an inexorable evolution causally unfolding itself within human society, disembarrass ourselves of the necessity for ethical valuations. This was the standpoint assumed by Marx in his ' materialistic ' interpretation of history, and nowhere is the fallacy of it more apparent than in the scientific socialism of which he was the father. However we interpret the evolution of society, we are bound to discern and to evaluate the conscious motives of men in maintaining or modifying or transforming the social order at every stage. It is almost a meaningless statement that Marx made to the effect that the ideal is but the ' reflection ' in the human mind of the material world, nor do we remove the problem of motive by declaring that human conduct is the ' resultant ' of, or ' reaction ' to, climatic or geographical or technological conditions. Marx himself betrayed his own theory by his unsparing and persistent criticism of the established economic system, and by his deliberate use of this criticism as a lever for its overthrow.[1] As soon as we enter the sphere of society we enter the realm of values, where existence and worth are no longer identical. The political, like the economic, thinker must relate the institutions of society to human intentions and social consequences. He is not scientific if he ignores the teleology which is anathema to the physicist—he is merely shirking his own problem. Here his problem is on the one hand to apprehend the mental attitudes which precede and accompany the building of political institutions, and on the other hand

[1] This point is well stated by Hans Kelsen, *Sozialismus und Staat*, Einleitung.

to reveal the significance of these institutions as means of serving, controlling, diverting, or repressing, the aims and ideals which men commonly accept as worthy to be pursued. So far it is surely possible, though hard, to remain objective. The difficulty grows when the thinker distinguishes his own conception of human welfare from that which appears dominant in the age he studies (itself no easy discovery in the complexity of human conduct), and seeks to relate such institutions to his own ideal.[1] It grows yet greater when he is bold enough to bring forward suggestions for the reform or reconstruction, or even the transformation of the political order in the name of an accepted ideal, or even, perhaps, of a personal interpretation of human welfare.

Within this region of incertitude this much remains as firm ground for the political thinker, that every social institution *is* dependent upon existent modes of thought, that every change in the social structure, however conditioned externally, *is* accompanied by changes in the mentality of those whose lives fall within it, and that every form of social order *does* have relation, more or less ascertainable, to the welfare of mankind. To discover these value-facts is the peculiar task of the social scientist, not least of the political thinker.

Although we have insisted on the purposive character of the state, as of every organized form within human society, it should never be forgotten that the practice of men outstrips their reflection, that institutions change under the pressure of needs that scarcely arise to consciousness, that in the building of the social structure men do not proceed like architects who have clear designs of what they intend to build, but rather like

---

[1] As, for example, Mill does in his *Essay on Liberty*.

' social animals ' whose nature fulfils itself through forms they scarcely understand. Political understanding for the most part lags behind political actuality. Thus even a statement of current constitutional practice seems to many to savour of dangerous radicalism. Oxford was burning in 1683 the works of such as dared to assert that sovereign authority derives from the people or that tyrants forfeit their rights. To-day the realistic study of the nature and limits of political sovereignty yields conclusions remote from the accepted tradition. In fact the task of political thought may be far more to clear away the prejudices which prevent men from seeing the state as they have made it than to offer doctrines of what the state ought to be. Facts are no less facts, laws are no less laws—they are only the more difficult to discern— because they belong to the region of values.

II

THE STATE AS POWER *VERSUS* THE STATE AS JUSTICE

No thinker, not even Treitschke, has ever contended that the state is merely a power-system. Power is means, and we cannot think at all without relating means to ends. But many thinkers have exalted the state as a power-agency, making the exercise of power its characteristic expression, estimating the achievements to be won by domination as of supreme importance, and regarding coercion as the primary condition of social order. Such views are associated either with the belief that human nature is essentially refractory and disposed to evil, and therefore needing always the bit and curb of political restraint, a belief encouraged by certain theological preconceptions, or with the aristocratic principle which treats the many as an inferior order whose mission is to serve the few. In either case those thinkers lay little stress on the common welfare and less on the common will. Sometimes, as in the Hegelian philosophy, they postulate a mysterious end which is served by the state and which transcends the welfare of its members altogether. A less esoteric form of the same principle is obscurely present in the crude glorification of the ' flag ' and the semi-adoration of the might and ' honour ' of the state.

Against these attitudes other thinkers have always protested, invoking the claims of human personality as such, denying the master-servant relation as properly applicable in the political sphere, appealing to the unity and potential solidarity of human beings, and minimizing the value of coercion as a means to welfare. Historically the protest has taken characteristic form as an assertion of the juridical nature of the state. As men naturally appeal from force to justice, they oppose the idea of the state as justice to the idea of the state as power. The juridical conception is itself very partial, though clearly applicable within limits. Justice is concerned primarily with the things that divide. It does not envisage the things that unite or are common. But the juridical ideal was historically the most serviceable conception in the conflict against the power-claims of the established state.

As we have seen, from the very beginnings of history the ideals of power and of justice have confronted one another in the making of the state. It was inevitable therefore that they should have reflected themselves, as political consciousness grew, in two antithetic conceptions of the state. There were elements in every state which supported either view. From below had always come the call for justice, and beyond it there lay a force, vague but formidable, dormant but capable of vast eruption, which the power-seeking ruler dared not wholly to resist. Moreover, the loyalties which the chief must cherish even for the sake of power, the traditions which generations slowly create out of the half-conscious instinct that the state owes something to those who serve it, the very sense of unity without the support of which government seems a precarious and monstrous engine and law an enemy of nature, all conspired to establish the idea of justice within the order of the state. Yet from above the impulse of power has constantly shaped the state to its own ends, instilling the policy of division and domination, inspiring fear and subservience, and fostering the principle that government exists in its own right, irresponsible, majestic, above the law which is nothing but its own command. The concentration of the instruments of power, whether political or economic, hardens the mind to power. The ignorance, prejudice, superstition, and helplessness of the mass permit government to grow despotic and the state to assume the pretensions of absolutism. The state as power finds its freest expression in war, for thus in the uncontrolled clash of state with state it can for a time achieve internal unity on the mere basis of power. Under those conditions, when the thoughts of men are turned to victory and defeat, power, because it is also a destroyer from without, arises as a saviour from within ; and the conquests achieved by a power-motived government appear as the glory of the whole state or its deliverance from external foes as the heroic goal of all endeavour.

The doctrine of the state as a power-system became conscious and insistent in the birth-process of the modern state. It was alien to the thought of Aquinas or Dante, even as it was inapplicable to the array of semi-independent principalities, of estates and *parlements*, of confused interminglings of secular and ecclesiastical jurisdictions, great and small, which found a place within the disarticulate body of feudalism. Its first characteristic expression is found in Machiavelli. Writing in the age of Alexander VI and Julius II, of Caesar Borgia and the Medici, of Maximilian and Louis XII, he was acutely aware of the destructive results of the conflict of unreconciled powers within the community. The only reconciliation was through subjection, the acknowledged and entire supremacy of the one prince. He set forth accordingly, drawing freely on his own observation and historical study, the methods by which his prince might subdue all opposition to his will. The prince must 'know well how to use both the beast and the man'. In the former lore he must imitate the qualities of the fox and the lion. Success justifies the means, for success brings the great end of stability. Like most advocates of power, Machiavelli is chiefly concerned with ways and means, and he states these with a candour appropriate to their simplicity. Let no scruples of faith or humanity obstruct the fulfilment of the first duty of the prince, to make his dominion sure.

Beyond this criterion of success Machiavelli refused to go. 'Right and wrong have nothing to do with government.' He meant thereby that government has one great object whose fulfilment requires the setting aside at need of the ordinary standards of rightness. If he had stated that object as the interest of the whole or of the governed, he could easily enough have reconciled his power-politics with clear ethical principle. For he might have claimed, what indeed is latent in his thought, that the value secured by a strong government is worth its necessary price, and that here we have a supreme case of that presentation of alternatives on which all ethical action depends.[1] But Machiavelli is addressing the prince and not the people, and speaks of the advantage of power to the potentate. The perception of values is thus obscured, and the insistence on ways and means is dissociated from the ends which alone could justify them. Machiavelli is less a philosopher than an engineer of politics. But in the background of his thought there lay the ideal of a well ordered state and beyond that the already significant sense of national unity. Though he addresses Lorenzo, he thinks of Italy, as the last chapter of the *Prince* reveals. In a time of violent disunion and vast insecurity men take refuge in the rock of power. The achievement of unity is enough to justify its most ruthless assertion. How far the security of the state demands the abrogation of the ordinarily accepted principles of conduct is another question. It is true that an age distracted by uncontrolled and unscrupulous ambitions, like that of Machiavelli, creates a desperate political problem which must be solved by methods repugnant to the time when order is already established. But the very exercise of ruthless power distorts the ideals of those who wield it, and the results of such methods seldom offer convincing grounds to justify, even in such times, the general rejection of those ethical standards to which the community has already advanced.

The philosophy of power in due time found a broader expression than mere personal advice offered to a prince. In the sixteenth century the absolute state had already

[1] *Community*, Bk. III, ch. v, § iii.

risen in France, and elsewhere was emerging from the shell of outworn traditions. There were forces at work effecting a tremendous revolution, that which transferred ' the allegiance of the human spirit from clerical to civil authority '.[1] Thus the way was prepared for the concentration of political power. Feudal prerogatives crumbled before the majesty of a state which no longer acknowledged any authority but its own. The unity of the state was reinforced by the awakening spirit of nationality. As the state was one, so was its power, so also was its law. And that power and that law were in the hands of its sovereign head. The rediscovered doctrine of absolute sovereignty won from the struggle a renown greater than it had ever possessed in imperial Rome, for the sovereign was now invested, in the proclamation of the ' divine right of kings ', with the spoils of his spiritual adversary. The first great exponent of this absolute power was Jean Bodin. He was concerned with the nature of the state, not, like Machiavelli, with the mere institution of government. But from the nature of the state he derived certain attributes of sovereignty. For the state is held together by law, and law must have a source, must issue therefore from a power not itself subject to law. This is sovereign power, absolute and perpetual, independent with regard to other states, so that it makes peace or war at will; unlimited within its own, so that it need never ask in anything the consent of any superior or equal. To Bodin this sovereignty spells monarchy, though he admits the case of a sovereign assembly.

Here we have the clear presentation of that legalist doctrine of sovereignty, one and indivisible, inalienable

[1] Figgis, in *Cambridge Modern History*, iii, ch. xxii.

and imprescriptible, which has been repeated by a long line of political thinkers down to the present day. As a formal definition of the purely legal aspect it did notable and necessary service. But as a comprehensive statement of the nature of sovereignty it is wholly inadequate. For it exalts the instrument above the function, the means above the end. ' The sovereign is above the law.' True, if we mean that the sovereign is the law-maker. But the doctrine is easily perverted into the principle that the sovereign is above the state. So it degenerates into a power doctrine, and the state is delivered to its master. The true logic of association is thereby defeated, and its purpose dimmed. If the sovereign makes the law, it has still to be determined who makes the sovereign, and for what end, and on what conditions. The theologian might answer as did Bossuet, that ' God has given to every people its ruler ', but the people were learning to ask for evidence. Nor was it enough, with Bodin and Hobbes and Austin and all their company, to set over against the supreme will of the sovereign the ' law of nature ', the obligation of conscience, the moral responsibility of that power which is politically free and independent. Conscience is no sufficient brake for the chariot of power. Though for the time being the trend was in the opposite direction, the future was to show that power could be made not only morally but politically responsible. The government may be—must in some sense be—above its creature the law, but not above its creator the state. The legal truth, when over-emphasized, becomes political untruth.

We need not follow out the numerous expressions of the state as power which filled the age of absolutism and still find echoes in the schools of law. Much ingenuity was expended in defence of the doctrine, and the more so, the more it was refuted by political developments. Theologians invested it with the authority of the Bible, with the borrowed dignity of the vice-gerent of God. Hobbes and others justified it by the fanciful construction of an original compact, formulated to show that the people surrendered, as the only way to peace and security, their whole persons to the will of the ruler. In such a view the state is inflexible and narrow, a police-state with corresponding means. It was right and needful to insist, as these writers did, on the general duty of law-abidingness. It was natural that the more timorous spirits, as the forces pent in by absolutism erupted in violence, should find in the fiat of an indisputable master the only safeguard against chaos. But it was at best a half-truth—and the wrong half for the times—which proclaimed power as the deliverer of mankind from its own effects. Behind the partial chaos of breaking absolutisms creative forces were at work which the philosophy of ' strong government ' did not comprehend.

Even through the age of absolutist pretensions there were never wanting those who denied that government existed in its own right or for any other purpose than the welfare of the governed. Against the claims of power they set the claims of justice. They repeated the famous saying of Augustine, that if you take away justice kingdoms are nothing but robber possessions. Religious divisions were particularly effective in strengthening the anti-absolutist claims. For when absolute government sought to enforce a state-religion it attacked the profound convictions of the persecuted and stimulated them to put forward not merely the doctrine of toleration but the more revolutionary distinction between legitimate rule and tyranny. From the latter it was an easy step to assert the right of the people to depose the tyrant, and so the doctrine of the ultimate sovereignty of the people was reborn. ' Lawful princes receive the laws from the peoples ', declared the author of the famous *Vindiciae contra Tyrannos*,[1] and Holman in his *Franco-Gallia* seeks historical grounds for the same principles. Like most of the doctrines which have made political history, it arose as the protest of the subject against a particular exercise of power. According as the wind of persecution blew from one quarter to another, this doctrine was asserted by Catholics and Huguenots and Lutherans and Calvinists alike. But it attained its broadest expression in countries like Scotland and Holland where the popular religious sentiment was stirred against a government which upheld another faith. Perhaps its finest product was the work of the German writer Althusius who, living near the frontier of the Dutch republic, was inspired by the successful revolt of the Protestant Netherlands against the domination of Catholic Spain.

The political thought of Althusius is remarkably clear and reasonable. It rests on the principle that the state is a contractual federation whose units of association are the smaller corporations of cities and provinces. These are not merged and lost in the state. They unite for a purpose, and for that purpose they establish kings and assemblies. The state is their agent, their instrument. The king is their magistrate. Ultimate sovereignty rests with the people, acting not as individuals but as corporate unities. This sovereignty belongs to the corporation as such, and through its proper agencies it can insist on the

[1] See Laski's Historical Introduction to the English version of the *Vindiciae*.

performance by kings of their obligations to the people, or, failing that, release the people from the duty of obedience. The state exists for their welfare, and Althusius would give it a wide control over both religious and secular affairs. But for all its range it is a delegated control, and has an inner and an outer limit. The inner limit is the law of nature, the principle of justice which is binding on the conscience of men, whether kings or subjects. The outer limit is the right of deposing governments which wantonly violate this principle.

This was as clear-cut a doctrine as the age and country permitted. It set up limits of obedience without sanctioning anarchy. It made sovereignty the will of a collectivity and not of a person, and thereby justified it without resort to mystical or theological arguments. It showed the necessity of relating the will of government to the will of the governed, making the former the agent of the latter and finding the ground of unity in the conception of the common welfare. The time was scarcely ripe, at the beginning of the seventeenth century, for proclaiming the indifference of the state to religious concerns. Nor was it possible for Althusius to show, what many people of our own day do not yet understand, that the state is not qualified to be a *censor morum*, the coercive guardian of morality. Althusius could vindicate the rights of majorities, but the harder problem of the rights of minorities could not be solved until the sphere of the state itself was demarcated.

Some advance in another direction was made by de Groot, who attacked the power-concept where it was most strongly rooted, in the region of international relations. But his doctrine, very significant as it was, failed to distinguish between the mere ethics of international justice and the political principles and practices through which it must be achieved. His *jus gentium* fluctuates uncertainly between positive law, established usage, and ideal. One reason why de Groot could not securely relate ethical to political principle was that he refused to accept, within the state, the constitutional responsibility of government to the people or the welfare of the people as the sole and necessary end of government. His reactionary doctrine of state sovereignty was not consistent with his enlightened vision of an inter-state order, and it brought obscurity and confusion into his reasoning.

The later seventeenth century increased the volume of critical thought which attacked the doctrine of the intrinsic and irresponsible right of government Three writers born in the same year, Spinoza, Locke, and Pufendorf, are pre-eminent in this regard. Spinoza [1] applied his profound and passionless logic to demonstrating the absurdity of absolute right, and dared to make liberty itself the primary object of the state. The common sense of Locke [2] revolted against the ' right divine of kings to govern wrong ', and insisted on the fiduciary character of government, so that it could be called to answer for violation of its trust by the people for whose good alone and by whose consent alone it had the right to govern. Pufendorf [3] adumbrates the distinction between society and state, and finds the essence of the latter in the creation and maintenance of rational law, this duty being the true determinant of its powers and limits. From many directions the demand for liberty within the state, not merely liberty against the

[1] *Tractatus Theologico-Politicus.*   [2] *Two Treatises of Government.*
[3] *De Iure Naturae et Gentium.*

state, was arising in strong protest against absolute claims. Its finest expression had already been given in Milton's *Areopagitica*. Milton boldly proclaimed two principles of profound importance. One was the immunity of the religious life from political regulation. The other was that doctrine which has been the strength of the best thought of individualism from his day to the present, to wit that the well-being of society requires the natural diversity of its members, and that coercive uniformity of morals and manners would spell the ruin and degradation of any people.

It took these many generations to bring to clear consciousness the elementary problem of the state, the reconciliation of liberty and law. It was a problem which the power-theorists could not even formulate, nor had it any significance for those who believed in authority independent of consent, whether belonging to status or derived from God. The first task of any politics that could be really called scientific was to relate authority to its positive source, to show its dependence on the whole social fabric, the customs and traditions, the modes of thought and the standards of life that prevail among a people. It was this outlook which so greatly distinguished the work of Montesquieu [1] from that of most of his predecessors. He really sought to understand society, to show the influence of underlying conditions, climatic, geographical, economic, to show that customs and institutions neither are made nor can be changed by *fiat*, to show that there is in every people a spirit or character which their laws must reveal. Montesquieu made politics concrete and realistic, not in the Machiavellian sense as an art by means of which the passions and

[1] *L'Esprit des Lois.*

follies of men are exploited to further the design of government, but in a deeper sense as a science through which the laws and institutions of the state are revealed as the expression of the whole complex life of a people. All government that defies the spirit of the people is doomed to fail; all law that would change it or even ' reform ' it is futile.

In Montesquieu we get beyond the alternatives of power and justice as political ideals. The state is an agency through which a people gives expression and order to its collective life. The laws exist for something more than ' justice ' or ' security ' or the ' preservation of property ', they are a support and framework of the national spirit. This realistic interpretation passed into the political consciousness of the nineteenth century. It was only in the undeveloped field of international relations that the old issue between power and justice retained significance as a struggle of principles. Thinkers like Kent and Bentham and Mill and Green took one side, while the Hegelians and the extreme nationalists like Treitschke took the other. So narrowed, the problem is one with which we have already dealt.

III

THE STATE AS BASED ON CONTRACT

The form of political theory which held the field from the sixteenth to the eighteenth century was that of the ' social contract '. In the age when strong assaults were being made on Renaissance absolutism this doctrine of the social contract had a great service to perform. For it helped to clear men's minds of the mystical preconception of sovereignty, of those fervent ideas of divine right and inherent irresponsible power to which multitudes clung in their horror of that great process which was undermining the foundations of the throne. It offered another and more intelligible creed alike to those who feared and those who hoped. It swept out of the way the endless deductive arguments based on subjective interpretations of the Scriptures, and refounded the state on its only true foundation, the will of men and the common purpose which inspires that will to institutional life. Moreover, it was capable of ingenious modifications to suit the changing times. For contract can imply anything from ' sacramental sanction ' to mere convention. The terms of the contract were filled in according to the persuasions of each thinker and each occasion, while yet its logic always tended towards the clearer recognition of those human purposes which the state can serve and which alone justify its existence.

The first great writer who freed the principle of contract from irrelevant ideas and made it the fount and being of the state was Thomas Hobbes. Profoundly impressed by the conflict for sovereignty between king and parliament, obsessed by the dangers of the revolutionary principles of the democratic party and especially of the Independents, and growing disturbed by the confused attempts to establish the state on doctrines derived from a no longer unified church, he found in the social contract a basis for a theory of absolute sovereignty, one and indivisible, unbounded and inalienable.[1] Unless there is one indisputable authority, a final court of appeal and ultimate source of law, set high above all conflicting claims and omnicompetent, there is no

[1] The *Leviathan* was conceived about 1640, but not published until 1651.

political firmament, no security against the riot of the passions of men. There is no order without intimidation, no security without supreme compulsion. There are but two alternatives open to mankind: the 'state of nature' which is a state of war, with all the misery of the unbridled strength of individuals, when every man's hand is against every man; and the civil state, where men are reduced to a common obedience. If we assume the exclusiveness of these alternatives—which Hobbes seeks to prove by a curious piece of psychological study—what more natural than that men should give up their quarrelsome liberties to save themselves? This is the great surrender, the contract, which is 'as if every man should say to every man, I authorize and give up my right of governing myself to this man or this assembly of men, on this condition, that thou give up thy right to him, and authorize all his actions in like manner'. 'This is the generation of that great Leviathan, or rather, to speak more reverently, of that Mortal God, to which we owe under the Immortal God our peace and defence.'

All the ideas that Hobbes weaves into this doctrine, 'natural rights', the 'state of nature', the ideal but unheeded 'law of nature', the contract, and the civil state, were current long before his time. Hobbes was not original in seeking to establish peace and harmony on a basis of contract—we find it so stated, for example, in the sixteenth-century French political tract called the *Vindiciae contra Tyrannos*. What is remarkable is the rigour of the Hobbesian contract. The surrender must be perfect. Hobbes indeed wavers for a moment when he reflects that men will not resign their 'rights' unless they thereby secure a *quid pro quo* in the form of security— what if the sovereign in his turn denies them this? But always he goes back to his insistent alternative—subjection or chaos. Hence he has no compunction in concentrating every kind and degree of supremacy on his sovereign. Men have transferred under the covenant all their rights to their sovereign, who thus has plenitude of power in everything, over property, over opinion, over the forms even of religious worship. If this last exercise of authority offends the conscience, Hobbes's reply—though it was far from satisfying his own age—is no other than that contained in the famous verse of Euripides, ' the tongue has sworn, the mind remains unbound '. ' Profession with the tongue is but an external thing, and no more than any other gesture whereby we signify our obedience.' The believer is suffered, nay more he is bound, to bow himself at need in the house of Rimmon.

But political thought, especially in a period when absolutism was beginning to break, was not likely to accept the first premiss of this absolutist and ultra-Erastian structure. Is it indeed true, men came to ask, that we have no alternative beyond complete subjection and the ' state of war ' ? Why should this contract be, unlike all others, for ever irrevocable ? Why cannot the subjects insist on the *mutual* observance of the covenant ? May not men, remaining in the civil state, institute a new sovereign ? First comes the agreement to form society, next the particular institution of the sovereign— may not the former agreement remain though the latter be changed ? Even if it means revolution, is that necessarily the fault of the subjects, and may it not be worth the cost ? These were the questions which led Locke to restate the theory, to bring it into harmony with the English Revolution of 1688.[1] Men, after all, want not mere order—that may exist in a menagerie or

---

[1] Locke's two treatises on government were published just after the Revolution of 1688.

in a slave state. They want a decent order, in which property is safe and justice is administered and liberty itself has meaning. ' The obligations of the law of nature cease not in society.' ' The end of the law is not to abolish or restrain, but to preserve and enlarge freedom.' So Locke develops the inherent logic of contract. The purpose of the state, as it appears to the reason of men, is not thrust back into a single moment of political institution, it becomes a living active determinant of the state. Locke's conception of political purpose may be defective. If Hobbes was inclined to limit it to defence and peace, Locke lays excessive stress on the ' preservation of property '. The individualism of his time allows him to play with the old notion of rights which men bring like bundles into society, out of an hypothetical and crudely atomistic ' state of nature '. But this apparatus of thought is becoming a scaffolding no longer required for the political structure. The idea is emerging again that man is really a ' social animal ', and that the mainstay of government is found in such inherent needs of human nature as the state can serve. Here is the principle, so obvious and yet so slow to be attained, which is the beginning of all wisdom concerning the state. This idea is further advanced in the last of the great trio of social-contract thinkers, Jean-Jacques Rousseau. If he still retains the already antiquated machinery of the social contract, with its transformation of the natural man into the citizen, it is but the conservative form through which he expresses a social philosophy poles apart from that of Hobbes. The secret of Rousseau's doctrine is found in the substitution for *a* sovereign of *the* sovereign. His sovereign is the ' general will ', and he is perfectly ready to apply to it all the sweeping attributes which Hobbes delivers to his ' one man or assembly of men '. It too is one and indivisible, inerrant, indestructible, omnicompetent. But the difference is profound. If Hobbes declares that liberty exists only in the interstices of law, if Locke reconciles law and liberty only by assigning to the former the sole task of reducing the field of the latter, Rousseau boldly makes law the very expression and fulfilment of liberty. The precarious liberty of the state of nature is well lost for the assured and enlarged liberty of the social order. The idea that law was not merely consistent with liberty, not merely a possible guardian of it, but the very form of its realization, was of profound importance for the true interpretation of the state. It gave a new and most significant setting to the problem of political obligation. For Rousseau that problem solves itself when government is vested in the true sovereign, the ' general will '. When that is attained, then ' each, coalescing with all, may nevertheless obey only himself, and remain as free as before '.

The heart of Rousseau's doctrine is therefore the conception of the ' general will ', whose exercise transforms mere government into self-government. The deep truth of this principle is, after all, just this, that society is an integral unity, and that the consciousness of unity is the sense of the common interest or welfare. We are all members one of another and ' the body cannot wish to injure its members '. It can will only their welfare, and so of the true sovereign. In all societies there must be this living and inherent identity of interest, to secure and enhance which is the task of government. If it seeks aught else its will is no longer the will of the state, but the will of a class or section usurping the place of the true sovereign.

Here was a principle capable of momentous development, but unfortunately Rousseau was too impatient and doctrinaire to do it justice. He might have shown, for example, how the general will is revealed in the spirit of nationhood, how it is the logic of all professions of loyalty, how in hours of crisis it may break through all the conflicts of particular and opposing interests and make itself the undisputed master of the state, how at other times it remains below the surface as the final check on disruptive forces. He might have shown how the general will creates through the ages that ' spirit of the laws ' which so impressed his predecessor Montesquieu. He might have shown how it is blindly present in the solidarity of the most primitive peoples, how it struggles to fuller, if yet always partial, expression in the evolution of what we call democracy. Lastly, he might have presented it as the *ideal* in the light of which the policies of government should be judged. But Rousseau wanted a hasty and impossible identification of the ideal and the actual, an attitude all too readily followed by his Hegelian disciples. He fell consequently into some dangerous fallacies, which vitiated his treatment of a fundamental truth. He accepted the facile identification of the ' will for the general good ' with the ' will of the generality ', and after defining his ' general will ' in the former sense continued as if it were simply the ' will of the people '. The latter may be the actual sovereign, but it may still be far from the ideal sovereign which Rousseau postulates. He was unwilling to consider the necessary implications of majority rule. The weight of a vote cannot be politically determined by the disinterestedness of the motive which inspires it. A whole people cannot legislate except in a tiny city-state, a stage to which the world, in spite of the 'citizen of Geneva', is little likely to return. Even if it could, it would still be at most majority, not unanimity, upon which government would rest. Rousseau sought his 'general will' on the surface, instead of in the hidden foundations of the state.

To make the older contract-theory serve for the new age, it had seemed enough to Rousseau to change the location of sovereignty without changing its nature. His abstract sovereign is as concretely absolutist as that of Hobbes. It is, by anticipation, the rule of the revolutionary assembly endowed with the omnicompetence of Louis Quatorze. His sovereign prescribes, for example, certain 'dogmas of civil religion' which every citizen, on pain of banishment, must accept. If thereafter he 'behaves like an unbeliever in them, he should be punished with death'.[1] So writes the apostle of liberty who would exclude all other creeds on the ground of their intolerance!

Such inconsistency does more than reveal the mind of Rousseau—it sets in a glaring light the ultimate defect of the whole doctrine of social contract. The state may well be, but society can never be, interpreted as a contractual fabric, and the theory identified society with the state. From this confusion the 'social contract' never escaped. Society, which is the very condition of human life, is made to depend on a rationalized and full-grown human will which itself is meaningless except for a remotely long process of social growth. Within this process the state has emerged as a 'will-organization', controlling and instituting those forms of order which prove amenable to political law. But the order established by the state never was and never could be, even

[1] *Social Contract*, IV, ch. viii.

under the extremest absolutism, coextensive with the primary and intrinsic order which reveals the social nature of man. Before the state began, there was society. When the state in its fullest pride of power claimed to be everything, society still said to it, 'thus far and no further', at first implicitly, at length in a clearer consciousness of its right over its own instrument. Sovereignty has its limits, but the social contract theory, because of this false identification, could not properly assign them.

The contract theory had firmly set the state on its true basis of will, redeeming it from the alien or irrelevant conceptions derived from mystical and traditional hypotheses. But it could not define that will. To do so it was necessary to abandon the whole mechanism of the state of nature and the ensuing compact. In Rousseau the theory seemed to reach its term of development. He had given the principle of will its deeper significance. He had expressed in its true form the problem which the state must solve. For he had perceived the high necessity of that which in some measure the state was beginning to achieve, the union of liberty and authority. He offered boldly, if mistakenly, a complete solution of the dilemma involved in the endlessly reiterated opposition of these two factors. Here at any rate was the ideal whose attainment could make the perfect state, though Rousseau could not translate the ideal into terms of political reality. Henceforth a more inductive method of inquiry was needed, concerning itself directly with the social purpose which the state, as seen in that historical evolution which the contractualists ignored, has been constructed and reconstructed in order to serve.

IV

THE STATE AS A MYSTICAL UNITY

From the earliest times the inquiring mind had puzzled over the problem of interpreting the unity of the state. The contract theory was at bottom individualistic. The state, nay society itself, was an organization resting on the specific will of its members, an edifice created by their *fiat* and having no deeper foundation than its convenience. There was truth as well as error in this doctrine. The chief error lay in the confusion of the superstructure with the foundation. Society is ultimate, inherent in the meaning of life, rooted in the nature of personality. The state is but one of its expressions, necessary but not ultimate. If man is a political animal, it is only because he is a social animal. The failure to make this distinction vitiated, until quite recent times, all attempts to reveal the nature of the state. This clearly appears in the different explanations offered by the advocates of the social contract. Some, like Hobbes and Locke, reduced society to that mere system of consentient wills which constitutes the institutional fabric of the state, a system both precarious and artificial unless it be related to a deeper unity. Others, like Rousseau, sought to include the profound significance of society within the terms of a political compact, to which no ingenuity could give a form adequate to the truth they sought to convey. The contractualists were right in basing the state upon will; but since the society with which they identified it does not also rest upon will, they could offer no adequate interpretation of either.

The adversaries of the social contract were no less

confused, and for the same reason. If they were right in denying the contractual derivation of society, they were wrong in refusing to acknowledge the relevance of that principle within the state. The contractualists had indeed performed a service which their opponents sought to undo. They had removed from the institutions of law and governments the beclouding mystery which set their worth apart from their function. Men like Burke sought to restore the mystery. In this respect at least they retarded the progress of political thought. In the hidden matrix of society there are forces deeper than our thoughts and stronger than our wills, but the state as a conscious organization must be related to, and justified by, our conscious purposes. It was no service to our understanding when Burke enveloped once more in mystic obscurity the office of government and in the sphere of politics appealed once more against reason to tradition and religion. Nor did it avail to transform, by an eloquent reinterpretation, the idea of contract into something even more sacramental and universal than it had appeared to Rousseau. Nor, again, was the process of thought advanced when Burke appealed to that old analogy of the organism in order to vindicate prerogatives which were already being swept into the past.

The contractualists could not explain society as a compact, nor could the anti-contractualists explain the state as anything else. It was natural to take refuge in analogy, but analogy was a dangerous guide. From the beginning men had likened the body politic to the 'individual writ large', or to the mind, or to the organism. It was helpful in suggesting the interdependence of men, and the reality and strength of the unity of which they are members. But the further these analogies were carried, the more misleading they became. Plato perverted the understanding of society by comparing the three ' parts ' of the mind to his three classes within society. Medieval theorists had carried the analogy of the body to the most meticulous and arbitrary extremes, as when Nicholas of Cusa discovered that in the ' corporal life ' of the state the offices of government are the limbs, the laws are the nerves, the emperor the head, and the subjects the flesh.[1] Physical analogies of this kind found favour throughout the later history of political theory, and even the individualist Hobbes entitled his state the Leviathan. When the contract-theory had run its course the idea found new and vigorous expression. To the mechanics of the social contract Burke opposed the doctrine of the living organism. This movement culminated in the work of Spencer and of Schäffle. It became thereafter speedily apparent that these elaborations of the organic conception, attributing for example to the state (or to society) an alimentary system, a nervous system, a circulatory system, and so forth, were fanciful and vain. Even the upholders of the doctrine protested when Bluntschli endowed the state with sex, describing it as having a male personality.[2] The organic theory lost its prestige, nor was it restored by those thinkers who took refuge in such expressions as ' contractual organism ' or ' spiritual organism '. Here the saving adjective was in fact a denial of the substantive.

From organism men turned again to mind or person in the quest for a true representation of the state. The state was the greater mind, the supra-person, whose will or purpose comprehends and transcends that of the individual

[1] See Gierke, *Political Theories of the Middle Age*, iv.
[2] Bluntschli, *Theory of the State*, Bk. I, ch. i.

minds or persons who compose it. This conception had found a certain support in Rousseau's interpretation of the general will. Rousseau had mystically distinguished the general will from the ' will of all '. His one and indivisible sovereign was something greater, something purer, something far more rational, than the conflicting wills of the members of the state. Fichte took over this notion, in the name of the unity and spirit of a nation. It found, however, its fullest development in the philosophy of Hegel.[1] The state is a living person (not merely an organism). Its unity is in its own self-consciousness. It is a collective person, a majestic being, a sort of God whose thoughts are not our thoughts and whose ways are not our ways. It was no mere ' legal personality ' which Hegel attributed to the state. In law the term ' personality ' has a perfectly definite and non-mystical meaning, but to Hegel the state was no convenient subject of rights and obligations. He sought under this form of expression to reveal the unity which makes a nation. We speak of the mind or the spirit of a people, meaning thereby the common qualities of mind or spirit which they reveal. But Hegel is not thinking simply of common qualities, of attributes shared by like-natured beings. He thinks of a mind that animates the whole ' body ' of a nation, that guides and governs it, a mind that is more real than the minds of its members, that works in history towards the fulfilment of its own purpose. Individuals are merely its temporary instruments, and epochs are but the revelations of its creative will.

How this mind is related to the minds we know remains a mystery. How it is to be identified with the state is a mystery still more inscrutable. Hegel's recent disciple,

[1] Hegel, *Philosophie des Rechts.*

Bernard Bosanquet, strove to show that the will of the state is the ' real ' will of its members, even though their ' actual ' will is at odds with it.[1] But even if we accept the extraordinary Hegelian identification of the ' rational ' with the ' real ', we are no nearer to understanding how the *de facto* will that undertakes the business of government is invested with superior rationality. If it is not, the real will of the state is something else than the will of government, and so becomes curiously unreal. Hegel himself was more forthright on this subject. Although he shrank from incarnating his nation-mind in the actual nation, he had little difficulty in discovering that his ' constitutional monarch ' was the very expression and organ of rationality.[2] So he restored, in happy conformity with his age and country, that divinity of government which history had mockingly denied to kings.

Viewed as an interpretation of the unity and nature of the state, all these conceptions, expressed in terms of a single mind or person or organism, are exposed to fatal objections. In the first place they confuse the state and the community. If there are any grounds for attributing to the community a profound and permanent integrity of being comparable to that of an enduring mind, there are none for identifying that being with the state. For, as we have seen, the state is an organization created by the community, with limited objects and modes of attainment. It is no self-substantial entity whose end is its own fulfilment, existing in its own right and for its own welfare. It is an instrument to serve the purposes of its members, and its

[1] Bosanquet, *Philosophical Theory of the State*, c. v. See my *Community* (3rd ed.), App. B. For a good criticism of the Hegelian school, see Hobhouse, *Metaphysical Theory of the State*.

[2] *Philosophie des Rechts*, sec. 273.

whole structure is meaningless save as it is built and maintained to further that service. The unity of the state is not to be found within itself at all. Its unity comes from without, it is kept together only by the community of those who use it as their instrument. Its sovereignty is nothing final or self-determined, but a form of trust, a derivative power, a commission. First we must learn the nature of social unity and then we shall be able to understand and distinguish the secondary unity which alone we can assign to the state.

In the second place, it is a logical error to seek to interpret the unity of a whole as though it were exactly correspondent to the unity of its members or components. A state consists of persons, and that fact alone makes it impossible to represent its unity as that of a person. A grove of trees is not a tree, nor a colony of animals itself an animal. It is no less absurd to think of a society of persons as a person. It is to lose the sense of relationship which brings persons into unity. The very thing we are seeking after, the social nexus, disappears if we identify the relationship with the nature of the objects to be related. We want to know how minds are related, and we are told that the system of relationship is itself a mind.[1] Such an easy but confusing answer would be impossible in the natural sciences. What would we think of a science which informed us that a system of atoms should itself be understood as an atom, or a system of stars as itself a star? No unity of like elements can possibly be described as equivalent in structure to that of its own elements.

The practical danger of this illogical identification lies in the mystical interpretation of the end or purpose of the

[1] Cf. McDougall, *The Group Mind*, ch. i.

social system. If the state is a person or greater mind, it has, like the persons we know, its own intrinsic value, its own fulfilment—which is not therefore the fulfilment of its members. The state comes to exist in its own right. It is not, according to the jargon of this school, the ' sum of its members ', and the denial of this meaningless expression is taken to imply that it has a goal other than the good of its members. It is a new way of justifying absolutism. I have elsewhere commented on this doctrine as follows : ' It regards humanity as something more than men, nationality as something more than the members of a nation. It suggests that it is possible to work for humanity otherwise than by working for men, to serve nationality otherwise than by serving the members of a nation. In so far as the end and value of society are regarded as other than the ends and values of its members taken as a whole, the latter count for less than before, becoming in so far mere means to an end which is beyond, not merely each as individual, but all as collective. Not only can we not give meaning and concreteness to such a value, but the postulation of it deprives of actuality the values we actually know. If the whole be such as to have an end which is realized otherwise than as the fulfil- ment of the ends of its parts or persons, then personality is in so far an illusion ; for it rests on the being of each as an end in itself, and all its striving is understandable only on the supposition that each person and the other persons for whom also he strives are ends in themselves.' [1]

The fallacies we have described occur alike in all systems which represent the whole as a large-scale type of its own units, whether they speak of the group-mind or of the

[1] *Philosophical Review*, September 1915, article entitled ' Personality and the Suprapersonal '.

social organism. We must abandon all such analogical methods if we are to understand either community or its creature the state. We must first appreciate the nature of social unity before we can proceed to the understanding of the state, for the clue to the latter lies outside its own organization, in the community which it serves, which brings it into being, and which holds it together. This we have already shown in part, and it will be the task of a later chapter to show it more completely.

XV

POLITICAL THOUGHT OF THE PRESENT

I. THE ISSUE BETWEEN INDIVIDUALISM AND COLLECTIVISM

THE establishment of formal democracy brought new issues into the foreground. On the one hand there arose the conditions of a new individualism which could not have developed at all within the class-state. The class-state rested too entirely upon governmental control to admit the doctrine that collective action is neither necessary nor desirable to guide the economic or the moral life of the community. It might indeed, distinguishing the 'secular' from the 'sacred', withdraw from the control of the latter, but to carry the principle into the former field would have been fatal to its foundations. Only after democracy was formally installed could the doctrine of individualism be anything but a revolutionary protest. This was especially true in respect of the economic order. Just as economic change was the most powerful solvent of the old class-state, so was the doctrine of economic individualism, as proclaimed for example by Adam Smith, the clearest witness of the fact that a new political age had dawned. But on the other hand this doctrine met opposition not only from the adherents of tradition but also in increasing measure from those who looked to the democratic state for deliverance from new or ancient economic ills.   So a new collectivism also arose.

The issue between individualism and collectivism provided the greatest political, as well as the fiercest economic, controversy of the nineteenth century, and yet taken in its earlier and strict interpretation, the issue is dead.   Not because it has been settled by the triumph of either side, but because the conditions they alike presupposed no longer exist.   The controversy has shifted to new grounds.

Let us examine briefly the argument of one of the foremost and best of the champions of individualism.   It is set out with fine sincerity in Mill's short *Essay on Liberty*.   It is partly a moral plea, that we should learn the devastating effects of intolerance, the attitude of men who make their own opinions and beliefs, their own customs and modes of behaviour, the norm and sole standard of the universe, regarding divergence as either crime or sin or folly, and narrowing the field of legitimate conduct to the fenced area of their own petty understanding.   Against this attitude Mill protested in the name of individuality.   He claimed that only through difference does life become rich and grow, and that it has generally been the despised and rejected of men who have been the movers and makers of the world.   Individuality is thus an essential element of well-being.   It is all too liable to be suppressed by the intolerant spirit of the tradition-bound masses and on the other hand by the tyranny of bureaucrats and officials, the unimaginative slaves of power.

As a moral plea Mill's argument stands unassailed. It rests on the incontrovertible fact that the right of the majority is not the rightness of the majority and that the keys of truth are not delivered to the owner of power. It emphasizes the always necessary doctrine that even good customs, if they harden to the uniformity of social pressure, may corrupt the world, and that no institutions may be judged by their mechanical efficiency, but only by the contributions they make to human welfare in the present and the opportunities they give for further development. It is a sound protest against at once the capricious tyranny of the mob and the too-well-ordered régime of bureaucratic authority. But to his moral plea Mill added, without adequate distinction, a political plea. He begins with a principle that ' the sole end for which mankind are warranted, individually or collectively, in interfering with the liberty of action of any of their number is self-protection'. This statement has a form which suggests that the full significance of the inter-dependence of social beings is hardly realized by Mill. And the suggestion is confirmed when he undertakes to distinguish, though with reservations, between acts which do and acts which do not concern society. There are ' distinct and assignable obligations ' the maintenance of which justifies the ' interference ' of the state. Outside these obligations every adult individual should be free to follow his own course.

Mill seeks to give us a political criterion, and at this point he fails us. Those ' definite and assignable obligations ' of which he speaks—who makes them, or do they belong in the nature of things? ' No person ', says Mill, ' ought to be punished for being drunk, but a soldier or policeman should be punished for being drunk on duty '. Suppose a person drives a car while drunk, is he violating a ' definite and assignable obligation ' to be sober while in charge of a car? Suppose a person has such a disposition that when drunk he is liable to do violent acts, must the law not intervene until the danger is fulfilled in violence? For the law cannot distinguish between temperaments so as to legislate only for such as by drunkenness create a public menace. Even if we accept Mill's conclusion on this matter we cannot feel satisfied with his criterion. Men might adduce Mill's own principle of self-protection as justifying the preventive as well as the punitive action of the state. Nor is ' self-protection ' itself a sufficient criterion of the range of law. Why should law not have a more positive function in promoting the end of well-being? Mill's argument is strong against the coercion of opinion or belief, but it is weak against the regulation of those external forms of conduct which may interfere with a desirable system of order or a programme of development. There are many acts which are not in themselves to be disapproved, but which nevertheless the law must forbid because the general well-being requires a certain uniformity of regulation. The most obvious examples of these *mala prohibita* occur in the economic sphere, and Mill himself, in his economic writings, admits the thin end of the wedge which has since his day fatally penetrated his criterion.[1]

The fact is that Mill, like most individualists, had not clearly liberated himself from the misleading assumptions of the social contract theory. To argue for individuality is not to argue for individualism, since individuality has

---

[1] Cf. Mill, *Principles of Political Economy*, Bk. V, ch. ii. In discussing the principle of a maximum working-day he admits that it may be a desirable thing and that it would probably involve for its establishment the sanction of law. Bk. IV, ch. vii, ' On the probable Futurity of the Working Classes,' is also out of harmony with his individualistic hypothesis.

its positive conditions in society, is in some sense itself a social product. The theorists of the social contract had thought of man as ' by nature ' wholly unsocial, until by the contract he was baptized into a wholly social being. Mill thinks of man as in certain categories social, but in others wholly ' individual '. But if we realize that the nature of man is a unity, that in every *aspect* he is a social being at the same time that he is also autonomous and self-legislating, so that his sociality and his individuality cannot belong to two different spheres, or, as the contractualists thought, to two different times—we must seek another form of reconciliation. And in that case we can no longer be content with an abstract doctrine of liberty. Mill tends to speak of liberty as an ultimate, an end of life. But even liberty must be justified as a means of life, and then it stands no more alone but in its relation to other means. Liberty itself is not one but manifold. There are so many forms of liberty, liberty of thought and of its expression, liberty of action in a hundred external spheres, civil liberty, economic liberty, and so forth—each of these again having many divisions, such as in the economic field, the liberties of contract and of competition. There are greater and lesser liberties, judged by the only possible standard, their relation to the general welfare. Moreover, these liberties conflict. As Mill perceived, the full liberty of competition may mean the subjection of the wage-earning class. We must then judge and choose between liberties. The great name of liberty cannot justify all its children. We are too deeply bound together to find the way of life in any mere principle of separation, and to the individualist liberty is little more. It is negative and formal. But the positive concrete reality, that well-being which we all seek within society, is ultimate alone and beyond any of its formal conditions, even liberty.

We have taken as our example the individualism of Mill because his argument is detached from those transient considerations which at first reinforced but speedily discredited most of the individualistic philosophies of the nineteenth century. Thus the economic individualism of *laissez-faire*, itself born of changing needs, could not withstand the demonstration of its inadequacy which the age afforded. Its doctrine of free competition gave even to the name of freedom a sinister as well as an unreal sound. It came to appear that the unequal are never free and that without protective laws the free are only the strong. Against such a destroying freedom man appealed again to the state, and the brief age of *laissez-faire* passed with its prophets. Belated champions came to their cause from the fields of science, proclaiming the struggle for existence and the survival of the 'fit'. But in the world of human civilization their doctrine seemed hollow and remote. The ingenious Spencer had a short-lived success, the popular repercussion of ideas whose scientific reign was already ended. The new or reborn science with which his own name was linked, that of sociology, was beginning to reveal again the profounder dependence of social beings on one another and on the whole structure within which they lived, showing that neither in health nor in sickness, in strength nor in weakness, do men live alone as competitive units, detached in splendid—or wretched—isolation from the common welfare.

The individualists had summed things up all too nicely in the antithesis between 'man' and the state. But the richness and multiplicity of social relations, once men came to recognize the facts, refused to support the conclusions based on so unreal a simplification. No doctrine could endure which failed to take into account in particular the great development of non-political forms of association. These bore witness to social needs which confounded the gospel of the individualist. For these at least were not to be explained by the grasping hand of power. Here all talk of the 'interference' of authority was vain. They could be explained only by the consciousness in men of common needs and common goals. The family, the club, the countless free groupings of every-day life, did not merely stand in contrast to the compulsive state ; they also revealed, in the light of the impulses which created them, the inner necessity of association, far above the realm of compulsion, the constructive mission that belongs alike to them and to the state.

The rival and opposite doctrine of collectivism is nevertheless the twin-brother of individualism and subject to a similar fate. If we look again into the rich complexity of human association, we must see how vain is the project which would place under a single centre of control not only the economic enterprises of individuals but also the activities of a multitude of economic groups, corporations and monopolies, trade-unions and co-operative societies, leagues of manu-facturers and of wholesalers and of retailers in their myriad forms, circle beyond circle of economic interests, financial and commercial and industrial and agricultural alliances seeking through union, inclusive and exclusive, the particular aims which distinguish them from the rest, to say nothing of the professional and technical objectives which are reinforced by the sense of a common economic motive. In the presence of these multifarious unities and divisions the older doctrines of socialism seem to belong to another world than ours. Marx was right in characterizing them as 'Utopian', but he avoided a like condemnation only because he laid stress on the evils of the economic system, stirring in those who suffered most grievously by it a fiery indignation, but refraining from any attempt to show how the state was to fulfil the tremendous new role which he assigned to it. He too simplified the variegated texture of society into the black-and-white of capitalists and proletarians, a useful method of propagandism which nevertheless utterly ignores the fertile experimentations of industrial society. Only in a relatively primitive régime like that of Russia, when its props of tyranny and superstition were overthrown by the calamities of war, could so vague an apocalypse make a successful appeal. In their desperation men simplify the conditions of good as well as of evil. But even under conditions so peculiarly favourable the collectivistic state had to modify its policy and to acknowledge the claims of economic interests, which its masterful leaders could not bring under their control. In the far more differentiated societies of western Europe and America a single centralized direction of the whole economic system would be an impossible task.

We are not arguing against the aims of collectivism, any more than against those of individualism. Our point is simply that the antithesis on which both doctrines rest, that of the individual and the state, is so far from representing the whole social fact, is so limited in the presence of the vast associational activity of modern days, that it cannot any longer be made the basis of a realistic theory. Individualism, looking only at the state, claims that the state should confine its control to the safe-guarding of individual liberties, but it ignores the significance of a thousand other associations, ' free ' associations, spontaneous expressions of the truth that nearly all the things men seek they seek through social means. Why then should the state alone be denied the right and the power to promote in positive ways the interests of its members ? Why, when it is endowed with the greatest of all the instruments of social man, the instrument of universal law, should it not apply it to its full capacity of service ? Moreover, if the state does not exercise this power, is it not abrogating it in favour of other associations—lesser ones with narrower aims, such as monopolies, trusts, trade-unions, the conflicting groups of the economic struggle ? Is the common interest so meagre as compared with these partial and contradictory interests, that the state must do nothing but keep the arena ? Collectivism again, also looking only at the state, claims that the state should assume the place occupied by these multitudinous groupings. It would restore, in the face of the whole development of modern civilization, the unity of economic and political power. But, as we have sought to show, an enforced unity of these two so diverse powers would put in a straight jacket the progress of society. That the state should maintain unity in difference is a hard enough task ; that it should itself constitute the unity of social life is a vain ideal.

Many collectivists, realizing the inadequacy of the state for so tremendous an enterprise, have cast about for an alternative agency of a directly economic character. This is the attitude of the syndicalists, who impetuously decry the state, and of the guild socialists, who would transform the present trade-unions into producers' associations, inclusive of all the producers, managers and workers, within an industry, while leaving to the state a certain control over the processes of distribution and a certain guardianship of the interests of ' the consumer '. We need not discuss the syndicalist position, if our whole argument goes for anything. The guild-socialist doctrine has much more significance, but nevertheless it attacks, in a more subtle way, what we regard as the business of the state. We may grant to it that a unified economic system would undertake great functions of control which its present divisions render impossible. But, as we have pointed out, the economic order is essentially one of inequality and of conflict. Some of its more extreme inequalities and some of its differences may well be removed in a more intelligent co-operation, but others belong to its very nature. The great cleavage which the guild socialists would abolish is that between the passive capitalist and the active worker. This end they would achieve by abolishing the former altogether, by denying all rights to rent and interest. It does not belong to our subject to examine the possibilities of so vast an economic revolution, but if feasible at all it would surely throw upon the state enormous new responsibilities which are hard to reconcile with the limited-state theory of the guildsmen. For their general teaching tends to belittle the sphere of the state. They attack the principle of political representation on the ground that one man cannot really represent a heterogeneous territorial group, but only specific interests, such as those of manufacturers or steel-workers or artists or teachers or Catholics. Political representation is indeed a rough device for the expression of the common interest, but for lack of a better one we must either retain it or fall into the greater confusion of opposing 'functional' parliaments. The sense of the commonwealth is still real, however beclouded by the particular interests of groups. Citizenship is still real, though men may identify its demands with their nearer purposes. The very idea of the common welfare irradiates the consciousness of sectional aims. The very existence of institutions which even formally stand for the general interest is of great service in directing towards it the thoughts of men. The danger is not that particular interests will not be focused and asserted, but rather that the general interest may suffer domination through their urgency. Against this danger the chief bulwark is the state, because its organization presupposes and in some degree realizes the activity of the general will. Besides, we must assume that through the rough method of political representation the 'pluses and minuses' of particularist and opposing aims will, as Rousseau said, in a measure cancel out. The extreme insistence of the guild socialists on functional representation becomes an attack upon the state itself.

The essential difference between other associations and the state lies just in this: that the other associations are limited primarily by their objective, which is particular, whereas the state is limited primarily by its instrument, which is particular, while its objective is general, within the limits so imposed. This difference is obscured by the guild philosophy. We may say that there are two forms of representation with two corresponding types of institution. One way is the representation of interests, the other of men. The former is definite and easy, but also partial and inadequate. It does not express at all the unity which makes society a real living growing truth. Men are not content to be represented simply as farmers or as engineers or as Anglicans or as lovers of music or any other art or recreation : they want also to be represented as citizens. Otherwise the unity of their individual lives is unexpressed, no less than the unity of society. This representation is achieved, no matter how roughly, through the development of the party system. We have seen that though parties are dominated by strong particular interests they are in idea and in principle the formulations of the broader attitudes of citizenship. Unless they were, the state would fall to pieces. But it endures in strength, witnessing to the fact that the sense of the commonwealth lives and works beneath all determinate interests of lesser range.

The scheme of guild socialism is an attempt to get away from the insignificance of locality, but it is also in effect an attempt to get away from the significance of the state. A parliament chosen in terms of occupation would inevitably either cease to be a state parliament or else, which is far more likely, would exercise general control in virtue of whatever specific group of interests was dominant within it. Such a result may occur under any system, but it is opposed to the principle of other systems. A nation is not simply composed of crafts and professions. These might logically elect an economic ' parliament ', but if it possessed also political sovereignty it would be a denial of the whole process which has differentiated economic and political centres of power. The state is retained in name but disappears in fact. Perhaps after all the insignificance of locality is necessary for the significance of the state. Political representation is real only because it is not based on any function but the function of citizenship.

The attack on the state, whether in the disguised form

we have been examining or in the open vehemence of the syndicalists, is the extreme manifestation of a more permanent movement of political thought—an attack not on the state but on the ancient tradition of its absolute sovereignty. We may now proceed to consider the lines along which this great assault has been progressing.

II

THE ATTACK ON ABSOLUTE SOVEREIGNTY

We have sought to show that the sovereignty of the state is no simple final power, as free and unconditioned over human life as the will of an over-ruling God might be supposed to be. It is the exercise rather of a function, limited by and dependent on the prevailing conception of what that function should be, and no less limited by, and dependent on, the kind and degree of organization established for its exercise. It is the attribute of an association and is no more absolute than the association itself. The theory of the state has too long been dominated by the legalist conception of sovereignty. While that conception may be useful enough in its own place, it becomes not only inadequate but false when it is applied to explain the substantial nature of sovereignty. In the first place, the legalist doctrine is formal. The fact that there may be no formal limitations on sovereignty, that in the extreme case of a unitary state without written constitutions government is formally free to legislate on anything and everything, has after all no great significance. Legally, the state is unlimited, because it is itself the source of legal enactment ; but it is no more absolute on that account than, say, the church, because it is the source of ecclesiastical law, or the Royal and Ancient Club, because it alone prescribes the laws of golf. We do not need to minimize the real and vital differences between political law and all other forms of social regulation. We merely insist that political law is but one form of social regulation. The state is *one* of the organs of community, and we must reconcile with this cardinal fact both its great services and its greater claims.

In the second place, the legalist doctrine speaks in terms of power and not of service. But power is only an instrument of service. In the last resort, it is only an ability to render service, which is recognized, constituted, and controlled by the kind of service it can render. It is possible of course to detach the means from the end. Men easily fall victims to that delusive habit of acceptance which makes them subservient to the institutions which should serve them. But they merely substitute in consequence a mystical for a real service. Always, in so far as they think at all, they must think of laws and other institutions as justified by their results. No one ever regards the service of the state as unlimited, and therefore the conception of unlimited sovereignty is dangerously false. To attribute power to government beyond the limit of its capacity for service is the grave error on which all tyranny is based.

The great difference between the political thought of our own times and that of the past is the definite assertion of the limited and relative character of sovereignty. In other ages men have protested against absolute power, appealing on moral grounds. They have put forward considerations of expedience and justice to which the ruler *ought* to give ear. They have proclaimed a 'higher law', the 'will of God' or the welfare of his subjects, which the ruler *ought* to obey. They have even justified rebellion or revolution when governments disregarded the duty annexed to power. But the duty was great because the power was so unlimited. The only definite bounds that men set to the exercise of sovereign power were in the religious or suprasocial sphere. In respect of secular or 'mundane' affairs, the sovereign was supreme. The question did indeed arise—who then is the sovereign? And while some still answered that it was the king and others that it was parliament, the more radical thinkers declared that it was the people themselves. But these disputes touching the residence of sovereignty did not raise the crucial issue of its socially (not morally) determined range. To Rousseau the sovereign was still as absolute as to Hobbes. The state was still, not an organ, but the organ, of community.

The newer doctrine arose out of the social developments of the nineteenth century. The trend towards democracy seemed to settle the question as to the residence of sovereignty, so that men turned rather to examine its nature. The complexity of social organization which the industrial age had brought, overthrew, as we have seen, the simple antithesis of the individual and the state. The real powers exercised by the numerous and often vast associations of the new age confounded the idea of a single all-comprehensive authority. It led men to seek a restatement of the character of political unity and of political power. It opened up a new and formidable problem. The older doctrine had at least envisaged society as a unity, under the direction of a sovereignty one and indivisible. But if sovereignty were limited, if there were other powers not reduced under the power of the state, where was the unity of society? Had it indeed any unity at all? This is our final question; but before we answer it we must consider the various influences which led certain groups of thinkers to reject the synthesis offered by the traditional doctrine.

There were at least three avenues of approach to the new theory of sovereignty. One of these, the nearest to the traditional doctrine, is well represented by the political philosophy of Green. Green made a careful distinction between the sphere of law and that of morality.[1] Political obligations can and should be enforced, whereas moral duties cannot: unless the latter express the free will of a moral being they lose their character. Political law therefore exists simply for the removal of obstacles in the way of free moral activity within society. It creates the order within which that freedom can exist. Hence the state has a limited sphere and cannot be identified with the whole activity of society. Since law must act though external sanction, it should refrain from touching those activities whose value is conditional on the motive or spirit with which they are performed. Thus the whole creative side of human thought and endeavour, including religion and morality in its proper sense, are outside the sphere of the state. Its place is determined by the fact that law is an instrument of limited range. The state should only, if it is true to its own nature, enforce those acts the doing of which, from whatever motive, is necessary for the good life within society.

---

[1] The distinction suffers because Green, with his Hegelian inheritance, appears to make all rights, ethical as well as political, depend on social recognition. This is not entirely consistent with his fundamental doctrine, that ethical rights express the nature of personality.

This principle, if related to the active forces which build up associations of other kinds than the state, was capable of far-reaching development. But to Green it remained somewhat abstract. He did apply it cautiously to certain practical problems, but wholly from an ethical point of view. Thus he considered, in the light of his criterion, the right and wrong involved in war, private property, political punishment, temperance legislation, and so forth. All through he is considering what the state can and therefore should do to secure the conditions within which men can act as free moral beings. But the poles of his thought are still the individual and the state. He does not consider how both are affected by the existence of other associations with other instrumentalities than political law. Had he done so he would have seen that the problem is not simply what the state *should* do, but also what the state is permitted to do, surrounded as it is by other powers, limited as it is by definite organizations of other kinds, fulfilling functions of their own in ways of their own. Green remains on the verge of the modern problem of sovereignty.

The second approach to a new doctrine may be called the evolutionary road. It is the road we have generally followed in this study. As we trace the development of social organization we apprehend the fact that the state has differentiated out of a communal system, which held together the potentialities of state and family and church, and all the newer associations of the economic and of the cultural sphere. Looking backwards we are apt to call this undifferentiated order by the specific name of the state, especially when it reached such a degree of centralized control as is found in, for example, the Greek city-community. But the state was still an aspect, not yet a form, of society. The city was the state, and much else besides—a kin system, a religious system, and so forth. In the historical process the state gradually emerged, until it became clear that the state was not the community, but a way in which the community was organized. Owing to the peculiar character of political power, it claimed to dominate the whole system within which it arose. This proud claim was never in fact realized, for custom and usage set sheer bounds in every direction to the exercise of sovereignty. But the significance of this fact only appeared when, as the interests of men grew more complex and varied, distinct associations took shape to promote objects which the state was itself not capable of securing, or which made an appeal only to particular groups. In the Western world the diversity of religious beliefs sharpened the issue between church and state, and in the end necessitated the withdrawal of the state from the control of one of the great communal interests. This was the first wave that broke over the doctrine of absolutism. It has been succeeded by others, and in our own days the conflicting currents of strong economic interests may well be said to have overthrown it altogether. Confronted with the determinate powers of the greater economic associations, the state could no longer pretend to be the one all-powerful agency of the social life. It had to accept the status of an association, one among others, no matter how essential its service.

Once this position is attained the whole subject of sovereignty appears in a new light. We have now to consider, not the ethical or discretionary limits of an indeterminate power over society, but the positive limits of a particular association, viewed alike in relation to other associations and to the specific means with which it is endowed. Here it is that the third line of advance, proceeding from a study of jurisprudence, brings reinforcement to the others. An association, recognized as such in law, becomes a corporation. The very name connotes definite limits, definite powers and responsibilities. At once therefore two very important questions arise. In the first place, what is the relation of the state to those corporate unities whose rights it recognizes and defines? In the second place, can we go so far as to call the state itself a corporation, a subject of definite rights and obligations, not only of rights which it must assert, but also of obligations which it too must, somehow, acknowledge?

Behind these questions lies another touching the nature of the corporation. We must here ignore the interminable juristic debate as to whether the corporation was a *persona ficta* or not. *In the legal sense* the corporation is a ' person ', a subject of rights and obligations which belong to it as a unity. In other words, it has rights and obligations which are not those of its members as individuals. A corporation may own funds collectively which its members cannot be said to own distributively. If it possess a franchise or monopoly it can be operated only through the accredited agents of the corporation. On the other hand, a corporation may be held responsible for the tortious acts of its agents—observe the significance of the fact that a corporation as such cannot commit a criminal offence (but only its agents or members), whereas it can be sued for damages. A corporation may prosper though its shareholders are in straits, or it may decline or grow insolvent while its shareholders flourish and pay their debts.

We cannot, for reasons already given,[1] accept the

---

[1] Bk. IV, ch. xiv, § iv.

attribution by Gierke and Maitland of a ' group-mind ' or a ' group will ' or a ' group personality ' to the corporation. A corporation is a unity but not an integrity. It is simply an organization through which its members pursue a common purpose. The purpose is not really the purpose of the organization but of its members. It expresses and develops an aspect of their personality, but an aspect only. Its meaning lies outside itself. There are only two unities which are integral, whose meaning in any sense lies within themselves—the individual and the community. Finally there are no purposes but individual purposes, and no values but individual values. But communities are whole areas within which these purposes and values are realized, whereas corporations are but specific means. A community is a union of individuals, but a corporation is only a union of members. The unity of membership, the unity of the corporation, is the unity of an aspect and no more. Thus one corporation may be identical with another in respect of membership, but such identity is quite meaningless in the case of communities. That is because we enter into corporations with only a part of ourselves, but we bring in a sense our whole selves into any community. If our argument holds, then the state itself does not embrace the whole personality of its members. We do not live within the state, but only by means of the state.

What then is the relation of the state to those other associations which it recognizes as corporations ? It gives them a special status defining their privileges and responsibilities. The state does not create the corporation but only regulates its legal character.[1] The association,

---

[1] This fact has been admitted in the courts. I quote by way of illustration the following statement from Bulletin No. 321 of the United

such as a professional group or a body of believers, exists apart from and prior to the state's act of recognition. The state cannot, for the most part, either make or unmake it. The state can dissolve a trust, but at most it is potent only to modify a mode of organization, and even so only with great difficulty, and under special conditions. The great associations are as native to the soil of society as the state itself. The state can scarcely even decide whether it will or will not recognize them. As Maitland pointed out, the state is practically bound to acknowledge the corporate character, the rights and responsibilities, of groups which operate as collectivities, and its formal recognition makes little difference to their character.

If then the state is not the creator, is it at least the superior of these corporations? It regulates them and defines their limits and forbids their transgressions of these limits, and curbs and penalizes them when they transgress. Is the state not after all their master? Can it fulfil its actual function of control and co-ordination unless it remains supreme? Is not the fact that it alone possesses compulsive power indicative of the world of difference between it and the corporation? And is not this legal fact the reflection of the profounder truth that all corporations stand for partial interests, while the state is the guardian and agent of the universal interests of men?

States Bureau of Labour Statistics (*Labour laws that have been declared Unconstitutional*, by Lindley D. Clark) : ' It was contended that corporations are the creatures of the state, and are not " persons " within the meaning of the Fourteenth Amendment ; but this was overruled on the authority of a decision by the Supreme Court of the United States, holding to the contrary.' (The reference given is Gulf, *C. & S. F. R. Co.* v. *Ellis* (1897), 165 U.S. 150, 17 Sup. Ct. 255.)

Here is the crucial question, and we cannot answer it unless we turn again from the legal form to the social reality. Let us remember in the first place that the state does not regulate the internal affairs of the other corporations; it does not and cannot determine their purposes or for the most part their methods. It marks their boundaries and brings them into relation within a common order. It does not treat them as its own agencies, as subordinates which it commands. Except as one group of interests encroaches on another, it does not deal with any of them in isolation from the rest. It does not say to the trade union, Go, and to the employers' association, Come, and to the church, Do this. These are the attributes of absolute sovereignty, and the state does not possess them. True, it stands for the common interest; but only so far as the common interest is sufficiently unified to admit of political expression, and only so far as it is sufficiently externalized to admit of legal regulation. True, it stands for the common interest; but not for the whole of the common interest. There is a common interest in customs, but it is not guarded by the state. There are common interests, such as that in the economic welfare of a country, which depend at least as much on the specific activity of various associations as on the general activity of the state. The common interest is no simple objective, attainable in its entirety by an inclusive authority. The partial interests of a thousand associations, cultural and economic, are also parts of the common interest.

Nor can we even maintain that the common interest, as sustained by the state, makes always and necessarily a superior and deeper appeal to the loyalties of men than interests which are less extensive in range, but which are, by contrast, more intimate and more closely bound with the traditions and beliefs of groups. On this account the doctrine of absolute sovereignty, if actually practised in the states of to-day with all their diversities of culture, would be fatal to the harmony of social life. A principle of unity, if carried beyond its proper range, becomes a principle of division. The state does certainly stand for the unity of society, for that basis of order which reflects the common needs and the common nature of social beings. No loyalty is more essential and none is more constant. The social experience of myriads of years has woven it into the texture of men's instincts. But if this experience has led men to endow the state with a peculiar and exclusive property, that of compulsive power, it has also discovered gradually the limits of its application. It has not only endowed the state with power; it has endowed it with a function to which the power is relative. And that function proves to be but one among the functions for which men organize themselves. Beyond the power, beyond the state, lies the will of social man. Thence in the last resort does the state derive what power it is permitted to exercise. The state makes rights for men, but men first make the rights of the state. As has well been said, ' The power of the state over its members depends upon the will of the members themselves, and on the fact that they allow the state to organize force which can indeed coerce individuals, but cannot coerce the whole community. The state, therefore, can have control over the corporations within it only if, and so far as, the citizens are prepared to give it such power.' [1]

---

[1] A. D. Lindsay, ' The State in Recent Political Theory,' *Political Quarterly*, February 1914. Strictly speaking, we should not say that these corporations are *within* the state, but within the community. Strictly

We may now seek to answer our remaining question : Is the state itself a corporation ? Is the state subject to legal obligation ? Have its members rights against it ? Are its rights, for example as a property owner, limited by those of other property owners ? The question might at first sight seem meaningless. How can the state be bound against its will by its own law ? It could not be so bound if law were simply the *fiat* of the state. But in the great book of the law the state merely writes new sentences and here and there scratches out an old one. Much of the book was never written by the state at all, and by all of it the state is itself bound, save as it modifies the code from generation to generation. The state can no more reconstitute at any time the law as a whole than a man can remake his body. The structure built through ages determines and limits its present conduct. In this sense there is truth in the argument so forcibly insisted upon by Krabbe, that the authority of law is greater than the authority of the state.[1] At any moment the state is more the official guardian than the maker of the law. Its chief task is to uphold the rule of law, and this implies that it is itself also the subject of law, that it is bound in the system of legal values which it maintains. Its task is incomplete, nay broken, if it seeks exemption from the legality which it also imposes. If the state were not responsible before the law for the acts of its agents, as any other corporation is responsible, there would be a fatal lacuna in the universality of law, a sheer denial of the universality. In part the state does admit, though sometimes through subterfuge, its own submission to law.

speaking, too, we should say that the powers of the state depend upon the will of men, not merely as citizens but as social beings.

[1] Krabbe, *The Modern Idea of the State*.

When it borrows funds, it accepts the obligation to pay interest. It allows, though it may be in form as a matter of grace or favour, individuals to obtain redress against itself (or its agents) through the courts. What is needed is a more explicit recognition of its corporate character. It is absurd that, as in England, the state should escape responsibility for the tortious acts of its agents. This liability would not impair the proper sovereignty of the state, and it would vindicate and complete what we may now call the sovereignty of law.

The state, then, we may conclude, has the essential character of a corporation. The theoretical difficulty, due to the relation of the state to law, to the fact that the state alone owns direct power to enforce the law, must be met by a more realistic interpretation of the state. It can be so met if we are frank to recognize that the state is a particular form of organization, itself sustained and controlled by that greater thing, that source and final judge of all it institutes, whereof all organization is but a mode or expression—the community itself.

XVI

A RE-INTERPRETATION OF THE STATE

I. THE STATE AS ORGAN OF COMMUNITY

In our last chapter we approached the great dilemma with which the political thought of the present is faced. We showed not only that the state must be regarded as an association among others, but also that it has, partly in fact and wholly in the logic of its function, the character of a corporation. It commands only because it serves; it owns only because it owes. It creates rights not as the lordly dispenser of gifts, but as the agent of society for the creation of rights. The servant is not greater than his master. As other rights are relative to function and are recognized as limited by it, so too the rights of the state *should* be. It has the function of guaranteeing rights. To exercise this function it needs and receives certain powers. These powers should be limited just as the function is limited. The function is limited both by its own nature and by the capacity of the agent, and that capacity becomes known to us by experience of its conduct, in the light of the means at its command. The state is not exempt from the imperative, ' thus far and no further ', to which all agencies are subject.

But here the dilemma threatens us again. How can the power which determines rights be itself subject to obligation ? How can the authority which alone has compulsive power be itself controlled? If the state be not the final authority, how can there be any other? And if there be none, how can order be secured? Who assigns to each association its place, who establishes its bounds, unless it is the state? How can law itself be supreme, unless the state also is supreme? And yet again, how can the state be supreme in the face of the indubitable fact that other associations are not its creatures, and that they possess powers and spheres of their own, which are not those of the state?

If we turn again, and for the last time to the criterion of law, we find the answer. Let us for a moment contrast law with custom. There are many customs which are observed at least as faithfully as political laws. Now customs are sustained by the community as such, not as a rule by the aid of any organization. Law, on the other hand, is sustained by the state. But ultimately they rest alike on the same basis, for the state itself is sustained by the community. Ultimately they are both expressions of the social sense, the sense of solidarity, the sense of common interest. In this subjective fact we find the root of the unity of society, not in the state, which is only a form through which that unity is expressed. We are here in the sphere of values, which must be felt before they are established. Just as, for example, all the objective values of the economic sphere, together with all the institutions and associations by which they are maintained and pursued, derive from the subjective valuations of economically minded beings, so in the whole area of society all forms of relationship, including those protected by the state, derive from the subjective valuations of social beings. It is they who create, according to the range of felt or recognized solidarity, states and churches and trade-unions and employers' associations. It is they who say what the state shall or shall not do or be, and set limits, directly or indirectly, to the activity of groups to which they belong or do not belong. The community is the matrix of all its inclusive and exclusive forms. It is not an organization but the source of organization. No structure, no form of government, can assure social unity. The final unity lies in the solidarity of men, not in the power of the state. There is social unity just in so far as the sense of common interest or common nature is stronger than that of dividing interests. Man is a social animal and the more fully he comes to realize it the stronger and the greater does the order of society become. In that realization lies the source of what unity exists or can exist.

The state is, as it were, the paved highway of social life, bordered by fields and cities. It is the common way which serves them all. All the business of life is rendered possible by its aid, and all who live along it must contribute to its upkeep. It is the basis of all social communications. Therefore, whatever else a man may be, he *must* be a member, or at least a subject, of the state. If he does not share the responsibility for the highway he must at least observe its rules. But he does not live on the highway, nor does man live for the state. His home is in the fields or the cities, and there he gathers the fruits of his labour. In the simpler days when there were only a few scattered houses along the highway, men learned to speak of it as if it included all that belonged to them. So the rule of the highway became a tyranny, because its guardians claimed to control the whole lives of men. Very slowly have they learned its true significance. They are only now learning that although they all have duties

towards the upkeep of the highway, this universal obligation does not sum up their social life. The fields and
cities now stretch far away from the thoroughfare. So
the many memberships of social life have grown explicit,
and refuse any longer to be summed in the one membership of the state.

The one membership remains still as a condition of all
the rest. It too has grown fuller and richer, the greater
means of more manifold purposes. The highway is
broader and more necessary than ever before. Now it is
the means whereby great groups and centres of social
life are kept in due relation to each other and to the
whole. But we must not on that account restore its
ancient claim, the former claim of its guardians, that
they should control the centres of life to which it
ministers. The highway is for the sake of the life that
is lived along it and beyond it. Nor, dismissing that
false claim, should we take the opposing extreme, which
would make the centres independent of the highway.
The greater community is still a community, and the
highway is still the chief external means that makes
it one.

All civilized men must be members or subjects of a
state, because they are all members of some community
and must share its external social conditions.[1] In this

[1] This distinction between the membership of the state and that of
other associations is generally put in a misleading way, and consequently
false deductions are made from it. Thus a recent writer, Mr. Norman
Wilde, in a generally well-balanced work (*The Ethical Basis of the State*),
remarks that ' all men are members of the state, but not of any other
association ' (p. 135). All men are subject to some one state, but not all
are members of it. Moreover, all men are members of families, and all
men are bound together in some economic system, though there is here
no association co-extensive with the system. The same writer adds that

sense the state is universal in extension, though on that very account it is peculiarly limited in its *mode* of action. Ideally the order of the state includes everybody everywhere, and its end is not fully achieved until all states are parts of a universal political order as extensive as humanity itself. This order may be achieved through the consent of particular states, each maintaining, to return to our metaphor, its own part of the one great highway. But the logic of political order requires a unity of system over the whole earth, and our traditions of independent and exclusive sovereignties have become mere obstacles to the recognition of this indefeasible truth. Within this unity all the intrinsic differences of groups can find their proper place ; apart from it they are distorted or exaggerated because they ignore the intrinsic likenesses, the common social nature, of humanity. If all men *must*, no matter what their differences, be included in some political system, all men should, by the logic of the same necessity, be included in one still greater order, the unbounded rule of law.

The same logic opposes the conception of a pluralistic society wherein great associations seek their several aims and when these clash must somehow decide their differences by the mere impact on one another of their respective forces. We too have insisted that the state is but one among the great associations, but its own peculiar function is no other than this, of giving a form of unity

---

the state ' is not merely one institution among many, but the condition of all '. This is true, at any rate if we substitute ' association ' for ' institution '. But it is a statement which can be made with equal truth of the family, and also, in the modern world, of its economic associations. If the state is unique in its own way, so are other associations in their ways. And if the state is absolutely necessary to our social life, so are they also.

to the whole system of social relationships. It can achieve this end, as successfully as other associations achieve their ends, without arrogating to itself again that omnicompetence which it has vainly sought to establish. There are times when it fails, as every human organization fails, but its success is far more notable and enduring. Ultimately it succeeds, because it does not act merely in its own right, because it is an organ of society maintained by it for that very purpose. It is the community, including therefore the members of all other associations, which assigns to it its function and lends it power.

We see this too if we reflect on the actual clashes which do occur between associations. We speak, for instance, of the conflicts between church and state, or between the state and the trade-union. But such conflicts have a very different interpretation from those that occur, say between church and church or between trade-union and employers' union. In the latter cases there is a sheer difference of attitude or of interest. The particular groups, wholly as groups, deny and oppose the aims of one another. The aims are themselves particular, and the conflict can be waged on a ground which leaves intact the general order of society. But it is otherwise when the issue involves the state and another association. It is never simply a conflict of two distinct groups, two distinct sects of interest, of which one is at stake. Take for example the Scottish Disruption or the Kulturkampf. These were conflicts *within* a state, because all directly concerned were its citizens. In the first instance it was also a conflict *within* a church. In the second it was a conflict, touching the proper spheres of state and church, between those citizens who accepted certain claims of the Catholic Church and those who denied them.

In the strict sense there cannot be a conflict between the state as a whole and any other association. The claims of the state, as insisted upon by a government or by a majority of its citizens, may be opposed to the claims of other associations. But it is always an internal struggle, and therefore, unless the state be dissolved altogether in the process, one modified by the common fact of citizenship. As the state has grown in experience, it has learned the unwisdom of making such claims as endanger the vital principle or the autonomy of any of the great associations to which its members may also belong.

The state can act thus as a unifying agent, but only in so far as it has itself undergone evolution towards democracy. For this reason we regard democracy as the form of the state proper, for only under democratic conditions can it achieve this proper function, this function, in other words, which it and it alone is capable of performing. Historically the interest of the state has been identified with that of ruler or ruling caste, military or landed oligarchy or later plutocracy. In these forms it was the organization of a class, and instead of standing for the interests we have shown to be its true concern it stood for the whole complex of interests belonging to a class. The land laws, enclosure acts, anti-labour acts, and so forth, which states have enforced were contradictory of the universality of law—they were not directed towards the common interests of those who were subject to the laws. The true nature of the state, here as always, is revealed in the fundamental character of law.

CONCLUDING REFLECTIONS ON SOVEREIGNTY

We have arrived at the days when the sovereign power, the maker of laws, the government, is told what it may and may not do. It is so instructed in the constitutions of nearly every modern state. In these states explicitly, in all states implicitly, there are many things which are forbidden to any or all organized authorities. The limits of sovereign power are particularly marked in federal states. In the United States, when 'in five years the courts of this country hold three hundred and seventy-seven statutes or an average of over seventy-one a year, unconstitutional',[1] it is surely obvious that the principle of sovereign power can no longer be stated in the old terms. Nor can the power which declares these acts of legislation 'unconstitutional' itself enact these or any other laws. Nor can any *constituted* authority reverse its decision. If there is here any absolute authority it is one that expresses itself only in a *veto*, and this authority is after all not absolute, for it never acts in its own name and right.

In whose name then does it act? Not in the name of government or party or majority, but in the name of a fundamental law which is superior to the will of any of these. It is superior because it is constitutive of the state itself. The traditionalists vainly try to save their doctrine by ascribing *the* political sovereignty to the will which is at irregular intervals and sometimes after long periods of inaction called into being to amend the fundamental law. But so inchoate a will has none

[1] Pound, *American Law Review*, January to February, 1910.

of the normal attributes of sovereignty. It is surely simpler and more convincing to find here the will, not of the state, but of the community, the ' general will ' on which the state is based, of which the state is an organ. The general will need not do the work of its own agent, it need not and cannot govern. It is not a *political* sovereign. But though it rarely acts, it never sleeps. Always it maintains the state, upholding the unity that is deeper than political divisions. Sometimes, in periods of crisis, it appoints a special organ to re-establish the foundations of the state. Sometimes at such periods, devices are framed, necessarily imperfect devices, accepted forms through which the general will may again at need find expression, and amend or repeal what it has established. But just as the general will is the will *for* the state, not *of* the state, so these devices, whatever their value, are institutions of the community, not of the state. They exist in order to control and limit the state, the agent of the community.

This interpretation is in keeping with the language and the spirit of modern constitutions. They assign, for example, duties to the state, not merely to the government.[1] They say what political power may do and how it shall be exercised. They declare that all power emanates from the people or the community. They profess to be based on the indefeasible or ' natural ' rights of persons, which are anterior to the legal and constitutional rights of citizens. Thus the Fourteenth Amendment of the United States forbids any of the

---

[1] The German Constitution of 1919 is particularly explicit in this matter. Note, as one of many examples, the following (Art. 119): ' It shall be the duty of the state (*Staat*) and of the municipalities to maintain the purity, health, and social welfare of the family.'

constituent states to deprive any *person* of life, liberty, or property, without due process of law, or to deny to any *person* the equal protection of the laws. They insist that certain rights before the law shall belong equally to all persons within its jurisdiction, whether citizen or non-citizen, without bar of race or nationality or social degree. They insist above all on certain liberties—as of opinion, or religion, of employment, of association, of *la vie privée*—which the state must respect. Unless these solemn protestations are vain, what do they mean except that the people, the community of persons, the general will, is setting limits to the state itself?

There remains indeed the problem of distinguishing between this profounder will, this communal will, and the sovereign will of the state. The system which requires a preponderant or more-than-majority decision to amend the constitution is, as we have pointed out, exposed to the defect that it gives the power of veto to a minority. The true distinction depends on the fact that there are certain fundamental principles which express the very nature of social man. When a constitution ' guarantees ' certain ' rights ' of personality, it says in effect that no laws *should* be made abrogating these rights, that it is wrong for *any* majority to abolish them. There are matters which properly belong to the sphere of policy, and these may well be determined by the will of the majority. There are other matters which should not be cast at all into the political arena. There are rights and liberties— however we care to name them—which belong to men as men, and of which no authority should deprive them. All differences between majorities and minorities are not made political issues—if they were, the state would be rent in pieces. But the social insight of men prevents this disruption. The state should determine only those matters in respect of which it is expedient or desirable that a common form of action should be established. As men come to apprehend this truth they learn the true limits of sovereignty. And sometimes they record the lesson in the form of a constitution. But the real guarantee that these limits shall be observed is the living sense of what society means, and of its relation to personality. This it is that prevents majorities from the blind appeal to the state to enforce their opinions and that saves minorities from oppression. The will that maintains the state learns also to assign its place.

In fine, sovereignty is the will of an association, not of the community. The state is given a function to perform and means wherewith to perform it, but that which assigns the function and provides the means is the unseen master-builder of society.

III

WHEREIN UNITY LIES

In dealing with the state we have been dealing with a form, a product, a resultant, and at the last, to understand its nature, we have had to turn from the form to the creative source. Our thought grows uneasy when it must pass beyond the apprehended form, when it must seek the relation between the form and the life. It is the border line between science and philosophy. If it were possible, we would avoid the peril altogether. But it is not possible, for unless we adventure beyond it the form becomes absolute, a tyrant against which the creative spirit must revolt or perish. Every organization is also a prison, every protection a limit, every shelter a barrier. Every custom, if blindly accepted, corrupts the world, and if it is a ' good ' one it only corrupts it the more, because it claims the more. The spirit of man must have a way out of every thing it builds.

In the social process it has devised two ways. One is the extensive way, whereby it passes, not from one community to another, but from a narrower to a wider circle of community. So it is liberated from the pressure of all-prevailing custom. The other is the intensive way, whereby it passes from one association to another, so that none can claim its whole allegiance, so that each membership will include only an aspect of its being, so that personality may be free to express itself not only through associations but also away from associations.

In our search for unity we come at last to the individual. We find that unity where many have discovered only its opposite, disharmony and strife, in the will of each to be himself and achieve the objects that are dear to him. We find it not in the surrender but in the fulfilment of personality, not in an imposed order but in one which is responsive to the inmost nature of every man. Enforced unity is precarious and unstable. Social order must be adjudged not only good but enduring in proportion as it expresses and is created by free personality. This liberty is the very condition of social development, and the structure of society gains vastly in intricacy and in strength as it grows in the consentient devotion of those whom it should serve. The endless conflicts of life do not touch its foundations, because of the eternal dependence of personality on society. The blindness and misunderstanding which trusts to force, which draws lines of sheer division between classes or nations, ends in defeat and disaster. The deeper bond of community is the character not of class nor of nation, but of free human personality which from within its own small circle is capable of reconciling in one community the whole world.

The state has had by slow experience to learn the meaning of its own limits. When it arose originally within the kin-community, it seemed to be itself the organization of the kin. But its true significance was found to be expressed in terms not of kinship but of citizenship. The kin was merely the convenient circle within which the state evolved the principle of citizenship. And when at a far later stage the state came to embrace the nation within its organization, its membership seemed to be identified with common nationality. But the circle of the nation was again merely the convenient area of community adapted to the establishment of a greater state. Within it too the principle of citizenship has to be redeemed alike from false exclusiveness and from excessive claims. The state of to-day is not the organization of a nation, for all the purposes which are active within the nation. It is the organization of citizenship, for definite purposes which are scarcely derived at all from the conception of nationality. And there are obvious signs of the coming of the group-nation-state. If that process advances the sense of nationality may well cease to be determinative of state limits, having in this respect fulfilled its historical function. Then it too will become, as kinship has become, a purely social factor, with little political significance. Or else the very idea of nationality will merge into the dominant idea of citizenship. Already it is becoming harder than it was in the early nineteenth century to say what nationality really is.

The state has also, for the achievement of its function, to be redeemed from its identification with force. Here there has been the greatest obstacle to the attainment of unity, alike within the single state and in the world of states. The force with which the state is necessarily endowed, instead of being regarded as a mere corollary and condition of the universality of the law which it assures, has been made its very substance. Instead of being the vindication of liberty it has been the instrument of repression. Instead of being the safeguard of unity it has been a sword of division. Within the state it has at length become, for the most part, the last guardian of the commonwealth. But to one another each state is still a ' power '.

If this fatal contradiction within the life of the state were removed ; if its external policy were harmonized, through an international system, with its great business of order and furtherance ; then it might benefit mankind in a measure yet unattained. For then the aspect of power would recede, and the sense of common interest would be enhanced. The state would relate itself more intimately to the needs which it can serve, gaining a truer vision of what these may be. In the seething tides and incessant changes of human affairs it would provide a rock of assurance ; in the endless struggle of our self-centred pursuits it would deliver us from the grosser perils of the competitive stress ; it would more fully than before consolidate the enduring elements of a myriad achievements ; and supported by all there is of kindliness and sympathy in man for his fellow-man, by that spirit of patriotism which has worked, darkly or clearly, throughout the whole process of human history, and by the instinct of co-operation which springs wherever we truly understand the need and the occasion for it, it would move with more enlightened will towards the high fulfilment of its appointed task.

INDEX